LONGMAN GUIDE TO LIVING RELIGIONS

Ian Harris
Stuart Mews
Paul Morris
John Shepherd

LONGMAN
CURRENT
AFFAIRS

LONGMAN GUIDE TO LIVING RELIGIONS

Published by Longman Group Limited, Westgate House,
The High, Harlow, Essex CM20 1YR, United Kingdom.
Telephone (0279) 442601
Telex 81491 Padlog
Facsimile (0279) 444501

◪DPA
DIRECTORY PUBLISHERS
ASSOCIATION

ISBN 0-582-252970

A catalogue record for this publication is available from the British Library.

Phototypeset by The Midlands Book Typesetting Company.

Printed in Great Britain by Redwood Books, Trowbridge, Wiltshire

Contents

Preface

The **Longman Guide to Living Religions** is a distinctive reference tool. It has been designed to offer the student or scholar of religion a most convenient and accessible resource for researching the variety and complexity of contemporary religious groups and movements. The title is intended to reflect the dominant emphasis on "living religions", that is, groups active in the current world. Groups of purely historical influence have been excluded and the usual approach adopted by encyclopedias and reference works of covering everything from Abraham to the State of Israel or Muhammad to the Ayatollah Khomeini has been avoided.

The inclusion of movements that appear primarily "political" reflects the broader understanding of the category of religion as evidenced particularly in relation to Islam, but to a lesser extent in a number of traditions. Despite the use of criteria such as these, the omission of certain groups and movements remains inevitable. Nevertheless, the range of entries included is considerable and represents an unprecedented attempt at producing a contemporary world guide to living religions.

The **Longman Guide to Living Religions** may be used in two main ways. The first is simply to look up groups and movements in the alphabetically ordered main entries of *Religious Groups and Movements*. Cross-references to other entries in this main section are picked out in bold on their first occurrence within each entry.

This method of proceeding presupposes that one already has a starting point for the search. However, it may be that one has a particular interest in one or more of the "world religions" (Islam, Buddhism, etc.), or one or other of the general categories of religious traditions commonly used in the study of religion (e.g. New Religious Movements). It is possible to gain an impression of groups and movements falling, at least approximately, into these categories by consulting the *Introductory Classification of Groups and Movements* arranged according to religious tradition or category of religion, on pp. x–xvi.

There is much material in the present work which is only likely to be tapped if the relevant entries are identified and approached in this way. There are obvious difficulties in classifying some of the entries appropriately. To take just one example, the Ahmadiya regard themselves as being Muslims, but are rejected as heretics or even apostates by other Muslims. Where, then, should they be listed? The solution adopted is to list them within square brackets under Islam, and then separately under New Religious Movements. Clearly, this could be contested and is controversial, so in some cases, groups are simply listed twice.

In addition, the book includes an introductory essay in which Prof. Ninian Smart provides a global contextualisation of living religions today.

Dr Ian Harris, S. Martin's College, Lancaster; *Dr Stuart Mews*, Cheltenham and Gloucester College of Higher Education; *Dr Paul Morris*, Lancaster University; *Dr John Shepherd*, S. Martin's College, Lancaster.

Contributors

Ahmed Andrews
University of Glasgow.
Khoja Ithna 'Asharis.

Elisabeth Arweck
Centre for New Religious Movements, King's College, University of London.
Church of Christ, Family of Love (& Children of God), Positive Thinking/New Thought, Unification Church/Moonies, Way International, Worldwide Church of God.

Professor Hugh Baker
School of Oriental and African Studies, University of London.
Chinese Folk Religion, De Jiao.

Dr Fiona Bowie
University College of North Wales.
African New Religious Movements, African Traditional Religions, Aladura, Bwiti Cult, Harris Movement, Khoisan religion, Kikuyu religion, Kimbanguist Church, Kitawala, Maria Legio, Nuer and Dinka religion.

Dr Bert F. Breiner
Centre for the Study of Islam and Christian–Muslim Relations, Selly Oak College, Birmingham.
Amal, Hizbollah, Islamic Jihad.

Dr Catherine Cantwell
University of Kent.
Entries written jointly with Robert Mayer.

Dr Peter Clarke
Centre for New Religious Movements, King's College, University of London.
Candomblé, Convince, Macumba, Obeah, Rastafarians, Santería, Umbanda, Vodun (Voodoo).

Dr Owen Cole
West Sussex Institute of Higher Education, Chichester.
Balmikis, Kabir Panth, Namdharis, Nirankaris, Ravidas Panth, Sikh Dharma of the Western Hemisphere, Sikhism, Udasis.

Dr Simon Coleman
St John's College, Cambridge.
Word of Life (Livets Ord).

Dr Peter Connolly
West Sussex Institute of Higher Education.
Buddhist Churches of America, Buddhist Society of Great Britain and Ireland, Chogye Chong, Chondo Gyo, Friends of the Western Buddhist Order, Sino–American Buddhist Association, Son, T'aego Chong, Viniyoga, Won.

Dr Guy H. Cooper
Matlock, Derbyshire.
Inuit Religion, Native American Religions, Pan–Indianism, Peyotism, Shamanism.

Thomas Daffern
Institute of Education, University of London.
Australian Aboriginal Religion, South American Traditional Religions; (and jointly with James Veitch): Maori Religion, Melanesian Religion, Polynesian Religion.

Ben Pink Dandelion
Society of Friends (Quakers).

Wendy Dossett
St David's University College, Lampeter.
Jinja Shinto, Jodoshinshu, Jodoshu, Komeito, Kyoha Shinto, Minzoku Shinto, Nichirenshoshu,

Nichirenshu, Nipponzan Myohoji, Omotokyo, PL Kyodan, Reiyukai Kyodan, Rinzai Zen, Rissho Koseikai, Seicho no Ie, Sekai Kyuseikyo, Sekai Mahikari Bunmei Kyodan, Shingonshu, Shinto, Shotokushu, Soka Gakkai, Soto Zen, Tendaishu.

Dr Gavin Flood
St David's University College, Lampeter.
Aghoris, Kashmir Shaivism, Lingayats, Nagas, Naths, Shaiva Siddhantins, Shaivas, Shaktas, Smartas, Shri Vidya, Tantrism.

Dr Theodore Gabriel
Cheltenham and Gloucester College of Higher Education.
Tribal Religions of India.

Dr David Gosling
Clare College, University of Cambridge.
Buddhayana, Burmese Theravada, Cambodian Buddhism, Cao Dai, Hoa Hao, Kasogatan, Laotian Theravada, Samnak Paw Sawan, Thai Theravada, Theravada Buddhism, Tridharma, Unified Vietnamese Buddhist Church, Vietnamese Buddhism.

Richard Gray
S. Martin's College, Lancaster.
Ramanna Nikaya, Sarvodaya Sramadana.

Dr Ian Harris
S. Martin's College, Lancaster.
Amarapura Nikaya, Arya Maitreya Mandala (AMM), Branch Davidians, Buddhism, Chinese Buddhism, Chinese Buddhist Association, Christianity, Compassion Society, Dasanamis, Free Presbyterian Church, Gedatsukai, Gelugpas, Great White Brotherhood, Hooppha Sawan, Hossoshu, International Society for Krishna Consciousness (ISKCON), Kanji Panth, Kavi Panth, Kegonshu, Lao United

Buddhists Association, Mahanikay, Maruyamakyo, Nanak Panth, Neo-Buddhism, International Network of Engaged Buddhists, Obaku Zen, Ramanandis, Ramdasis, Sant Nirankari Mandal, Santi Asok, Satya Samaj, Sauras, Self-Realization Fellowship, Shugendo, Shwegyin Nikaya, Siddha Yoga, Siyam Nikaya, Thammakaai Religious Foundation, Thammayutika Nikaya,Trailokya Bauddha Mahasangha Sahayaka Gana, Unity Sect, Vinaya Vardhana Society, Vipassana Movements, Vishwa Hindu Parishad, World Fellowship of Buddhists, Zen.

Bradley Hawkins
University of California, Santa Barbara.
Bharatiya Janata Party (BPJ), Dehra Dun Ashram, Radha Soami Satsang, Ramakrishna Mission, Rashtriya Swayamsevak Sangh (RSS), Sandipani Sadharalaya, Shiv Sena, Tiruvannamalai, Vedanta, Yoga.

Dr Paul Heelas
University of Lancaster.
New Age.

Richard Hoch
University of California, Santa Barbara.
Ashkenazi, Bene Israel, Conservative Judaism, Havurat Judaism, Jewish Feminist Groups, Kibbutz, Orthodox Judaism, Reconstructionist Judaism, Reform Judaism, Samaritans, Sephardi. Beta Israel, Jewish New Agers, Karaites (jointly with Paul Morris).

Dr Will Johnson
University of Wales, College of Cardiff.
Buddhist Society of India, Digambara Jainas, Irani Zoroastrians, Jainas, Parsees, Svetambara Jainas, Zoroastrians.

Claudia Liebeskind
*Royal Holloway and Bedford New
College, University of London.*
Bektashiya, Chishtiya, Malangs.

Dr Denis MacEoin
Newcastle-upon-Tyne.
'Alawis, Ahl-i Haqq, Babis,
Bahais, Dhu'l-Riyasatayn,
Druzes (Druses), Fiver Shi'ites,
Imamis, Isma'ilis, Ithna 'Asharis,
Ja'faris, Mandaeans, Musta'lis,
Ni'matullahiya, Nizaris, Nusayris,
Sevener Shi'ites (Seveners),
Shi'ism, Twelver Shi'ites, Yazidis,
Zaydis.

Stewart McFarlane
University of Lancaster.
Confucianism.

Dr Freda Matchett
University of Lancaster.
Bauls, Mahanubhavs, Pushtimarga,
Shri Shankaradeva Sangha, Shri
Vaishnavas, Swaminarayans,
Vaikhanasas, Vaishnava Sahajiyas,
Warkaris.

Robert Mayer
*School of Oriental and African
Studies, University of London.*
(Entries written jointly with
Catherine Cantwell.) Bonpos,
Drukpa Kagyudpas, Kagyudpas,
Karma Kagyudpas, Mongolian
Buddhism, Nyingmapas, Sakyapas,
Tibetan Buddhism.

Dr Stuart Mews
*Cheltenham and Gloucester College
of Higher Education.*
Anglicans, Anglo-Catholics, British
Israelites, Episcopalians, House
Churches, Moral Re-armament,
Nippon Kirisuto Kyodan,
Nippon Sei Ko Kai, Old Catholic
Mariavite Church, Scientology,
Seventh-Day Adventists, Uniate
Churches, United Church of Christ,
Wesleyan Church, World Congress
of Christian Fundamentalists,
World Council of Churches.

Dr Peter Moore
University of Kent at Canterbury.
Armenian Church, Autocephalous
Churches, Coptic Church, Greek
Orthodox Church, Nestorians,
Orthodox Church (Byzantine),
Oriental Orthodox Churches,
Russian Orthodox Church, Syrian
Jacobite Church, Syro-Indian
Churches, Zoe.

Dr Paul Morris
University of Lancaster.
Agudat Israel, Arunachala Ashram,
Aurobindo Ashram, Baba Lovers,
Belz Hasidism, Bratslav Hasidism,
Cochin Jews, Donmeh, Ger
Hasidism, Gush Emunim (Block of
the Faithful), Haredi (Haredim),
Kabbalah, Karlin-Stolin Hasidism,
Lubavich Hasidism, Hasidism,
Hinduism, Judaism, Mafdal
(Mizrahi, National Religious
Party), Messianic Judaism, Musar
Movement, Neo-Hasidism, Neturei
Karta, Satmar Hasidism, Sephardi,
Sephardi Torah Guardians Party
(SHAS), Society of Jewish Science,
United Torah Judaism (United
Torah Party), Vizhitz Hasidism,
World Jewish Congress, World
Union for Progressive Judaism.
Beta Israel, Jewish New Agers,
Karaites (jointly with Richard
Hoch).

Keith Munnings
Bristol.
Cargo Cults, John Frum (jointly
with Dr James Veitch);
Anthroposophy, Freemasons,
Occultism, Paganism (Neo-
Paganism), Rosicrucianism,
Satanism, Witchcraft (Wicca).

Dr Francesca Murphy
S. Martin's College, Lancaster.
Benedictines, Carmelites,
Carthusians, Chaldean Uniate
Church, Cistercians, Dominicans,
Eastern Rite Romanian Church,
Eastern Rite Ukrainian Church,
Franciscans, Jesuits, Maronites,
Melkites, Opus Dei, Pax

Christi, Roman Catholic Church, Ruthenian Church.

Dr Petya Nitzova
University of Sofia, Bulgaria.
Qizilbash.

Dr Michael S. Northcott
New College, University of Edinburgh.
Angkatan Belia Islam Malaysiam (ABIM), Darul Arqam, Parti Islam Se-Malaysia (PAS).

Dr Sarah Potter
West Sussex Institute of Higher Education.
Black Muslims, Moorish (–American) Science Temple of America, Nation of Islam.

Elizabeth Puttick
Centre for New Religious Movements, King's College, University of London. Ananda Marga, Brahma Kumaris, Elan Vital/Divine Light Mission, Gurdjieffian Groups, Krishnamurti Foundation, Sahaja Yoga, Satya Sai Baba Satsang, Subud, Theosophical Society, Transcendental Meditation.

Prof. Francis C. R. Robinson
Royal Holloway and Bedford New College, University of London.
Ahl-i Hadith, Ahl-i Quran, Ahmadiya (Qadianis), Ahmadiya (Lahoris), Barelvis (Barelwis), Deobandis, Islamic Modernists (South Asia), Jama'at-i Islami, Tablighi Jama'at.

Dr John J. Shepherd
S. Martin's College, Lancaster.
Aga Khanis, Alevis, Ansar, Badawiya, Bassij-i Mostazafin (Mobilization of the Oppressed), Bohoras, Catholic Action, Church of the Cherubim and Seraphim, Church of the Lord (Aladura), Daudis, Da'wa Party (Hizb al-Da'wa), ECKANKAR, est, Ethiopian Churches, Free Russian Orthodox Church,

Front Islamique du Salut (FIS), Halveti-Cerrahis, Hamas (Algeria), Hizb al-Nahda (Renaissance Party; MTI; Ennahda), Human Potential Movement, Ibadiya, Iglesia ni Cristo (jointly with James Veitch), Islam, Islamic Council of Europe, Islamic Foundation, Islamic Renaissance Party, Islamic Revolutionary Guards, al-Jama'at al-Islamiya, Jihad Organization/al-Jihad, Jihad-i Sazandigi (Reconstruction Crusade), Kardecismo, Khojas, Kumina, Mahdiya, Maitatsine, Maria Lionza, Milli Görüs, Mouvement Croix-Koma, Muhammadiyah, Muslim Parliament of Great Britain, Muslim World League, Nahda Movement/Party, Nahdatul Ulama, Nañiguismo, Nurçus, Organization of the Islamic Conference, Pocomania, Primal Therapy, Psychosynthesis, Qalandars, Qimbanda, Rajneeshism, Republican Brothers, Republic Sisters, Revival Zion, Shakers, Shango, Shouters, Society of Militant Clergy, Spiritual Baptists, Sufism, Süleymancis, Sunnism, Swedenborgianism, Taro Cult, True Orthodox Church of Greece, UK Islamic Mission, Winti, World Conference on Religion and Peace, World Congress of Faiths, World Muslim Congress, 'Yan Tatsine ('Yan Izala), Yasawiya, Zar cult, Zionist Churches.

Dr Elizabeth Sirriyeh
University of Leeds.
Hamas (West Bank and Gaza), Hanafis, Hanbalis, Malikis, Maraboutism, Mawlawiya, Muridiya, Muslim Brotherhood, Naqshabandiya, Qadiriya, Rifa'iya, Sanusiya, Shafi'is, al-Takfir wa'l-Hijra, Wahhabism.

Prof. Ninian Smart
University of California, Santa Barbara.
Guide to Living Religions.

Dr Nasir Tamimi
School of Islamic Studies, Jakarta.
Muhammadiyah, Nahdatul Ulama
(jointly with John Shepherd).

Dr James Veitch
Victoria University of Wellington,
New Zealand.
Iharaira, Maori Religion, Maori
Religious Movements, Melanesian
Religion, Polynesian Religion
(jointly with Thomas Daffern);
Ratana, Ringatu; Cargo cults,
John Frum (jointly with Keith
Munnings); Iglesia ni Cristo (jointly
with John Shepherd).

Rosemary J. Watts
Westminster College, Oxford.
Adventists, Amish, Assemblies of
God, Baptists, Catholic Apostolic
Church, Christadelphians, Christian
Science, Congregationalists,
Conservative Catholic Churches,
Disciples of Christ (Restorationist),
Dutch Reformed Church,
Exclusive Bretheren, House
Churches, Hutterites, Jehovah's
Witnesses, Lutherans, Mennonites
(Anabaptists), Methodists,
Moravians, Mormons, Nazarenes,
Old Catholic Churches, Open
Bretheren, Pentecostal Churches
(Charismatic), Protestantism,
Presbyterians (Reformed),
Reformed Catholic Churches,
Salvation Army, Southern Baptists,
Spiritualists, Unitarians.

Dr Richard Wilson
University of Essex.
Mesoamerican Traditional Religion
(Mayan).

Introductory Classification of Groups and Movements

Square brackets denote entries that are listed under more than one grouping (see Preface)

BUDDHISM

Amarapura Nikaya
Arya Maitreya Mandala (AMM)
Buddhayana
Buddhism
Buddhist Churches of America
Buddhist Society of Great Britain and Ireland
Buddhist Society of India
Buddhist Sunday Schools Movement
Burmese Theravada
Cambodian Buddhism
Chinese Buddhism
Chinese Buddhist Association (CBA)
Chogye Chong
Clean Government Party
Drukpa Kagyudpa
Friends of the Western Buddhist Order (FWBO)
Gedatsukai
Gelugpas
Hooppha Sawan
Hossoshu
Hua Yen
Jodoshinshu
Jodoshu
Kagyudpa
Karma Kagyudpa
Karmapas
Kasogatan
Kegonshu
Komeito
Kyo Chong
Lao United Buddhists' Association (LUBA)
Laotian Theravada
Mahanikay
Maruyamakyo
Mongolian Buddhism
Neo-Buddhism
Nichirenshoshu
Nichirenshoshu of the UK (NSUK)
Nichirenshu
Nipponzan Myohoji
Nyingmapa
Obaku Zen
Pure Land School
Ramanna Nikaya
Rinzai Zen
Sakyapa
Santi Asok
Sarvodaya Sramadana
Shin Buddhism
Shingonshu
Shotokushu
Shwegyin Nikaya
Sino-American Buddhist Association (SABA)
Siyam Nikaya
Son
Son Chong
Soto Zen
Sri Lankan Theravada
T'aego Chong
Tendaishu
Thai Theravada
Thammakaai Religious Foundation
Thammayutika Nikaya
Theravada Buddhism
Thomayat
Thuddama Nikaya
Tibetan Buddhism
Trailokya Bauddha Mahasangha Sahayaka Gana (TBMSG)
True Nichiren School
True Pure Land School
Unified Vietnamese Buddhist Church
Vietnamese Buddhism
Vinaya Vardhana Society
Vipassana Movements
Won

World Fellowship of Buddhists (WFB)
Zen

CHRISTIANITY

Adventists
Aladura
Amish
Anglicans
Anglo-Catholics
Armenian Church
Armenian Gregorian Church
Armstrongism
Assemblies of God
Assyrian Church
Autocephalous Churches
Baptists
Benedictines
Branch Davidians
Brethren
[British Israelites]
Bwiti Cult
Carmelites
Carthusians
Catholic Action
Catholic Apostolic Church
Catholic Tridentine Church
Chaldean Uniate Church
Children of God
Christadelphians
Christian Science
Christianity
Church of Albania
Church of Alexandria
Church of Antioch
Church of Bulgaria
Church of Christ
Church of Constantinople
Church of England
Church of Finland
Church of Georgia
Church of God of Prophecy
Church of Jerusalem
Church of Poland
Church of Romania
Church of Scotland
Church of Sinai
Church of the Cherubim and Seraphim
[Church of the Latter Day Saints]
Church of the Lord (Aladura)
[Church of the Twelve Apostles]
Cistercians
Congregationalists
Conservative Catholic Churches
Coptic Church

Coptic Evangelical Church
Dominicans
Dutch Reformed Church
East Syrian Church
Eastern European Congregational
  Churches
Eastern Orthodox Church
Eastern Rite Churches
Eastern Rite Romanian Catholic
  Church
Eastern Rite Ukrainian Church
Elim Fellowship
Elim Pentecostal Church
Episcopalians
Ethiopian Churches
Ethiopian Orthodox Church
Euseibia
Exclusive Brethren
[Family of Love]
Franciscans
Free Churches
Free Presbyterian Church
Free Russian Orthodox Church
Friends
[Harris Movement]
Harvestime Group
House Churches
Hussite Church
Hutterites
Ichthus Movement
Iglesia ni Cristo
Irvingites
[Jehovah's Witnesses]
Jesuits
[Kimbanguist Church]
[Kitawala]
Latin-Rite Catholics
London Church of Christ
Lusitanian Church
Lutherans
Malabar Christians
Malankarese Uniate Church
[Maria Legio]
Mariavites
Maronites
Mar Thoma
Melkites
Mellusians
Mennonites
Messianic Judaism
Mission Covenant Churches
[Moonies]
Moral Re-armament
Moravians
[Mormons]

Mouvement Croix-Koma
Nazarenes
Neo-Catechumenal Way
Nestorians
[New Church of Jerusalem]
New Testament Church of God
Nippon Kirisuto Kyodan
Nippon Sei Ko Kai
Old Catholic Church
Old Catholic Mariavite Church
Olive Tree Church
Open Brethren
Opus Dei
Order of Friars Minor
Order of Preachers
Oriental Orthodox Churches
Orthodox Church (Byzantine)
Orthodox Church of Cyprus
Orthodox Church of Greece
Orthodox Church in America
Orthodox Church in Australia
Oxford Group
Pentecostal Churches (Charismatic)
Pioneer
Plymouth Brethren
Polish National Catholic Church
Presbyterians (Reformed)
Primitive Methodism
Protestantism
Quakers
Reformed Catholic Churches
Reformed Church
Roman Catholic Church
Russian Orthodox Church
Ruthenian Church
Salvation Army
Serbian Orthodox Church
Seventh Day Adventists
Slavonic Orthodox Church
Society of Friends
Society of Jesus
Southern Baptists
St Thomas Christians
Syrian Jacobite Church
Syrian Orthodox Church
Syro-Indian Churches
Trappists
True Orthodox Church
True Orthodox Church of Greece
True Orthodox Church of Romania
Ukrainian Uniate Catholic Church
Uniate Churches
[Unification Church]
Unitarians
United Methodist Church

United Reformed Church
Way International
Wee Frees
Wesleyan Church
Word of Life (Livets Ord)
World Congress of Christian
  Fundamentalists
World Council of Churches
Worldwide Church of God
Zoe

HINDUISM

Aghoris
Aurobindo Ashram
Baba Lovers
Balmikis
Bauls
Bharatiya Janata Party
Brahma Kumaris
Dashanamis
Dehra Dun Ashram
Hinduism
International Society for Krishna
  Consciousness
ISKCON
Kanphatas
Kapalikas
Kashmir Shaivism
Krama
Lingayats
Mahanubhavs
Manbhavs
Nagas
Naths
Pushtimarga
Radha Soami Satsang
Ramakrishna Mission
Ramanandis
Ramdasis
Rashtriya Svayamsevak Sangh
Ravidas Panth
Shaktas
Self-Realization Fellowship (SRF)
Shaiva Siddhantins
Shaivas
Shiv Sena
Shri Sankaradeva Sangha
Shri Vaishnavas
Siddha Yoga
Smartas
Swaminarayans
Tantrism
Tiruvannamalai
Udasis

Vaikhanasas
Vaishnava Sahajiyas
Vaishnavas
Valmikis
Vatakalai
Vedanta
Vedanta Society
Viniyoga
Virashaivas
Vishwa Hindu Parishad
Warkaris or Varkari Panth
Yoga

ISLAM

Aga Khanis/Nizaris
Ahl-i Hadith
Ahl-i Haqq
Ahl-i Quran
[Ahmadiya]
'Alawis
[Alevis]
Amal
Black Muslims/American Muslim
  Mission/Nation of Islam
Angkatan Belia Islam Malaysiam
  (ABIM)
Ansar
Barelvis/Barelwis
Bassij-i Mostazafin
Bohoras/Bohras
Darul Arqam
Da'wa Party/Hizb al Da'wa/Islamic
  Call Party
Deobandis
[Druzes/Druses]
Front Islamique du Salut—FIS/Islamic
  Salvation Front
Hamas—Algeria
Hamas—West Bank and Gaza
Hanafis
Hanbalis
Hizb al-Nahda/Ennahda
Hizbollah (Islamic Resistance)
Ibadiya
Islam
Islamic Call Society
Islamic Council of Europe
Islamic Foundation
Islamic Jihad
Islamic Modernists—South Asia
Islamic Renaissance Party
Islamic Revolutionary Guards/Pasdaran
Isma'ilis/Sevener Shi'ites
Ja'faris

al-Jama'at al-Islamiya/Islamic Groups/
  Islamic Leagues
Jama'at-i Islami
Jihad-i Sazandigi
Jihad Organization
Khoja Ithna 'Asharis
Khojas
Mahdiya
Malikis
Milli Görüs
Muhammadiya (Aisiah)
Muslim Brotherhood
Muslim Parliament of Great Britain
Muslim World League
Musta'lis (Daudis)
Nahdatul Ulama
Nizaris/Aga Khanis
Nurcus
[Nusayris]
Organization of the Islamic
  Conference
Parti Islam Se-Malaysia (PAS)
Qizilbash/Kizilbash
Republican Brothers/Republican
  Sisters
Shafi'is
Shi'ism
Society of Militant Clergy/Association
  of Combatant Clergy
Sufism
  Badawiya
  Bektashiya
  Chishtiya
  Halveti-Cerrahis
  [Malangs]
  [Maraboutism]
  Mawlawiya (Dancing Dervishes,
    Mevlevis)
  Muridiya
  Naqshabandiya
  Ni'matullahiya (Dhu'l-Riyasatayn)
  Qadiriya
  [Qalandars]
  Rifa'iya (Howling Dervishes)
  Sanusiya
  Yasawiya
Süleymancis
Sunnism
Tablighi Jama'at/Jama'at Tablighi
al-Takfir wa'l-Hijra
Twelver Shi'ites/Imamis/Ithna 'Asharis
UK Islamic Mission
Wahhabism
World Islamic Call Society
World Muslim Congress

Winti
Ahmadiya (Qadianis, Lahoris)
Ananda Marga
Babis (Bahais)
Black Muslims/Nation of Islam
Cao Dai/Dai Dao Tam Ky Pho Do
Cargo Cults (John Frum Movement)
Catholic Apostolic Church/Irvingites
Christian Science
Chondo Gyo/Religion of the Heavenly
  Way
Church of Christ
Compassion Society/Tz'u Hui T'ang
De Jiao/Tak Kaau
Elan Vital/Divine Light Mission
est
Family of Love/Children of God
Freemasons
Great White Brotherhood
Gurdjieffian Groups
Heavenly Virtue Church
Hoa Hao/Buo Son Ky Hong
Hooppha Sawan
Human Potential Movement
I Kuan Tao
Iglesia ni Cristo/Manalistas
International Society for Krishna
  Consciousness (ISKCON; Hare
  Krishna Movement)
Jehovah's Witnesses/Watchtower
  Society (Kitawala)
Krishnamurti Foundation
Maori New Religious Movements
  Iharaira
  Ratana
  Ringatu
Moral Rearmament
Mormons/Church of Latter Day Saints
New Age (Jewish New Agers)
Occultism
Olive Tree Church
Omotokyo
Paganism (Old Religion)
Pan-Indianism (Peyotism)
PL Kyodan/Church of Perfect Liberty
Positive Thinking
Primal Therapy
Psychosynthesis
Rajneeshism
Rastafarianism
Reiyukai Kyodan/Society for
  Companions of the Spirits
Rissho Koseikai/Society for the
  Establishment of Righteousness and
  Harmony

Rosicrucianism
Samnak Paw Sawan
Satanism
Scientology
Seicho no Ie/House of Growth
Sekai Kyuseikyo/World Messianity
Sekai Mahikari Bunmei Kyodan (Sukyo
  Mahikari)
Self-Realization Fellowship
Soka Gakkai
[Soka Gakkai International (SGI)]
Spiritualists
Subud
Sukyo Mahikari
Swedenborgianism
Taro cult
Tenrikyo/Religion of Heavenly Wisdom
Theosophical Society
Transcendental Meditation
Tridharma/Sam Kauw Hwee
Unification Church/Moonies
Unity Sect (Lui-ist, Sunist)/I Kuan Tao
Way International
Witchcraft/Wicca/Craft
Worldwide Church of
  God/Armstrongism

PRIMAL/TRADITIONAL/FOLK
RELIGIONS

African Traditional Religions
  Nuer and Dinka Religion
  Zar Cult/Sar Cult
Australian Aboriginal Religion
Chinese Folk Religion
Inuit Religion
Maori Religion
Melanesian Religions
Mesoamerican Traditional Religions
Native American Religions
Polynesian Religions
Shamanism
South American Traditional Religions
Tribal Religions of India

SHINTO

Association of Sect Shinto
Association of Shinto Shrines
Jinja Shinto
Kyoha Shinto
Minzoku Shinto
New Sect Shinto
Sect Shinto
Shinto

Shrine Shinto
Tokumitsikyo

SIKHISM

Health, Happy and Holy Organization
   (3HO)
[Kabir Panth]
Khalsa Sikhs
[Kuka Sikhs]
[Nakali Nirankaris]
[Namdharis]
Nanak Panth
Nihangs
[Nirankaris]
[Sant Nirankari Mandal]
Sikh Dharma of the Western
   Hemisphere

Sikhism
Three HO

OTHERS

Alevis
Bahais
Bonpos
Chinese Folk Religion
Chinese Taoist Association (CTA)
Confucianism
Druzes
Irani Zoroastrians
Mandaeans
Parsis
Shugendo
World Conference on Religion and
   Peace
World Congress of Faiths
Yazidis
Zoroastrians

Guide to Living Religions

Ninian Smart

During the 20th century religions have undergone remarkable changes and vicissitudes. The rise of totalitarian ideologies, notably Fascism, Nazism and Communism, has caused considerable suffering to religious traditionalists, notably to Jews and **Tibetan Buddhists**, but to many other groups as well. The collapse of Nazism and Fascism at the end of World War II has been followed by the demise of Marxist régimes in Eastern Europe and in the former Soviet Union. All this has brought significant change to traditional religions. But other factors too have brought about transformation. The emergence of a global civilization characterized by instant communication, extensive travel, migrations and an increasingly unified global capitalist system, has encouraged various developments: the emergence of new emphases on ecumenism in many religions, the increased prominence of diaspora groups (such as **Sikhs** outside India supporting movements within India), solidarity between religions and nationalisms (in Iran, Sri Lanka, Ireland and elsewhere), a new self-consciousness of the global significance of each major religion, tendencies towards syncretisms, wider backlashes against religious modernism or liberalism, the growth of new religious movements, a wider spread of individualism and with it a new voluntarism in religion, and the adoption of modern technology in the preaching and spread of religion.

Also, the balance of power has shifted both within religions and between them. The end of the 19th century and the beginning of the 20th was the heyday of the colonial system, and Christian missionaries rode on the backs of empires in a remarkable effort at proselytization, being successful particularly in sub-Saharan Africa and the Pacific region, though not inconsiderable impacts were made in Asia. But particularly since World War II the dignity and power of other traditions have been reasserted. Included here are the relatively small-scale societies of Africa and Native America, which have evolved a wider alliance to express **African religion** as a whole and **Native American religion** (not thus confined to a particular tribe or nation). Meanwhile the post-colonial era has shifted balances. Thus, the majority of Christians now live in the Southern Hemisphere, in sub-Saharan Africa, in Central and South America and in the Pacific region. The majority of Muslims live in South Asia and South-East Asia (notably in Indonesia), and so demographically the Arab region, the traditional heartland of **Islam,** is less significant. **Buddhism,** still (1994) largely suppressed in Marxist countries, from Vietnam to China and North Korea, has assumed a more Western incarnation. Likewise **Confucianism** and **Taoism** are more vigorous outside than inside China. **Judaism** since World War II has two major epicentres, Israel and the United States, while its older vitality in Central and Eastern Europe has been largely snuffed out by the Holocaust: its presence in Muslim lands has decisively diminished.

Another phenomenon in the modern period especially has been the growth of new religious movements, both in the West and in most other regions of the world, especially in Africa, where numerous independent churches are making spectacular progress. Some of these new movements are blends of elements from diverse traditions—for instance, African themes intertwined with **Christianity,** Hindu doctrines and Gurus adapted to Western conditions, transformations of indigenous religion as in the **Cargo Cults** of the South Pacific, modernized forms of Japanese **Shinto,** etc. Indeed to some degree all religions have been altered by the impact of capitalism, colonialism and the new globalism. Mainline **Protestantism** for instance is heavily influenced by liberal attitudes and modern scholarship, while Catholicism since Vatican II has felt the impact of the same forces. So in a sense all religions are "new religions". Nevertheless we should not neglect the force of the smaller new religions, which taken together have a lot of power.

It is useful at this point to survey the distribution of the major religions and ideologies in the world, as they have emerged from the colonial period into the new global order—a period which has seen the universalization of the conception (though not always the reality) of the nation-state. The earth's land surface is virtually covered by independent nations, even if there are nations still struggling for such political self-expression.

First, there is a great region, from Europe to North America and from the Arctic to portions of the South, such as Australia and New Zealand, which is predominantly Christian and White. This has been the powerhouse of colonialism, capitalism and a more or less liberal ethos, especially under the influence of Protestantism. Into this Western civilization are mixed in other forces, notably Judaism, especially in the United States of America. But other minorities are important too—Muslims in America, Britain, Germany and France particularly, Chinese and Japanese Buddhists in California, indigenous peoples in North America, Scandinavia, and so on. Attached as a Southern wing of this great bloc of Western culture are Australia and New Zealand, and in an ambiguous way South Africa. Although formally much of the West is Christian, and perhaps more intensely in the USA than elsewhere, it is deeply affected by scientific humanism and a pragmatically agnostic attitude to religion. During the period since World War II the main trends have been democratic, with dictatorships in Southern Europe being overthrown in Greece (1977), Spain (1975) and Portugal (1974). While the whole region of White civilization, both North and South, has been deeply influenced by Christian values, it has entered a phase in which many choose to leave those values behind. At the same time this area has vital minority influences. To signify this transcendence of traditional Christian ideas I shall refer to it as the TransChristian West.

This region abuts upon the countries of Eastern Europe and the former Soviet Union. These are currently in a state of turmoil. There was a period, after World War II, after the Chinese Communist victory in 1949, and subsequent developments in South-East Asia, when the whole region from the River Elbe to Vladivostok, and from Murmansk to Ho Chi Minh City, was Marxist and totalitarian, with little room for traditional religions. In effect Marxism functioned as the state religion. But this Marxist bloc has recently (namely from 1989) been progressively torn apart, with the collapse of Communist régimes in Eastern Europe in 1989, and the demise of the Soviet system in 1991. Actually, though Marxism was like a religion it turned out to be an ineffective one. The emerging countries of the ex-Soviet Union and Eastern Europe have a variety of dominant and militant religions. Poland, Hungary, Slovenia, Croatia, and the Czech and Slovak Republics are predominantly Catholic. Serbia and other parts of ex-Yugoslavia are mainly **Orthodox** (with Muslims an important presence). The warring sides in Bosnia—Croatians, Serbians and Bosnian Muslims—are divided along religious lines. Bulgaria and Romania are mainly Orthodox. So too are Ukraine and Belarus, Russia (with its many embedded minorities), Moldava, Armenia and Georgia. But the Central Asian republics are chiefly Muslim. In the Baltics, Protestantism dominates. It looks as if the Muslim republics will join what I below dub "the Islamic Crescent". Meanwhile we may call the area from the Elbe to Vladivostok the TransChristian East.

The third major bloc in the world is constituted by the countries of the Islamic Crescent. Islam dominates from beyond the Australian littoral through Indonesia, Malaysia, Bangladesh, Pakistan (and the Republic of India, which has more than 80,000,000 Muslims within its borders), Afghanistan, Central Asia, Iran, the Arab Middle East and North Africa, to Mauritania and parts of West Africa. There are vital outposts in East Africa. This Crescent is divided primarily between **Shi'a** and **Sunni** Islam, with the latter being most preponderant. Today it is undergoing revival and a new ecumenical self-consciousness, fostered by jet-borne pilgrimage to Mecca.

Within the Arab and related lands there are anomalies. Thus, Turkey, through the reforms and initiative of Kemal Ataturk (1881–1938), became a secular state, attempting, in effect, to join Europe. Its support for Islamic causes has been therefore ambiguous. While some other states in the area, such as Egypt and Iraq, have followed modernist paths, espousing Arab nationalism rather than Islamic solidarity, Turkey has progressed further along the path of modernism than others. The other anomaly in the Islamic Crescent has been the state of Israel, which has (from a Muslim point of view) stuck like a thorn in the flank of Islam: an outpost, in the eyes of many Muslims, of Western imperialism and Jewish–Christian influence.

Another cultural region of the world is Latin America, from just north of the Rio Grande (where its influence on US culture is growing) to Patagonia in the South, comprising largely Spanish-speaking nations, though also the huge Portuguese-speaking Brazil and the multilingual Caribbean. Here the main influence is **Roman Catholicism,** springing from the colonial conquest of the Americas, in this case primarily by Spain and Portugal. In recent times there has been throughout this region a strong surge of Protestantism, especially in its conservative and **Pentecostal** forms. Newish religions, created out of a synthesis of African and other elements are also present, since, especially in Brazil, there is a large African population. The Latin South (as I shall call it) has its own character, and liberal modernism in the Western mode is less dominant.

Below the northern part of the African continent, stretching from Morocco and Mauritania in the West to Egypt, Sudan and Somalia in the East the continent is largely Christian, mostly through modern activities by missionaries, though Ethiopia has its ancient form of Christianity, allied to the **Coptic Church** in Egypt. Sub-Saharan Africa also has many adherents of classical African religions. New, largely Christian, movements are also well represented, even if mainstream Churches often try to deny their legitimacy. Moreover, some parts of sub-Saharan Africa, notably Nigeria and Tanzania, are deeply affected by Islam. Still, Black Africa (as I shall call this zone) is largely Christian, despite its classical African and Islamic minorities.

We have already glanced at the Marxist dominance of East Asia, though it is true that aspects of capitalism are beginning to invade China, especially in the south and around Hong Kong (due to join the People's Republic in 1997, with Macao joining two years later). China has not wished to follow the line of *glasnost* taken by the former Soviet Union. As such political rigidity, with stern suppression of separatism in Tibet and other non-Han outposts of the Chinese Empire, with special apprehension towards Central Asia, goes hand in hand with economic liberalization, what will emerge is obscure at the time of writing (1994). Anyway, China, together with North Korea and much of former Indochina, retains a Marxist autocracy, which is already crumbling, since totalitarian rule is not being efficiently maintained in the face of market liberalization and increasing problems of centralizing the bureaucracy. There is therefore some revival of traditional religions in China. This area can be called the Marxist Bloc.

The final major cultural area in today's world is the region where traditional Asian, mainly Buddhist and Hindu values, have been maintained. In South Asia, there is the predominantly Hindu state of India, though—as we have seen—with a strong minority of Muslims, not to mention smaller minorities of Sikhs, **Parsis**, Christians, **Jainas** and Buddhists. To the South is largely Sinhalese Buddhist Sri Lanka, with, however, powerful minorities of Tamils and Muslims (the former engaged for more than a decade in insurrection). South-East Asia, namely in particular Thailand, Myanmar (Burma), Laos and Cambodia, is **Theravada** Buddhist, and Vietnam is partly Buddhist. Thailand has a substantial minority of Muslims. Vietnam is partly Buddhist, with a Catholic minority.

As well as these areas indebted greatly to Indian civilization there are areas in Asia outside the Marxist Bloc which are chiefly Chinese in culture, such as Taiwan, Hong Kong and Singapore, together with South Korea (having its distinctive Korean tradition). All these countries are to some degree influenced by Buddhism, and so have an affinity to South Asia. All this underbelly (so to speak) of Asia we can here nominate as the area of Traditional Asia. Actually, it is not that traditional, since some parts of it are hurrying along a modern capitalist path. In the region we need of course to include Japan, with its own distinctive and largely Buddhist civilization, but with ingredients of Shinto, Confucianism, Taoism and Western liberalism, especially in the settlement after World War II.

One might add as a final area the islands of the South and Central Pacific. Though it is now substantially Christian in religion, there are differences of culture from the Northern scene, for here we find Polynesian, Melanesian and other cultural motifs woven into Christian values. And so we can call this the Pacific Region. In short, we have established a number of large cultural areas or blocs in the world, namely: the TransChristian West and the TransChristian East, the Islamic Crescent, the Latin South, Black Africa, Traditional Asia, and the Pacific Region.

These different regions are in differing relations to one another, and to themselves. Generally speaking, the TransChristian West has a majority religious representation side by side with an active minority. Most of the major Christian Churches are either traditionalist or liberal; a more radical fundamentalist wing is dynamic in its opposition to the majority as well as being very energetic in mission. This evangelical minority is also active in the TransChristian East. Similarly, in the Jewish tradition there is an active conservative radicalism, which fastens particularly on developing an outreach in Israel, through such parties as the **Gush Emunim** (Bloc of the Faithful). In the case of Islam, the reaction against modernism and compromise with the West is reinforced by the feeling of opposition to colonialism and possible capitalist oppression. Though so-called fundamentalist movements, such as the **Muslim Brotherhood,** active particularly in Egypt, and analogous movements in Algeria, Pakistan and elsewhere, have a modernizing aspect, at least in practical affairs, they also see themselves as restoring original Islamic values. Similarly the Shi'ite revolution in Iran advocates and implements the notion of an Islamic Republic (an innovative idea), yet also sees itself as restoring a long-betrayed past. In South Asia there are reformist but conservative national movements, among both Hindus in India and Buddhists in Sri Lanka.

Partly because of these more radical movements, there are tensions between the blocs. Already of course there were conflicts between the Islamic Crescent and the West over Israel, regarded as an intrusion on rightful Islamic territory (the *Dar al-Islam*). But especially since the Islamic revolution in Iran there have been difficulties in Western–Islamic relations. These became obscured during the Gulf War of 1991, with differing Islamic nations taking opposing sides.

Conversely, the tensions between the (Asian) Marxist Bloc and the West, on the one hand, and the Islamic Crescent, on the other, have diminished, despite the Beijing massacre of 1989. The TransChristian East and West have largely reconciled their previously bitter differences. While the Southern regions of the world are worried, to put no finer point on it, by economic disparities and a perceived plunder of the South, the fact that these regions are dominated by Christianity modifies the resentment. On the whole, the lands of Traditional Asia have successfully entered the general capitalist system and religions such as Buddhism, **Hinduism,** Confucianism, Taoism and Shinto are happy enough in their, on the whole, fruitful interface with Western and Christian values.

As we have noted, the new global civilization has also tended to foster new religions and borrowings between religions. Forms of both Hindu and Buddhist **yoga** have made their way into Christian practice here and there, and more generally into Western culture. Conversely, Eastern religions have often adopted Western styles of self-presentation and organization. Many works written in English have incorporated Western philosophical ideas into Eastern doctrine. For instance, Swami Vivekananda's articulation of a modernized form of **Vedanta** as presenting the true meaning of the Hindu tradition, which remains popular among the Hindu élite, draws in some degree on motifs derived from 19th century idealism; while both Wittgensteinian and empiricist themes have entered into Sri Lankan Buddhist modernism. As we have noted, there are also conservative movements which represent a reaction against too much accommodation with both modernism and the new global order. They also reflect ways in which tensions between particular religions reinforce or are reinforced by ethnic tensions. Thus religious factors are important in various ongoing trouble zones, as well as some new ones opened up by the demise of the Soviet Union and the devolution of the old system into diverse republics.

The most obvious of the older, partly religion-based conflicts, are those in Northern Ireland and Israel. The division between the two Irish communities is in fact defined by religion, as between the Protestants and Catholics. We have noted how the Jewish state is resented by the Arab countries, partly because it

is seen as an alien non-Arab intrusion, but also because of the principle that the
territory of Islam (*Dar-al-Islam*) should not be violated by non-Islamic political
entities. Conversely, the concern for the land of Israel is more and more being
seen as a sacred one, not just as a secular quest for a homeland for the Jews
after the tragedy of the Holocaust. But there are plenty of other partially
religious conflicts elsewhere. Thus, the Sinhalese nationalist conflict with Tamils
(mainly Hindus and Christians) is partly grounded in the belief that Sri Lanka
is the true guardian of the Buddha's Law or *Dhamma*. This is reinforced by
appeal to the chronicles which piously detail Sinhalese history from a Buddhist
perspective. Again, the conflict between India and Pakistan over Kashmir turns
on the fact that Kashmir, a largely Muslim state, joined the Republic of India
after partition in 1947, because of the action of its then ruler, a Hindu. The rise
of revivalist Hindu sentiment in India is seen in the formation of the **Bharatiya
Janata Party,** which threatens to disturb the pluralist constitution and policy of
the Republic of India. In Afghanistan, much of the energy which motivated
the guerrillas (and now the government) fighting against the Soviet Union, and
then against the Marxist régime was energized by Islam. The civil war in the
South of the Sudan is partly fuelled by the dislike of Christians and adherents
of classical African religion for the imposition by the government in Khartoum
of Islamic law (*shari'a*). The fighting from 1989 on in Armenia and Azerbaijan
is dependent on the perception of national identities which are grounded both
in language and religion. Similarly, in Yugoslavia conflict between Croatians
and Serbians is heightened by religious differences. There are other struggles
in Myanmar (Burma), the Philippines, Thailand, Cambodia (Kampuchea), and
elsewhere which have a partly religious character.

It is now time to look a little more closely at developments in the various
blocs whose disposition in the modern global civilization we have sketched
above. First, in the TransChristian West there have been some notable
developments. The most significant probably was Vatican II (1962–1965): by
bringing *aggiornamento* (updating) to the Church Pope John XXIII (1881–1963)
effectively opened the way to liberal modernism within Catholicism. This in
turn greatly accelerated Catholic impulses to participate in the ecumenical
movement. The latter has brought a high degree of *rapprochement* between
most mainline Christian denominations. While Protestant mainline churches
in North America and elsewhere have experienced decline, the total impact
of liberal Christianity has gained because of the Catholic Church. But this has
in turn sparked conservative reactions, particularly over abortion, as a symbol
of the division between liberals and others. But also in the late '70s and '80s
evangelical and fundamentalist Christianity has shown renewed vigour. This in
turn has helped to fuel Protestant missionary activities, significant particularly
for Latin America. While in the TransChristian West as a whole new religions
have a diminished role, after their flourishing period between the late '60s
and the end of the '70s, there has been a growth more generally in themes
loosely collected together as the **New Age.** In the United States in particular
there has been a significant growth in people who have constructed private
religions, drawing on sources in both Christianity and in Eastern religions.
Significant too has been the increasing confidence of exponents of **Native
American religion**, beginning too to form alliances with analagous ill-treated
minorities such as the **Maoris** and **Australian Aborigines.** More significant is
the rooting of originally migrant groups in the West professing traditions

not hitherto regarded as Western: notably Muslims from Pakistan and India, North Africa and Turkey in Britain, France and Germany. Other groups such as traditional Sikhs, Hindus and Buddhists, as well as migrants of all kinds, have given most Western countries a pluralist feel. Most major cities contain sizeable groups from all the world's major cultures. This trend will doubtless continue, as frontier controls become more and more ineffective in restraining immigration into the richer countries from the poorer, including the former Soviet Union.

Meanwhile the revival of religion after the Soviet period is evident in the TransChristian East. While Marxism as an ideology is not as dead as might have seemed from the sudden collapse of the system in Eastern Europe and the former Soviet Union, the new freedoms allow churches to recruit and build, while a massive migration of Jews to Israel is beginning to alter the demographics of that country. Also the traditional religions of relatively small-scale groups among Siberian **shamanists** and so on are liable for revival. Russia also has within its border sizeable pockets of Muslims, as in Tatarstan. Islamic minorities in South-Eastern Europe, notably in Bulgaria and in Bosnia-Herzegovina, are significant, while Albania is resuming its role as the only predominantly Muslim state in Europe. Some Western influences are also beginning to penetrate the East, such as Christian evangelicalism and New Age concepts.

The Islamic Crescent possesses a variety of problematical developments. There remains a continuing crisis of Islamic identity. This is due to several factors. First of all, the period after World War II has been characterized by anti-colonial struggle, in the Middle East and North Africa, in South Asia and South-East Asia, and most recently in former Soviet Central Asia. Only in China does there remain a sizeable Islamic minority which has not achieved significant autonomy. During the first phase of anti-colonial nationalism the struggle was often conceived in socialist terms. Thus in the Arab lands, from Algeria to Iraq the primary model was modernizing and not Islamic. Hence the dominance of secular, non-religious régimes in the principal countries, under the aegis of the *Front de Libération Nationale*—FLN in Algeria, the Ba'ath parties of Syria and Iraq, and post-Nasserite régimes in Egypt. Second, the relative failure of these movements in delivering economic strength has led to the growth of neo-Islamic parties and governments, such as the Muslim Brotherhood in Syria and Egypt, suppressed sometimes with brutality, and régimes in the Sudan which have imposed Islamic law. Saudi Arabia has continued a conservative social stance, based on the **Wahhabi** movement dating from the late 18th century but revived as a state ideology from the 1920s. The most spectacular backlash both against monarchism in the Islamic world and against secular modernism was the Islamic revolution of Ayatollah Khomeini in Iran. A less strongly revivalist Islamic régime prevails in Pakistan (a country which was founded on Muslim values in 1947, though a break between the Western region and Bangladesh occurred in 1971—Islam alone being an insufficient bond between the two halves).

The relative ease with which Muslims, even from as far away as Indonesia, can get to Mecca reinforces the sense of unity among the pious. In consequence, a greater unification of practice and belief is becoming evident. There are tendencies opposed to traditional practices not perceived as truly Islamic, such as many of the rituals surrounding the cult of holy men, e.g. in North Africa, and there has been a great erosion of **Sufism,** because fundamentalist

revivalism pins some of the blame of the poor state of Islam under the impact
of colonialism on the fact that Muslims have not always practised a pure Islamic
faith. Though Sufism has had a modest appeal in the West it was suppressed
in westernizing Turkey. It maintained influence during the Soviet period in
Central Asia, partly because it was adapted to transmitting Islam in a private
and secret way. Disillusion both with traditionalism and with secular modernism
is a major factor in the new influence of radical revivalism, sometimes called
"fundamentalism".

Meanwhile in Israel the struggle between Palestinians and the Jewish state
has been largely conceived in secular nationalist and pan-Arab terms. But
religious factors are changing, through the growth of influence of the religious
right in Israel, notably through the Gush Emunim. In addition, among the
Palestinians, the rise of the Islamic revivalist **Hamas** is of increasing significance.
The spectrum of Jewish opinion remains highly diverse, from the secular and
often socialist **Zionism** of **kibbutz** pioneers, through the religious agnosticism
of many Israelis, to anti-Zionist Jewish conservatism and radical politically-
oriented religiosity.

The Latin South has long been dominated by the Roman Catholic Church,
which proselytized fairly successfully under the Spanish and Portuguese empires.
But since Vatican II in particular there has been some polarization. Liberation
theology has been a largely Latin American phenomenon, blending Catholic
and Marxist motifs and stressing the Church's need to maintain solidarity with
the poor and under-privileged. The establishment of new forms of spiritual and
social welfare through the setting up of base communities has helped to foster
a new self-consciousness, especially among Indians. Such a polarization of the
Church between the more radical priests and the old establishment attitude has
expressed itself in a strong tension in areas particularly of civil war (during the
late '70s and '80s in Nicaragua and El Salvador). In Peru the Sendero Luminoso
or Shining Path movement has exhibited a ruthless and anti-Catholic ideology.
But the main tendency in the '80s in Latin America was towards democratic
systems, going beyond both older authoritarianism and new revolution. During
the '70s and '80s the renewed vigour of conservative Christianity among North
American Protestants has helped to fuel a remarkable growth throughout Latin
America of Pentecostalism and evangelical faith. Such recruitment is in part
among tribal groups but is also evident among Catholics. Also important in
Latin America and the Caribbean are a number of African-based new religions,
combining often traditional African with Catholic and other elements. Notable
among these are the **Santería, Umbanda** and **Candomblé** in Brazil (though the
first originated in Cuba and has been spread in the US, Venezuela and elsewhere
by exiles from the Castro revolution of 1959). In Surinam and throughout the
whole Caribbean region we find varying groups and movements, perhaps the
most important being the **Rastafarians,** who look to Ethiopia and the late
emperor Haile Selassie (Ras Tafari) in hope, and Haitian **Voodoo.** All these
movements have penetrated into America through migrations.

Black African religion has had to contend with the need to come to
terms with the modern world: the impact of colonialism, modern science,
capitalism, a new nationalism somewhat arbitrarily expressed in terms of
colonial boundaries, struggles for independence, most recently in Zimbabwe
and South Africa, and missionary work. The traditional, largely smaller-scale,
societies have on the whole accepted Christianity (in some areas Islam).

Naturally, classical African religions have maintained themselves to some degree. The second and related problem is the need to synthesize some of the traditional values and those flooding in from the global civilization and from the West. The most important vehicle for such a synthesis are the new religious movements (over 10,000 in sub-Saharan Africa and over 3,000 in South Africa) which are mainly Christian and express through their black leadership a replacement of the previously European-dominated character of the mainline churches. Of these the most prominent perhaps is the **Kimbanguist Church,** originating in Zaire, and now admitted to the **World Council of Churches.** Its founder, Simon Kimbangu (died 1951), was both healer and prophet, and indeed martyr. The themes of prophetism and healing are prominent in indigenous revivals. The independent churches amount to more than 15 per cent of total Christian membership in Black Africa. In South Africa, taken together, they constitute the single largest religious movement (around 8,000,000).

The missionary churches have been prominent in the struggle for African freedoms. It is true that the **Dutch Reformed churches** of South Africa have generally speaking expressed an ideology of racial separateness. But otherwise the missionary movements, being close to Africans and inspired by ecumenical ideals, have fostered both the education and empowerment of African leaders.

The Marxist bloc, centered on China, has witnessed various vicissitudes. The clampdown associated with the massacre of Tiananmen Square in 1989 cannot conceal the degree of popular disillusion with the Marxist system. While in the '60s and '70s Maoist philosophy itself effectively constituted an evangelical kind of religion, being replete with rituals of solidarity, devotion to the leader, a revolutionary doctrine, a new ethics, and a new mythology, the period since Mao's death in 1976 has seen little new inspiration and much regret at the destruction caused to the fabric of Chinese society by Mao's vision. Further, though restrictions on religion in most of China have been eased, the colonialist oppression of Tibet remains, and to a lesser degree that of other minorities such as the Muslim Uighirs. The influence of Tibetan religion has paradoxically greatly increased through the dispersal of learned Tibetan monks throughout the world and through the example and teaching of the Dalai Lama.

In Marxist South-East Asia much of traditional religion, especially in Cambodia during the Khmer Rouge period (1975–1979), was suppressed. The Khmer Rouge preached a kind of nationalist hermitism, in which Cambodia was to be purified of modern elements, and cut off from the global capitalist system.

The region which I have called Traditional Asia contains varying tendencies. Some Buddhist countries have experimented with socialism, such as Burma and for a time Sri Lanka. There has been since World War II a revival of the Order or *Sangha,* partly through the greater emphasis on meditation methods, and partly through a new revival of Buddhist learning, fostered also by Western scholarship. New directions have occurred in lay participation and social revival. Meanwhile in India not only have new religious movements sprung up within Hinduism (such as that associated with Sai Baba, not to mention older trends such as that expressed through the **Aurobindo Ashram** and the continuing work of the **Ramakrishna Mission**). Most importantly there has been a new assertion of Hindu chauvinism, sparked in part by recognition that upper-class Hindus can be disadvantaged by affirmative action to uplift the scheduled castes (viz untouchables and others). The older pluralist philosophy is fading, and a new

Hindu self-consciousness is being developed throughout the Hindu diaspora (in the West Indies, South Africa, Fiji and Canada, etc.).

There has been some revival of Confucianism, especially in Singapore. New scholarship is restoring a sense of the Taoist heritage. Meanwhile in Japan and Korea there have occurred vigorous reinterpretations of **Zen,** and in Japan **Pure Land School** Buddhism. The new religions of Japan continue to play a role in adapting to new urban social configurations. There has been some revival of Shinto values, going back to the Meiji period (1867–1912) when they were given national prominence. The resurrection of Japanese patriotism in recent years is significant.

Finally, the South Pacific has seen some revival of traditional interests. The notion of a Pacific Way animates the small nations of the South Pacific, while Maori activists in New Zealand have begun to establish a more important place for traditional **Polynesian religion** in the fabric of New Zealand self-understanding.

One of the late questions on the agenda of non-Western cultures is how to synthesize the varying demands for religious recognition. Within Christianity there are diverse notions deriving basically from the 1970s, such as Black theology, African theology, Asian theologies, Red (Native American) theology and so forth. All the religions are moving into a period when they will need to express both their particular cultural embodiments and their universal or global significance, especially in relation to one another and to the various global ideologies.

Finally, a significant though minor change has been the development of cross-cultural religious studies, which helps to promote mutual understanding between the traditions but also a more objective and analytical knowledge of religion worldwide, without sacrificing the importance of empathy.

A

Adat Israel. See **Orthodox Judaism.**

Adventists. There are many Adventist groups, of which by far the largest is the Seventh Day Adventists, so called because they celebrate the "seventh day" i.e. Friday sunset to Saturday sunset, as the day of rest.

Adventists trace their origin to William Miller, a Baptist preacher in Massachusetts USA, who in 1836 concluded that Jesus Christ would come again to earth in 1844 (the "Second Advent"). When 1844 came most of his followers fell away. However a few remained and announced that Miller's interpretation of the Bible had been correct, but the event foretold was not Christ's return but the beginning of an investigation in heaven of those who have died, to determine who is worthy of resurrection.

In 1863 Adventists, under Ellen G. White, organized themselves into a denomination with its headquarters at Battle Creek. The first missionary was sent out in 1874, and the movement began in England in Southampton in 1878 with the work of W. Ing.

Adventists receive communion four times a year in a service preceded by foot-washing, and practise believers' baptism. Tithing (giving one-tenth of one's income to the church) is expected of all members. They favour vegetarianism and avoid tobacco, alcohol and other drugs.

Seventh Day Adventists are enthusiastic missionaries and have churches throughout the world. Since 1903 the headquarters has been in Washington DC, USA. The Adventist movement has proliferated significantly over the years. Other important groups include the Second Adventist Church which has many followers in the USA and **Branch Davidians** who, though small in number, are well known because of events in Waco, Texas, in 1993. Total global membership of Adventist churches stands at about 6.25 million. **Jehovah's Witnesses** and **Christadelphians** are sometimes classed as Adventist movements.

African New Religious Movements. There has been a steady increase in the number of New Religious Movements (NRMs) and their adherents since the turn of the century, although NRMs in Africa date back to the 17th century with the Antonian sect in the Kingdom of Congo. The vast majority are in sub-Saharan Africa, where by 1978 there were an estimated 10,000 movements with 10,000,000–12,000,000 active members. They are often messianic or millenarian in character, with prophetic leaders and an emphasis on healing, visions and dreams. The extent to which NRMs engage in political or welfare activities varies, both with regard to one another and within one movement over time. Some are highly fissiparous (such as the **Harris** churches in West Africa), and may decline or dissolve on the death of a charismatic founder (e.g. Alice Lenshina's Lumpa Church in Zambia). Others continue to expand and to adopt structures closer to the pattern of mission churches (e.g. the **Kimbanguist Church** in Zaire).

Attempts have been made to classify African NRMs along a continuum between traditional religion and mission **Christianity** (their degree of religious

syncretism), according to origin, or by reference to organizational and leadership structures. At best such descriptions can only provide a rough guide
with few NRMs falling neatly into any one category. Three broad types are
commonly recognized: (i) The most numerous and fastest growing are the
African Instituted, Independent or Indigenous churches, also known as **Zionist,**
prophet-healing or spiritual churches. They are broadly **Pentecostal** in character
with an emphasis on charismatic leadership and healing (e.g. the prophetic
Aladura, Harrist and Kimbanguist churches; the messianic Mai Chaza Church
and Johane Masowe's Apostolic Church in Zimbabwe, and the millenarian
Kitawala (Watch Tower movement); (ii) Separatist, African, Orthodox or
Ethiopian Churches, so called because of their separation from a parent body
(usually a mission church) in response to a desire for greater independence and
indigenization of leadership, sometimes with accommodation of customs such
as polygyny. The Jamaa Movement (Zaire), **Maria Legio** (Kenya) and Catholic
Church of the Sacred Heart (Zambia) originated in **Roman Catholic** missions
while the Church of Christ in Africa (Kenya), Providence Industrial Mission
(Malawi) and the Cameroon **Baptist** Convention separated from **Protestant**
bodies. The ancient **Coptic** Church in Ethiopia and Old Testament prophets
often provide inspiration for a more African form of Christianity than that
offered by the mission churches; (iii) Neo-traditional or syncretist movements
which attempt to reform or revive traditional customs while incorporating some
Christian (or occasionally Muslim) elements (e.g. the **Bwiti** cult in Gabon, the
Poro and Sande cults among Mande-speakers in West Africa and the National
Church of Nigeria).

African Traditional Religions. Traditional religions, Christianity and Islam
have coexisted for many centuries in Africa and have frequently interacted,
influencing one another's practices and beliefs. The term "African Traditional
Religions" (ATRs) is used to refer to the oral religious traditions of peoples
who have not subscribed to either of these two "religions of the book",
and are found mainly south of the Sahara. The pervasive, implicit nature
of African Traditional Religions led some early Western observers to deny
the existence of "religion" among peoples without a written tradition. More
recently, however, scholars have appreciated that the term "religion" is itself
a Western cultural construct. Examples of African "religiosity" abound, but
based upon a cosmology in which the entire world can be viewed as a source
of power to be held in balance, controlled, checked, and channelled, rather than
on Western notions which distinguish between the sacred and secular, natural
and supernatural.

There has been some discussion as to whether it is correct to speak of
African Traditional Religion, or only of a multitude of different religions. While
anthropologists have tended to examine the specificity of particular religious
traditions, African theologians have sought to map out the common ground
between traditional religions. Geographical, historical, linguistic and social
forces have certainly produced a bewildering variety of religious expressions and
customs, yet some common characteristics do emerge, particularly regarding
underlying attitudes and assumptions about the nature and role of human
beings and their place within the world. The comments that follow indicate
some features which are common to many ATRs, none of which, however, are
ubiquitous, or take precisely the same form in different societies.

African Traditional Religions have been described as forms of "diffused monotheism" or "refracted theism". There is a common belief in a supreme creator, who is generally beneficent and can be petitioned directly in times of crisis, (known as *kwoth* among the Nuer of the Southern Sudan), and may even be associated with a particular sacred place (Mount Meru in Kenya for the Kikuyu) but who acts more commonly through intermediaries in the form of lesser divinities, spirits or ancestors. These intermediaries may be regarded as symbols or conceptualizations of the power inherent in the world and in people (as for the Shona of Zimbabwe). For the Uduk, of the Sudan/Ethiopian border, deities emanating from outside, be it from Muslim neighbours, Christian missionaries or Nilotic peoples to the south, can be contrasted to an implicit form of "moral knowledge" based on their experience of the hunt, human existence and mortality and conceptualized as an animating life force (*Arum*), which has become differentiated within the world.

Creation myths commonly relate a time when a creator god lived close to human beings, who were immortal. Through accident, chance, or as a result of human misbehaviour, the creator withdrew from intimate contact with human society and the connection between heaven and earth was severed, introducing mortality. Cosmogonies are usually explanatory—they describe the situation in which human beings find themselves—rather than apportioning blame, suggesting a means of salvation, or the restoration of a primordial state. The world as it is experienced, the reality of life, mortality and regeneration, is the starting point for ritual activity and worship.

The degree of centralization and elaboration of religious authority mirrors the political and economic situation of a particular people. In the medieval centralized kingdoms of West Africa, Zimbabwe and the Sudan, traditions of divine kingship sought accommodation with older more diffuse sources of authority. Among the Yoruba peoples of Nigeria, Benin and Togo, for instance, modern rituals re-enact struggles between local cults and a centralized imperial religion. In agricultural societies the king or chief is often associated with the fertility of the land and will usually sacrifice at a sacred shrine on behalf of his people. For the Zulu of southern Africa fertility is conceptualized as a female deity, who plays an important role in girls' initiation ceremonies in this patrilineal society in which women, through marriage, form a link between clans. Zulu women are also frequently healers and ritual specialists, suited by their social role to mediate also between the spirits and human society, or to repair rifts in the social fabric. Nomadic peoples, such as the Mbuti of Zaire, the Khoisan peoples of southern and south-west Africa, or the **Nuer and Dinka** of the southern Sudan, with a decentralized or segmentary social structure, are unlikely to recognize centralized spiritual authorities or shrines with permanent religious specialists to serve them.

Continuity between the living and the dead is expressed through contact with ancestors, particularly the recent or "living dead" (also referred to in the literature as "shades"), who have the power to intervene in individual or communal affairs. When they have no one left alive who remembers and pays respect to them, seeking their good will and mediation through libations by offering sacrifices to their skulls or to carved wooden ancestor statues (as among the Bangwa of south-west Cameroon), they may become disembodied spirits, lacking in individual personality. Access to ancestral skulls is, for the Bangwa, itself a source of political and spiritual authority. The male successor of the patrigroup sacrifices skulls on behalf of those related to the deceased. For women, who can inherit the skulls of female, but not male kin, and whose skulls do not form patrigroup lineages, prayer is more personal and the relationship between a deceased woman and her children less threatening. For the Mbuti the spirits of the dead merge with the other spirits of the forest and can become a potential menace to those who dwell there.

Belief in multiple selves or disparate psychic powers within an individual are common. Thus that part of a person which represents continuity with a family or clan can be reincarnated, while the dead individual retains his or her position as an ancestor. Other "selves" may manifest their presence through dreams or witchcraft activity, either volitionally or without the knowledge of the conscious self. Witchcraft may be used for the benefit of the individual or community, or for anti-social ends (sorcery—associated with night time activity, shape-changing, cannibalism, incestuous behaviour and the beasts of the bush or forest). Witch-curing cults, which ward off or counteract the activities of sorcerers and witches, have gained in popularity in recent years, as have healing cults in general. All sickness has a potentially "supernatural" source, as it is the diminution of personal power either through possession by a deity, spirit or ancestor, or the maleficent effects of sorcery or witchcraft. Divination, often by a specialist using some form of oracle, determines the source of the illness and allows for appropriate remedies. (Western understandings of curing can sometimes co-exist with traditional beliefs, as the former are more concerned with mechanical processes than with the underlying rationale of sickness and health.) Where sickness results from spirit possession the afflicted individual may become a mouthpiece for that particular deity or spirit, and can build up a reputation as a **shamanic** healer.

The powers and forces which are possessed by and emanate from people, as well as from other animate and inanimate sources, continually interact, and must be kept in balance. Music can play an important part in restoring harmony, as in the Mbuti *elima* female initiation ceremony, in which the slumbering forest is reawakened. Securing the blessings of life, and maintaining fertility, economic prosperity and harmony within the community, while countering the threats of war, disease, drought and death, require continual vigilance and appropriate ritual activity. Christianity and Islam may be harnessed as sources of power and directed towards these ends (cf. Shona Spirit Churches and other **African New Religious Movements**). Traditional religions are far from static, with new cults (such as the **Bwiti** in Gabon), rituals and religious responses developing and interacting with one another in reply to 20th century demands. ATRs show little inclination, as some 19th century missionaries had assumed, to wither away with the advance of **Christianity** and "Western civilization".

Aga Khanis. In 1817 the Shah of Iran conferred the honorific title Aga Khan (or Aqa Khan) on the spiritual leader (Imam) of the **Nizaris,** the larger of the two main surviving branches of **Isma'ili Shi'ism** within **Islam.** Following an unsuccessful rebellion against the Shah in 1841, the Aga Khan fled to India, eventually making Bombay his headquarters in 1848. The hereditary title has passed to his successors as Imams, and as a result "Aga Khanis" has come to be used as a common designation for the Nizari sect within Isma'ili Shi'ism. Thus the Agha Khanis and the Nizaris are one and the same group, with the different names indicating different aspects of their history and tradition.

The Aga Khanis are sometimes also referred to as **Khojas,** but strictly speaking this is inaccurate: it is not the case either that all Khojas are Aga Khanis, or that all Aga Khanis are Khojas.

Not all Khojas are Aga Khanis: a few are not Nizaris at all, but **Twelvers** (and indeed a few are even Hindus). Conversely, not all Aga Khanis are Khojas: some Nizaris within India, and those elsewhere (e.g. in Syria and Iran), are drawn from quite different groups.

The confusion has presumably arisen because, under the Agha Khan's leadership, the Nizari Khojas have become a wealthy and widely distributed community, with a major presence in East Africa.

The religious centres of the Nizaris are known as *jama'at khanas*, being assembly and prayer halls which also function as mosques. Aga Khan III (d. 1957) established the practice of using these for the dissemination of modern adaptations of the faith, both in religious matters and also on social issues: he regularly sent *farmans* (religious guidance) to be read out in all jama'at khanas. He encouraged not only younger people, but also women, to lead public prayers.

Aga Khan III was also—playing a non-sectarian role—one of the main forces behind the foundation of the All-India Muslim League in 1906, and was elected President of the League of Nations in 1937. The tradition he established of a variety of charity work—building schools, hospitals, clinics, welfare organizations—has been continued by Aga Khan IV, now resident in France, who in 1967 established the Aga Khan Foundation to promote humanitarian and cultural causes. The Aga Khanis remain a well organized and influential community both within India and beyond.

Aghoris. Aghoris are Indian ascetics living in and around cremation grounds, renowned for their unorthodox and antinomian practices. They are the successors to the, now defunct, ascetic tradition of the **Kapalikas.** The Aghoris worship Shiva in his terrifying form as Aghora; imitating their god by wearing long, matted hair, going naked or draped in a stolen shroud, covered with ashes from the cremation ground, garlanded with bones, carrying a skull begging bowl taken from a corpse found in a river and behaving as if mad. The ascetics aim at liberation from *karma* and the cycle of reincarnation by embracing the impure and abandoning social norms. In some rituals the Aghori worships Shiva seated upon the chest of a corpse and might consume the corpses's flesh, as well as excrement and urine. Aghori ritual involves the use of the five "m"s of **Tantrism,** namely alcohol, meat, fish, parched grain (perceived as an aphrodisiac) and performing sexual intercourse with a menstruating or low-caste woman or prostitute. Through these rites the Aghori is breaking brahmanical taboos and acting out his monistic theology. At death an Aghori is buried in a meditation posture in a tomb called a *samadh*. This becomes a place of reverence for devotees. Few Aghoris remain in India, though there is a centre or *ashram* at Varanasi established in the 18th century by the sect's founder Kina Ram, who is said to have been an incarnation of Shiva.

Agudat Israel. (*See also* **Hasidism; Orthodox Judaism; Zionism.**) Agudat Israel (Hebrew, Association or Union of Israel) is the single most important, international Jewish **Orthodox** organization, and later also an Israeli political party. It was founded in Kattowitz (Upper Silesia) in 1912 as an attempt to preserve and protect the strictly Orthodox way of life against a plethora of modern challenges. Like **Zionism** it sought to develop a mass movement among the Jews of Europe. The actual context of the formation of Agudat Israel was to counter the growing Zionist Organization but other threats included **Reform Judaism,** the assimilation of Jews into European culture and socialism. The founders, who included some of the greatest rabbinic authorities of the day (e.g. Rabbis Israel Meir Hacohen, Haim Soloveitchik of Brisk, Haim Oser Grodenski of Vilna and Abraham Mordecai Alter of **Ger (Hasidism)**), sought to re-establish the historical position of the great rabbis of the Jewish community as its leaders. They formed a Council of Torah Sages (Moetzet Gedolei Hatorah) as Agudat's ruling advisory body and a Great Assembly (Kenesiyyah Hagedolah) which included representatives of German Neo-Orthodoxy; Polish and Lithuanian Orthodoxy (Hasidic and non-Hasidic) and Hungarian Orthodoxy. Thus under the umbrella of Agudat Israel were a wide variety of opinions and styles of Orthodox Judaism. Agudat centres, youth movements and women's groups were established throughout the **Ashkenazi** world.

Jewish education was a priority concern. The movement was particularly influential in Poland and took an active part in Polish politics with a number of Agudat candidates being elected to the Polish parliament.

Agudat's attitude to the Zionists' aim of Jewish resettlement in Israel was ambiguous—while supporting Orthodox Jewish communities in Israel, the idea of a non-religious state was rejected. The rise of Nazism in the 1930s gave rise to a change in Agudat policy and settlement in Israel was supported and Agudat members were encouraged to emigrate there. Also Israel came to be recognized and accepted as the centre of Jewish Orthodox life. The Holocaust wiped out the European heartland of Agudat Israel and the movement, while still represented in most centres of Jewish population, is now based in Israel and the USA.

In America since 1939, Agudat Israel supports Jewish educational and other facilities and publishes the monthly *Jewish Observer*. It opposes the inclusion of non-Orthodox elements in communal organizations.

In Israel since 1919, Agudat Israel set about the task of building a separate **Ultra-Orthodox** community in the land, totally independent of the Zionist Organization and Jewish Agency. Immigrants after 1935, particularly from Poland, led to a change in their separatist policy and the development of a more accommodating stand on working with the Zionists. This development led to **Neturei Karta** and other extreme anti-Zionist groups leaving Agudat Israel. From Agudat Israel's ranks the Agudat Workers' Party had also emerged in Poland. In time this party became independent and pursued separate policies and later took part in a number of Israeli coalition governments.

Agudat Israel joined the provisional government of the State in 1948 and was part of the ruling coalition until leaving following a dispute over religious education in 1952. In 1953 Agudat established an independent religious school system that was government funded. Agudat has, and is, represented at the national and municipal levels. From 1952 until 1977, when Agudat joined Menahem Begin's ruling Likud coalition, Agudat did not participate in the government. In 1973 it re-combined with its Workers' Party. Its position is still somewhat ambiguous in that it does not fully recognise the legitimacy of the non-religious state yet it takes part in the political process and even accepts senior committee posts.

Agudat Israel has consistently fought for the support of its institutions and over issues of *halakhah* (Jewish law) and the state. It insists on fighting what it understands as "secular" coercion, such as the conscription of religious women, abortion, etc., and holds that values cannot be generated by society alone and thus there is need for the authoritative interpretation of religious texts as the guide for contemporary values. Traditionally it sought to develop the Torah-state in Israel and limited its energies to direct religious issues, however, in recent years Agudat has developed concerns relating to foreign policy and national security. For example in the 1988 elections, largely under the influence of the **Lubavich** Rebbe, Menahem Schneersohn, it took a hard line on the return of the occupied territories ("not an inch").

Agudat Israel was for a generation the only major **Haredi** party and the second religious party in Israel after the religious Zionist, **Mafdal** party. In 1984 **Shas (Sephardi Torah Guardians' Party)** was formed to counter the **Ashkenazi** domination of Agudat, thus splitting the Haredi vote. Just before the 1988 general election, a further split took place when a new **Haredi** party was founded, Degel Hatorah (Torah Flag) to counter the Hasidic domination of Agudat Israel (largely by **Ger** and **Lubavich**) and give a voice to the Lithuanian Haredi (and **Belz** Hasidic) communities. Degel Hatorah took two seats in the Knesset (Israeli parliament), Agudat gained five seats and Shas an unexpected six seats, giving the Haredi community as a whole an unprecedented 13 seats. After the 1988 elections it appeared as if there had been an increase in the power of Agudat and the Haredi community as a whole. However for the 1992 Israeli general election in an unsuccessful attempt to consolidate the Ashkenazi Haredi vote, Agudat Israel and Degel Hatorah joined forces as **United Torah Judaism.** This new alliance took only four seats, while Shas retained its six seats. While Agudat is no longer the sole political voice of the Ultra-Orthodox, it still represents the voice of the Ashkenazi, especially Hasidic communities.

Ahl al-Da'wa. This is the name—meaning "People of the Call"—under which the Algerian branch of the **Muslim Brotherhood** is known.

Ahl-i Hadith. The Indian Muslim movement known as *Ahl-i Hadith*, which means "People of the Traditions", came from a similar intellectual background and shared similar concerns to those of the **Deobandis**. They were, however, more extreme in their ideas, more intense in their commitment, more élitist in social background, more consciously sectarian in their behaviour, and less influential. Many came from once great Muslim families which had fallen on hard times. By the 20th century the movement had developed madrasahs, mosques, journals, and from 1912 its annual All-India Ahl-i Hadith Conference.

Like the Deobandis, the Ahl-i Hadith are committed to purifying Muslim behaviour of all practices not sanctioned by Islamic law. In doing so, however, they reject the decisions of the medieval law schools, and use only the Quran and the Traditions as guidance, and only those jurisprudential techniques sanctioned by the Traditions as method. Their approach means very great individual responsibility for the believer; they condemn almost all expressions of Islamic mysticism.

The ways of the Ahl-i Hadith are puritanical. They insist, for instance, on simple marriage celebrations and scrupulous fulfilment of the requirements of the faith. Their style is sectarian and embattled; they sport their own cut of beard and insist on their form of prayer which involves, amongst other things, saying *Amen* aloud and a different positioning of the hands. In British India they were often the focus of disturbances. Furthermore, as is not unusual in the case of such intense ideological sects, a group split off in the late 19th century to form the **Ahl-i Quran**. There is much similarity between the Islamic stance of the Ahl-i Hadith and that of the **Wahhabis** of Saudi Arabia. They have spread with the South Asian diaspora of the 20th century and currently have branches in all the major cities of Britain as well as in Europe.

Ahl-i Haqq. The *Ahl-i Haqq* ("People of the Truth") are adherents of a small but scattered religion found in western Iran and parts of north-eastern Iraq and Soviet Central Asia. There are also members in most major Iranian cities. Followers are often misleadingly termed 'Ali-Ilahis ("believers in the divinity of 'Ali"), but in fact the **Shi'ite** Imam 'Ali plays only a minor part in their system. The sect combines extremist Shi'ite beliefs with elements from **Sufism** and local legend. Doctrine centres around the notion of successive manifestations of the divinity and repeated metempsychosis, while religious practices have clear links with those of some Sufi brotherhoods, including entry into trance states, during which burning coals are handled. The Ahl-i Haqq are split into numerous ethnic, tribal, and religious groups. There is no central organization, nor do they have a canonical scripture.

Ahl-i Quran. The Ahl-i Quran stem from a splinter group of the **Ahl-i Hadith**, led by Maulana Abdullah Chakralavi in Lahore, which asserted from the late 19th century that only the Quran could be used as a source of authority. They are exclusive and have a history of strife with the Ahl-i Hadith. A notable developer of the position of the Ahl-i Quran was the Pakistani thinker Ghulam Ahmad Parvez (1903–1985). His followers, the Parvezis, are based in London and hold annual functions.

Ahl-i Sunnat wa Jama'at. This is the self-designation, as "true Sunnis", of the Indian Muslim movement known as the **Barelvis**.

Ahmadiya (Lahoris). A group of highly educated men who split from the **Ahmadiya (Qadianis)** in 1914 over the succession to the leadership of the community. They felt that the leader should be selected; the bulk of the community wanted to confine the choice to the family of the founder, Ghulam Ahmad. The Lahoris have gradually edged their way back to the mainstream of Islam.

Ahmadiya (Qadianis). The Ahmadiya were the last major Islamic movement to develop in 19th-century India. The founder was Mirza Ghulam Ahmad (1839–1908), who came from an old Mughal service family of the Punjab, a province wracked by competition between Christian and Hindu missionaries. Ghulam Ahmad began as a champion of Islamic orthodoxy, but in the process claimed to be an incarnation of the Hindu God, Krishna, the true Christian Messiah (Jesus, he argued, had not died on the Cross but had lived to carry his mission to northern India and was buried in Kashmir), and a Muslim prophet

— Muhammad, he declared, had been the last of the law-giving prophets, but he, Ghulam Ahmad, was a prophet as a reviver of religion (*mujaddid*). These claims were bitterly contested by nearly all Muslims. Ghulam Ahmad and his followers were forced to separate from the **Sunnis** and pray in their own mosques, being known as Qadianis.

The Ahmadiya are one of the most highly organized Muslim communities. Leadership has passed down through the descendants of Ghulam Ahmad, who are regarded as having the gift of prophecy—a claim opposed by the rival **Ahmadiya** (**Lahoris**). They are most efficiently organized as a great multinational concern, with their headquarters first at Qadian and then, after the partition of India, at the purpose-built town of Rabwa in Pakistan. All members of the community pay a tithe of 6.5 per cent of their income each year.

The Ahmadiya are also amongst the most vigorous proselytizers of **Islam.** Currently they have a presence in 120 countries, and missionaries at work in 48. Around 10,000,000 followers are claimed worldwide; the most successful area of proselytization outside Pakistan has been West Africa. Ahmadis are present in all Western European countries. In Britain they have 45 branch associations and two notable centres, the London Mosque at Wandsworth, and Islamabad, near Tilford in Surrey, where they have printing facilities in 30 different languages. The London Mosque is the movement's designated international headquarters. The movement also runs a daily satellite television service (MTV—Muslim Television). This provides "Islamic programmes" four hours each day, capable of being received throughout the world.

The Ahmadiya are hated by all Muslims, being deemed to have betrayed Islam by the nature of their heteredox beliefs. They have suffered appalling persecution in Pakistan and in other Muslim countries; the current head of the community lives in exile in London. They have many similarities with another (erstwhile) Islamic messianic movement, the **Bahais**, who emerged in 19th-century Iran. There is, however, one difference; the Bahais have left Islam, the Ahmadiya have not—although they have in effect been expelled.

Aladura. Aladura (Yoruba, "owners of prayer") is a term used to describe various prophet-healing churches, going under names such as the Celestial Church of Christ, the Brotherhood of the Cross and Star and the numerous Cherubim and Seraphim societies, primarily in Nigeria and neighbouring West African countries, although there are offshoots in Europe and the USA. Aladura churches originated around 1918, with considerable expansion in the 1930s under Jospeh Babalola's mass healing movement, and gaining in respectability and size since Nigeria's independence (1960). Although now also making converts in Nigeria's Muslim north, the majority of members are still drawn from former mission churches, appearing less élitist and offering greater scope for participation and leadership, particularly for women. Relations between Aladura churches are generally cordial but attempts at union have met with little success. Links with Western **Pentecostal** churches are common, and Oshitelu's **Church of the Lord, Aladura,** with over 1,000,000 members, is affiliated to the **World Council of Churches.**

'Alawis. This is a general term applied to various political and religious groupings with particular connections to the **Shi'ite** Imam 'Ali. Nowadays it is mainly used to refer to the **Nusayri** sect found in Syria and to a lesser extent in Turkey, especially around Antakya.

The Nusayris, under the label 'Alawis, should not be confused with the **Alevis** of Turkey.

Alevis. The Alevis are a heterodox Islamic group in Turkey, where they are claimed by some observers to constitute as many as a quarter of the total population—a claim which, however, it is impossible to verify. They are sometimes confused with the **'Alawis,** some of whom are also found in Turkey, but the distinction remains clear if the latter are referred to by their other name, **Nusayris**.

One thing that Alevis and 'Alawis do have in common is, as these names imply, a veneration for 'Ali, the nephew and son-in-law of the Prophet Muhammad, and for this reason they are often classified as **Shi'ites**. The **Twelver Shi'ites** of Iran, however, although they have begun to establish links with the 'Alawis of Syria, reject the Alevis as heretics. Nor do the Alevis regard themselves as being Shi'ites. They are close to, if not indeed identical with the **Qizilbash**.

They distinguish themselves from their **Sunni** neighbours, however, in several ways additional to their veneration of 'Ali, to whom they attribute divinity. They reject the Sunni practice of prayer five times a day as mere external ritual; they reject the month of fasting at Ramadan—replacing it with 12 days (in memory of the 12 Imams of the Twelvers, and generally observed during the month of Muharram when Twelvers commemorate the martyrdom of Imam Hussain at Karbala); they reject the pilgrimage to Mecca; and they observe less strict rules of ritual purity. Distinctive of them too is their veneration of the rabbit, against the eating of which there is a taboo.

They have their own independent religious organization in eastern Turkey (many Alevis are Kurds), which is hierarchical in structure: in a given region a *mursid* (professor) is in charge, with elders or *pirs* under him, and guides or *rehbers* under them in turn. *Mursids* and *pirs* both come from sacred lineages, and intermarriage with ordinary villagers is forbidden, being widely regarded as equivalent to incest.

The pir—known too as the *dede*—visits villages in his jurisdiction, and the villagers collect funds to give him. He also presides over the central annual ritual known as the *ayn-i cem*, (service of union). This involves prayer, the sacrifice of a ram (symbolic of submission—*islam*—to God as in the story of Abraham's readiness to sacrifice his son) followed by a communal meal in which food and wine are shared by all equally; preaching, singing, slow-turning dances similar to those of the Whirling Dervishes (**Mawlawiya**), and communal recitations of the oft-repeated name of God (*zikr*), in a session which lasts the whole night until the following morning.

There are clear similarities here to practices of certain **Sufi** orders, especially the **Bektashiya**, whose founder, Hajji Bektash, they particularly venerate (along with Jalal al-Din Rumi, the famous mystic-poet founder of the Mawlawiya). Indeed, the Alevis may have originated as an offshoot of the Bektashis, and the two groups—along with the Nusayris—are regarded as in some sense kinsfolk.

Another practice which reinforces the Alevi sense of community is the tradition of each young person being "paired" with another (known as a *musahip*) from a very early age; and of married couples being paired too (known as *eş tutma*).

Within Turkey Alevis have been regarded with suspicion by the Sunni majority, both because of their allegedly grave heresy, and because of their alleged links with Kurdish nationalism and/or extreme leftism/Communism. They in turn have sought to claim the equality that is their due according to the principles of the Kemalist secular state. In 1966 they began publishing a bi-monthly political and cultural journal, *Cem*. This has often contained attacks on two modern Sunni movements, the **Nurcus** and the **Süleymancis.**

From the '60s on, there has been a trend towards politicizing the faith, and particularly among Alevi migrant groups in Germany, for example, songs in praise of egalitarian social justice have been introduced into the Ayn-i Cem alongside the traditional devotional ones. Cassettes and videos celebrating, say, the life of Pir Sultan Abdal, the great Alevi poet, as a battle on behalf of the poor and powerless against a strong and tyrannical centralized power, are also in wide circulation: they have clear contemporary implications, and the Turkish state remains suspicious.

'Ali-Ilahis. A term erroneously applied to the **Ahl-i Haqq.**

Amal. AMAL is an acronym for the Arabic *afwaj al-muqawamah al-lubnaniyah* (Lebanese Resistance Detachments) and forms the Arabic word for "hope". AMAL—or commonly "Amal"—was founded by Imam Musa al-Sadr in July 1975 as the military and political wing of an organization known as *Harakat al-mahrumin* (The Movement of the Deprived). Imam al-Sadr was a charismatic **Shi'ite** leader who became president of the Supreme Islamic Shi'a Council of Lebanon in 1969, two years after its foundation as the first recognized political institution to represent the interests of the Lebanese Shi'ites. In 1974, he founded the Movement of the Deprived which grew out of his deep concern for the plight of the Lebanese poor, many of whom were Shi'ites. He worked closely with the **Melkite** Bishop George Haddad in their common fight for the rights of the poor. The formation of a militia by a religious and political movement is typical of Lebanese communalism, where most political groups represent a religious constituency and have their own militias (for example the **Maronite** Christian Phalangists and the **Sunni** Muslim Murabitun).

Imam al-Sadr's disappearance while visiting Libya in 1978 remains a mystery. Following his disappearance his leadership role was divided. Shaikh Shamsuddin continued as deputy head of the Supreme Shi'ite Council, and by mid-1980 Nabih Birri, a lawyer, was President of the Amal Leadership Council. In spite of personal rivalry between the two leaders, the leadership of both organizations remained generally faithful to Imam al-Sadr's vision as expressed in the 1975 Charter of the Movement of the Deprived and later accepted as Amal's Charter. The Charter comes out strongly against traditional Lebanese confessionalism and in favour of complete equality of all Lebanese citizens. It argues that the political confessionalism of the Lebanese system hinders constructive political development and divides the citizenry into mutually exclusive categories which destroy national unity.

In contrast to its more radical rival, **Hizbollah**, Amal's aim is for a reformed Lebanese system rather than the establishment of an Islamic state modelled on Iran. In this it differs too from Islamic Amal. It has opposed Hizbollah's policy of hostage-taking, and fierce fighting broke out between the two groups in 1988 and 1989 over a number of issues. This fighting was followed by a ceasefire and an agreement which may, however, prove to be purely temporary.

Amarapura Nikaya. One of the three main divisions of the **Theravada** Buddhist *Sangha* in Sri Lanka. Founded in the 19th century as a protest against the royal sponsorship and casteism of the **Siyam Nikaya**, its ordination lineage derives from the **Shwegyin** order based at Amarapura, Burma, hence its name. Once established on Sri Lankan soil entry to the order was not dependent on caste, though as time has progressed caste specific sub-groups have emerged. Of the current 18 fraternities, the most prominent are the Mulavamsa, Saddhammavamsa, Kalyanavamsa and Dhammarakkhitavamsa. Organization is rather loose and the united order is presently presided over by Ven. Balangoda Ananda Maitreya, a scholar, visionary and astrologer. Amarapura's approximately 3,000 monks reside in about 1,000 monasteries throughout the island and are thought to be more puritanical than members of other orders. Distinctively, they cover both shoulders with their robe and leave their eyebrows unshaven.

Amish. The Amish are a branch of the **Mennonite** Church. They were originally followers of Jakob Ammann, a Swiss 17th-century Mennonite elder who set high, rigid standards of behaviour and dress and withdrew his followers from the mainstream Mennonites. Amish families migrated to America in the 18th century and settled in Pennsylvania, later spreading out to other states. The movement eventually died out in Europe.

Old Order Mennonite Amish live in settlements of up to 200 people each. There are no church buildings; members meet in each other's homes. The leader of the settlement is the bishop, aided in worship by preachers and deacons. Services are conducted in a distinctive language known as Pennsylvanian Dutch (a mixture of Old German and English).

Amish men have beards (but not moustaches) and their clothes fasten with hooks and eyes, not buttons. They wear distinctive broadbrimmed black hats. Women wear long full dresses without jewellery, black stockings and shoes, plus bonnets and shawls. They do not have electric light, telephones or motor cars, but despite refusing to use modern machinery have a high reputation as farmers. Each community is independent, and a community may divide into two if it is too large.

The Amish practise adult baptism and celebrate Holy Communion and foot-washing. It is believed there are over 50,000 Amish.

Anabaptists. *See* **Mennonites.**

Ananda Marga. Ananda Marga is a new religious movement founded in 1955 in Bihar, India, by Shri Anandamurti (b. 1921). He taught a form of **Tantrism** based on chanting, meditation and Yoga. It is highly structured and ascetic, with strict regulations on cleanliness, conduct, diet (vegetarian), and sex. Fully committed members (*acharyas*)—estimated at several hundred thousand worldwide—wear Indian dress, take an Indian name, and are celibate, though part-time members blend in with society.

The movement has been accused of violent terrorism, and believes the use of force is justified against tyranny and exploitation. It was banned in India during the 1970s emergency, when its leader was imprisoned, though finally acquitted, on murder charges.

The movement used to have a large following in Europe, especially Germany, but numbers are now diminishing. It runs schools, orphanages and projects for the poor in several Third World countries.

Angkatan Belia Islam Malaysiam (ABIM). ABIM, the Malaysian Islamic Youth Movement, is one of the most important *dakwah* (Muslim renewal) organizations in Malaysia. Founded by students of the University of Malaya in 1971, this campus-based movement was in the 1970s responsible for the radicalizing of Malay students at home and overseas. ABIM's founders saw **Islam** as a force for change throughout society, including political change, and as a comprehensive way of life relevant to all areas of society. ABIM lays much emphasis on international Muslim brotherhood, and on justice in all spheres, campaigning for example against government corruption. Close ideological similarities are claimed with two well-established Islamic movements abroad, the **Jama'at-i Islami** and the **Muslim Brotherhood.**

Like most *dakwah* organizations, ABIM operates through a network of cell groups, on campuses and in university halls. It also publishes magazines and pamphlets, and promotes training and education in true Islamic principles. Its influence has changed the whole nature of student life in Malaysia, symbolized perhaps by increasingly strict Islamic dress becoming standard on campus. For a while, especially between 1979 and 1981, it also commanded increasing respect in rural areas through its championing of social as well as religious issues.

ABIM is now a relatively declining force. UMNO (United Malay National Organization), the main, Malay–Muslim, party in the government coalition, moved to counter its influence, for example by setting up rival schools, and rival programmes of talks and seminars. In 1982 UMNO actually recruited the charismatic ABIM president, Anwar Ibrahim, to its ranks—in which he quickly ascended to ministerial level. This "defection" induced many ABIM members to transfer their allegiance to the fundamentalist opposition group PAS (**Parti Islam Se-Malaysia**), leaving ABIM appreciably weakened. Its progressive emphases have been displaced by more radical fundamentalist groups and influences, including **Darul Arqam.**

Anglicans. Adherents of the Church of England are called Anglicans in Britain. All the churches which belong to the Anglican Communion trace their origins to the Church of England and send bishops to the Lambeth Conference. They are independent, autonomous churches, except in England where the mother-church has restrictions placed on it by Parliament. Anglicanism outside Britain is largely the result of missionary and imperialist outreach. The beliefs and practices of the Church of England were carried to the American colonies (where they were originally under the episcopal oversight of the bishop of London), to Canada. India, Australia and New Zealand, and to those parts of Africa, Asia, and the Caribbean where British colonies were established.

The Church of England claims to be a reformed Catholic Church. The Reformation in England was partly an act of state, decided by King Henry VIII, but made possible also by the influence of **Protestant** ideas from the continent, and by an upsurge of popular piety. In England, the authority of the Pope was renounced by the *Act of Supremacy* in 1534. The *Book of Common Prayer* was authorized in 1559, and for centuries provided the only permissible forms of service which could be used in Anglican churches. Doctrine and ritual were defined in the *Thirty-nine Articles* of 1571, and the Bible was translated into English in the Authorized Version of 1611. The Church of England attempts to be inclusive, and contain those with widely differing theological emphases. These include Evangelicals, who include the present Archbishop of Canterbury, Dr George Carey, who stress individual commitment to Christ. The Archbishop of York, Dr John Habgood, on the other hand, values the historical role of the church of the kingdom of England, by law established, with the monarch as Supreme Governor, and bishops in the House of Lords. There are high churchmen, sometimes called **Anglo-Catholics,** who see themselves as heirs to a fusion of the Celtic Church pioneered in the north by Aidan of Lindisfarne in 634, and also of the mission from Rome sent by Pope Gregory and led by Augustine who reached Canterbury in 597. As an episcopal church, value is placed on the historic succession of bishops.

The creation of bishops outside England inevitably presented problems for united action. In 1867 Archbishop Longley invited all the diocesan bishops to a conference at Lambeth, and his successors have normally repeated the invitation every 10 years. Lambeth Conferences provide an indication of the Anglican instinct on a wide range of doctrinal, moral and social questions, but their decisions are not legally binding.

The issue of the full ordination of women, first raised at the 1988 conference, has resulted in vigorous and, at times, ill-tempered debate. Nevertheless the predicted mass conversion of traditionalists to **Roman Catholicism,** except for a few well-publicized cases, has so far failed to materialize and the first ordination ceremonies took place on March 12, 1994. As a compromise, two "flying bishops" have been created to serve the needs of congregations unable to accept the priesthood of women.

The financial security of the church has been significantly undermined in recent years, not least because of disastrous stock-exchange dealings by the Church Commissioners. This major setback, allied to a push towards disestablishment in some influential quarters, make the future of Anglicanism very difficult to predict.

Anglo–Catholics. The name given to those priests and people in the Church of England who hold high church views. They value the apostolic succession conveyed in the laying-on of hands by a bishop at ordination. Anglo–Catholicism is a product of the Oxford Movement which was a reaction to government interference in the affairs of the church in 1833. It came to value ritual, the wearing of vestments, and the use of incense. Supporters often long for the recognition of Anglican orders by the Pope. Some of them work in the downtown parts of cities and feel a particular commitment to Christian Socialism. Through the *Alternative Service Book 1980,* Anglo–Catholics have largely succeeded in one of their aims which was to make Holy Communion the principal service of the Church of England. In recent years some of those who accept the Catholic vision have become concerned that it has become associated with opposition to women priests and a tolerance of homosexuality. The bishop of Edinburgh, Richard Holloway and the theologian, Rowan Williams, have launched Affirming Catholicism to emphasize the positive aspects of this tradition.

Ansar. The Ansar (Helpers) are a Sudanese religious movement loyal to the memory of Muhammad Ahmad (1848–1885), the Mahdi. Originally a revolutionary messianic movement, or **Mahdiya,** which established an Islamic state in the Sudan from 1885 to 1899, they have survived as a religious grouping with a powerful influence in the Sudan through support of their political extension, the Umma Party. Their militancy can still be reactivated, despite their military defeat by President Nimeiri's forces in the attack on their Aba Island base in 1970. At the height of Nimeiri's Islamization programme in 1984, they marched in force to the Mahdi's tomb to pledge an oath of allegiance to a great grandson of the Mahdi, Sadiq al-Mahdi, as their leader and the Mahdi's successor. Sadiq, leader of the Umma Party, and one of the leading politicians of independent Sudan, was a vocal critic of Nimeiri's shari'a policy. With Ansar support, he played a key role in the brief democratic interlude between the elections of 1986 (Nimeiri was deposed in 1985) and the military *coup* of 1989.

Anthroposophy. Anthroposophy (wisdom of humanity) shares the same tenets as Theosophy (wisdom of God—see **Theosophical Society**), but emphasizes the central place of humanity in the spiritual science. It was founded by Rudolf Steiner in 1913 when he broke away from the Theosophical Society in Germany. Knowledge of higher worlds is attained through mental, physical and spiritual exercises and the celebration of the sacrament is central to the Anthroposophical Society's Christian Fellowships. Steiner's ideas have been used as the basis for experimental work in agriculture and education. Steiner schools are most numerous in Germany, but are held in high regard in all countries where they occur.

Armenian Church. The Armenian Church, officially the "Armenian Apostolic Church", represents one of three main traditions among the **Oriental Orthodox Churches.** The ancient kingdom of Armenia was the first nation officially to adopt **Christianity,** converted by St Gregory the Illuminator around 300, whence its alternative title of Armenian Gregorian Church. It became separated from the mainstream Church in 506, after repudiating, partly for ecclesio-political reasons, the decrees of the Council of Chalcedon (451), which made the Church at least nominally monophysite in its theology. Armenian worship, celebrated in an archaic form of Armenian but based substantially on the Byzantine (Greek) Liturgy, preserves some of the oldest forms of Christian chant. The supreme head is theoretically the Catholicos-Patriarch of all the Armenians, whose seat is at Etshmiadzin monastery in the independent republic of Armenia. The hierarchy's alleged complicity with the Soviet régime led many Armenians to acknowledge the Catholicos of Sis (resident near Beirut) as supreme head.

The Armenians have suffered centuries of invasion and persecution, becoming widely scattered outside their original homeland (now divided between the Armenian Republic and north-east Turkey). During World War I, c.500,000 Armenians were massacred by the Turks, while in Soviet Armenia the Church was all but completely suppressed. Throughout, the Church has remained a potent symbol of Armenian national identity. Today Armenian communities preserve their religious traditions in many countries of the Middle East, Europe and the Americas, numbering around 4,000,000 individuals worldwide. There is a small but well-known community in Jerusalem. Since 1742 there has also been a **Uniate** Armenian Church, governed by a Patriarch residing in Beirut and numbering around 1,000,000 faithful. These have shared the suffering and exile of the Oriental Orthodox Armenians, and communities exist in many parts of the Middle East and North America.

Armstrongism. This name, based on that of the founder, Herbert W. Armstrong, is an alternative designation for the **Worldwide Church of God.**

Army of Shiva. *See* **Shiv Sena.**

Arunachala Ashram. Ramana Maharshi (1879–1950) was a South Indian Hindu saint who at 17 experienced what he later referred to as his "awakening". He left home and established himself at Tiruvannamalai, the site of the sacred hill Arunachala, where he remained for the rest of his life. Although he never founded a formal movement, he attracted a large following. Ramana's teachings were collected and published by his disciples, a number of whom were Europeans. There are also several published biographies.

Ramana considered that the spiritual path towards freedom, or God-realization, was hard and required total commitment. His teachings were centred around his famous question "Who am I?" as the basis for a sustained programme of self-enquiry leading to the surrender of the self to the supreme Self.

A number of ashrams devoted to his teachings and based on the Arunachala model have been established in America under the auspices of the Arunachala Ashrama Bhagavan Ramana Maharshi Center, Inc.

Arya Maitreya Mandala (AMM). A Buddhist organization founded in north India by the Tibetan monk, Tomo Geshe Rinpoche, in 1933. Its importance today is mainly due to its German "second patriarch" Lama Anagarika Govinda (born Ernest Hoffman, 1898–1985). The AMM was introduced into Germany in 1952 as a vehicle for the ordination of monks and nuns in the Vajrayana tradition. In 1975, a Society of Friends of the AMM was formed to cater for an expanding lay interest in the movement and today the order comprises ordained Order members, candidates awaiting ordination and Friends. In his many writings, Lama Govinda has brought together **Theravada,** Mahayana and **Tibetan Buddhist** teachings and practices into a form deemed suitable for Westerners living in the late industrial epoch. Both organizationally and intellectually, the AMM has much in common with the **Friends of the Western Buddhist Order (FWBO),** though it is primarily active in Germany with significant outposts in Hawaii, South Africa and the USA. Leadership of the Order passed to Advayavajra (born Karl-Heinz Gottmann in 1919) in 1989.

Ashkenazi. (*See also* **Sephardi.**) Refers to Jews from Central and Eastern Europe and their descendants. The community began in the Middle Ages along the Rhine valley in Northern Germany and France, being referred to by the name of the Biblically-mentioned Ashkenaz (Genesis 10:3, 1 Chronicles 1:6 and Jeremiah 51:27) for reasons that are disputed among scholars. The originally geographic designation became the label for a specific Jewish cultural tradition. The Ashkenazim gradually spread throughout Central and Eastern

Europe as well as to England and later to America. Following the outbreak of the Russian pogroms (1881), Ashkenazim fled in large numbers to America and in lesser numbers to the land of Israel. Ashkenazim outnumbered Sephardim (Jews from Spain and Portugal) from the 17th century onwards, comprising 90 per cent of world Jewry before the Holocaust.

Ashkenazi and **Sephardi** cultures developed their own cultural, liturgical and linguistic differences (differing pronunciation of Hebrew along with Ashkenazim speaking German-influenced languages such as Yiddish). Though upholding both the Written and Oral Torahs, Ashkenazi and Sephardi interpretations of Jewish law differ to some degree, being most pronounced during Passover when Sephardim permit and Ashkenazim prohibit certain foods.

Today, Ashkenazim comprise the majority of Jews in Europe, North America, South Africa, Australia, and New Zealand, and just less than half of the population of Israel. The Ashkenazim in Israel have their own Chief Rabbi and systems of education and law courts.

Assemblies of God. (*See also* **Pentecostal Churches—Charismatic.**) The Assemblies of God is the largest Pentecostal denomination in the United States. It was founded from a number of pentecostal groups at Hot Springs, Arkansas in April 1914 at the initiative of Howard Goss.

The church has an ordained ministry and a democratic system of church government. It administers a number of Bible Colleges and a publishing house, and sends missionaries throughout the world.

As in all pentecostal churches the gifts of the Holy Spirit are expected and practised, in particular speaking in tongues, healing and prophecy.

Association of Combatant Clergy. This Iranian **Shi'ite** organization is described under the alternative name of **Society of Militant Clergy.**

Association of Sect Shinto. A Japanese religious organization formed to oversee the administration and development of **Kyoha Shinto.**

Association of Shinto Shrines. Also known as Jinja Honcho, this organization was founded in 1946 to co-ordinate the affairs of Shrine or **Jinja Shinto.**

Assyrian Church. This is an alternative name for the **Nestorian Church**.

Aurobindo Ashram. Shri Aurobindo Ghose (1872–1950) was the founder of an international spiritual movement. Following a western education and an academic post, he became an ardent Indian nationalist. While in prison for his political activities, Aurobindo read the *Bhagavad Gita*, began the practice of **yoga,** and had a vision of the Hindu god, Krishna, with the result that he renounced politics and in 1910 established an ashram in Pondicherry in South India. He soon attracted both Indians and Europeans. One of his followers, Mira Richard (1878–1973), a French woman, known as "The Mother" after being called so by Aurobindo, became his "co-*guru*". She regarded Aurobindo as an avatar (an "incarnation of the divine") and after his death became the group's chief inspiration and administrator. In 1956, she announced herself as an avatar and was responsible for much of the international dissemination of Aurobindo's teachings.

She founded the New Age Association in 1962, and in 1968, with the backing of UNESCO, she inaugurated the Auroville ("City of Human Peace") project. In the 1950s a number of groups in the West were set up to promote Aurobindo's philosophy, such as the Cultural Integration Fellowship (1951) in San Francisco, and the East-West Cultural Centre (1953) in Los Angeles. New centres developed in the 1960s and 1970s, including the California Institute of Asian Studies (1968), Matagiri in New York (1968), and the Atmaniketan Ashram in California (1971). The Pondicherry ashram continues to attract large numbers of adherents and is still the focal point for the thousands of followers of the movement as a whole.

The core of Aurobindo's spiritual path is to be found in his report that in 1926 he experienced the "Overmind" (the Divine presence, or super-consciousness). He taught that humanity could evolve spiritually to this highest level, at which point the material world was transformed and individual consciousness perfected. In his writings, particularly *The Life Divine*, he developed a system of spiritual discipline, yogic practices, and devotion, known as Integral Yoga.

Auroville. *See* **Aurobindo Ashram.**

Australian Aboriginal Religion. The Australian Aborigines retain one of the oldest of all living religious traditions on the planet, having lived for millennia untouched in Australia before the coming of the Europeans.

The understanding of human nature in Aboriginal religion is profound in that each person is seen as a partial incarnation of a totemic ancestor, with all people having two souls, one being from its human parents, and the other being immortal and deriving from its totemic ancestor. This latter soul returns at death to the sacred realm of the dream time. The totemic ancestors are seen as archetypes pre-existing in nature out of which the shapes and forms of the natural world, including the animal and human realms, are created. It is thanks to their continued activity that life as we know it is possible. The greatest of all totemic ancestors is the Great Rainbow Snake who is conceived as the primary totemic deity of the dream time, the giver of life, dweller in deep pools, with a body shining like quartz, brilliant with light, shimmering like mother of pearl. In its moistness and effervescence the Rainbow Snake is the giver of all fertility, liquid, blood, water and hence life itself. The Rainbow Snake is also seen as underlying the energy of sexuality and is hence accompanied by sexual companions, the "Green Parrot Girls". For Aboriginal culture the sacred and the secular co-exist; sacred time, "Altajiranga" or the "dream time", comprises the depth and resonance within which our own world is sustained.

Central to Aboriginal spirituality is the idea that certain particular regions of the landscape or certain sacred objects are more deeply charged with the numinous than others, and act as channels or interconnection points between the different levels of being in the cosmos as a whole. "Tjurunga" are particular sacred objects or activities which act as agents of intersection in this manner, such as the bullroarer, or tshals, or yams, or special boards with elongated ends. Aboriginal religion is concerned with the control and channelling of the sacred into forms which can sustain and uphold the community, through individual or collective initiation rites. This process of initiation is important to Aboriginal culture and involves elaborate and painful mutilations, periods of fasting and solitude, and the ceremonial decoration of one's body through sacred cosmetics. Collective times of transformation included "corroborees", namely festive ceremonies which involved the re-enactment of myths seen as co-existing in the dream time performed on sacred ground, which has been decorated and prepared in advance. The Aboriginal sense of art, including colour and design, is closely interlinked with their spirituality, and integrated into their religious practices, unlike more sophisticated cultures where "art" is seen as something other than spirituality.

Aboriginal spirituality remains a living tradition for the minority indigenous population of Australia, comprising some 2 per cent of the population, namely 250,000 people. It remains a rallying force in the face of the growing contemporary problems of the country, such as racism, unemployment, and landlessness.

Autocephalous Churches. These are so-called because each is completely independent of the jurisdiction of any other church. The term is primarily used for **Orthodox Churches (Byzantine)** outside the direct control of the Ecumenical Patriarch. In general these are national churches of Greek or Slavonic character, such as the Churches of Romania and Bulgaria and the **Serbian Orthodox Church.** The four ancient patriarchates of Antioch, Alexandria, Jerusalem and Constantinople are also, of course, autocephalous. With the break-up of the Soviet empire and the rise of nationalism more churches, once under the control of the **Russian Orthodox** authorities, are likely to fight for autocephalous status.

B

Baba Lovers. The followers of the Indian spiritual teacher, Meher Baba (1884–1969), are usually called Baba Lovers, a reference to his claim that the perfect love of him by his devotees had salvific value. Born Merwan Sheriaji Irani to a Persian family, he was influenced by both Hindu and Muslim teachers. In 1921, following the declaration of his *guru,* the Hindu saint Upasani Baba, that he was the avatar of our time ("the incarnation of the divine"—the latest in a series that included Zoroaster, Buddha, Krishna, Rama, Jesus and Muhammad), Meher Baba ("Caring Father") began to gather round him a group of disciples. The ashram that he established in the 1920s near Ahmednagar in the Deccan, known as Meherabad, continues to be the centre of the international activities of the Baba Lovers.

Taking a vow of silence in 1925, Meher Baba communicated by means of an alphabet board and a system of hand signals. He spoke only once again in 1966 to his disciples in order to deliver his final message to the world. After his first non-Indian followers joined him in 1938, he travelled extensively in the West and founded centres around the world. These include: The Friends of Meher Baba; the Society for Avatar Meher Baba in New York; the Baba League; and Meher Durbar. The works of Meher Baba are published and

his teachings disseminated by the Universal Spiritual League of America and
Sufism Reorientated Inc.

Babis. Babism began in Iran and Iraq as a radical millenarian movement
within **Twelver Shi'ism**. The founder, Sayyid 'Ali Muhammad Shirazi, the
Bab (1819–50), was a merchant who had been deeply influenced by **Shi'ite**
esotericism. In 1844, following the death of the head of the semi-heterodox
Shaykhi school, Shirazi proclaimed himself the Gate (*bab*) to the twelfth Imam,
the Shi'ite messiah.

Subsequently, he claimed to be the Hidden Imam in person and a prophet
bringing a new faith to abrogate **Islam**. Large numbers converted throughout
Iran, leading to widespread controversy. The Babis themselves adopted a militant
policy, anticipating a holy war and the inauguration of a theocratic state.

Defeat in fierce clashes with state troops led to the collapse of the movement's
appeal as an instrument for social and political change. The Bab himself was
executed in 1850, and the remaining leadership forced into exile in Baghdad in
1852, after an abortive attempt on the Shah's life.

By the 1860s, a split had occurred between the Bab's appointed successor,
Mirza Yahya Nuri Subh-i Azal (c. 1830–1912) and his half-brother, Mirza
Husayn 'Ali Baha Allah, whose followers created an independent religion,
Bahaism. Only the small minority remaining faithful to Azal retained the beliefs
and laws of the original movement.

Many **Azali** Babis became prominent in radical Iranian politics around
the turn of the century, but Babism has remained an insignificant minority
movement increasingly marginalized from wider society and lacking a clear
leadership or organization. There are now only a few hundred Azali families
in Iran.

Badawiya. The Badawiya is one of the most important **Sufi** orders in Egypt. It
was founded by Ahmad al-Badawi, a Moroccan educated in Mecca who began
to have mystical experiences when he was about 30, followed by a vision
impelling him to go to Tanta in Egypt. Here he remained until his death in
1276, attracting disciples and establishing a reputation for miracles, mysticism
and saintly conduct.

Today a large city in the Egyptian delta, Tanta remains the centre of the cult
of "Sidi Ahmad". Its highlight is a week-long autumn festival which attracts
well over 1,000,000 pilgrims. Other Sufi orders are prominently represented
too, setting up their tents, displaying their flags, and taking part in the colourful
procession which culminates in the present leader of the Badawiya entering the
great mosque-tomb for a special Sufi service.

The government is also well represented at this gathering, although among
sophisticated Egyptians there is a tendency to dismiss the whole thing as
popular superstition. At the popular level, certainly, the Sidi Ahmad cult
remains spiritually potent throughout Egypt today.

Bahais. With a world membership claimed to lie between 3,000,000–4,000,000,
over 100,000 centres in almost every part of the globe, and an active international missionary campaign, Bahaism (the Bahai Faith) may yet prove the
most successful of the numerous new religions that have come to prominence
since World War II. The question of how to "place" Bahaism is a little

problematic. Although it originated as a sectarian movement within **Shi'ite** Islam, there is now no sense in which Bahais would regard themselves as Muslims, nor would they be recognized as such by any branch of **Islam**.

Bahais themselves have for some time now proclaimed their faith to be a "world religion" on a par with Islam, **Christianity,** and other established creeds. This however, presents obvious problems in the case of a movement at most 150 years old, without a distinct culture, and lacking a major presence in any one country. Actual status varies from place to place. In Iran, the movement's birthplace, Bahais represent the largest religious minority (about 300,000), but are the object of severe official and popular disapproval and periodic persecution. Elsewhere in the Muslim world, they are a negligible minority subject to legal and social restrictions or, in many cases, an absolute ban.

Since the 1960s, there has been considerable growth of the movement in developing countries, to the extent that Bahaism, it has been said, has started to become a predominantly Third World religion. "Mass conversion" of largely rural peoples in Latin America, Africa, and Asia has been the chief cause of expansion in the modern period. The largest Bahai community in the world is now that of India, where there are almost 1,000,000 adherents.

The faith's founder, Mirza Husayn 'Ali Nuri Baha Allah (Baha'u'llah) (1817–1892) was the son of an Iranian government official. One of the first individuals in Tehran to convert to the radical **Babi** sect in 1844, Husayn 'Ali came to prominence following the death of the Bab and most of his leading disciples (drawn from the ranks of the Shi'ite clergy) by 1852, and went on to become the most prominent of a new generation of non-clerical claimants to divine inspiration in the 1850s.

In the course of successive exiles (Baghdad 1853–1863, Istanbul, Edirne 1864–1868, and Palestine 1868–1892), Husayn 'Ali, now terming himself Baha Allah (the Beauty of God), transformed the militant sect of the Bab into a semi-pacifist, universalist religion that owed much to Islam but proclaimed the advent of a new dispensation in which all earlier religions would be fulfilled.

Both Baha Allah and his son and successor, 'Abbas Effendi 'Abd al-Baha (1844–1921) did more than just modify the eccentricities of Babism. Influenced by Western ideas on matters such as the equal status of men and women, the harmony of science and religion, universal peace, world government, or the adoption of an international language, they created an eclectic movement designed to be attractive far beyond the Islamic confines within which it had had its origins. 'Abd al-Baha in particular preached a universalist creed equally divorced from Islamic legalism and Far Eastern mysticism, and from the 1890s the faith attracted a following in Europe and America, principally among middle-class religious dilettantes.

'Abbas's successor, Shoghi Effendi Rabbani (1897–1957) carried the Westernization of Bahaism much further. He was one of the first spiritual leaders in this century to introduce Western managerial techniques into the realm of religious organization, creating bye-laws and administrative methods for the numerous local and national "Spiritual Assemblies" which formed the basic units of an increasingly complex organizational hierarchy. By his death in 1957, he had successfully laid the basis for the continued international expansion and bureaucratization of the movement and, like his predecessors, bequeathed to its followers a substantial body of writing (including numerous original works and translations in English).

It had originally been intended that Shoghi be the first of a line of Bahai

Guardians (modelled on the Shi'ite Imams), but he left neither children nor will, and in 1963 an internationally elected body known as the Universal House of Justice took control of the faith. The vast majority of Bahais gave their allegiance to this nine-man council, although a number of small splinter groups have challenged their authority and advanced their own leaders.

Bahai belief is a complex development of Islamic doctrine modified by general Shi'ite and Babi concepts and manifestly influenced by modern Western social and political theory (although Bahais ascribe their beliefs solely to divine inspiration). Within the Bahai system, a transcendent divinity periodically reveals Himself to mankind through the medium of "Manifestations" (*mazahir ilahiyya*), among whom the most notable have been Moses, Jesus, Muhammad, the Bab, and Baha Allah. Bahais include among the prophets of the past several figures not recognized in conventional Islamic doctrine, such as Zoroaster, Krishna, and Buddha.

Apart from spiritual teachings modelled on Jewish, Christian, and Islamic norms, Baha Alla "revealed" a body of laws and social teachings deemed to constitute a shari'a or legislative canon binding on believers and covering such areas as prayer, fasting, pilgrimage, marriage, divorce, burial, inheritance, punishments for criminal offences, and taxation. This rudimentary system may in future be supplemented (but not abrogated) by the Universal House of Justice, which is regarded as a divinely inspired legislative body.

Modern Bahaism since 'Abd al-Baha has laid much emphasis on religio–social teachings such as those mentioned above, and there tends to be a greater emphasis on administrative than devotional activities. A small number of Bahai temples (*Mashriq al-Adhkar*) have been built on a continental basis, but in most places meetings take place in rented premises or believers' homes. The Bahai world centre at Haifa, Israel, has been elaborately developed and landscaped, and is the focus for pilgrimage in the absence of access to holy sites in Shiraz (Iran) and Baghdad.

Bahais are formally prohibited from engaging in politics, but the writings of Shoghi Effendi in particular make it clear that the long-term aim of the movement is to enter the political process through the creation of theocratic states, leading to the eventual emergence of a universal Bahai commonwealth ruled by the Universal House of Justice and subsidiary national Houses of Justice.

Balmikis. This is the Punjabi form of the name of the author of the **Hindu** *Ramayana*. He is said to have been a member of the *chuhra* (i.e. sweeper) caste. Many *chuhra* attempted to improve their status by converting *en masse* to **Sikhism** in the late 19th and early 20th centuries. They discovered, however, that religious acceptance did not necessarily improve their depressed social position so they adopted Balmiki as their guru and have established a *sabha* (society) which is neither Hindu nor Sikh, though in their places of worship, also known as *sabhas*, copies of the *Guru Granth Sahib* and *Ramayana* will be seen installed side by side. Balmikis tend to adopt the uncut hair of **Khalsa Sikhs**.

Baptists. In 1611 Thomas Helwys returned from Amsterdam, inspired by the teaching he had received from John Smyth. He founded a church in Newgate Street, Spitalfields, London. Its distinctive belief was in believers' baptism, rather than the infant baptism practised by the established church. In addition, members supported Armenian theology which maintained that Christ died for all, but that it was possible even for Christians to fall from grace and resist the work of the Holy Spirit. Though the movement flourished, it was soon ruptured by disputes between Particular and General Baptists over the Calvinist doctrine of "election".

Both these groups grew during the 17th century, despite persecution. A lasting legacy from this time is *The Pilgrim's Progress* written by a Baptist pastor, John Bunyan, whilst in prison.

In 1792, following the work of William Carey, the Baptist Missionary Society was formed at Kettering, Northamptonshire, "for propagating the Gospel among the Heathen". This was the first Protestant missionary society and inspired other denominations to set up their own similar societies during the next 10 years. Once established in India as a missionary, William Carey translated the whole Bible into six different Asian languages with the aim of making God's word available to all.

The Baptist Church spread to America in 1639 with the founding of the community at Providence, Rhode Island by Roger Williams. It has grown to be one of the largest denominations in the USA and was the origin of the black Baptist Church movement which has its own denominations. As in England there were doctrinal schisms: the **Southern Baptist** Convention (with over 14,000,000 members and extensive worldwide missionary work) is more fundamental and conservative than its northern equivalent the American Baptist Churches in the USA (2,000,000 members). The civil rights leader Martin Luther King came from the black Baptist church; Billy Graham, whose evangelistic campaigns take place all over the world is also from the American Baptist tradition.

In Europe Baptist doctrine "returned" in 1834 through work in Hamburg, and spread throughout the continent. In the communist period, Russian Baptists were subjected to particular oppression because of their refusal to compromise with state suppression of religion and their insistence on evangelizing. The work of Baptist missionaries has spread the Baptist church into all continents.

Most Baptist churches in Britain now belong to the Baptist Union of Great Britain and Ireland, though some more conservative Baptist churches have formed their own groupings (in Wales, Scotland and Ireland). Baptists are divided about church unity, some support ecumenical bodies such as the **World Council of Churches**, others refuse to work with other denominations, particularly **Roman Catholics**.

Church leadership is from ministers with the assistance of elected deacons (lay). Worship usually consists of hymns, prayers and a sermon, with regular celebration of the Lord's Supper which Christians of other denominations are mostly welcome to share. Worldwide membership is estimated at 40,000,000 (not including the black Baptist churches).

Barelvis (Barelwis). The Barelvi movement is derived from one of several attempts by the Muslims of South Asia to find ways of being Muslim under colonial rule. However, whereas most of these attempts had their origins in a process of Islamic revival and reform, those of the Barelvis were in large part in resistance to this process. If the **Deobandis** wanted to conserve Islam as they found it in the law books of the Middle Ages, the Barelvis wished to conserve it as they found it in 19th-century India, laden with local customs and imbued

with the belief that saints could intercede for men with God. The movement
crystallized in the late-19th century around the scholar and polymath, Ahmad
Riza Khan of Bareilly (1856–1911), whose followers call themselves the true
Sunnis, *Ahl-i Sunnat wa Jama'at*.

All Muslims honour the Prophet Muhammad. In the teaching of Ahmad Riza
Khan, however, the Prophet is pre-eminent. He stresses the **Sufi** concept of
the Light of Muhammad (Nur-i Muhammadi), which was derived from God's
own light and which existed like the Word in Christian theology from the
beginning of creation. It had played a part in the very process of creation; it
was omnipresent; it meant that the Prophet, though human, was also more than
human. He could intercede for man with God. In consequence, Ahmad Riza
Khan's followers display enormous respect for the Prophet in their religious
practice, paying great attention to *maulud* (celebrations of the Prophet's birth),
to a particular moment in *maulud* when it is believed the Prophet is present, as
well as to the annual death celebrations of many saints who, it is believed, also
have intercessory powers.

Under the British the Barelvis tended to avoid politics, although eventually,
like other non-reforming groups, they supported the demand for Pakistan. Since
Independence in 1947, the movement has burgeoned both inside and outside
South Asia. In Pakistan its organization is the Jam'iat ul-Ulama-i Pakistan,
which boasts at least one notable political figure in Maulana Noorani. In
Britain they form the largest group of Muslims and one which has been
notable for its continuing quarrels with the Deobandis and the **Ahl-i Hadith**,
and for the leading role its members played in the agitation against Salman
Rushdie's *Satanic Verses*.

Bassij-i Mostazafin. Bassij-i Mostazafin, or Mobilization of the Oppressed, is
an Iranian paramilitary organization which has become a vehicle of mass
participation in the defence of the Islamic Republic by tens of thousands
of volunteers, mostly young people under 18 years of age. In the 1980–1988
Iran–Iraq war they featured prominently in human wave attacks, being labelled
by some observers the "boy warriors". Dedicated to the cause of **Islam**, the
bassijis saw it as their duty to court martyrdom.

The Bassij has functioned under the Pasdaran organization, the **Islamic
Revolutionary Guards,** since its inception in 1980.

Bauls. A Bengali **Hindu** movement noted for the poetic quality of its songs
and the strangeness of its members' appearance. The name *baul* means "mad",
and the tattered garments of these low-caste wandering mendicants give an
impression of wildness which is in keeping with their refusal to accept social
or religious conventions. They have neither ritual nor ceremonies, regarding
their songs as their only worship and their spiritual path as the reverse of what
is usually accepted. They have affinities with both the **Vaishnava Sahajiyas** and
the **Sufis,** and come from both Hindu and Muslim families. The content and
style of Baul songs was an influence upon the poetry of Rabindranath Tagore
(1861–1941). He and his associates preserved many Baul songs, which had
formerly been part of a completely oral tradition.

Bektashiya. The Bektashiya is a **Sufi** order founded by Hajji Bektash Wali
(d. about 1337) in the 14th century; its organization and practices were reformed

in the 16th century by Balim Sultan. It was one of the most important orders in the Ottoman Empire and flourished particularly in areas with a Christian population, in Albania and South Anatolia. Today it is found still mainly in Turkey, although there are a few centres in Yugoslavia (in Macedonia and Kosovo), and it may be expected to resurface in Albania, where it continued until its suppression, along with all organized religion, in 1967. (An Albanian Bektashi community is also to be found in Detroit.)

Registered officially as a **Sunni** organization under Ottoman rule, it might more aptly have been designated **Shi'ite**. Bektashi worship centres around 'Ali, adherents having evolved the concept of a trinity uniting 'Ali with Allah and Muhammad. The order has placed no great emphasis on the formal requirements of **Islam**, preserving some pre-Islamic Turkic **shamanic** traditions (e.g. a taboo on contact with the hare, or the necessity of revering the threshold of a door). It also includes Christian elements in its practices, such as the participation of women with unveiled faces in rituals, the confession of sins with absolution, and the distribution of wine, bread and cheese to new members. After the impressive initiation ceremony, men and women dance together.

The Bektashi order has a strict authoritarian structure with a *celebi* (chief) at its apex. It is famous for guarding a great secret, about whose content—whether theological, political, or social—there has been a variety of speculation.

The fortunes of the order have varied considerably. It was closely connected with the Janissaries (the slave military corps of the Ottoman army raised from the Christian population), and the destruction of these in 1826 was followed by a persecution of the Bektashiya. The order revived by the mid-19th century and played its part in politics through an alliance with the Young Turks. During World War I the order supported Kemal Ataturk. Together with all other Sufi orders, however, the Bektashiya was prohibited in Turkey in the autumn of 1925. It went underground and only re-emerged with the introduction of party politics after World War II. The Bektashis' main lodge, in Hacibektaş in central Anatolia, was restored and opened as a museum in 1964. The annual celebrations have been promoted as a tourist attraction, although they have at times become rather politicized: they have also become a rallying point for **Alevis**. The fate of the Bektashiya has continued to depend from year to year on which government is in power.

The survival of the Bektashiya has depended on its flexibility in re-interpreting its role in Turkish society. The order began to re-interpret its history according to political necessities. Great emphasis has been placed on Turkishness, and the order's contribution to the Turkish language and literature. The Bektashis have also described their founder as an opponent of foreign influences, such as capitalism and fascism. The Bektashiya became very politicized; its structure and emphasis on secrecy have been a useful political resource for opposition to Turkish central government. Through re-interpretation of its tradition the Baktashi order has coped with the repression of various authorities over the centuries. It is cautiously finding a new mode of co-existence with the contemporary secular state.

Belz Hasidism. (*See also* **Judaism; Orthodox Judaism; Zionism.**) One of the Eastern European Hasidic dynasties re-established after the Holocaust in the land of Israel (Jerusalem, Bene Berak, Haifa, Ashdod) with centres in

Europe (London, Manchester, Antwerp) and North America (New York, Montreal, Toronto). It comprises part of the **Haredi (Ultra-Orthodox)** sector of contemporary Jewry. Named after the town, in Galicia, where the founder, Rabbi Shalom Rokeah (1779–1856), established his "court". Under his leadership and that of his family dynasty, Belz became the major Hasidic centre in Galicia, with other centres at Lvov and Cracow, and through their involvement in communal affairs, Belz Hasidim came to exercise great influence on the development and character of Galician Hasidism. Shalom Rokeah was a renown Talmudic scholar and began the traditional Belz stress on Rabbinic learning in addition to the practice of the commandments and Hasidic practices. He was also an opponent of the Haskalah and the Belz who were, and still are, noted for their opposition to innovation and modernization. In Galicia the Belz were anti-**Zionist** and initially opposed to **Agudat Israel,** a tension that has re-surfaced in recent times.

Rabbi Aaron Rokeah (1880–1957), the fourth Rebbe (master), who helped establish the influence of Belz Hasidism among Hungarian Jewry (1914–18), moved to Israel in 1944. Establishing *Yeshivot* in Israel and a Belz centre in Tel Aviv, Aaron sanctioned the Belz affiliation with Agudat Israel. His grave in Tel Aviv is a place of pilgrimage for the Belz Hasidim. The current Rebbe is Rabbi Issachar Dov (1948) who moved his court to Jerusalem, now the centre of Belz life.

In recent years the Belz have resisted the growing dominance of Agudat Israel by **Ger** and **Lubavich Hasidim** and were the only Hasidic group to join the Lithuanian-dominated *Mitnaggdim* to form the Degel Hatorah party for the 1988 Israeli general election. The Belz supported the **United Torah Party** (created for the 1992 elections and made up of Agudat Israel and Degel Hatorah).

The Belz are characterized by their attention to their distinctive version of traditional Hasidic modes of dress, the absolute centrality of the Rebbe, Torah study and their attempt to preserve in its entirety the structure of their Hasidic lifestyle. Although their numbers are comparatively small, the Belz Rebbe and his Hasidim play a major role in the Haredi world, both in Israel and the diaspora.

Bene Israel. The Bene Israel ("Sons of Israel") comprise the largest Jewish community in India, centred around Bombay (there are smaller communities in **Cochin,** Calcutta and Surat). Unknown to other Jews until the 18th century, the Bene Israel maintained a separate Jewish identity while having a unique niche in the caste system as well as adopting Hindu practices such as the prohibition of the eating of beef and the banning of widows from remarrying. According to their own traditions they are descendants of the lost 10 tribes of Israel and came to India as early as the 2nd century BCE. The Bene Israel underwent something of a "renaissance" in the 19th century and have since adopted **Sephardi** rites and traditions.

From a base of some 6,000 in the 1830s, their numbers peaked at more than 20,000 in 1948, but since then the majority have emigrated to England and Israel (some 7,000), where after some controversy over their Jewishness they were fully accepted by both the **Ashkenazi** and Sephardi Chief Rabbis in 1982.

Benedictines. Members of **Roman Catholic** monastic communities which observe the Rule of St Benedict of Nursia (c480–542), which seeks ". . . to establish a school of God's service, in which we hope to ordain nothing which is harsh or burdensome". The Rule departs from the severe asceticism and the hermetic individualism of Egyptian monasticism. Benedictine monasticism is cenobitical, or communal. The monks' "work" is to praise God in the liturgy. There are seven daily offices: these are Lauds, Prime, Terce, Sext, None, Vespers and Compline. Obedience to the Rule is intended to impress upon the monk the successive stages of the ladder of "humility", and to train him in the performance of the liturgy.

The Benedictines have never been an order, answering to a central authority. Within the framework of adherence to the Rule each abbey has relative autonomy.

The Rule has been applied to diverse circumstances with ease, becoming, by the eighth century, the basis of all European monasticism, and of much of its civilization. After the Oxford Movement, Victorians such as J. H. Newman depicted the Benedictines as the heroes of the Dark Ages, quietly rebuilding Europe after the depredations of the Vandals and Goths.

The near death of Benedictine monasticism in the 18th century, and its recovery by the late 19th, may be a source of optimism today, when numbers have once more fallen. The French Revolution, Napoleon and Joseph II of Austria each laid waste to the Benedictines. In 1800, only 30 Benedictine abbeys remained. By 1914, numbers had doubled. In the 1850s, the Benedictines returned to England, there to found the abbeys of Downside and Ampleforth: there are now 10 English abbeys. One major debate among modern English Benedictines has been whether monks should be first and foremost "missioners" or monks within the abbey: the latter have won the day. The present finds 21 Benedictine Congregations: the largest, the Subiaco, is a group of 34 abbeys; an average Congregation contains 10 abbeys. The Benedictines now muster 9,453 monks, 8,425 nuns, and 11,564 sisters. An Abbot Primate presides over the united congregations. Since 1977, he has been the Reverend Dom Victor Dammertz, though Benedictines still vigorously subscribe to the principle of the subsidiarity of individual abbeys. Benedictine practice is thus diverse. Some French abbeys are contemplative, whilst the largest abbey, St John's, in Minnesota USA, is home to a university campus.

Beta Israel. Literally the "House of Israel" (in the Ge'ez language), the self-designation of Ethiopian Jews. Their oral traditions recall "coming from the west" and following Jewish traditions from ancient times. They are often referred to as "Falashas" (Ge'ez for "strangers"), although this name is not used by the Beta Israel themselves. In the past century their population declined from 250,000 (according to one report) to approximately 40,000. Identified by some traditionalists as the lost Israelite tribe of Dan, dating from the 8th century BCE and by other scholars as 4th century CE converts to **Judaism**, their origins are still a matter of debate. Their "Judaism" is very different in that unlike most Jewish communities, shaped by the mainline rabbinic developments in theology and practice as reflected in the Oral Torah, the Beta Israel had no access to these sources and have a number of their own specific traditions. They studied the Bible in Ge'ez translations.

In the mid-1970s American Jews took up their cause and after some questioning of their Jewish status, Israel began bringing them out covertly. The first major rescue attempt, Operation Moses, in 1984 brought out more than 8,000 and was only halted due to publicity. Operation Solomon was launched in May 1991 to rescue Ethiopian Jews caught up in the civil war. More than 14,000 were brought to Israel in 24 hours. By April 1992, a further 2,560 had emigrated with the last 1,500 expected in Israel before the end of the year. The Beta Israel leadership patterns (the *kes* or "priest") have been somewhat assimilated to Jewish norms with a number of their leaders being ordained as **Orthodox** rabbis who encourage the community to follow contemporary Jewish rabbinic norms. Although recognized as Jews by the **Sephardi** Chief Rabbi in 1973 and the **Ashkenazi** Chief Rabbi in 1975 there have been some difficulties over issues of marriage and legitimacy. There is also evidence of tensions between the traditional religious leaders and a new generation of non-religious spokesmen. More than 30,000 Beta Israel now live in Israel.

Bharatiya Janata Party (BJP). Formed in April of 1980, the BJP represents a coalition of **Hindu** sectarian groups which has attempted to wrest power from the ruling Congress Party. Its major component is formed of former members of the Bharatiya Jana Sangh (BJS). Originally strongest in Uttar Pradesh, Madhya Pradesh, Rajastan, the Punjab, and around Delhi, the BJS managed in 1967 to wield enough power to exert considerable influence on the coalition governments of the period, but its influence declined in the early 1970s. After the lifting of the Emergency in January, 1977, it joined with other parties to form the Janata Party which held power until 1980.

The BJP has strong links with the **Rashtriya Svayamsevak Sangh** (RSS), an influence that has been openly acknowledged by L. K. Advani, the party's leader since 1986. The party's doctrine of Hindu supremacy (*Hindutva*) ensured significant gains in the 1989 and 1991 Indian elections, though its electoral influence has now declined as part of the backlash against its involvement with other groups such as the **Vishwa Hindu Parishad,** in the destruction of a mosque in Ayodhya in December 1992. Following this event, Advani was temporarily arrested for fomenting anti-Muslim feeling.

Black Muslims. The scholar C. Eric Lincoln first used this term to describe the Nation of Islam, a 20th century movement of black Americans to restore a black nation. It began as a "proto-Islamic" religion with Christian and black nationalist elements, but through its influence most new converts to **Islam** in North America are now African-Americans, totalling about 1,000,000 in a number of organizations, in an American Muslim population of some 4,000,000.

In 1913, Noble Drew Ali founded the **Moorish-American Science Temple** in Newark, teaching that blacks must recognize their true Islamic identity and reject the name "negro" by which whites stripped them of their heritage. In 1929 in Detroit, Wallace D. Fard (also known as Wallace Fard Muhammad), an immigrant possibly of Turco-Persian parentage, claimed to be Noble Drew Ali reincarnate. He became leader of part of this movement which grew into a separate organization under the new name of (in full) the Lost-Found Nation of Islam in the Wilderness of North America (generally abbreviated to Nation of Islam), but proclaimed a similar message to the effect that blacks must be restored to Allah and their original high status as the Asiatic tribe of Shabazz.

After Fard disappeared mysteriously in 1933, Elijah Muhammad (born Elijah Poole, son of a Baptist preacher in Georgia, who moved to Detroit in 1923) headed the movement from 1933 to his death in 1975. He believed that Fard was Allah, and that he himself was Allah's messenger to African-Americans. Black Muslims expected the imminent destruction of white rule, when blacks would inherit the earth, and taught that Original Man was black and that whites had been selectively bred by a wicked scientist, Yakub, and are wholly inferior and evil.

This racial mythology, and Elijah Muhammad's claim to prophethood, were in fact beliefs contrary to authentic Islam, as was impressed upon him during extensive journeying in the Muslim world in 1959, but he found it impossible to repudiate them. His message of black pride and separatism was significant in the black nationalism which opposed integration and the focus on civil rights in the 1960s and '70s.

Malcolm X, the leading Black Muslim minister from 1953 to 1964, and a hero for blacks today, was a prominent black nationalist. His autobiography is the chief primary source on the Black Muslims, as well as an outstanding account of religious conversion, but by the time of his assassination in 1965 he had moved to embrace orthodox Islam and an advocacy of human rights, leaving the Nation of Islam to found his own Muslim Mosque Incorporated and Organization of Afro-American Unity. Although the Nation of Islam grew rapidly during his ministry to perhaps 100,000, membership was limited by its "black Puritanism", which included abstention from smoking, alcohol, drugs and gambling; refusal of military service (Elijah Muhammad was imprisoned during World War II as a conscientious objector, and Muhammad Ali's boxing career was notoriously interrupted in consequence of his refusal to fight in Vietnam); and an emphasis on an ordered family life, clothing and dietary restrictions, hard work, economic and educational self-help, as well as daily prayers and regular mosque attendance.

Elijah Muhammad's son and successor, Warith Deen Muhammad (also known as Wallace D. Muhammad), changed the profile of the movement, rejecting the earlier racial mythology of black superiority and the claims, unacceptable to orthodox Muslims, to the divinity of Fard Muhammad and the prophethood of Elijah Muhammad. Thus he has led his followers to mainstream **Sunni** Islam, and has relaxed some of the lifestyle restrictions. All blacks are now known as Bilalians, after Bilal, the black ex-slave who was Muhammad's first *muezzin,* and the enemy is now racist states of mind rather than "white devils"—indeed some whites have been admitted into membership.

In 1976 the name was changed to World Community of al-Islam in the West, and again in 1980 to American Muslim Mission, its current title. The organization moved to establish good relations with the previously excoriated US government, as also with a number of foreign Muslim governments and associations. In 1985, however, the organization's national structure was disbanded (Warith Deen Muhammad resigning as leader), and the movement became completely decentralized.

Meanwhile in 1978 the controversial Black Muslim Minister, Louis Farrakhan (formerly Louis X), whom many had thought would succeed Elijah Muhammad as leader, claimed to have been excommunicated from the World Community of Islam, and revived the Nation of Islam with its original black nationalist apocalyptic and lifestyle, and with its disciplined order of men—some would say its security force—the Fruit of Islam.

One authority suggests, without statistical evidence, that the American Muslim Mission is now more middle-class, as well as closer to the American mainstream, while Farrakhan retains the increasingly dispossessed urban working-class male membership which was the original strength of the Black Muslims. The black separatist position is now, however, a minority stance among African-American Muslims, who have mainly joined the Islamic mainstream.

Bohoras. The Bohoras (Bohras) are an Indian community who mostly adhere to the Daudi branch of the **Musta'li** sect of **Isma'ili Shi'ism** within **Islam**. Their name derives from the Gujarati word *Vohoras*, meaning "traders". They are often regarded as identical with the Daudis, although strictly speaking this is inaccurate: some Daudis in the Yemen are not Bohoras, while conversely a few Bohoras belong to the rival branch of the Musta'li sect, the Sulaymanis, and a few are **Sunnis** or even **Hindus.**

The reasons for this confusing configuration lie in their history. This goes back to successful Musta'li missionary activity in Gujarat as early as the 11th century, which resulted in a thriving Musta'li community, perhaps based on the conversion of a whole caste or caste grouping. These converts became known as Bohoras. By the late 16th century, these Indian Musta'lis emerged as more important than the Musta'lis in the Yemen, which had been the centre of the movement since the twelfth century, and the centre was transferred to Gujarat.

At this point, however, there occurred the split between the Daudis and the Sulaymanis. Most Bohoras identified themselves with the Daudis, a situation that has continued until today. A few, however, became Sulaymanis.

Meanwhile in the mid-15th century a schism had occurred amongst the Bohoras, one group becoming Sunni. These Sunni Bohoras have developed independently as a largely agricultural community.

In general, however, as their name implies, the Bohoras have a well-founded reputation as prosperous traders. While Gujarat remains their centre, Bohoras are to be found in most towns in the sub-continent, and there are numbers in the commercial centres of East Africa, and in Mauritius, Myanmar (Burma) and elsewhere. They are unusual in following the old Fatimid code of religious law. Some estimates put their number at around 1,000,000, while others suggest fewer than half that figure. In any event, their significance is disproportionate to their numbers.

Bonpos. "Followers of the Bon Faith", an ostensibly non-Buddhist religious minority of about one per cent of Tibetans. A monastic tradition, the Bonpo curriculum is identical to that of **Tibetan Buddhism** in all but name; yet the Bonpos claim greater antiquity, accusing Buddhism of plagiarization. This has earned the Bonpos occasional persecution from irritated Buddhists.

Bonpos believe their religion was founded in the distant past by Lord Shenrab Mibo, in the Olmo Lungrig district of Tajik (modern Iran?), from where it spread throughout the world, reaching Tibet centuries before Buddhism via the old western Tibetan kingdom of Zhang Zhung. Although there were priests called Bonpos in pre-Buddhist Tibet, Bon since the 10th century effectively became a multiform of **Buddhism**, and Bonpos extensively participate in Buddhist institutions and doctrines. Hence Bonpo logicians freely study and debate with their **Gelugpa** or **Sakyapa** counterparts, while others partake of the **Nyingmapa** (Great Perfection) or *Terma* traditions.

The basic Bonpo scriptures (*Kanjur*) fill 113 volumes, and their commentaries (*Katen*) a further 293, mostly copied from Buddhist prototypes. Their pantheon is huge and their main symbol is the *svastika*. Before the Chinese invasion of 1959, Bonpos had some 330 monasteries in Tibet. They have successfully established a refugee monastery in Dolanji, India, and, as an endangered cultural minority, have attracted vigorous support from western academics. They retain their reputation for exemplary piety and discipline.

Brahma Kumaris. The Brahma Kumaris World Spiritual University was founded in India in 1937 by a diamond merchant and devout **Hindu** now known as Prajapita Brahma (1877–1969), who believed he was sent to save chosen souls from a forthcoming cataclysm. The millennialist dimension is played down in the West, where the movement presents itself as primarily educational and philanthropic.

The teachings, called Raj **Yoga**, aim to realize one's essential nature as soul, purifying the body through an ascetic régime, including vegetarianism and celibacy.

The movement is unusual in being run almost entirely by women, as teachers and administrators. Its headquarters are in Mount Abu, India, with centres throughout the world. Estimated numbers are 250,000 worldwide (about 800 in Britain), though the movement's influence is much larger, with many sympathizers and patrons in high places. Its latest peace project, Global Vision, is backed by the United Nations, to which it is affiliated as a non-governmental organization.

Branch Davidians. Victor Houtess seceded from the Seventh Day Adventists (*see* **Adventists**) and founded the Shepherd's Rod, later renamed the Davidian Seventh Day Adventists, in Los Angeles in 1929. The Branch Davidians are the sixth splinter group to emerge from Houtess' highly fissiparous legacy. Vernon Howell, *aka* David Koresh, was "disfellowshipped" by his fellow Seventh Day Adventists in 1981 and became the charismatic leader of the Branch Davidians in 1988. He rapidly established a personal harem of the women members of the group and made a series of increasingly messianic claims. He also launched a recruiting drive among disenchanted Seventh Day Adventists, particularly in Canada and the UK. On Feb. 28, 1993, the Mt Carmel compound, Waco, Texas, headquarters of the sect since 1959, was unsuccessfully raided by officers of the Bureau of Alcohol, Tobacco and Firearms on suspicion of a "massive arms build-up". The resulting 51-day siege ended on April 19, when the group deliberately set fire to the compound leaving c. 80 members dead, including 20 children. Koresh had previously predicted that members would be "sucked up to heaven" in the fire. It is reported that some of the survivors have remained in the Waco area awaiting Koresh's second coming.

Bratslav Hasidism (Bratslaver). Rabbi Nahman of Bratslav (1772–1811), a great-grandson of the Baal Shem Tov, was one of the most original Hasidic teachers and the founder of a new movement within Hasidism. Nahman made a pilgrimage to the land of Israel in 1798 and taught small groups of disciples in the Ukraine and in the Podolian town of Bratslav (1802–10). During his short life he was involved in a series of acrimonious controversies with other Hasidic leaders. Nahman died at 39 in Uman (Ukraine) and his grave was, and is, a place of pilgrimage for his followers. His devotees, in accordance with their master's instructions, dance around his grave on the annual anniversary of his death.

In a number of ways his teachings differ from those of other Hasidic Rebbes *(Tzaddikim)*, most significantly in relation to his "doctrine" of the *Tzaddik* (Rebbe) itself. Whereas other Hasidic movements developed dynastic and hereditary, charismatic patterns of leadership, Nahman taught that there can only ever be one "true Tzaddik" (referring to himself), with whom it was essential to be in contact. Further, the Messiah would be an incarnation of this "true Tzaddik". This messianic doctrine marks off the Bratslav from other Hasidic groups, adding an historical element to their concerns largely absent in the others. Bratslav Hasidim have maintained this tradition and even after Nahman's death they have continued to "be led" by their dead Rebbe—they are often referred to as the *Toiter* (Yiddish, "dead") Hasidim.

Nahman's teachings were collected and disseminated by his disciple, Nathan Sternhartz (1780–1845), including the famous collection of 13 folk tales, *The Tales of Rabbi Nahman* (1815). These stories have secret, allegorical and mystical interpretations taught only to initiates.

Bratslav Hasidism developed a following in Poland in the late 19th century and there was a centre in Uman until recent years. Nahman was influenced by Lurianic **Kabbalah** and taught that doubt in God's existence was part of the structure of creation itself. He was strongly opposed to the study of Jewish philosophy, undermining reason while greatly emphasizing the vital importance of faith ("Better a superstitious believer than a rationalistic unbeliever"). Only faith, and he limited this, in the main, to faith in himself as the true Tzaddik, was of true spiritual value and this should be developed along with practice of the commandments.

Nahman insisted that his followers spend a period of each day in total solitude for prayer, which he understood as a dialogue between man and God. This stress on intense, isolated meditative dialogue *(hitbodedut)* with God is one of the distinctive features of Bratslav Hasidic practice. Others include moving with a shuffling gait during communal prayers in order to lose the "ego" ("Man must lose himself in prayer and entirely forget his own existence"); attendance at three annual sessions at the Jerusalem centre (originally the tradition was a thrice-yearly meeting with Rabbi Nahman himself) and a concern with the spiritual importance of music ("Melody and song lead the heart of man to God"), in particular the Hasidic melody *(niggun)*.

There are Bratslav centres in Brooklyn (New York) and in Israel. Rabbi Nahman's influence can be discerned in a number of different quarters. Rabbis Shlomo Carlebach and Zalman Schachter-Shalomi and others draw heavily on his teachings in their presentations of New Age Judaism (*see* **Jewish New Agers**). The continued popularity of Martin Buber's interpretations of Hasidism which include his retelling of Nahman's *Tales* (*see* **Hasidism**) also attest to this influence. The works of major figures such as the Jerusalem-based Talmudic authority Rabbi Adin Steinsalz evidence the impact of Nahman's writings.

There are also two distinct bands of direct "devotees"—a number of "inner circles" of disciples and groups of more general followers. The former includes the circle of Rabbis Rosenfeld and Fleer in Brooklyn, where membership is limited to initiates who have already made at least one pilgrimage to Nahman's tomb in Uman, and Rabbi Gedaliah Koenig's circle attached to the main Bratslav synagogue in Jerusalem. There is also a Bratslav community in Bene Berak in Israel. Although the number of devotees is comparatively small, Rabbi Nahman continues to be a spiritual force in contemporary **Judaism**.

British Apostolic Fellowship. *See* **Apostolic Church**.

British Israelites. Those who believe that the British, and perhaps, more widely, the Anglo–Saxon peoples, are the literal descendants of the 10 lost tribes of Israel which were deported by the Assyrians in 722–721 BC. Acceptance of the theory, partly on a literal interpretation of the Bible, carries the assumption that the British are a chosen people. Believers in this theory have not found it necessary to form a sect, but have been found, particularly in the 19th century, when Britain ruled the waves, in all churches and sects. Their teaching aroused particular opposition from **Christadelphians**.

Buddhayana. The Indonesian Buddhayana Council or Majelis Buddhayana Indonesia (MBI) was first established at Watu Gong, Semarang, in Central Java, in 1954, as a result of the initiative of Sthavira A. Jinarakkhita, an Indonesian **Buddhist** monk who had been ordained in Burma. MBI is based on three scriptures, the Pali and Sanskrit *Pitakas* and the Indonesian *dan Kawi Pitaka*. Members worship Sang Hyang Adi Buddha and always begin sessions with the invocation "*Namo sang Hyang Adi Buddhayana*", from which the name derives, expressing homage to the Buddha. Tjoetjoe Ali Hartono is currently the sect's leader.

Buddhism. A tradition based on the teachings of a north Indian holy man, the Buddha, "the Enlightened One", (c. 536–476 BCE). Over the last 2,500 years the tradition has developed from a simple form of religious mendicancy based on the charismatic figure of its founder into a series of sub-groups which stress a variety of meditational, devotional and philosophical positions. Geographically, Buddhism has spread from its original sites in northern India throughout the subcontinent, coming to play a social, political, educational and cultural role in Tibet, China, Korea, Japan, Sri Lanka, Myanmar (Burma), Thailand, Laos and Cambodia. As such, Buddhism has helped define the 20th-century movements of political liberation in a variety of South and South-East Asian states and today Buddhists address themselves to a raft of social and economic issues undreamt of at its inception. More recently, with the structural collapse of many states in its Asian heartlands, Buddhism has adapted in the West to such an extent that Tibetan monasteries, Vietnamese meditation centres and Cambodian temples are to be found across Europe and North America.

According to legend, prince Siddhartha was traumatized into rejecting his luxurious life at the age of 30 after witnessing suffering represented by sightings of old age, disease and death. Seeing a mendicant monk, he vowed to relinquish his life in the protected surroundings of the royal household and take up a life that would lead to a full understanding of the nature of existence. Leaving the palace, Siddhartha studied with two eminent teachers of **yoga** and followed this up with a life of severe asceticism. Close to death, he realized the necessity of steering a middle path between the extremes of sense indulgence and mortification of the flesh. For this reason Buddhism is known as the religion of the Middle Way. Withdrawing to the foot of a tree on the outskirts of the city of Gaya, Siddhartha woke up to the truth that he had been seeking for so long. The essence of this truth was delivered in his first sermon and is known as the four noble truths: (i) there is a basic lack of ease in our lives; (ii) this is rooted in our selfish desires; (iii) this dis-ease can be brought to an end; (iv) the method by which the goal may be accomplished is the Noble Eightfold path, comprising ethics (right action, right speech, right livelihood), mental discipline (right effort, right mindfulness, right concentration) and wisdom (right view, right thought). Actions (*karma*), motivated by ignorance, bind us to existence in this life and the next, for ancient Buddhism, like other Indian religions, accepted the concept of rebirth (*samsara*). The Buddhist middle path is said to disrupt this endless cycle and bring an end to all craving. The root of ignorance in this life and in the future is held to be the false imputation of substantiality to things as if they endure over time. The Buddha taught that all things are in a permanent state of flux. Our attachment to a permanent self as the centre of our being is the most deep-rooted manifestation of this ignorance, and gives rise to all our sufferings. The Buddha analyzed our imaginary self into five impermanent factors, i.e. materiality, sensations, perceptions, intentions and consciousness. Full knowledge of the truth of impermanence, non-self and sufferings is *nirvana*. It cannot be learnt or taught in the conventional sense, but unfolds existentially.

By the 4th century CE most of the major schools of Buddhist thought had come into existence. Many have failed to survive down to the present, though the **Theravada** and Mahayana in its various forms continue to flourish. Despite their differences, particularly on matters of monastic discipline, all schools preserved the basic insight of the Buddha into the radical impermanence of things. This insight was conserved most radically by Nagarjuna (2nd century CE?), the founder to the Madhyamaka school of the Mahayana, in his concept of "emptiness". Another Mahayana school, the Yogacara, founded a few centuries after Nagarjuna, while accepting this basic position, focused more on the activities of the mind as the ground of all transitory imaginings. The Vajrayana, yet another branch of the Mahayana, seems to have borrowed some of the meditative and yogic procedures of Hindu **Tantrism** to produce a rich tradition which ultimately came to dominate **Tibetan Buddhism.**

Monasticism has, until recent times, been the bedrock of the Buddhist tradition. The great Indian monastic universities of Nalanda and Vikramasila were influential in the debates that helped to form the various schools in the classical period of Buddhist history and their teachers, libraries and curricula attracted students from as far afield as China and Tibet. In consequence, scholarship and education have been one of the great legacies of Buddhism throughout Asia. Only recently have these traditional institutions been eroded by the forces of Westernization and secularization. Monasteries have also provided the focus for meditational and related activities, though not all Buddhist schools stress the importance of meditation as much as is popularly thought in the west. The Sino-Japanese meditation (Ch'an or **Zen**) school is perhaps the most widely known in this context. There were many disagreements with regard to the nature of meditational practice and theory, though most early schools accepted a distinction between the two complementary techniques of calming (*samatha*) and insight (*vipassana*), the former stressing the value of highly concentrated states of mind, while the latter emphasized investigation of impermanence, etc. Another recurring theme in this connection was the debate over whether enlightenment comes suddenly or as a result of gradual meditational and ethical praxis.

Since the Buddha laid down the means by which enlightenment can be accomplished, the status of Buddha is not confined to him alone. Founders of many surviving forms of Buddhism, e.g. Padmasambhava for the **Nyingmapas,** Bodhidharma for Chan/Zen, or Nichiren for **Nichirenshoshu** etc., are regarded by their followers as supremely enlightened. This has allowed a good deal of flexibility to be tolerated within the overall tradition. In the Mahayana, the spiritual exemplar of wisdom (*prajna*) and compassion (*karuna*) is known as the *bodhisattva*. He or she is regarded as the embodiment of Buddhist ethical behaviour and insight. On many occasions the Buddhist saint is also seen as a locus of spiritual power and cults of these saints, e.g. Padmasambhava, Milarepa, or Naropa are particularly common in Tibetan Buddhism, including as they do stories of miraculous and magical exploits. This has led to the transformation of the Buddha and later Buddhist saints into mytho-cosmic characters upon which an elaborate series of rites, meditations and so on are centred. Thus, in Japan, the **Pure Land Schools** hold that the Buddha Amida (Amitabha) saves those who simply utter his saving name in absolute faith. However, in many recent South-East Asian reformist movements such as **Santi Asok,** this almost theistic devotion is firmly rejected, while in contemporary Burma, Thailand and Japan certain monks are revered by the laity for their supernatural powers of healing, prophecy, and the like, as much as for their wisdom and ethical behaviour. Images of the Buddha and his relics are clearly connected with these popular practices, while places associated with such objects, often monasteries, eventually became significant centres of large-scale lay piety. This in time leads, as is still the case today in Thailand, to an image of the monastic centre as a highly complex institution embedded in the cultural, social, economic and political environment in which it plays such an important part.

In common with other major religions, the Buddhist ritual year is marked by a sequence of festivals with *Visakha Puja*, marking the birth, enlightenment and death of the Buddha, being the most important for the Theravada, who hold that all three events miraculously occurred on the same date. Ancient agricultural rites are also retained, though recast in a Buddhist light. This is particularly so in Japan, Tibet and Thailand, where the new year festival serves as an act of sympathetic magic to call up fructifying rains, together with good fortune, while at the same time making vague links with significant moments in the Buddha's life story. Unlike Judeao-Christianity, Buddhism has only sought to associate itself with one rite of passage, namely death. The fact that there is no equivalent to baptism, initiation or the wedding ceremony makes it exceedingly difficult to be certain about the numbers of practising Buddhists in the world. In some areas, most notably in Tibet and in China and Japan, where the tradition has been influenced by Confucian and Taoist elements, death rites can be highly elaborate and doctrinally sophisticated.

Buddhism has developed in diverse ways, but has always maintained its insistence on the validity of ethical behaviour, based on the virtues of equanimity, generosity and loving-kindness to humans and the animal realm. In recent times, H. H. Dalai has spoken out on a range of issues from the degradation of the natural environment to AIDs. The Vietnamese Zen monk Thich Nhat Hahn has similarly taught a message of Buddhist social activism. The age of the Buddhist-inspired kingdoms of South Asia such as Sri Lanka, Myanmar (Burma), Thailand, Laos and Cambodia, often based on the historical model of the Indian emperor Ashoka (3rd century BCE) now seems at an end, though even at its zenith Buddhism often had to compete with rival philosophies to retain power. More recently, the fortunes of Buddhism in Asia have fluctuated. Buddhism played a significant role in the nationalist overthrow of colonialism in Burma and Sri Lanka in the 19th and early 20th centuries, while the efforts of the **United Vietnamese Buddhist Church** to steer a middle path between the policies of China, USSR and the USA were significant, though they ultimately failed. In Japan, **Komeito,** a political party aligned with **Soka Gakkai,** is a major influence in the nation. In other parts of Buddhist Asia, notably in China, Tibet and Cambodia, the Buddha's teachings and followers have fared less well.

The contemporary period has been particularly difficult as Asian Buddhism has struggled to come to terms with new politico-economic realities in which a monarchical, subsistence, village economy has been largely overtaken by urban, developing modern nation states. As a result, Buddhism has taken on a markedly more international character. The interest in Buddhism in the west has its origins in the 19th century with the foundation of organizations like the **Buddhist Society of Great Britain and Ireland,** though Asian, particularly Chinese and Japanese immigrants in the USA, also founded organizations to serve their own needs, such as the **Buddhist Churches of America.** As a result of sizeable refugee populations from Buddhist Asia the interaction between Asian and western Buddhists is likely to increase dramatically. Organizations such as the **World Fellowship of Buddhists** and the **International Network of Engaged Buddhists** give an indication of the extent of this process.

Buddhist Churches of America. The Buddhist Churches of America constitute the American wing of the **True Pure Land School (Jodoshinshu)** and are formally affiliated to the western branch of its Japanese headquarters in Kyoto. Originally, the Churches were called The Buddhist Mission of North America, founded in 1899 by two Jodoshinshu missionaries, Rev. Shuei Sonoda and Rev. Kakuryo Nishijima. The aim of the Mission was to serve the religious needs of the Japanese immigrant community on the West Coast. During World War II many American Japanese were relocated to the interior of the country and after the war many of them remained in their new places of residence. In this way the movement broadened its geographical base. It was also during the war years (in 1942) that the Mission changed its name to the Buddhist Churches of America.

Doctrinally, the Churches subscribe to the tenets of Jodoshinshu (or **Shin**) **Buddhism** with their emphasis on the saving power of Amida Buddha. Services are simple and are usually conducted in Japanese, though special English-language ceremonies are becoming more frequent. The head of the Churches is the bishop, who is assisted by a Board of Directors and a Ministerial Association made up of Jodoshinshu clergy.

At the present time the Buddhist Churches of America claim over 100,000 adherents, almost all of whom are of Japanese extraction. One of the major issues facing the Churches as they approach the 21st century is, therefore, that of whether to seek expansion into the wider American community or to simply maintain a stable Japanese-rooted membership.

Buddhist Society of Great Britain and Ireland. The Buddhist Society was founded in 1907 " . . . to welcome and serve as the vehicle for the teachings of . . . Ananda Metteya", the first Briton to ordain as a Buddhist monk and return to teach. Two years later the Society published a journal, *The Buddhist Review*, which appeared fairly continuously until 1922.

During this same period Buddhists within the Theosopical Society began to organize themselves and founded a Buddhist Lodge in 1924. The following year they began publishing a journal, first under the title of *The Buddhist Lodge Monthly Bulletin* and then as *Buddhism in England*. In 1926 the Lodge detached itself from the Theosophical Society and, under the presidency of Christmas Humphreys, became The Buddhist Society, London; the journal was renamed *The Middle Way*. Both titles are in use at the present time.

The aims of the Society are " . . . to publish and make known the principles of Buddhism and to encourage the study and application of these principles". The Society adheres to no one school of **Buddhism** and is concerned to offer the newcomer an impartial introduction to the variety of Buddhist teachings and practices. Hence members can attend classes on one or more of **Theravada, Zen** and **Tibetan Buddhism.**

In 1979 the Society published *The Buddhist Directory*, a guide to Buddhist groups in the UK and, in a more limited fashion, abroad. This has been revised every few years since then and is probably the most up-to-date publication on the British Buddhist scene. At the present time the Society has around 3,000 paid-up members.

Buddhist Society of India. Founded in 1951 as the focal organization for the "neo-Buddhism" established in India by Dr B. R. Ambedkar (1891–1956). Although interested in **Buddhism** for most of his life, it was not until two months before his death that Ambedkar and his followers officially converted at a dramatic public ceremony in Nagpur. That occasion was merely the prelude to the rapid conversion of almost 4,000,000 people, most of them from the untouchable or "scheduled" caste to which Ambedkar himself belonged (the *mahars* of Maharashtra).

A major impetus in Ambedkar's espousal of Buddhism was his conviction that untouchables could only find freedom outside Hinduism. His interpretation of **Theravada** Buddhist texts, as propagating his own ideals of egalitarianism, justice and rationality, made Buddhism seem the perfect vehicle for this liberation.

Many of his untouchable followers came to regard him as a *bodhisattva* or "saviour", and since his death they have built Buddhist temples throughout Maharashtra state, as well as publishing much literature, mainly in Marathi, on various aspects of Buddhism. Ambedkar's grandson, Prakash Ambedkar, is now the head of the Society. The early growth of neo-Buddhism in India has now peaked at about 6,000,000 persons, and some reconversion to Hinduism has taken place in recent times. **TBMSG** is an offshoot of this movement.

Buo Son Ky Hong. A modern Vietnamese millennial movement, also known as **Hoa Hao.**

Burmese Theravada. Burmese **Buddhism** is essentially **Theravada.** It was preceded, however, by the animistic beliefs of the hill tribes and by the **Hinduism** of early traders from India, and these have profoundly changed its cosmology.

According to Burmese cosmology, *nats, devas, nagas, garudas* and gods of many kinds are an integral part of everyday life. They feature prominently in Burmese architecture.

It has been said that for the Burmese, *nats* serve much the same purpose as do saints in relation to popular **Roman Catholicism.** Theravada Buddhists cannot turn to the Buddha in times of need, but if the *nats* are suitably appeased with offerings of flowers, food and money, or approached through soothsayers, they may be of assistance.

Originally each tree and field in a village was inhabited by a *nat*, and there were additional *nats* of the wind, rain and harvest. The unification of Burma as a great centre of Buddhist culture in the 11th century led to the suppression of many *nats*, though 36 managed to survive under the aegis of Thagyamin (or Sakka; similar to the Hindu god Indra), who was elevated by King Anawrahta for the purpose of keeping the others in line with Buddhist principles.

During the next centuries Burmese Buddhism contributed much to the stability and progress of Asian Buddhism, and became famous for its *Abhidhamma* tests. The Fifth Great Council was held in Mandalay in 1871. British rule from 1886–1948 provoked a strong feeling of nationalism which combined the desire for political independence with the need to protect and promote national religion. The Sixth Great Council, celebrating the 2,500th anniversary of the Buddha's demise, was held in Rangoon in 1954 and lasted two years.

Monks (*pongyis*, literally "great glory") played a prominent part in the early independence movement, and actively supported U Nu's election campaign in 1960. U Nu's distinctive Buddhist socialism, with its goal of *loka-nibban*, the perfect society on earth, was influenced by U Ba Swe, a prominent Burmese Marxist, who used Buddhist terminology to denote social liberation through revolutionary struggle. Thus, for example, the Burmese strike slogan "turn down, turn down" is based on the traditional phrase for a refusal by *pongyis* to accept alms by inverting their bowls against the givers.

In 1965 many young *pongyis* denounced the revolutionary government of Ne Win as anti-religious; many were arrested, and the Sangha has subsequently become much less influential in political and national affairs. Eighty-five per cent of Burma's population of 42,000,000 is Buddhist. There are now estimated to be between 100,000 and 300,000 *pongyis* in Burma, of which 30,000 to 50,000 are novices. Among the various groups of Burmese Theravada, the **Thuddama** is most numerous, while the **Shwegyin** is important and influential. There are also a number of Theravada sub-groups which accommodate, to a greater or lesser extent, animism and *nat* veneration and reflect the importance of various sacred sites and temples. The Shwedagon Pagoda in Rangoon, which dates back to the 11th century, is a focal point of Burmese religious and national aspirations.

Bwiti Cult. The Bwiti Cult, also known as the *Église des Banzie* ("Church of the Initiates"), is one of the **African New Religious Movements**. It originated among the Fang of Gabon as a neo-traditional movement which attempted to revitalize an ancestral cult, incorporating beliefs and rituals from neighbouring peoples. The Cult has since adopted a messianic/prophetic type of leadership similar to some **Zionist** churches, with increased synthesis of Christian and indigenous elements. Converts are now drawn from mainstream Protestant and **Roman Catholic** churches, as well as from **African traditional religions**.

C

Cambodian Buddhism. Hindu, **Theravada** and Mahayana influences all played a part in Cambodia's religious life to varying degrees until approximately the 12th century, when Buddhist reforms in Sri Lanka and developments in Thailand brought the Theravada to prominence. In 1887 Cambodia became part of the French *Union Indochinoise*, with the result that Cambodians became exposed to a wide range of external influences, some of which were readily assimilated, while others provoked hostility and rejection. The *Sangha* was stimulated to modernize its schools and raise their standards to college level. The Université Bouddhique Preah Sihanouk began functioning in 1961, and monks became increasingly involved in educational and community welfare projects. As in Thailand, there were two "orders" of **Buddhism** known as **Mahanikay** and **Thomayat**, the latter being smaller, royalist and more conservative, with close links with Thailand. Unlike Thailand, though, the Cambodian orders each had their own patriarchs, the last of whom was publicly disembowelled by the Khmer Rouge.

In 1970 it was estimated that there were 3,369 monasteries in Cambodia, of which 3,230 were Mahanikay and 139 Thomayat. The total number of monks was 65,000, of which 62,700 and 2,300 respectively were members of the two orders.

In 1975 Cambodia's capital, Phnom Penh, fell to Pol Pot's Khmer Rouge, and four years later the Vietnam-backed People's Revolutionary Council of Cambodia replaced them. Between 3,000,000 and 4,000,000 Cambodians died, including possibly as many as 50,000 monks. Tens of thousands of refugees, fleeing from both Pol Pot and the Vietnamese, took refuge in holding centres inside the Thai border. At two of these, Sa-kaeo and Khao-I-Dang, a remarkable Cambodian monk, Phra Maha Ghosananda, set up temples and organized days of prayer and meditation for peace between April and June 1980. These were attended by more than 150,000 refugees of all religions, and messages of support were received from the Pope, the Dalai Lama and other major religious leaders. Under the Heng Samrin régime the two monastic fraternities were merged as "our monks are neither Mahanikay nor Thomayat but are Nationalist monks" (1985).

As far as one can tell, religious observance, though greatly curtailed, is much as it was in the past, though strongly coloured by Mahanikay custom and practice. Government restrictions, determined by considerations of a vastly reduced population, allow ordination of monks only over the age of 50. Similar restrictions are placed on potential nuns, though the government Office of Religious Affairs has difficulty in enforcing the law in rural areas. Monastic education is in a particularly poor state and Buddhist literature sent from neighbouring states tends to be held up by an unsympathetic bureaucracy. It is hoped that, with the return of Prince Sihanouk to the country, the *Sangha* will rapidly regenerate.

Candomblé. Candomblé, more than likely an onomatopoeic term referring to an African musical instrument, was brought by African slaves to Brazil during the trans-Atlantic slave trade and began to establish itself as a religion in its own right in the first quarter of the 19th century in the states of Bahía, Maranhão and Pernambuco in north-eastern Brazil. It is known by different names in different regions: as **Shango** (Portuguese: *Xangô*)—the name of the Yoruba god of thunder—in Pernambuco, **Macumba** in Rio in the south-east, Tambor de Mina and Nagô in Maranhão, and Pajelança, Catimbó and Batuque in the central regions. The congregations of believers remain independent of each other, with no moves comparable to those in **Umbanda** to seek to develop a national organization, and this, together with the variety of names, is a reflection of Candomblé's origins as the continuation in Brazil of local or tribal **African traditional religions** which are centred on worship and rites of spirit possession.

Based today very largely on Brazilian versions of Yoruba myths and rituals, Candomblé mixes, or as some would say juxtaposes, African and **Roman Catholic** beliefs (notably the conflation of Catholic saints with African deities), and to a lesser extent Amerindian ones, but, in contrast to Umbanda, not the spiritism of Allan Kardec (**Kardecismo**). Members are in the main Afro–Brazilians, largely from underprivileged groups in society. In Bahía especially, the mediums of the Yoruba gods are women.

Although persecuted in the late 19th century, and again during the Vargas dictatorship (1937–1945), Candomblé, like Umbanda (and perhaps because of it) is now legal, and participation in the various cults is open.

Cao Dai. Cao Dai, more formally known as Dai Dao Tam Ky Pho Do, is a syncretistic Vietnamese sect, founded in 1926. It tries to draw together **Confucianism, Buddhism, Taoism** and **Christianity** into a single religion of the Way (Tao). Its full title means "The Great Way of the Three Epochs of Salvation". During the first two epochs God used different religions to save humanity from materialism; now, during the third, all these religions are coming together. Thus Confucianism traces the road to a just society, Buddhism serves as a guide to devotion and charity, and Taoism teaches the value of truth and discipline of character.

Cao Dai teaching is derived from texts based on revelation by mediums, often teenagers, who claim to be in touch with either the Supreme Being (*Cao Dai*) or the spirits of famous historical figures. These include the Buddha, Confucius, Jesus Christ, Muhammad, Sun Yat-sen, Victor Hugo and Joan of Arc. The Cao Dai hierarchy was modelled on that of the **Roman Catholic Church,** having a pope, cardinals, archbishops, etc. The movement rejects family worship and the role of apostle healers, both characteristics of the related **Hoa Hao.**

By 1935 Cao Dai had grown extensively and had split into about 10 different branches, each with its own leader, and until 1955 even fielded its own army. Resolutely anti-Communist, its hope was for an independent Vietnam which would lead a "middle way" between the superpowers. In the mid-1960s such an approach harmonized with the moderate elements of the **Unified Vietnamese Buddhist Church,** and contributed to the collapse of the Diem government.

Cao Dai and Hoa Hao have been described as millenarian movements, in that they represent the fusion of the secular and the sacred to form a socio–religious grass-roots movement. Both await the imminent return of Maitreya, the future Buddha. The current membership of Cao Dai is still large in traditional areas.

Cargo Cults. Cargo cults are new religious movements that have sprung up in great numbers this century, primarily where traditional religions in New Guinea, Melanesia and the Pacific Islands have encountered European colonization. They are based on a belief that the greater wealth and happiness associated with Western materialism can become available to indigenous groups through certain religious rituals.

Western material prosperity became apparent with the arrival of bulk supplies of European, later American, goods (cargo), by air or sea. In cargo cults, further supplies are sought which are to be delivered supernaturally by God or the gods, perhaps aided by the spirits of the dead or to be brought by returning ancestors. Wharves, airstrips and warehouses were built, facilities prepared and new rituals created to replace traditional customs in order to hasten the arrival of this new order of equality with whites (so that observers have often characterized the cults as millenarian movements).

Cargo cults sprang up most notably in Irian Jaya, Papua New Guinea, the Solomon Islands, Fiji and Vanuatu. In the last of these, the **John Frum movement** made its appearance in 1939–40, and maintains a following still today.

Carmelites. The Carmelites have been from the outset one of the strictest penitential Orders in the **Roman Catholic Church**. There are two wholly separate branches of the Order, both originating in the 12th century, among certain Christian settlers in Palestine. The Rule was devised by St Albert between 1206 and 1214 and authorized by Pope Innocent IV in 1247. It required that "All . . . remain in their own cells . . . meditating on the Law of the Lord day and night and watching in prayer".

Driven back to Europe upon the dissolution of the Latin Kingdom, the Carmelites dispersed and became preaching friars. Arriving in England in 1242, they built friaries in Aylesford in Kent and in Hulne, Northumberland. Expelled thence by Henry VIII, they returned to England in 1926 and to Aylesford in 1949. There are now 2,000 friars, 900 nuns and 3,000 sisters. Numbers are in some places beginning to climb. The original Order of Carmelites ("O. Carm.") retain a 12th-century devotion to Elijah, and to the Mother of God; they are still inspired by St Albert's Rule. They are divided into 23 provinces worldwide. Fr John Malley oversees the Order as a whole, as Prior-General.

The two names for the reformed order are the Order of Discalced Carmelites ("O.D.C."), because they wear peasants' sandals ("Discalced", shoeless), and the Teresian Carmelites, after their foundress, St Teresa of Jesus (1515–1582).

St Teresa, with her friend and spiritual director St John of the Cross, have remained at the heart of Teresian Carmelite contemplation, which has sometimes been characterized as specifically "feminine". St Thérèse of Lisieux (1872–1897) taught the "Little Way" to God in her autobiography, *The Story of a Soul,* and in her "hidden" life. She was the woman who in the first half of this century most fired the devotional imagination of Catholics. The saint concealed beneath their sentimental glossings still inspires Carmelite nuns and priests. The German Jewess, Edith Stein, who has lately been beatified as Sister Teresa Benedicta of the Cross, is another Carmelite woman of distinction. Born on the Day of Atonement, 1891, Edith Stein took her doctorate in Göttingen under Edmund Husserl, and became the great phenomenologist's assistant. She was converted by reading St Teresa of Avila's *Autobiography.*

The Order of Discalced Carmelites is growing in numbers throughout the world. The most fruitful areas are Latin America, Asia and Africa. There are now 3,681 Teresian Carmelite Brothers and Friars and 11,402 nuns. Sixty congregations are affiliated to the order. "Secular" or lay orders of Teresian Carmelites also thrive. Teresian Carmelite women live in enclosed houses. The men combine contemplation with preaching. All of their houses attempt to observe a rule of silence. Daily prayer includes the saying of the Liturgy of Hours and two hours of personal prayer. Carmelites are divided by country into Provinces. Vincent O'Hara is Father-Provincial of the Teresian Carmelites of Ireland and England. The Father General of the Order is Fr Camilo Maccise.

Carthusians. In the late 11th century, many monks and nuns were driven to return to the austere and hermetic way of life which characterized primitive Egyptian monasticism. St Bruno, the founder of the Carthusian order, was one of these. He left his post as rector of Reims University to live as a hermit in the wilds outside Grenoble. Having been joined by several like-minded fellows, he founded in 1084 the monastery of the Grande Chartreuse; the monastery and the **Roman Catholic** Order to which it gave rise take their name from the nearby village of Cartusia. The Carthusian rule, the *Consuetudines,* was composed by St Guigo and published in 1136. The basic principle of the Order was, and remains, commitment to solitude: each brother was to live in his own cell, within which he said his Office; each was to cultivate his own garden, and to prepare his own meals from its produce. Members of the Order are still committed to a life of complete solitude and unbroken silence. They are occasionally permitted short walks, for a chat with a fellow Carthusian. There are currently 394 Carthusian monks, 86 nuns, 14 postulants and 36 novices. There are now four Carthusian monasteries in Spain, two in Italy, and one each in Germany, Slovenia, Switzerland, Brazil, Portugal and the USA. Two Carthusian convents survive in Italy, two in France and one in Spain.

Catholic Action. A **Roman Catholic** lay movement promoted by Pope Pius XI, and strongly influenced by the thought of French philosopher Jacques Maritain. Beginning in the 1920s, it became active in Latin America where it encouraged the development of a social conscience among the upper class initially, although in recent decades it has become heavily involved with the poor.

In France it has been completely reorganized in the wake of the Second Vatican Council, and exercises considerable influence. It is accorded a certain priority, compared with other groups, by the hierarchy, and in turn it influences the appointment of priests and bishops. It has developed special programmes, e.g. for workers, or in the field of education, and through these it draws in an estimated 8 per cent of practising Catholics.

Catholic Apostolic Church. The Catholic Apostolic Church began in Britain in 1832. Based initially at the Newman Street church in London (off Oxford Street) partly inspired by former Scottish Presbyterian minister Edward Irving, the sect is sometimes referred to as Irvingites.

The church was charismatic and catholic, members spoke in tongues but developed elaborate rituals out of a belief in the "Real Presence" and "Perpetual Reservation". Membership was achieved by the "Sacrament of Sealing" which included the person among the 144,000 mentioned in Revelation 7.

Believing that the Second Coming of Christ was imminent, the church chose 12 "apostles" who together with the original 12 would occupy the 24 thrones of Revelation 4. In 1836 these new apostles delivered a statement to King William IV and the Anglican Church. In 1842 a service book was issued created from Roman Catholic, Greek and Anglican sources. By 1853 a new church had been built in Gordon Square.

The 12 new apostles were each given an area of Europe or America to evangelize. However, no provision was made for a replacement when an apostle died. Furthermore, once the 144,000 members had been "sealed" no additional sealing of members was possible, so the movement has now almost died out.

In 1863 in Germany a new apostle was recognized after the original Apostle to Germany had died. This caused a split with the Catholic Apostolic Church and a New Apostolic Church was formed, with a Patriarch, regarded as the Apostle's successor, rather as the Pope is regarded as the successor of St Peter. When Hitler came to power the then Patriarch called him "God's special emissary".

A number of other splits have occurred in the New Apostolic Church and the movement is now strongest in Germany and the Netherlands with offshoots in areas with German and Dutch immigrant communities such as the USA and South Africa. Global membership is approximately 25,000.

Catholic Tridentine Church. *See* **Conservative Catholic Churches.**

Chaldean Uniate Church. Nearly all of Iraq's Christians are Catholics; nearly all of these are Chaldean. The Church as a whole numbers 335,000; a small group of 93,000 reside in Eastern Syria. Iraq's Christians were originally Nestorian. The efforts which were made after 1200 to recover them for the Catholic Church led to a reunion pact in 1553, resulting in the Chaldean **Uniate** Church. The Chaldeans were predominantly rural in northern Iraq. From the mid-1970s, violent repression of the Kurds by the Iraqi government, and tensions between Christian minority and Muslim majority, have encouraged those Chaldeans who have not abandoned Iraq to move to the cities, especially Baghdad, which is seat to their Patriarch, and home to the Church's central administration. Raphael I Bidawid has been the incumbent of the See since 1989. Some Western journalists view his failure to criticize Saddam Hussein, President of Iraq's military–socialist government, in a poor light. The Chaldeans have abstained from ordaining married men since 1948. They have 17 bishops.

Iraq's major seminary, shared between Chaldean and Syrian Catholics, is in Mosul.

Children of God. This was, during the first decade or so of its existence, the name of the new religious movement currently known as **Family of Love.**

Chinese Buddhism. It is exceptionally difficult to determine the condition of **Buddhism** in China at the present time. Neither the numbers of monks, nuns and laity nor the denominational allegiance of believers are known with any certainty. What is certain is that Buddhism is only slowly recovering from the horrors of the Cultural Revolution (1966–1979). In that 13-year period public worship was suppressed, many clergy were imprisoned or forced into labour camps and temples, monasteries and Buddhist libraries were destroyed. The temple complex at Zhaojue, for example, was turned into a municipal zoo in this period, though some temples, for reasons not fully understood, were protected by order of Zhou Enlai. Since the early '80s the situation has improved a little and the government-sponsored **Chinese Buddhist Association** has encouraged clergy training on a limited scale. A monastic training school, the Buddhist Institute, is established in Beijing and a similar institute for nuns exists in Sichuan. Courses last from two to four years depending on previous schooling and it is estimated that the countrywide figure for enrolment in all institutes and temples is about 1,500 persons per year. A 15-day ordination ceremony of 800 monks and nuns was reported at a temple in Guangdong Province in 1988 but the numbers of fully trained members of the *Sangha* are still woefully low. Temples are expected to be self-supporting. Those on the tourist routes prosper, but most must rely on profit-making enterprises such as weaving, bookbinding or agriculture. Donations from visiting ex-patriots can be a significant element of income. The government decrees that "all monks shall take part in productive labour", though this is interpreted in a more liberal manner as time passes. Nevertheless many restrictions remain. Monks are prohibited from holding religious services in homes of the faithful, a traditional duty, and no new monasteries may be built.

Conditions for Buddhists in the Tibetan Autonomous Region remain poor and any statistics to the contrary may be regarded with the utmost suspicion. The vigour of **Tibetan Buddhism** before the 1959 Chinese invasion will take many centuries to recover. Of the 6,254 monasteries standing in 1951, virtually none remain. The vast majority of the monastic population are either dead, imprisoned, forcibly returned to secular life or in exile in India and beyond. Nevertheless many party officials recognize that 30 years of atheist propaganda have been a failure in Tibet and outside observers have noted that, despite the absence of a thriving monastic sector, lay pilgrimages and other devotions continue to attract large numbers. There are now some signs of a softer official approach. The Dalai Lama's family have visited the Lhasa area within the last few years and some temples and monasteries have been reopened. The number of monks officially allowed in residence is however strictly limited. Buddhist higher education is almost non-existent. On a more positive note, the establishment of a **Gelugpa** training institute in 1985 marked the reintroduction of a 10-year course leading to the degree of *geshe*, though the central government's 1994 reiteration of a directive to the effect that all religions must adhere to "patriotic" ideals is unlikely to improve the prospects of Buddhism in the People's Republic.

Chinese Buddhist Association (CBA). Founded in 1954 this central-government-sponsored organization oversees the development of Buddhism throughout the People's Republic. It is not clear how provincial delegates are chosen for the "national representatives meetings" but the primary task of the CBA is to "help the government in implementing the policy of freedom of religious belief". To this end the Association attends to the training of monks and nuns, produces and circulates Buddhist scriptures and related literature, fosters Buddhist research and promotes exchanges with Buddhists from other lands. The national CBA has little direct control over individual temples and monasteries though it does determine the monasteries which may be reopened. The organization disburses government funds but also has the authority to solicit donations from ex-patriot benefactors in Hong Kong and overseas. The current president is Zhao Puchu; the Panchen Lama was honorary president until his death in 1989. The CBA produces a quarterly journal, *Fa Yin*.

Chinese Folk Religion. In the 19th century when the population was thought to be about 400,000,000, it was common to call China "the land of 400,000,000 Buddhists". It would have been equally true to call it "the land of 400,000,000 ancestor-worshippers" or "of 400,000,000 Taoists" or "400,000,000 nature worshippers". The vast mass of the Chinese people were all of these. The population now is over 1,100 million, but no figures or even estimates are available for the number practising any or all of these beliefs—probably it is a long way short of the old figure of 400,000,000.

The most deeply held of all Chinese beliefs is ancestor worship, and many of the very earliest writings describe ancestor worshipping ceremonies. When a mature person dies, his or her soul survives as a kind of minor god which can be worshipped by the children and by other later descendants. The worship confers benefits both ways: on the ancestor, because without the care of the living the dead soul is thought to fade away to extinction, and on the descendants, because the ancestors are considered able to bring spiritual influence to bear on their worldly well-being. It is assumed that the ancestors inhabit an after-world much like this one, and worship consists largely of providing the goods necessary for comfortable existence in that world—food, money, housing, clothing and transport. The food is real (eaten by the worshippers after the ancestors have taken their spiritual fill), but the other goods are made of paper and are burned to transmit them to the after-world.

Buddhism came to China from India in about the 1st century AD, and was soon embraced by the common people to whom it promised salvation. They did not cease to worship the ancestors, however, and for those (few) who worried about such things it became necessary to think of a split soul, part of which went on as an ancestor god and part of which went through the cycle of rebirths. One of the Boddhisatvas, Avalokitesvara, under the name Kuan Yin ("Hearer of cries") has been probably the most revered deity in all China, worshipped by all in need of help.

Taoism began as a philosophy which stressed man's unity with nature, but Taoists began to seek eternal life as a means of emulating nature's constant renewal, and they turned to alchemy and to dietary, breathing and sexual techniques designed to prolong life. By about the same time as Buddhism arrived they had separated soul from body and begun to worship ancient nature gods and the deified souls of great men. Magical practices such as rain-making and plague exorcism remain associated with Taoism.

Chinese folk religion developed as an amalgam of different religious elements. In addition to worshipping ancestors, Buddhist gods, Taoist gods, and nature gods, people worshipped "heaven", an impersonal force much like "destiny". They also took care to make offerings to the hordes of evil spirits which swarmed around them and might otherwise do them mischief. The mix of religious practice varied (and varies) from area to area, from village to village, and from home to home, so that it would really be more true to speak of Chinese folk religions rather than of one folk religion.

Chinese Taoist Association (CTA). A government-sponsored organization designed to regulate Taoism in much the same way that the **Chinese Buddhist Association** oversees the development of **Buddhism**. Taoism is the most difficult Chinese religion to accurately evaluate and the number of priests and nuns is unknown. Perhaps 200 Taoist monasteries and temples are now functioning and a small proportion of these are officially permitted to train priests. The CTA runs a one-year clergy-training course in Beijing and this appears particularly popular with young women students. Popular Taoism, essentially unregulated by the state, retains some vigour, with temples packed during major festivals.

Chishtiya. The Chishtiya is the most widespread and most popular **Sufi** order in South Asia today. Its original seat was in Chisht near Herat in present-day Afghanistan. Khwaja Abu Ishak of Syria has been credited with founding the order, and through him it is traced back to the Prophet Muhammad. Its effective founder, however, was Khwaja Mu'in al-din Chishti (d. 1233) who introduced the order to India in the late 12th century. His shrine at Ajmer today attracts the largest number of pilgrims in South Asia, especially at the annual *'urs*, or festival celebrating the anniversary of his death. The early development of the order was shaped by a number of charismatic "great Shaikhs", venerated still as saints, who were active in the northern part of the subcontinent—the tomb of Baba Farid (d. 1265) at Pak Pattan in the Punjab also attracts huge crowds each year on the occasion of the *'urs*. The disciples of the "great Shaikhs" then disseminated the order in most areas of South Asia. This early branching out in the 14th century explains the mass following of the Chishtiya today, and its supra-regional appeal.

The two most important branches of the order, the Nizamiya and the Sabiriya, developed in the 14th century.

The Nizamiya derives its name from Nizam al-din Auliya (d.1325), whose tomb is situated in Delhi where it functions as a centre of pilgrimage and is visited by many Hindus and Sikhs as well as Muslims. Visits by diplomatic representatives from various Muslim countries serve further to underline its importance. Silsilas (lines of discipleship), spread all over the subcontinent, are traced back to him, jointly constituting this branch of the Chishtiya.

The Nizamiya experienced a revival and reorganization from the 18th century onwards as a response to the declining central power of the Mughals. Emphasis was placed on the active propagation of **Islam** and the internal spiritual regeneration of Muslims. Successors of the Sufi revivalist saints became active in politics in the 20th century, joining the cause of the reformist *ulama* (Jam'iat ul-Ulama-i Hind), and using their mass appeal in electoral processes.

The silsilas of the Sabiriya are traced back to Alauddin 'Ali ibn Ahmad Sabir (d. 1291). This second branch, however, did not come into prominence until the 15th century when Ahmad 'Abd al-Haqq set up a great mystic centre at Rudauli in Awadh, Uttar Pradesh. The Sabiris spread especially in North India, their main centres developing in Uttar Pradesh. Leading representatives of the branch in the 16th and 17th centuries were Shaikh 'Abd al-Quddus Gangohi (d. 1537) and Shaikh Muhibullah Allahabadi (d. 1648). The latter, especially, promulgated liberal and syncretic trends in Indian Islam, reinvigorating the theory of *wahdat al-wujud*, or ontological monism, promulgated by Ibn al-'Arabi. Amongst the most notable Chishti-Sabiris of recent times have been Haji Imdadullah (d. 1899), the spiritual master of many **Deobandis,** Ashraf 'Ali Thanvi (d. 1943), the leading North Indian mystic of the early 20th century, and Muhammad Ilyas (d. 1944), the founder of the **Tablighi Jama'at.**

The early ideological concepts of the Chishti saints were firmly based on the concept of *wahdat al-wujud*, the negation of private property, and the undesirability of working for one's living. Their desire was to live for God alone. They avoided contact with, and dependence on, the state. An important feature was that they did not demand formal conversion to Islam before they initiated a new disciple: ideally they expected such conversion to come out of that person's religious experiences. Up to the present day many Chishti saints are venerated not only by Muslims but also by Hindus.

A characteristic of the Chishtiya is the practice of *sama*, the listening to hymns and mystical songs sung with or without the accompaniment of instruments. Khwaja Muin al-din Chishti gave this institution a new dimension, a local colour and character. Listening to music was a contentious issue among Sufis, and if it was allowed, then only in front of a spiritually immaculate audience. Other practices of the Chishtiya involve the silent and loud repetition of phrases, contemplation and confinement of a person for a prescribed period. A more indigenous feature used by the order is the practice of regulating their breath.

Migration from South Asia does not mean that followers relinquish their ties with the order. Devotees will return to the shrine of their saint on the annual feast day (*'urs*). Those who cannot do this will organize their own festival in their new local community. This then centres around a descendant of the shrine who can act as a regional representative.

Chogye Chong. The first distinctively Korean school of **Son (Zen) Buddhism**; also the name given to the single, unified school of Korean Buddhism which was established in 1935. After the Japanese occupation of Korea (1910–1945) the Chogye Chong was the school which represented the traditional Korean approach to monastic life, emphasizing celibacy and discipline. They are opposed by the **T'aego Chong,** a school representing the more liberal Japanese tradition of married monks.

Chondo Gyo. Chondo Gyo, the Religion of the Heavenly Way, was founded in 1860 by Ch'oe Suun. Ostensibly based on Ch'oe's personal revelation, the teaching is a synthesis of **Confucian, Taoist** and native Korean thought. Initially it was propagated under the name Tonghak (Eastern Learning) as a counterweight to **Christianity**, referred to by the Koreans as Sohak (Western Learning). In 1905 Tonghak was renamed Chondo Gyo and its numbers grew rapidly. Today it claims over 1,000,000 members in South Korea.

Doctrinally the Chondo Gyo could be described as a form of pantheism. There is one God (*Hanullim*) who embraces the whole of existence. Human beings are thus part of God and carry the divine within them. The aim of the religion is to help people realize their innate divinity and to bring about a heaven on earth. This is achieved through a combination of religious practice, ethical conduct and charitable works. Christian influences are discernible in some of the movement's practices such as prayer, reading from scripture, singing hymns and also, perhaps, in the earthy focus of its utopian aspirations.

In the years following its establishment and also during the period of Japanese occupation (1910–1945) the movement was heavily involved in the political struggle of the common people for democratic government and for Korean independence. At the present time, however, it is not an active participant in South Korean politics.

Christadelphians. The Christadelphians ("Christ's Brethren") were founded in America in 1848 by John Thomas. He initially joined the **Disciples of Christ** but broke away to form his own movement. The doctrines spread to England through the work of Robert Roberts.

Christadelphians base their faith on the Bible, particularly the Hebrew prophets and the book of Revelation which they use to predict future events. In the **Adventist** tradition, they believe Jesus will return and reign for 1,000 years in Jerusalem, but reject the doctrine of the Trinity. Salvation is received on the basis of good works and an acceptance of Christadelphian doctrines; members are baptized by immersion.

They have no ministers or clergy and publish no statistics on membership. There are believed to be 30,000 members in the United Kingdom. Churches meet in rented halls or private homes, the Christadelphian message is spread through literature and public lectures.

Christian Science. Christian Science was founded by Mary Baker Eddy (1821–1910) and is based on the teaching in her book *Science and Healing with a Key to the Scriptures* published in 1875. Mary Baker Eddy came from New Hampshire USA and had been healed from various illnesses by a spiritual healer, P. P. Quimby.

Christian Scientists are sometimes described as neither Christian nor Scientist. They believe that God is spirit, and that matter, sin, suffering, and illness are unreal. Death is an illusion: in consequence Jesus did not die on the cross. Accepting these beliefs leads to salvation.

The first church was opened in Boston USA in 1879 and the movement spread to England and Germany. Churches are run according to Mary Baker Eddy's directives in *The Manual of the Mother Church* (1895). There are no sermons, comment or interpretation: instead there are readings from the Bible and Mary Baker Eddy's writings. Church buildings are referred to as Reading Rooms. There are no ordained clergy, the movement is run by a board of directors.

The *Christian Science Monitor* is a newspaper published by the movement which has an international reputation for the quality of its reporting. It does not accept advertisements for alcohol or tobacco.

The entertainer Joyce Grenfell was a Christian Scientist. Present worldwide membership is over 1,500,000, of whom 1,000,000 are in the United States.

Christianity. With Europe, North and South America, Africa south of the Equator and Australasia predominantly Christian, this is the largest of the world's religions. Associated with the wealth and power of its traditional heartlands in Europe and more recently in North America, Christianity has been, and remains, hugely influential. Despite continuing signs of vitality in the west, it has been acknowledged for some time that the impact of modernity has done much to erode traditional allegiances, with countries such as France and England perhaps more accurately post-Christian than Christian. Despite the impact of secularization and the rise of scientism in the West, Christianity continues to attract adherents in very large numbers across the southern hemisphere, with Africa and Latin America now the principal regions of Christian vitality.

Based on the 2,000-year-old teachings of the Jewish prophet, Jesus of Nazareth, the tradition gradually shook itself free from its Jewish roots, though Hebrew writings still constitute three-quarters of its sacred book, the Bible. As such Hebraic notions of a chosen people, ethical monotheism, prayer and prophetic utterance have been retained, while the ritual and dietary regulations of **Judaism** have been more or less abandoned. The Hebrew scriptures were regarded by the writers of the New Testament as pointing to Jesus, the new covenant established through his death being mysteriously communicated to his followers.

The figure of Jesus, variously interpreted as radical moralist, miracle worker, supreme messenger of God, or crucified and risen one, yet also the Christ of faith, is central to the Christian movement. While Jesus is recorded as having written nothing, his teachings and activities, as recorded in the Gospels, range from the this-worldly ethics of the Sermon on the Mount to the triumph of the resurrection. Jesus proclaimed the "kingdom of God", yet whether this kingdom is to be realized in this world or the next is never fully resolved in the sacred writings of Christianity. This ambiguity has helped to ensure that there is always likely to be a varied range of Christianities, each interpreting the words of its founder in its own way.

The origins of a self-conscious Christian church took some time to develop. Despite the centrality of the concept of the church in Paul's writing, Jesus has next to nothing to say on the subject in the Gospels. Beyond baptism and the symbolic repetition of the Last Supper, early Christians observed very few rituals and developed no formal code of law. Gradually the network of scattered groups of Christian Jews, later swelled by Gentile recruits throughout the towns of the Mediterranean region, were linked by itinerant apostles such as Paul. They had little in the way of institutional structure. Nevertheless a powerful sense of universal community was maintained and has been a feature of Christianity down to the present, despite the fissiparous tendencies found in all major Christian traditions.

The major divisions in the Church may, in part, be traced to the ambiguity of the New Testament record itself. The important distinction between Latin and Greek/Byzantine theology perhaps follows from the two most prominent New Testament theologians, Paul and John, though the two cultures here represented are a mere part of the overall scope of the early Church which included Syrian, Coptic, Armenian and Ethiopian elements as well.

The position of the apostle Peter is another important factor in the development of subsequent traditions. Commissioned by Jesus to a clear leadership role, Peter died a martyr's death in Rome. While not the actual founder of the Roman church, the church of Rome and its bishops see themselves as heirs and successors to him. In the early period we therefore witness a gradual rise to primacy of the Church of Rome with its bishop as head; this process supported by the prestige of the city itself. The Church's relations with the State were transformed by the "conversion" of the western emperor Constantine in 312. This was quickly followed by toleration, a growth in the influence of Christianity and the proscription of "pagan" religion. In this way Christianity was transformed from an almost pacifist and apolitical movement of those on the margins of society into a mass movement and state religion justifying force on secular and religious grounds.

A little before Constantine's "conversion", monasticism and the ideal of celibacy had emerged in Egypt following the example of St Anthony. In a very short time the eremitical life was supplemented by organized monastic communities, each bound by their own "Rule". The explosion of the movement, with monasteries appearing in most parts of the Christian world, was in part a reaction to the increasing worldliness of the church and more and more monks were chosen to be bishops. The ideal of celibacy for the first time became associated with the church's regular ministry.

Doctrinal struggle, particularly over the nature of Christ and the Trinity, characterizes the 4th and 5th Christian centuries. The major problem was the correct relationship between the man Jesus and God. Alexandria stressed the divinity of Christ, while Antioch emphasized his humanity. Arguments at Alexandria between Arius and his bishop led to a Council at Nicaea (325) at which the Father and the Son were held to be of one nature. Further arguments led to councils at Ephesus (431) and Chalcedon (451). At the former, Jesus was affirmed as a single divine person and Mary truly "Mother of God", while the latter, which was a Roman compromise between Alexandrians and Nestorians from Antioch, affirmed that the one person possessed two natures, the fully human and the divine. These councils generally satisfied the "orthodoxy" of the Latin and Greek churches, though Christians to the East of Antioch remained **Nestorian,** or in the case of Egypt and Ethiopia "Monophysite". The breach between Greeks and Latins came in 1054 as result of a variety of doctrinal, ritual and ecclesiastical factors, including the strident claims of primacy by the bishops of Rome. By roughly this time, Europe as far north as Scandinavia and east to Poland and Hungary were Latins, while the Bulgars, Serbs, Ukrainians and Russians owed their conversion to Constantinople, not Rome. Despite Arab and Turkish Muslim pressure, the strength of the Eastern **Orthodox Church (Byzantine)** was ensured by the conversion of Russia. By the 13th century western Europe was unified as a religious society by "papal monarchy". With an enlarged canon of law and the emergence of scholastic philosophy, this age of Aquinas, Dante and the great Gothic cathedral represents the high water mark of **(Roman) Catholicism.**

The worldliness and politicization of the medieval western church, combined with an intensification of miscellaneous devotional practices centred on relics, pilgrimages, indulgences and the like led to calls for reform from a growing literate urban population. Early protests of John Wycliffe (14th century) and John Huss (15th century) were suppressed only to emerge with renewed vigour in the 16th-century movement of Reformation, inaugurated by Martin Luther. Justification by faith rather than reliance on the "works" of ritualism were asserted and the papacy and monasticism came in for severe criticism. "Scripture alone", not the ecclesiastical hierarchy, were to be the source of authority for the living church. Given this common core, **Protestantism** fractured into a variety of movements based on the writing of theologians like Luther, Calvin and Zwingli, since appeal to scripture inevitably brought disagreement. In due course **Anabaptists, Quakers, Anglicans** and **Methodists** emerged, to name but a few. With the decline of papal authority many of the reformed churches took on a strongly national flavour and on the radical wing of the movement a series of **"Free" Churches** developed.

Early Protestant theology tended to reject the rationalist philosophy of the scholastics and though "conservative" at its inception had, by the 18th century, gradually evolved a "liberal" strand which sought to restate the Christian message in terms of contemporary thought. The so-called quest for the historical Jesus dates from this time. In reaction to these developments, main-line Protestants became more narrowly scripturalist and conservative Evangelicals. On the other hand, Roman Catholicism, reformed in moral discipline yet with a renewed sense of authority at the centre, revived immensely, particularly from the late 16th century, with new conversions aplenty in the Asian and American empires of Spain and Portugal. The period of Protestant missions is somewhat later and coincides with imperial expansion, particularly in the case of Britain. Not all of this vast effort was successful, though as the 20th century opened, Africa was taking shape as a vast new Christian world. Alongside a wide range of Protestant denominations, hundreds of new churches drawing on indigenous traditions emerged in this continent. The **Harris Movement** and the **Kimbanguist Church,** based on the prophet utterances of their charismatic founders, are cases in point.

Approximately half of the world's Christian population are now within the Roman Catholic communion, the other half comprising groups as disparate as the **Armenian Church** and the **United Church of Christ.** This highly divided state of the non-Catholic churches led to the largest general development in 20th-century Christianity, the Ecumenical movement and the establishment of the **World Council of Churches** (1948). The success of this movement has, for a variety of reasons, not been as great as had originally been hoped. On the Catholic side of the divide, fissiparous factors have also been at work, particularly since the Second Vatican Council (1962–1965) which, by endorsing measures such as liturgical reform and a more active laity, represented a decisive break with medievalism. The current Roman reaction against the forces liberated by the council and encouraged by the Polish Pope John Paul II have tended to stifle the changes allowed by the council and in consequence have held back the wider ecumenical movement. Nevertheless, the 1960's "theology of liberation", feminist theologies and the ordination of women, among other matters, continue to alter and shape Christian thinking and behaviour in new ways. In a sense the ambiguities at the root of the tradition continue to manifest themselves in the tensions between modernizers and conservatives in the 1990s.

Chundo-Kyo. *See* **Chondo-Gyo.**

Church of Albania. *See* **Orthodox Church (Byzantine).**

Church of Alexandria. *See* **Orthodox Church (Byzantine).**

Church of Antioch. *See* **Orthodox Church (Byzantine).**

Church of Bulgaria. *See* **Orthodox Church (Byzantine).**

Church of Christ. Its parent church is the Boston Church of Christ, founded in 1979 by Kip McKean and wife Elena, though its roots go back to The Crossroads Church of Christ in Florida which McKean had started as a student convert to **Christianity.** Theologically the Church is akin to the **Baptists,** though there seems to be a claim to absolute truth which explains efforts to recruit members of other churches.

The structure of the movement is based on "shepherding", with a "discipler" in charge of converts to monitor their "spiritual growth". This means continuous contact, passing on instructions and involvement in personal matters.

By the late 1980s the movement had about 70 centres worldwide, their leaders often being highly motivated young couples. In the UK, significant congregations have emerged in London, Birmingham and Manchester.

Church of Constantinople. *See* **Orthodox Church (Byzantine).**

Church of England. *See* **Anglicans**.

Church of Finland. *See* **Orthodox Church (Byzantine).**

Church of Georgia. *See* **Orthodox Church (Byzantine).**

Church of God of Prophecy. This is a West Indian **Pentecostal** church which is one of the black churches which has become well established in the UK with a national headquarters and regional organizations.

Church of Jerusalem. *See* **Orthodox Church (Byzantine).**

Church of North India. *See* **United Churches.**

Church of Perfect Liberty. A Japanese new religious movement, more commonly known as **PL Kyodan.**

Church of Poland. *See* **Orthodox Church (Byzantine).**

Church of Romania. *See* **Orthodox Church (Byzantine).**

Church of Scotland. *See* **Presbyterians (Reformed).**

Church of Sinai. *See* **Orthodox Church (Byzantine).**

Church of the Cherubim and Seraphim. This church is established in the UK, mainly in London and the West Midlands, but is in origin a Nigerian sect in the **Aladura** tradition. It is not **Pentecostal,** although services bear certain similarities to those of black churches of West Indian origin such as the **New Testament Church of God.** During their services, members are barefoot and wear long white prayer gowns. Powerful congregational singing creates a mood of excitement, and individuals may engage in acts of prophesying. Preaching, on the other hand, is little emphasized, being in effect displaced by the interpretation of dreams and visions, which, however, must be in accordance with the Bible treated in a fundamentalist manner. Strongly authoritarian, the church insists on separate offices for men and women, but there is no emphasis on a distinctive ethical lifestyle.

Church of the Latter Day Saints. *See* **Mormons.**

Church of the Lord (Aladura). An important independent indigenous prophet-healing church based in Nigeria, and a product of the wider **Aladura** movement. It was founded in Nigeria in 1930 by a former Anglican teacher and catechist, Josiah Oshitelu, and then after World War II it branched out into Liberia, Sierra Leone and Ghana in particular. In 1964 the first branch outside Africa was established, in Britain.

Membership entails baptism by immersion. The ministry has a dual hier-archical structure, with apostles and bishops at the head of the two strands respectively. The Apostles are pre-eminent in a line of prophets, with gifts of visions, revelations and prophecy; the bishops are pre-eminent in a line of evangelists, with gifts of preaching, pastoral care and administration. An apostle ranks above a bishop, and above everyone stands the primate. Women have found gradual acceptance in these roles. The church has over 1,000,000 members, and is now affiliated to the **World Council of Churches,** as well as being linked to the **Pentecostal** movement.

Cistercians. A **Roman Catholic** religious order, the Cistercians spring from the reformist groups which, in the late 11th century, broke away from the **Benedictine** Order. They found its monastic practice overly leisured, its cuisine unduly filling, for a monastic order, its liturgy cluttered, and its architecture, as typified by the great Abbey at Cluny, unsuitably elaborate. The first Cistercian house was founded in 1098 at Cîteaux in Burgundy, by Robert of Molesme. Their *Institutes* were composed shortly afterwards by St Alberic. In the 12th century, St Bernard of Clairvaux explained that the aim of the Cistercians' hard penitential life is the soul's mystical union with God.

There are now two separate Cisterician orders, a consequence of a revolt against the laxity of the monks of what later came to be named the "Cistercians of the Common Observance". The newer group are the "Order of Cistercians of the Strict Observance"—OCSO, or in the vernacular, Trappists. Their founder was Armand-Jean le Bouthillier de Rancé. In 1664, de Rancé imposed reform upon the French Cistercian house at La Trappe. His legacy survived, and as a result of the French revolution, which drove those monks who survived it to emigrate, spread to Switzerland, and thence to Belgium, Germany, Spain, and Italy.

After Napoleon's demise, the French Cistercians of the Strict Observance flourished once more. Their house at Port du Salut has become renowned for its eponymous cheese. In 1848, they sent a successful expedition to Kentucky, where the first American Cistercian abbey was founded, at Gethsemani. The reformed Order was fissiparous until 1892, when Pope Leo XIII directed all Cistercian abbots of the Strict Observance to volunteer to become a single Order. Thomas Merton (1915–1968) was a monk of Gethsemani: his autobiography, the *Seven Storey Mountain* was a bestseller in the 1950s. Merton's flirtation in the 1960s with, amongst other things, **Zen** Buddhism, may indicate the openness of the Order to new religious styles; or it may reflect the mood of the time.

Cistercians of the Strict Observance are still vegetarians, fast for half the year, live by manual labour within the monastery confines, keep a rule of silence which has entailed the elaboration of a Cistercian sign language, and wake in the middle of the night for prayer. There are currently 2,000 Cistercian nuns in the Strict Observance, and 3,000 Fathers. Numbers are slightly lower in the Common Observance. Members of the Common Observance work in parishes and in schools. Clothed in white cassocks, they are known as the White Fathers.

Cochin Jews. Jewish communities developed in the city of Cochin (now in the Indian State of Kerala) and in a number of the surrounding areas. Although scholars have traced the history of Jewish settlement back to the 10th century CE, and its origins are obscure, one of the communities (the Pardesi, see below) celebrated its 1,900th anniversary in 1968. Jews organized themselves into three discrete and endogomous communities somewhat along Indian caste lines. The "Black Jews" were physically similar to the local population, had their own synagogues and were engaged in trade and crafts. The lighter skinned, "White Jews" (or Pardesi, "foreigners") were a combination of Jews from the area together with **Sephardim** (from Spain, Holland and the Middle East) and **Ashkenazim** (from Germany). Professionals and merchants, they had their own synagogues following a largely Sephardi rite with Ashkenazi elements. A third group (*meshuhrarim*–"emancipated") was made up of freed slaves who joined either community but did not have communal rights until the 20th century.

The communities, centred around an area still known as Jew Town, were protected by the Rajah of Cochin during the period of Portuguese control (1502–1663) and thrived under Dutch rule (1663–1795) with the increased opportunities for trade and commerce. Links were established between the Cochin and Amsterdam Jewish communities and subsequently with the wider Jewish world. Cochin Jews produced religious works in Hebrew and local languages. The emergence of the **Zionist** movement in Europe was supported by Cochin Jews and after the establishment of the State of Israel (1948), in a process initiated by the "Black Jews", many emigrated there in the 1950s. Approximately 5,000 Cochin Jews currently live in Israel. Small communities remain in the Cochin area represented at the national and state levels by the South Indian Jews' Association.

Compassion Society. Also known as Tz'u Hui T'ang, this modern Taiwanese group was founded in the eastern part of the island. Its prime deity is the

Venerable Mother, or Golden Mother of the Jasper Pool, who rules over a paradise of immortals in the mountains of the west. Society members believe that she revealed herself to the spirit medium Su Lieh-tung near Hualien in 1949. The movement places great emphasis on spirit writing and has a large body of sacred texts, many of which come from this source. There are thought to be about 200 "Branch Halls" and 400 smaller groups throughout the island with the main temple situated in Hualien. Members total between 10,000 and 15,000 and the society possesses a quite complex administrative structure. A small splinter group exists called the Palace of Sacred Peace, though relations with the Society remain cordial.

Confucianism. Confucian values and teachings have underpinned much of the moral, social and religious life of traditional societies in China, Korea, Japan, and Taiwan, and they have influenced established Chinese communities in countries such as Malaysia, Indonesia, Singapore, as well as affecting the beliefs and values of Chinese settlers in the Western Europe and the USA. The term "Confucian" is based on an English latinization of the name of the Chinese sage K'ung Fu Tzu (551–479BCE).

The most common term for followers of traditional Chinese values and humanistic ideals is *ju*, a term which is often translated as "scholar". The general term for educated followers of the Confucian school and apologists for Confucian values is *ju chia*. Confusingly, the term "Confucian" is used in western discussions to refer to a range of related but distinct processes, phenomena and traditions. The particular teachings and policies of the sage Kung Fu Tzu are described as Confucian. In addition, any Chinese conforming to traditional values of loyalty to the (pre-revolutionary) state, filial piety, ethical and social propriety and self restraint, is described as a Confucian. Scholars trained in the Confucian Classics and admitted to the official examination procedures in those Classics, are also described as "Confucian". In Imperial times (pre-1912) the term could be applied to those who participated in or believed in the effectiveness of the State Cult of China. This involved annual sacrifices to Heaven and Earth and the fundamental forces of nature, the Emperor and Imperial Ancestors, the god of Grain, and a range of other ancestors and deities, including the soul of Confucius himself. In addition the term "Neo-Confucian" applies to a range of teachers who refined and developed Confucian ideas from the 11th century onwards. Teachers such as Chou Tun-yi (1017–1073CE), Chang Tsai (1021–1077), Chu Hsi (1130–1200) and Wang Yang-ming (1472–1529) produced new syntheses of Confucian ethical and social teachings combined with elements of traditional Chinese cosmology and elements of **Taoist** and **Buddhist** theory. These syntheses became the dominant intellectual and ethical influences in China, Korea and Japan from late medieval times until the mid-19th century.

The sage Confucius was a ritual specialist who believed in the power of moral example and noble historical precedent as the right means of ordering human society. He, and his early successors such as Mencius (371–289 BCE), saw the moral force of humanity as ultimately derived from Heaven (*T'ien*), but best practised by careful attention to the rites and proprieties governing family and social relationships. The model and starting point was always one's relationship with one's parents and by extension with one's ancestors. Filial piety, respect for elders and for legitimate authority, as well as self-restraint, respect for classical

Confucian learning, ritual and protocol, became characteristics of Confucianism in traditional Chinese societies.

With the collapse of Imperial China in 1911, the Confucian State Cult, and official examination systems based on the Confucian Classics, were no longer sustainable but the values of filial piety, family loyalty, a generalized respect for tradition, personal self-restraint and the desire for harmonious and rather formally expressed family and social relationships, continued to be respected by Confucian traditionalists. With the emergence of Japan, Taiwan, Korea, and Singapore as major economic forces, attempts have been made to attribute economic success to the influence of Confucian values and traditions. Kung Te Cheng (1920–) a resident of Taiwan and a direct descendant of the Sage Confucius, is a leading spokesman for Confucian values in the modern world and has often made such claims.

In general terms, it may be possible to link the Confucian respect for hard work and self-sacrifice, regardless of personal discomforts or incentives, as a factor in the rapid economic growth in these countries. Another factor may be the success of small and medium-scale family business enterprises which could be partly attributable to the Confucian preference for non-contractual, informal business relationships based on networks of mutual trust and reciprocity, otherwise known as the *guanxi* system. Some scholars are critical of the claim that Confucianism has facilitated the East Asian economic boom. They point out that rapid economic growth in these regions has always followed the introduction of western forms of economic and business organization, and in fact the merchant classes of traditional China were in many ways the least Confucian-inspired members of traditional society. In this account the traditional Confucian preference for classical learning and bureaucracy rather than trade is stressed. A different response to the modern world is expressed by the contemporary Japanese Confucian teacher Okada Takehiko (1908–). He advocates Confucian meditation (*seiza*) or "quiet sitting" both as a method of moral cultivation and as an antidote to the dehumanizing effects of modern technology.

Congregationalists. Congregational churches are united not by a tenet of theology but by a system of church government. Taking seriously the words of St Paul, "Christ is the head of his body, the church" (Col. 1. 18) and the description of Christians by Peter "You are the chosen race, the King's priests, the holy nation, God's own people" (1 Peter 2. 9), Congregationalists reject external authority and give every local church the right to make its own decisions.

This has led to both liberal and evangelical strands in the church. Most Congregational churches believe in the need for a personal faith in Christ, and express this through the sacraments of Baptism and the Lord's Supper.

Since the 19th century Congregational churches have worked together through national and later international councils. Since 1970 they have been part of the World Alliance of Reformed Churches which also includes the **Presbyterians**, with which they often have a theological affinity.

As well as Congregational churches all over the world arising from missionary activity initiated in the USA and the UK, two other main areas have a strong Congregational tradition. These are the Mission Covenant churches of Scandinavia, and the Eastern European Congregational churches, particularly in Bulgaria, Czechoslovakia and scattered communities of Armenians.

In England most Congregationalists have united with the Presbyterian Church to form the United Reformed Church. However the Congregational Union in Scotland and the Union of Welsh Independents (Welsh-speaking) have remained separate. Worldwide specifically Congregational membership is estimated at over 2,000,000.

Conservative Catholic Churches. These are a group of about 60, mostly small, denominations, which opposed recent reforms in the **Roman Catholic Church,** particularly those of the Second Vatican Council (1962). In Britain they are represented by the Catholic Tridentine Church which supports the beliefs of Archbishop Lefebvre. Following his insistence on the Latin Mass and other traditional practices, Archbishop Lefebvre (d. 1992) defied the pope by training and ordaining priests, leading to his excommunication in 1988 from the Roman Catholic Church. The organization is based at Écône, near Geneva.

Although fragmented, the movement is worldwide and numbers over 250,000.

Conservative Judaism. Conservative Judaism simultaneously teaches that the Jewish people must be committed to *halakhah* (Jewish law) but they are also empowered to modify it, as long as such changes are consistent with what are seen to be the dynamic processes of change in the *halakhah* and **Judaism**. The movement has its origins in the thought of Zecharias Frankel (1801–1875) who called for a "positive-historical" approach to Judaism, arguing that while post-Biblical Judaism had developed historically, and thus, change was permitted, any alterations of *halakhah* must come slowly, reflecting the will of the Jewish people. At first he found common cause with some moderate Reform leaders but in 1845, he left a Reform-organized rabbinic conference in Frankfurt after a majority approved a measure stating that use of Hebrew prayers was "advisable" but not mandatory. In 1854, Frankel was chosen over Abraham Geiger, the noted radical Reform scholar, to head the newly-formed *Jüdisch-Theologisches Seminar* ("Jewish Theological Seminary") in Wroclaw (Breslau) which became the centre for what was then known as "Historical Judaism".

In America, the Conservative movement also began as a reaction to **Reform Judaism,** which by 1880, had become the dominant strand of Judaism. Some traditionalists and moderate Reform rabbis united in 1886 to found the Jewish Theological Seminary in response to the 1885 "Pittsburgh Platform" which, although not formally approved by the conference, was clearly favoured by many of its members, becoming the guiding principle of American Reform for the next 50 years. (The platform was adopted by the founding meeting of the Central Conference of American Rabbis, the Reform rabbinate, in 1889). The traditionalists and moderate Reform leaders were shocked by the Platform's rejection of rituals such as *kashrut* (the dietary code), the beliefs in Heaven, Hell, and the coming of the Messiah and the re-establishment of Jewish sovereignty in their ancestral home. The Seminary was the centre for both those who favoured moderate change, while accepting the Bible and *Talmud* and those who opposed change, although there were traditionalists who did not support the Seminary. By the end of the century, the Seminary was floundering, as Reform Jews maintained their ties and the new immigrants from Russia tended towards **Orthodox Judaism** (or secularism).

Under the urging of men like Cyrus Adler, Louis Marshall, and Simon Guggenheim, the Jewish Theological Seminary was reorganized in 1902 with Solomon Schechter (1850–1915) at its head. Now, the Seminary aimed to help "Americanize" the new immigrants by training rabbis who could both appeal to the tradition and integrate their congregants into America. Under Schechter's leadership, the Seminary and the movement, began to grow in influence and call itself "Conservative Judaism". In 1913, Schechter organized a union of congregations to support the seminary, the United Synagogue of America, but at its start, it was not clear if this was to be a specifically Conservative organization (as was desired by some *alumni* of the seminary) or if it were to be an "Orthodox–Conservative" union, as other leaders (including Schechter) wanted. Eventually, it became an organization of exclusively Conservative congregations.

Under the leadership (1915–1940) of Cyrus Adler, the movement grew, with the seminary, the United Synagogue, and the Rabbinical Assembly of America (reorganized in 1929 after its original founding in 1901; renamed in 1962 as the Rabbinic Assembly, the international association of Conservative rabbis) all being strengthened. The movement grew rapidly under the 1940–1972 tenure of Adler's successor, Louis Finkelstein. During those three decades, Conservative Judaism became the largest American denomination, meeting the needs of a large number of congregants who wished to feel part of both modern America and tradition. This blend can be seen in the 1960 decisions of the Rabbinical Assembly of America to permit the use of electricity on the Sabbath, which Orthodoxy considers unethical, as well as driving automobiles to synagogue on this day.

In recent years, this modernizing trend has continued with the Jewish Theological Seminary's 1981 decision to admit women into its rabbinic and cantoral programmes. This change of policy led to some dissent, with a group of Conservative rabbis, led by David Novak, splintered from Conservative Judaism, founding the Union of Traditional Conservative Judaism, later renamed the Institute for Traditional Judaism (Rabbi Novak remained a member of the Rabbinic Assembly and was otherwise involved in Conservative Judaism until 1988). In 1985, the Rabbinical Assembly voted to accept women rabbis, with Amy Eilberg becoming the first Conservative woman rabbi. After some controversy, women were also admitted into the Cantors Assembly, although a group of cantors opposed this decision. The International Federation of Traditional Cantors was formed in 1991, with Cantor Eliezer Kirshblum as Acting President.

That there are limits on the movement's liberalism were shown in the 1985 decision to reaffirm the traditional position that only those whose mothers are Jewish or have been converted according to *halakhah* are Jews (a rejection of Reform's decision that people with Jewish fathers and non-Jewish mothers or whose conversion was not conducted accorded to *halakhah* are considered Jews) as well as the 1992 decision not to maintain the "status quo" and not admit gay and lesbians to the Jewish Theological Seminary or Rabbinic Assembly (the decision prohibits any expulsion of gays or lesbians in the groups and established a commission to further study the issue).

Conservative Judaism is represented in Israel by the Masorti ("Traditional") movement, with more than 40 congregations and its own rabbinic seminary in Jerusalem, *Beit Midrash le-Limodai Yahadut* ("Institute for Jewish Studies" founded in 1984), where American rabbinic students also study for a year. The movement also established **Kibbutz** *Honaton* in the Galilee region. Currently, the Rabbinical Assembly has more than 1,200 members and the United Synagogue of America represents more than 830 congregations (approximately 1,250,000 persons).

Worldwide, the movement is represented by the World Council of Synagogues (1959). In addition to its seminaries in America (JTS and the Los Angeles University of Judaism where students may do part of their studying after their year in Israel) and Israel, there is the Seminario Latinamericano in Buenos Aires (1959). Currently, there are an estimated 2,000,000 Conservative Jews worldwide.

Convince. A small ancestral cult in eastern Jamaica where the ritual centres on Bongo ghosts, that is, the spirits of people who belonged to it during their lifetime. Unlike **Candomblé, Voodoo, Shango** and **Santería,** which comprise a syncretic mix of **African traditional religions** and **Roman Catholicism,** Convince combines elements of African religion with others typical of **Protestant** Christian worship, such as prayers, hymns and Bible readings. An annual ceremony of animal sacrifice is held, and spirits of the ancestors may possess a devotee during Convince rituals. However, the movement has declined rapidly in the last two or three decades, providing little more at present than occasions for festivities.

Coptic Church. From the arabized Greek word for Egyptian, the term "Copt" has come to mean an Egyptian Christian of the monophysite tradition. The Coptic Church is one of the main **Oriental Orthodox Churches** and the largest of three rival representatives of the ancient Patriarchate of Alexandria, the others being the Greek-speaking Patriarchal Church of Alexandria (Byzantine Orthodox tradition) and the **Uniate** Coptic Church (Roman Catholic) established in the 18th century. The now independent **Ethiopian Orthodox Church** was under the jurisdiction of the Coptic Church until 1959.

Up until the Muslim conquest in the 7th century most Egyptians were Coptic Christians. Their descendants today probably number somewhere between 6–8,000,000, roughly 15 per cent of the total population.

The primate, who bears the title "Pope of Alexandria and Patriarch of the See of St Mark of Egypt, the Near East and All Africa", has in modern times resided in Cairo. The best known of the dioceses outside Egypt is that of Jerusalem. The Coptic liturgy, based on the originally Greek Liturgy of St Mark, is celebrated in an ancient form of Coptic to which much Arabic has been added. Monasticism, which in the early Christian Church largely developed in Egypt, remains an important part of the Coptic tradition.

Throughout most of their history the Copts have suffered discrimination and occasional bouts of persecution, and have enjoyed complete freedom of religion in the modern sense only since the end of the 19th century. The current primate, Pope Shenouda III, was from 1981 to 1985 banished to a desert monastery following unrest between "revivalist" Copts and "fundamentalist" Muslims. The government has tried to act even-handedly, but as a minority the Copts are bound to find themselves increasingly under pressure if militant **Islam** gains significant ground in Egypt.

Coptic Evangelical Church. A **Presbyterian** church in Egypt and the largest single **Protestant** grouping in the Middle East.

Craft. "The Craft" is a common designation for **Witchcraft**.

Cumina. *See* **Kumina**.

D

Dai Dao Tam Ky Pho Do. A syncretic Vietnamese sect, more widely known as **Cao Dai.**

Dancing Dervishes. A colloquial designation for members of the **Mawlawiya Sufi** order.

Darul Arqam. The Darul Arqam is an important and controversial *dakwah* (Muslim renewal) organization in Malaysia. Established in 1968, it attracted numerous followers in the 1970s from among the young and educated, being in this respect a rival to ABIM (**Angkatan Belia Islam Malaysiam,** the Malaysian Islamic Youth Movement) in its quest for student support. More recently its activities have been centred in three rural villages in particular, where its followers practise an austere communal lifestyle. Its members dress in green or black—the men with turbans and a long green shirt, the women in black or green purdah dress. Instead of waiting for the creation of an Islamic state in Malaysia, Darul Arqam seeks to establish an alternative Islamic community on its own land. It aims to convert society by converting individuals to a truly Islamic lifestyle (and criticizes the Islamic fundamentalist political opposition group PAS—**Parti Islam Se-Malaysia**—for having failed to inculcate true spiritual strength in its members). It imposes strict segregation of the sexes, among both adults and young school-age children. Great emphasis is placed on correct practice, not just on religious ritual (as tends to be the case with one of the other *dakwah* groups, the **Jama'at Tabligh**) in all areas of life, familial, social, economic and political.

Its emphasis on separateness from the wider plural society of Malaysia, and its radical social vision, which includes a commitment to economic self-sufficiency, set it apart from other *dakwah* organizations in Malaysia.

Besides its three communes, Darul Arqam runs various schools, kindergartens, student groups, agricultural projects and halal food factories. In its social form as well as its practice and teachings, Darul Arqam is effectively a New Religious Movement in an Islamic context, similar to commune based NRMs in the West such as **Hari Krishna**.

Its radical critique of the partnership of UMNO (United Malay National Organization) with non-Muslims in the ruling coalition governments since independence in 1957, as of wider social and political arrangements, has earned it the disapprobation of government leaders and of the state *ulama* (clerics).

Both ABIM and PAS have also been targets of sharp criticism by Darul Arqam, as have Islamic movements abroad, including the **Jama'at-i Islami** and the **Muslim Brotherhood.**

In recent years the leadership has been involved in a series of theological controversies, and has attracted much unfavourable publicity in the government-controlled media. Its appeal has consequently been considerably weakened. In 1991 the federal government declared Darul Arqam a proscribed organization.

Dashanamis. The Dashanamis are constituted by 10 orders of Hindu renunciants (*samnyasins*) founded, according to legend, by the great Indian philosopher Shankara (c. 788–820). These orders are, more or less, caste specific, with four of the 10 being assigned exclusively to brahmins. The philosophical outlook of the movement is non-dualist (*advaita*) **Vedanta** and the majority of sub-groups demonstrate a strongly **Shaiva** orientation. Dashanami ascetics, on full initiation by a *guru*, sever links with their family and reside within a monastery (*math*) usually situated in an urban environment and often associated with the temple dedicated to an important deity. Bhubaneswar, in the east Indian state of Orissa, possesses many such *maths,* the earliest of which date back to, perhaps, the 10th century, though many are quite modern.

Maths are fully autonomous institutions usually presided over by a head ascetic or pontiff who is regarded as the ultimate arbitrator in theological disputes. He may be aided in the day-to-day running of the community by a management committee and on his death headship tends to pass in a hereditary line running through the nephew. Some *maths* contain schools and/or dispensaries for traditional medicaments. Dashanamis are physically distinguished by an ochre loincloth, a necklace of 54 *rudraksa* beads, a single-pronged staff and three horizontal white forehead markings.

Da'wa Party. The Da'wa Party (Hizb al-Da'wa al-Islamiya, or Islamic Call Party—not to be confused with Libya's **Islamic Call Society**), is one of the most important of the **Shi'ite** Islamist groups in Iraq. It apparently began in Najaf in the late 1950s as a renewal movement inspired by the important Shi'ite writer and religious authority, Ayatollah Muhammad Baqir al-Sadr (1933–1980), and in response to the growing threat of atheistic Communism in the period 1958–1963 under the republican rule of 'Abd al-Karim Qasim. By the late 1970s, however, it had become much more political, and a target of repression by Saddam Hussein's Ba'th government, in power from 1968 onwards.

Baqir al-Sadr, who had developed a theory of an ideal Islamic state under "the rule of the jurist" rather similar to that of Ayatollah Khomeini (himself in exile in Najaf between 1964 and 1968), was executed by the Ba'thist régime in 1980. So too was his sister, Bint Huda. By this time the Da'wa had begun to attack police posts and Ba'th party offices. Since then it has also been engaged in sabotage actions elsewhere in the Gulf, for example in Kuwait and Bahrain. In the 1980s it had some involvement with international terrorism, but this has ceased.

Al-Da'wa is a strong supporter of Khomeini's Iran, where it has a large number of members, mostly Iraqi refugees, and where it has established a multitude of cultural and social organizations. It also has an organized unit in the Iranian army.

There are some branches in Britain, and they publish several magazines supportive of their cause. Further branches exist in Syria, Lebanon and Afghanistan.

Since the severe repression at the time of al-Sadr's execution, the leadership has become less clerical and more lay. The Da'wa now opposes the theory of the rule of the jurist (*wilayat al-faqih*).

Al-Da'wa was fiercely critical of Iraq's invasion of Kuwait, and dismayed by the considerable popularity enjoyed by Saddam Hussein in the **Sunni** world in his subsequent confrontation with the West. As longstanding critics of American imperialism, they could hardly condone the presence of American soldiers on Muslim soil; yet they were apparently not opposed to limited military intervention by Muslim troops (although fearful of the possible military destruction of Iraq). They were actively involved in the post-war Shi'ite uprising in the south, but with what degree of influence is not clear.

De Jiao. De Jiao (Tak Kaau in Cantonese) means "Religion of Virtue" and originated in the Chaozhou (Teochiu) area of South China in about 1939. It is most firmly established in Singapore and Malaysia, where there are more than 60 "churches", but is also found in Hong Kong and among other Chinese communities. Adherents believe that there is truth in all the major world religions, and they worship before an altar on which are figures of Laotse (**Taoism**), Kuan Yin (**Buddhism**), Confucius, the Virgin Mary or Jesus Christ, and Muhammad. They recite from scriptures which are made up of extracts from the Taoist *Tao Te Ching*, Buddhist sutras, the **Confucian** *Analects*, the Bible and the Quran, and their leaders act as spirit mediums to give advice and healing, usually employing the technique of writing in sand with a stick to convey the spiritual message. Many of the groups look after the social welfare of their members through burial clubs, youth clubs, and medical clinics.

Dehra Dun Ashram. Dehra Dun ashram, at the foot of the Himalayan mountains in north-west India, was founded in 1932 by Shri Anandamayi Ma (born Nirmal Bhattachari in 1896). It was the first of a number of ashrams and later charitable organizations (under the auspices of the Anandamayi Charitable Society) established in India dedicated to the practices and personality of this Hindu woman spiritual teacher. She was renowned for her charisma and playful, almost flirtatious manner of dealing with people and taught the need for personal devotion to her as *guru,* meditation, and mild yogic techniques (see **yoga**) within the framework of a monist philosophy (see **Vedanta**). Beginning in the mid-1960s, a number of centres have been set up in the West, including the Shri Anandamayi Ma Monastery in Oklahoma.

Deliverance Church. One of the largest independent African **Pentecostal** churches in Kenya (and, to a lesser extent, Uganda). It has links with the Morris Cerrullo Ministries based in California, and is working to establish a wider international base.

Deobandis. The Deoband movement emerged from one of several attempts by the Muslims of South Asia in the 19th century to find a way of being Muslim under colonial rule. Education was the Deobandi answer to being good (**Sunni**) Muslims without political power. The focus of the movement was a *madrasah*

(Islamic secondary school) founded at Deoband, a small country town some 90 miles north-east of Delhi. The *madrasah* has subsequently grown to the extent that it is now regarded by many as the most important traditional university in the Islamic world after al-Azhar in Cairo. The movement itself has been spread in large part by the foundation of *madrasahs* associated with Deoband. By 1900 it acknowledged 40 attached schools; by its centenary in 1967, 8,934.

Deoband offered a way of being Muslim with as limited a relationship as possible with the state. In terms of beliefs this meant following the Islamic holy law as it had been handed down from the Middle Ages, tolerating only those expressions of **Sufism** that admitted no hint of intercession, and avoiding forms of behaviour which might suggest **Shi'ite, Hindu** or Western influences. It was a scriptural religion. Knowledge of God's word was central to knowing how to behave as a Muslim. As the state was controlled by a non-Muslim power, Muslims had to get their knowledge for themselves and ensure that they followed its meaning, the promptings of individual human conscience being the main sanction. Appropriately this has come to be termed a "protestant" form of **Islam**, which in its association, for instance, with literacy, the printing press and personal responsibility, bears comparison with **Protestantism** in Christian Europe. In the Islamic world it is to be compared with the **Muhammadiyah** of Indonesia and the **Salafiya** of North Africa.

In terms of organization Deoband's concern to sustain Islamic society outside the framework of the colonial state meant total dependence on public subscription, bureaucratic provision of guidance in Islamic law, a programme for the translation of Arabic and Persian Islamic texts into the vernaculars, and most vigorous use of the printing press. A typical Deobandi book is Maulana Ashraf 'Ali Thanvi's still popular *Bihishti Zevar*, which was first published in the 1890s and offers complete guidance to women on how to behave as Muslims. (For a translation and commentary see B. D. Metcalf, 1990, *Perfecting Women*, Berkeley: University of California Press.)

Deoband's Islamic stance has, by and large, been reflected in its politics to the present. Having created systems to operate outside the state, their adherents' idea of a properly ordered society was ultimately one ruled by scholars like themselves. Consistently with this they did not as a group support the movement for Pakistan, since they envisaged that it would be an Islamic state in name only, ruled by secular Muslims. They preferred a future in a secular independent India where, somewhat optimistically, they hoped some form of jurisprudential apartheid would be achieved between secular Hindu India and themselves.

Since 1919 their main voice in Indian affairs has been the Jami'at ul-Ulama-i Hind, which after Partition developed a Pakistani wing, the Jam'iat ul-Ulama-i Islam. Deobandis have spread with the South Asian diaspora of the 20th century. They remain notable for their concern to maintain a traditional Islamic education, and for their bitter disputes with the **Barelvis** over a range of issues but, most particularly, belief in intercession at saints' shrines. They are sometimes referred to by their Barelvi critics as **Wahhabis**: it is not intended as a compliment.

Dhammayut. An alternative rendering of the Thai **Theravada** monastic fraternity, the **Thammayutika Nikaya**.

Dhu'l-Riyasatayn. A branch of the Iranian **Ni'matullahi Sufi** order, one of the few **Shi'ite** Sufi movements.

Dianetics. This is the "science of mental health" taught by the Church of **Scientology**.

Digambara Jainas (Sky-clad Jainas). One of the two major sects of the **Jainas,** so-called because their monks go naked. They hold that the possession of clothing is tantamount to remaining a householder and therefore acts as a disqualification from the mendicant path to liberation. For this reason, they deny that **Svetambara** mendicants are monks at all. They also differ from the Svetambaras in their contention that souls cannot be liberated from female bodies. Digambaras reject the Svetambara canon as inauthentic, referring instead to other works, especially those ascribed to Kundakunda (2nd century BCE, or later).

Digambara mendicants are restricted to a single begged meal daily, which they receive in their upturned palms. Their *Sangha* presently contains perhaps as few as 65 full (naked) monks, 60 "junior" (clothed monks) and 50 nuns, although mendicant numbers have always been relatively small.

Traditionally, Digambara strength has been in south-west India—Maharashtra and Karnataka. The pilgrimage site of Sravana Belgola (in Karnataka) contains what has become probably the best known Jaina image, the monolithic figure of Bahubali. Its ritual "heat-anointing" every 15 years attracts tens of thousands of Jainas from all over India. Such sites are usually under the direction of a non-mendicant official, who may at various times combine the functions of caste *guru*, teacher and librarian. The status of this official is peculiar to the Digambaras, and especially to those of the Bisapanthi sub-sect. However, the Terapanthis (not to be confused with a Svetambara sub-sect of the same name) reject his authority. A further sub-sect, the Taranapanthis, are opposed to image worship. In this century the **Kanji Panth** has attracted a large Digambara following through Kanji Swami's reinterpretation of Kundakunda's teachings.

Disciples of Christ (Restorationist). In 1809 Alexander Campbell arrived in America to join his father, a minister of the presbyterian Church of Scotland. Following the influence of his father he came to believe that existing churches had wandered away from the ideals laid down in the New Testament. In 20 years they had founded a denomination which became known as the "Disciples of Christ" based on the principles of Christian life and church government which they believed were found in the Bible. They campaigned for other churches to unite by "restoring" what they claimed was God's original intention for the church.

In 1905 a major split occurred in the movement, partly caused by questions on the interpretation of the Bible in the light of modern Bible criticism. The more conservative members called themselves the **Church of Christ** and are now the larger of the two bodies. Most of the membership is still in the USA (7,000,000) but there are strong churches in Britain, Australia and New Zealand. Both groups have a weekly Communion service, practise believer's baptism and regard the New Testament as the sole authority for church life, rejecting other ecclesiastical traditions.

Worldwide membership is over 8,000,000.

Divine Light Mission. The Divine Light Mission is a new religious movement of Indian origin and known in the West since the visit to England in 1971 of the "boy-guru" Maharaji. Since the early 1980s it has been known by a different name, **Elan Vital**.

Dolma. A sub-group within the **Sakyapa** school of **Tibetan Buddhism**.

Dominicans. The Dominican Order, conceived by St Dominic as theologically knowledgeable missionaries, received Papal recognition in 1216. The Dominicans or Order of Preachers were, alongside the **Franciscans**, the first Order of friars. Friars were expected to be more flexible than their landed, monkish forebears. The Dominicans' first task was to catechize the untutored populace of Europe's new cities and to recover those of the French *intelligentsia* who had succumbed to various heresies.

The Dominican contribution to the Church has been broadly in the realm of ideas. The Dutch Fr Schillebeeckx draws on the experientialism originated by the **Protestant** theologian, F. D. Schleiermacher (1768–1834), while Matthew Fox propagates a peculiarly Californian fusion of the spirit of **Christianity** with that of nature. Numbers have dropped steadily since 1958: there are now 7,000 Dominican friars, 4,500 Dominican nuns, and 40,000 sisters. Half live in Europe, a quarter in the Third World.

Dominicans prefer to live and to pray in community. Their priories contain at least six friars; smaller groups are called houses. The priory elects its own prior; the houses' superiors are chosen by the Provincial. The Provincial is selected by a Chapter of priors and house delegates. He has four years in office. The Master is elected by the provincials and other Dominican officials. He has nine years' tenure and cannot be re-elected. The last was Fr Damian Byrne. The new Master, elected in 1992, is Fr Timothy Radcliffe, the first Englishman to hold the office in the Order's 777 years' history.

Donmeh. The Donmeh (Turkish, "apostates"), also known as Sabbateans, are the followers of the 17th-century Jewish "messiah" Shabetai Tzvi. Born into an **Ashkenazi** family in Izmir (Smyrna) in 1626, Tzvi, after studying *Talmud* and **Kabbalah** and always something of an eccentric, was banished from the community for religious deviations. He travelled extensively and lived in Jerusalem and Cairo before being proclaimed the long-awaited messiah by one Nathan of Gaza. He renounced many of the commandments and advocated a series of antinomian practices (his doctrine of the "holy sinner"). Thus began a wave of messianic fervour that swept across Europe and the Middle East as large numbers of Jews prepared for the imminent "end-times". Tzvi's campaign came to an abrupt end in 1666 when he was captured, taken to Istanbul and given the option of death or conversion to Islam. The Jewish world was stunned by Tzvi's decision to accept the latter! A few hundred families followed him into **Islam** and became known as the Donmeh. Tzvi died in exile in Albania in 1676.

The Donmeh formally and outwardly followed Muslim traditions but maintained secret Jewish and Shabbatean practices, including an orgiastic spring equinox festival which included wife-swapping. Salonika, proclaimed a holy city by Tzvi, became the centre of Donmeh life. In the late 17th century the Donmeh split into two groups—the Izmirilis (following Tzvi) and the Yakubis (followers of Tzvi's brother-in-law, Jacob, heralded as a reincarnation of Tzvi). In the early 18th century a second schism occurred and a new "incarnation" of Tzvi, in the person of Baruhiah Russo, led a third faction known as the Karakash. None of the "sects" permitted intermarriage with Donmeh of other groups and the groups themselves were distinguished by status and occupation—the Izmirilis were merchants and intellectuals; the Yakubis, clerks and officials; and the Karakash, artisans and workers.

In 1913 there were some 16,000 Donmeh in Salonika (out of more than 60,000 Jews) and in 1924 the Donmeh, rejected by Salonika Jewry, were moved into Turkey. Donmeh were influential in the Young Turk movement and the 1909 government included three Donmeh ministers. By the end of World War II the Yakubis and Izmirilis had largely assimilated into Turkish society, leaving only the Karakash as an active Donmeh group. Presently there are approximately 3,000 Karakash, mainly in Istanbul where they have their own synagogue containing a statute of Baruhiah Russo brought with them from Salonika. Continuing outwardly as part of the broader Muslim community, the Karakash do not let outsiders into their homes and only reveal their secrets on wedding days to brides and grooms. They await the imminent return of their messiah.

Drukpa Kagyudpas. "Dragon Kagyudpas". Second largest of the four surviving **Kagyudpa** schools of **Tibetan Buddhism,** the Drukpas are divided into three sub-groupings of "Middle", "Lower" and "Upper". Founded by Ling Repa (1128–1189), and his disciple Tsangpa Gyare, the school received its name from a vision of nine roaring dragons which filled the sky during the consecration of one of their early monasteries. The Drukpas are renowned for their renunciation, simplicity and deep commitment to practice, and are one of the few Tibetan schools to still maintain the tradition of *Repas*, "cotton-clad yogins" who practice *Tummo* or "inner heat", thereby living in freezing caves above the Himalayan snow-line with virtually no food or clothing. Despite their tendency to decentralization, the Drukpas became the state religion of Bhutan, where they survive in great strength. Noted for their skill in the arts, especially mystic songs, the Drukpas also produced a very great scholar in Pema Karpo (1527–1592), whose current reincarnation, the 12th Drukchen Rinpoche, is the Drukpa's major incarnate lama. With bases in Ladakh and Darjeeling, and fluent in English, H. H. Drukchen Rinpoche is now a popular teacher all over the world.

Druzes (Druses). A quasi-Muslim community of between 200,000 and 400,000, mainly found in Lebanon, Syria, Jordan, and Israel. The religion began as a branch of **Isma'ili Shi'ism,** originating in a belief in the divinity of the sixth Fatimid caliph, the despotic al-Hakim (d. 1021), a doctrine first preached in Syria by an Isma'ili missionary called al-Darazi (who gave his name to the sect). The Druze era begins in the year 1017, when an Iranian disciple, Hamza ibn 'Ali, proclaimed the faith of al-Hakim to be independent of both **Sunnism** and Isma'ilism.

The Druze still believe that al-Hakim (whom they regard as still alive) will return at the end of time as their Messiah. They do not observe either Sunni or Shi'ite beliefs or practices, but their particular doctrines have generally been kept secret, even from the majority of Druzes themselves. The essential belief is a strict monotheism centred in the divinity of al-Hakim. As in several forms of

Shi'ism, there is a cyclic theory of seven prophets, and a belief in reincarnation common to several extremist sects. The central scriptural text is a collection of letters by different individuals, known as the *Rasail al-hikma*. The community is sharply divided between a religious élite known as *'uqqal* and the remainder (*juhhal*—the ignorant).

Dutch Reformed Church. The Dutch Reformed Church is a branch of the **Presbyterian (Reformed)** tradition, and is highly influential in South African politics. Dutch immigrants to South Africa organized the church into a main white denomination, the Nederduitse Gereformeerde Kerk (NGK), and three "mission" churches for African, Coloured and Indian members.

The NGK held to a theological defence of apartheid until 1986. However in 1990 the newly-elected Moderator of the NGK, Pieter Potgieter, publicly confessed his church's guilt in supporting the policy which he now believed to be wrong. However other minority white denominations, notably the NHK and the newly formed APK (1987) have not withdrawn support for apartheid. The present vice-president of South Africa, F. W. de Klerk, belongs to the Gereformeerde Kerk, a branch of NGK.

The Coloured church (NGS) has been the most liberal and prominent of the mission churches, under the leadership of Dr Allan Boesak. In 1990 he resigned as Moderator of the church after admitting an extra-marital affair, although he is still active politically. The Dutch Reformed Church is the largest church tradition in South Africa with c. 15.6 per cent of the population.

E

East Syrian Church. This is an alternative name for the **Nestorian Church**.

Eastern Rite Churches. *See* **Uniate Churches.**

Eastern Rite Romanian Catholic Church. (*See also* **Orthodox Church— Byzantine.**) Eastern Rite Romanian Catholics use the Byzantine rite. Their Church came into being in 1698, when, under the less-than-casual influence of the Austro–Hungarian Empire, the Orthodox Church of Transylvania forged a union with Rome. Most current members of the Eastern Rite Church of Romania are Hungarians who, due to the demise of that Empire, found themselves domiciled in Transylvania. Theirs was a national church from 1919 until the Communist seizure of power after '1945. At the Synod of Cluj in 1948, the Church was compelled to be assimilated into **Russian Orthodoxy.** After this, Romanian officialdom knew Orthodox and Latin Rite Christians, but not the Church of the Eastern rite. Thousands of clerical and lay Romanian Eastern Rite Catholics received jail sentences; six were bishops, of whom the last to die in prison was Juliu Hossu, in 1970. In 1975, there were an estimated 900,000 secret Eastern Rite Romanians. They were enabled to practise their faith by the bravery of hundreds of underground priests. The

overthrow of President Ceaucescu at Christmas 1989 has allowed the Eastern
Rite Romanian Catholic Church to come above ground. It has met continuing
Romanian dislike of Hungarian "separatists". Its good health as a Christian
community will depend on its capacity to outgrow its enforced absorption in
private devotion alone.

Eastern Rite Ukrainian Church. *See* **Ukrainian Uniate Catholic Church.**

Edah Haredi. *See* **Orthodox Judaism.**

Elan Vital. Formerly known as the Divine Light Mission, this new religious
movement was founded in the 1930s by Shri Hans Ji Maharaj (d 1966), but
only became known in the West when the founder's youngest, 13-year-old son,
the "boy-guru" Maharaji, came to England in 1971. The teaching is called
"Knowledge", and this knowledge is achieved by training the senses to focus
on inner rather than external experiences. Part-time members lead a normal
lifestyle and can marry, but contribute 10 per cent of their income to the group.
Ashram members are unmarried and donate their salaries.

The movement grew rapidly, until Maharaji fell out with his mother after
marrying his American secretary. She took over in India, where his brother is
now recognized as head of the movement, but he is still in control in the West.
Elan Vital (as the movement began to be called in the early 1980s) then became
less Indian, and adopted a lower profile. Numbers, once claimed as hundreds
of thousands, are down to about 7,000 in Britain and 15,000 in the USA, but
growing slowly.

Elim Fellowship. An association of classical **Pentecostalist** congregations and
ministers, which grew out of revivals in Northern Ireland (1911–1920) and
subsequently in England and Wales. Their earliest full title was Elim Foursquare
Gospel Alliance.

Elim Pentecostal Church. *See* **Pentecostal Churches (Charismatic).**

Ennahda. This is a name sometimes used for the Tunisian Islamist organization
described here under the heading **Hizb al-Nahda**.

Episcopalians. Some settlers in the American colonies took their **Anglican**
beliefs and traditions with them and accepted the ecclesiastical oversight of
the Bishop of London. After the War of Independence, in 1789 the name
"Protestant Episcopal Church in the USA" was adopted. Samuel Seabury
was elected bishop by the clergy of Connecticut and consecrated by Scottish
Anglican bishops. In 1967 "The Episcopal Church" was accepted as an
alternative name. It claims 2,750,000 members, which include former President
George Bush. It belongs to the Anglican Communion. One of their most
controversial leaders is Bishop Spong of Newark.

est. Erhard Seminar Training is one of the movements which have been called
Self Religions, and which may also be seen as part of the **Human Potential
Movement.** Thousands of Americans and Europeans have been attracted to
it, with many claiming that its notorious method of enhancing personality by

encouraging participants to scream and shout abuse at each other has proved surprisingly effective.

Ethiopian Churches. (*See also* **African New Religious Movements.**) This is the label used primarily in a South African context to refer to African independent churches which have largely maintained the patterns of worship and doctrine of the older, European-based churches, but differ from them in having been founded by Africans for Africans. Most were founded in the period from 1890 to 1920 in reaction to the prevalent link between the older churches and colonialism, and the paternalism which kept control of the churches firmly in the hands of missionaries or whites. As well as differing from the European-based churches, the Ethiopian churches also stand in contrast to the **Zionist** churches.

Ethiopian Jews. *See* **Beta Israel.**

Ethiopian Orthodox Church. Ethiopia became Christian in the 4th century, falling within the jurisdiction of the original Church of Alexandria. Since the monophysite controversy of the 5th century, the Ethiopian Church has followed the theological and ecclesiastical traditions of the **Coptic Church**. Until the mid-20th century its primate and senior bishops were Copts rather than native Ethiopians. In 1959 it became completely independent of Coptic jurisdiction, and now constitutes a separate body among the **Oriental Orthodox Churches**. It numbers around 8,000,000, nearly half the country's population.

The Ethiopic liturgy is a version of the Coptic liturgy translated into the originally vernacular but now defunct Ge'ez language. A distinctive feature of Ethiopian worship is the use of percussion instruments and dance. The Ethiopians have over the centuries been variously subject to native African, Islamic and especially Jewish influences. From **Judaism** they have adopted circumcision, a Saturday Sabbath, and certain dietary observances. The Patriarch-Catholicos, or *abuna,* resides at Addis Ababa. Since the 19th century there has also been a Roman Catholic Uniate Church in Ethiopia, also using the Ethiopic rite.

Eusebia. *See* **Zoe.**

Exclusive Brethren. The Exclusive Brethren came into being as a result of a split in the Brethren movement in 1849 (*see* **Open Brethren**). They were originally the followers of J. N. Darby (Darbyites), a former lawyer and Church of Ireland minister who was associated with the start of the Brethren. Darby rejected everything he regarded as evil, and was involved in many conflicts over doctrine and behaviour.

Exclusive Brethren try to avoid the influence of "the World", for example by not watching television, attending only Exclusive Brethren meetings, not drinking alcohol etc. They do not share Communion with other Christians. Leaders are chosen from within the Church and some may be supported in full-time ministry. The movement has continued to fragment over doctrinal differences and at times extreme members have attracted hostile media attention. Worldwide membership is over 150,000, mostly in Britain but also in America and Australasia.

F

Falashas. *See* **Beta Israel.**

Family of Love. This movement was founded in California in 1968 by David Brandt Berg, later known as Moses David or "Mo". It was first called Children of God or Mission South, and emerged out of the Jesus Movement of the late 1970s in America. The headquarters moved to London in 1971. By the mid-1970s the movement had spread to 60 different countries.

The Family claims to be a truly Christian movement based on the Bible and the "Mo Letters", written by the founder as a modern equivalent to St Paul's epistles. Their often pornographic content provoked outrage and opposition, as does the practice of "flirty fishing": female members are exhorted to prostitute themselves (become "hookers for Jesus") in order to win new members.

Berg teaches that mankind is living its Last Days and that the signs of the Second Coming are close: capitalism and communism are on the verge of being destroyed by God and will be replaced by "godly socialism".

The structure of the movement is pyramidical, with Berg at the top, and counsellors, bishops, shepherds and under-shepherds beneath. The grassroots members "forsake all" their possessions to the movement, to which they devote themselves full-time. Mo's word holds the final authority over the teachings which are revealed to him from God. A distinction is made between "acts done in the spirit" and "acts done in the flesh", the latter belong to the "deluded" outside world and support "the system". Being a member and acting "in the spirit", i.e. in faith and obedience to Berg, all one's actions become sanctified and free from "worldly" laws, which explains the virtual absence of restrictions on sexual behaviour, both for adults and children alike. In the late 1970s, the movement changed from a large-scale community to widely scattered, mobile family units and small groups. These are encouraged to support themselves through jobs, hold bible study meetings and get involved in existing churches. Membership worldwide has been claimed as up to 10,000. This is a considerable overestimate.

FIS. *See* **Front Islamique du Salut.**

Fiver Shi'ites. The label Fiver Shi'ites (or simply Fivers) is sometimes given to the **Zaydis** as a convenient way of distinguishing them from both the **Isma'ilis** (or Sevener Shi'ites) and the **Twelver Shi'ites.** It derives from the fact that the Zaydi line of leadership deviates from those of the two other groups at the fifth Imam.

Flower Garland School. *See* **Kegonshu**.

Franciscans or the **Order of Friars Minor.** John Bernardone (1182–1226) was a spiritual "troubadour", dedicated to "Lady Poverty". He was known to his friends as "Francis", the "Frenchman", and to posterity as St Francis of Assisi. He was called to live in great austerity and to preach the Christian gospel. He gathered a group of friends who lived by begging alms in order to share the lot of the very poor.

The *joculatores domines* ("jugglers of God") sought acceptance at Rome. Their way of life was informally condoned by Pope Innocent III in 1209. By 1217, they had spread from Italy to Europe; the groups were now divided into "provinces", over which St Francis appointed ministers. The homeless and mendicant origins of the barefooted *fratres minores* led to the creation of one of the two new preaching orders of Friars of the 13th century (the other being the **Dominicans**).

In 1221, St Francis was asked to write a more detailed Rule for his Order. When this was taken to be too arduous, he composed a third: this was formally ratified by Pope Honorius III in 1223. St Francis regretted the social, human, or ecclesiastical compulsion to fix and to modify his rule. In popular **Roman Catholic** belief, St Francis was the first "stigmatist", bearing on his body the marks of the crucifixion.

There are now 25,000 Franciscan friars and priests, living in most countries of the world. They are prominent in Japan. The Franciscans still take the call to evangelization as their most serious duty.

An **Anglican** Society of St Francis was founded for men in 1922, but was preceded by a Community of St Francis, created in 1905 for women.

Free Churches. A general term for any Christian group unwilling to submit to the authority of an established church. In the UK this has come to signify non-conforming protestant churches, e.g. **Baptists, Methodists,** etc., that reject the teaching, discipline and governance of **Anglicanism.** The Free Church Federal Council was founded in 1940 to represent the interests of these churches.

Free Presbyterian Church. In Northern Ireland this Church is closely associated with Rev. Ian Paisley, though each congregation maintains a strong sense of autonomy. Founded in the early 1950s by conservative **Presbyterians** disturbed by a perceived shift towards liberalism, latest estimates put membership at c. 12,000 in over 50 congregations. Vehemently anti-Catholic, self-consciously Fundamentalist, and "loyalist" in political outlook, the church has strong links with the Democratic Unionist Party, led by Rev. Paisley.

The Free Presbyterian Church in Scotland (the Wee Frees), founded in 1900 as a conservative splinter from the Church of Scotland, has approximately 1,000 members. Lord Mackay of Clashfern, the present Lord Chancellor, is a prominent member. He was recently castigated by his co-religionists for attending the funeral of a Roman Catholic colleague.

Free Russian Orthodox Church. This is the name of the branch of the emigré Russian (Orthodox) Church Abroad which now operates within Russia. Its first parish was established in June 1990, and the number is increasing rapidly although there is fierce opposition from the Moscow Patriarchate and many priests still operate from their flats. It has three bishops who are subject to the Synod of the Russian Church Abroad located in New York. The senior of the three, Archbishop Lazar of Tambov and Moshansk, was for many years a member of the underground **True Orthodox Church**, and many other True Orthodox members are now joining FROC. Members of both organizations actively opposed the *coup* of August 1991, but they are in competition for churches and parishes, and FROC, in line with its parent organization, repudiates the validity of most True Orthodox priestly orders and sacraments.

Freemasons. Freemasonry today has a large membership, nearly 2,000 lodges existing in the Greater London area alone. As one of the world's oldest fraternal societies of men concerned with spiritual values, its members learn its mysteries through a series of rituals whose symbolism is based around the tools and customs of the stonemason. The basic principles of Freemasonry are Brotherly Love, Relief (assisting the community) and Truth.

The Brotherhood has come in for considerable media attack in recent years on grounds of corruption and misuse of power. Masonic meetings have a total ban on discussion of politics and organized or official religion, and freemasonry expresses no opinions on such matters. The recent public attention, by arousing a self-scrutiny of its own ranks, has probably strengthened Masonry.

Friends. Quakers are known as Friends, and their organization is the **Society of Friends**.

Friends of the Western Buddhist Order (FWBO). This group was founded in 1967 by Maha Sthavira Sangharakshita (formerly Dennis Lingwood). Born in 1925, he was stationed in India during World War II and was ordained as a novice in 1949. The following year he took full ordination as a monk in the **Theravada** tradition. Whilst resident in India, Sangharakshita studied both **Tibetan** and **Zen** traditions and worked extensively with ex-untouchable converts to Dr Ambedkar's **Neo-Buddhism.** On his return to London in 1964 the need for a kind of **Buddhism** that Westerners could practise in a Western context impressed itself upon him. The result was the founding of the FWBO and, in 1968, the Western Buddhist Order (WBO).

At the heart of the movement are the Order Members. These are male and female, some married, some single; the latter practise celibacy. They are the Order's equivalent of monks and nuns, though they do not observe traditional Buddhist *vinaya* rules.

The next level of involvement is that of the *mitra* (lit. friend). These are lay Buddhists who have made a formal commitment to the FWBO. All have close contact with Order Members, two of whom become the *mitra's* "spiritual friends" and take a special interest in his or her welfare. At the third level are the "friends", sympathetic and supportive lay people who want to be involved without making the degree of commitment expected from a *mitra*.

Each local group is attached to a Centre, which will accommodate at least five order members. The Centre provides a focus for friends, *mitras* and Order Members. Most operate Right Livelihood businesses such as vegetarian restaurants, wholefood shops and building companies. All Centres donate a portion of their income to finance centrally organized activities and the Indian wing of the organization, the **TBMSG**, which, because of its predominantly ex-untouchable membership, is dependent on donations for its effective functioning. The FWBO has extended its activities to Europe and North America in recent years.

Front Islamique du Salut (FIS). The FIS (al-Jabha al-Islamiya li-Inqadh, or Islamic Salvation Front) was founded in 1989, the first Islamic political party to appear in Algeria, and by far the largest. Within a year it had achieved 54 per cent of the vote in municipal and provincial elections in June 1990, gaining control of two-thirds of Algeria's Popular Assemblies (i.e. in 32 out of 48 of the provinces). Its further astonishing success in the first round of the national election in 1991 led to the suspension, in January 1992, of the second round of the election which was universally expected to pave the way for the formation of a fundamentalist Islamic government.

FIS's roots lie in the broad movement of Islamic renewal, **Ahl al-Da'wa,** that emerged in Algeria in the late 1970s and flourished after the death of President Boumedienne in 1978. This period also coincided with the success of the Islamic revolution in Iran, but in Algeria Islamist tendencies had been apparent already in the 1960s, their inspiration going back indeed to the **Salafiya.**

The FIS aims to re-establish the state and the society on the basis of Islamic law, the shari'a. The stricter lifestyle it advocates would include traditional restrictions on women, some of whom claim to have been ordered to vote for FIS by their husbands. Presenting itself as the necessary solution to Algeria's severe problems, which include large-scale youth unemployment, it has so far produced little in the way of practical policy. Appealing as it does to a wide variety of constituents, this may reflect a deep-seated difficulty, rather than being simply the consequence of its rapid success. Nevertheless, it is clearly extremely well organized, and capable of mobilizing very considerable numbers of people, using its own network of mosques as a popular base.

The Iraqi invasion of Kuwait in 1990 led to a crisis: the leadership, conscious of the need to secure continued financial support from the Saudis (and Kuwaitis), had little option but to support Saudi Arabia, while at the grassroots level there was massive popular support for Saddam Hussein.

Following the army intervention of 1992 to prevent certain FIS victory at the polls, the movement's leaders were detained, leaving the initiative to more militant elements within the movement. Sporadic acts of violence occurred, perpetrated in part, it is thought, by former mujahideen fighters in the war in Afghanistan, for which a number of Algerians volunteered. FIS was declared illegal, leading to increased violence and the emergence of the Armed Islamic Movement (MIA—Mouvement Islamique Armé), whose campaign included the targeting of Europeans in Algeria as potential victims of assassination.

FWBO. See **Friends of the Western Buddhist Order.**

G

Gedatsukai. A Japanese new religious movement which blends together elements of **Shinto** practice and **Buddhist** Shingon/Mikkyo doctrine. Founded by Okano Seiken (1881–1948) after a series of revelations at Kitamo, 50 miles from Tokyo, which remains the sacred ground (*goreichi*) of the movement, Gedatsukai teaches the equivalence of the central deities of Shintoism and **Shingonshu.** It also upholds ancestor worship, family and agrarian values, and the cult of the emperors. Members must observe three annual pilgrimages and the major spring and autumn festivals. Possession or "miraculous shaking" is a feature of Gedatsukai worship.

Gelugpas. "The Virtuous Ones." A monastic order of **Tibetan Buddhists** known as "Yellow Hats" because of their distinctive ceremonial headgear. Its most prominent member is H. H. Dalai Lama though, strictly speaking, he is not the head of the order. The *Gelugpas* originated in 15th-century Tibet as a reform movement placing great stress on strict monastic discipline and the elimination of certain magico–sexual practices that had begun to dominate the **Buddhism** of the region. The founder, Tsong-kha-pa (1357–1419), was able to harmonize *Mahayanist* philosophical thought into a coherent system for the benefit of his followers. He also laid the foundations of a graduated intellectual and meditative training scheme, modelled on a curriculum established at the great monastic universities of northern India. Monks are expected to progress through a rigorous study of selected philosophical texts to the degree of *geshe*. Beyond this stage a candidate may opt for further spiritual training in the Buddhist tantras.

The first monastery, Ganden, was established by Tsong-kha-pa in Lhasa and the influence of the school gradually extended throughout the country, though the *Gelugpa* powerbase has always been in Central Tibet. In the 16th century, the third successor to Tsong-kha-pa was influential in converting the Mongols to the Buddhist faith and was awarded the title "Dalai" (Ocean) by Altan Khan. Since this time it has been customary to regard successive Dalai Lamas as serial incarnations of the celestial bodhisattva Avalokitesvara. The present Dalai Lama (1935–), who is 14th in the line, was forced to flee from Tibet following the Chinese invasion of 1959. Now settled in Dharmasala, North India, with a considerable number of fellow Tibetans both monastic and lay, he is the head of the Tibetan government in exile. His changed circumstances are such that he is the focus of the spiritual and nationalist aspirations of all Tibetans irrespective of precise religious affiliation. The second most prominent lama in the order, the Panchen Lama, was forced by the Chinese authorities to spend his adult life in Beijing. He died in 1989. In recent years the *Gelugpas* have begun an extensive printing project, the Library of Tibetan Works and Archives based in Dharmasala, aimed at preserving the literary culture of Tibetan Buddhism. The Gelugpas have also had good success in gaining converts, mainly through the tours of prominent teachers such as Lamas Thubten Yeshe, Zopa, and Geshe Kelsang, founder of the New Kadampa Tradition, and there are now a considerable number of Western *Gelugpa* monks, nuns and lay people located in centres throughout the world. In Tibet itself *Gelugpa* monks have been an influential focus of popular discontent with the Chinese occupation and have suffered accordingly.

Ger Hasidism (Gur). (*See also* **Orthodox Judaism.**) Following the destruction of the major centres of Jewish life in Eastern Europe during the Holocaust, a number of Hasidic dynasties, including the Ger, were re-established in the land of Israel, with centres in Europe and North America. Thousands of Ger Hasidim and others pay visits to the Jerusalem court of the current Ger Rebbe, Rabbi Israel Alter, each year. He is one of the major figures in the Jewish world and his influence is widespread in both Israel and the diaspora.

Ger Hasidism is named after the small town near Warsaw, Poland, of that name (Hebrew, "Ger"; Yiddish, "Gur"; Polish, "Gora Kalwaria"), where their founding Rebbe, Rabbi Isaac Meir Alter (1799–1866), established his family dynasty (1859). A noted scholar, Isaac Meir was influenced by the

Przysucha-Kotsk school of Hasidism and promoted Torah study among his followers. He, and his successors, were active in public affairs and evidenced a particular concern with the situation of the Polish Jewish masses. His grandson, Rabbi Judah Aryeh Leib (1864–94), introduced a philosophical element into his teachings, drawing on the writings of Rabbi Judah Loewe of Prague.

Ger Hasidism became the most powerful Jewish Orthodox movement in Poland and the Ger Rebbe the pre-eminent spokesman for Orthodoxy until the Holocaust. This was particularly evident under the leadership and organization of Rabbi Abraham Mordecai Alter (1866–1948), the great-grandson of the founder, who was recognized as the leading figure in European Orthodox Judaism and was one of the founders of **Agudat Israel.** He was especially active in the creation of youth movements and educational institutions. In 1940 he moved to Israel. The current Rebbe is his son.

The Ger were one of the few Orthodox groups who were supportive of the programme of the return of Jews to the land of Israel and the rebuilding of Jewish life there. They are still, along with the **Lubavich Hasidim**, the main groups within Agudat Israel.

Ger Hasidim are characterized by their traditional garb including the tall fur hat (spodik), their Torah study and strict observance of the commandments, and represent the continuity of Polish Hasidism in the contemporary Jewish world.

Great White Brotherhood. An East European new religious movement that claims 150,000, mainly young, followers in Ukraine, Russia, Belarus and Moldova. Founded by Marina Tsvygun (*aka* Maria Devi Christos), a former journalist and Young Communist League activist, and her husband Yuri Krivonogov (*aka* the Holy Father), a **yoga** teacher and ex-worker into the military application of hypnosis and mind-altering drugs, the movement is best known for its prediction that the world would end on Nov. 24, 1993. To prevent a potential mass suicide of group members, and as a response to public panic, the police authorities of Kiev, described as the "new Calvary" by the Brotherhood, arrested the couple several days before this date on a charge of "hooliganism". As a result, Armageddon has been postponed indefinitely. Built up from fragments of apocalyptic **Orthodox** Christianity, Slavonic occult practices and **Hindu** mysticism, the central doctrine of the Great White Brotherhood is the complete divinity of the founding couple, who represent the two polar aspects of theistic reality. In particular, Maria Devi Christos is termed the "living God on earth" by her followers.

Greater World Christian Spiritualist League. *See* **Spiritualists.**

Greek Orthodox (Church). Institutionally there is no such entity as the "Greek Orthodox Church". The term has sometimes been used to describe the entire **Orthodox Church (Byzantine)** tradition, but very misleadingly in view of the important role played by the Slavonic (and other) elements in this tradition. A misleading usage identifies the term with the Orthodox Church of Greece, since a number of institutionally quite distinct Orthodox Churches can be described as "Greek Orthodox". These include the Church of Greece, the Church of Cyprus, the Ecumenical Patriarchate of Constantinople (the original

Church of the Byzantine Empire), the Patriarchal Church of Alexandria, and (at least nominally) the Patriarchal Church of Jerusalem, together with the semi-independent Church of Sinai. The Ecumenical Patriarchate (based in Istanbul in Turkey) also has jurisdiction over four semi-independent Churches located within the territory of modern Greece but for historical reasons never incorporated into the Church of Greece: those of Patmos, Crete, the Dodecanese islands, and Mount Athos. What basically defines a Church as Greek are the common language of worship, and the associated culture and customs. To what particular Church a Greek-speaking Orthodox belongs is not always obvious.

Gurdjieffian Groups. George Gurdjieff (c.1872–1949) attracted many leading members of the inter-war *intelligentsia* (for instance Katherine Mansfield) with his radical teachings, developed during his travels throughout Asia, and bearing many resemblances to **Sufism**. His theory was that most human beings are so mechanical and "asleep" that they do not develop souls, unless they receive a "shock" to wake them up. His method, known as the Fourth Way and also as "the Work", involved supreme tests of energy and endurance, but also meditations and sacred dances, which are still preserved in the Gurdjieff schools.

The main centre of his work in Britain is now the Gurdjieff Society, which currently has about 600 members. There are many other small groups, often at odds with each other, some of which have no direct link with Gurdjieff. There are about 1,000 Gurdjieffians in Britain. There are also groups practising the "System" of P. D. Ouspensky (1878–1947), Gurdjieff's most famous disciple, who founded his own movement.

Gurdjieff's therapeutic approach was one of the main influences on the **Human Potential Movement**. His unusual cosmology, including the doctrine of "reciprocal maintenance", was influential on the "green" movement. Along with **Krishnamurti** he is the most highly-regarded of contemporary Eastern spiritual teachers, even in academic circles, and his books are still widely read. Considerable impetus came too from the very clear summary of his teachings in Ouspensky's posthumously published book *In Search of the Miraculous*.

Gush Emunim (Block of the Faithful). (*See also* **Zionism.**) The major settlement group in Judea and Samaria (the "administered" or occupied territories) is the Gush Emunim, founded in 1974 (although its origins can be traced back to the Gahelet youth group in 1952). It is held to be "the major extra-parliamentary force within Israel", and its members, after supporting Likud in 1977, have since voted for a variety of parties. They represent a faction developing out of **Mafdal** and number only about 2,000. No other group has raised the core issues of the meaning of the Jewish state and the relationship between **Zionism** and **Judaism** so forcefully.

Gush Emunim offers a theological "answer" to the tensions between traditional **Orthodox Judaism** and modern secular Zionism—"there is no Zionism without Judaism and no Judaism without Zionism". This "answer" is based on the teachings of the spiritual leader of the Merkaz Harav *Yeshivah,* Rabbi Abraham Isaac Kook, and his son and successor, Rabbi Tzvi Yehuda Kook. The major figures in the Gahelet youth group were students at the Yeshivah and it represents the link between this group and the Gush Emunim.

Rabbi A. I. Kook, the first **Ashkenazi** Chief Rabbi of Palestine, taught that the apparently secular activities of the Zionist pioneers were, when correctly understood, to be seen as possessing the "hidden spark" of the sacred. In explicating his doctrine of the "sacralization of the secular", he had recourse to a number of analogies, such as the building of the Holy of Holies in the Jerusalem Temple (the Jewish "state") where the holiness was preceded by the activities of "secular" workmen. His "theological" efforts failed to unite the different factions of pre-state Palestinian Jewry. His son, Tz. Y. Kook, understands the state to be of ultimate religious significance, and the in-gathering of the exiles and the re-establishment of Jewish sovereignty in the land to be signs of the impending redemption. The Gush Emunim share their teacher's views of the sanctity of the "whole" land of Israel.

The Gush Emunim are generally tolerant of secularists and understand the present state of Israel to be "the kingdom in the making", although they insist that God's law always takes precedence over the democratic process. They seek to unite the different elements of Jewish Israel by their practical activities, that is, the establishment of religious settlement-communities (legal and illegal) in the occupied territories ("divinely mandated Israel"), and see themselves as the true heirs to the Labour-Zionist pioneers. Their settlement plans have been both supported and opposed by both major political parties.

In the 1992 general election the Labour alliance gained victory on a platform of advancing the peace process, leading to the peace accords with the PLO. This will almost certainly entail calling a halt to the building of new settlements in order to promote the signing of a full peace treaty. These developments will limit the future options open to the Gush Emunim and will almost certainly lead to the decline of their broad appeal to the Israeli Jewish populace.

H

Habad (Chabad) Hasidism. *See* **Lubavich Hasidism.**

Halveti-Cerrahis. The Halveti-Cerrahis are a Turkish **Sufi** order whose weekly meetings in Istanbul are often attended by visiting foreigners. There are branches in Germany and the USA, but Istanbul remains their centre. The movement's leaders are learned and respected.

The non-Turkish version of their name, Khalwatiya-Jarrahiya, discloses their identity as a branch of a larger order. They are also known as Howling Dervishes because of the particular sounds uttered as part of their *dhikr*.

Hamas (Algeria). Hamas is the acronym for Al-Haraqa li-Mujtama' Islami, the Movement for an Islamic Society, founded in Algeria in 1990. In contrast to the **Front Islamique du Salut (FIS),** it advocates Islamic renewal within society prior to, and as a necessary condition of success in, exercising government power to reform the state along Islamic lines. Nevertheless, electoral support of FIS is not ruled out.

The choice of name is an allusion to the **Hamas** active in Gaza and the West Bank, but there are no known organizational links. Hamas in Algeria represents the development into a political party of an earlier non-political association known as Guidance and Reform (Al-Irshad wa'l-Islah). The leader in both cases is Shaikh Mahfoud Nahnah.

Hamas (West Bank and Gaza). Hamas is, in this case, the acronym for Harakat al-Muqawama al-Islamiya, Movement of Islamic Resistance, a Palestinian Islamic organization founded in August 1988 by Shaikh Ahmad Yasin, a local leader of the **Muslim Brotherhood**, in order to participate in the *intifada* (uprising) to confront the Israeli occupation authorities in the West Bank and Gaza. In May 1989 Yasin was arrested and on Oct. 16, 1991 an Israeli military court in Gaza sentenced him to life imprisonment plus 15 years for ordering the killings of Israeli soldiers and Palestinians collaborating with the Israelis. Hamas is opposed to any peace negotiations with Israel and does not accept any plan to partition historic Palestine into Jewish and Arab states. It has declared its readiness to continue and escalate the *intifada*. Its supporters have clashed with Palestinians in favour of the peace process, and Israel has deported some leading activists. Money from its supporters around the world has been used to set up charities, clinics and mosques. Its leaders are generally well educated, and well versed in the Quran. Nevertheless its ideology is anti-semitic rather than simply anti-Zionist.

Hanafis. The Hanafi school or rite (*madhhab*) is the oldest and largest of the four **Sunni** schools of Islamic law (the other three being the **Maliki, Shafi'i** and **Hanbali**). It was founded in 8th-century Iraq by Abu Hanifa (d. 767), a silk merchant, whose system was to be granted official recognition by the 'Abbasid caliphs of Baghdad and later to enjoy the same status in the Ottoman and Indian Moghul Empires.

Early Hanafi jurists had considerable powers to make use of their personal opinions in forming judgements. Later on these powers were curtailed, but, where the Quran and Traditions offered no clear guidance, they frequently resorted to analogical reasoning (*qiyas*) in order to deal with new situations. This could be done in two ways. The first was to look for material similarities with a case already decided by the sacred texts, thus burglary could be considered similar to theft because both involve taking another's goods. The second was to establish the motive behind the Quranic or Prophetic ruling, hence since the consumption of wine is to be punished because of its intoxicating effects, similarly the consumption of drinks and substances that intoxicate is to be punished in the same way. Hanafi jurists generally laid stress on the need to consider the public interest in reaching their decisions, and to adapt the law to meet changing circumstances.

At present the Hanafi school is predominant in Turkey, the Indian sub-continent, Afghanistan and Central Asia. There are also large numbers of Hanafis among the Arabs of the Fertile Crescent, and most Chinese Muslims are Hanafis.

Hanbalis. The Hanbali rite or school of Islamic law (*madhhab*) takes its name from Ahmad b. Hanbal (d. 855), a famous collector and teacher of Traditions in Baghdad. Ibn Hanbal is the author of a number of works, including the *Musnad,* containing some 28,000 Traditions arranged according to the transmitters rather than the topics. He admired al-Shafi'i, founder of the **Shafi'i** school and agreed with him on the importance of the Prophetic Traditions as a source of law. However, he differed from him in holding to the view that only the Quran and Traditions constituted the sources of the Holy Law. Hanbalis since his time have normally rejected analogical reasoning (*qiyas*), although they have admitted a consensus confined to the early Islamic community.

The Hanbali school had few followers after the 14th century, but experienced a revival in the 18th century with its adoption by the Arabian **Wahhabis**. In modern times its thought has also influenced the reform movement of the **Salafiya**. It is usually regarded as the strictest of the four **Sunni** schools (the remaining three being **Maliki, Hanafi** and Shafi'i), but it can accommodate developments in more liberal directions. An example of this is its doctrine of permissibility, according to which acts are judged to be permissible where there is no specific reference in Quran or Traditions prohibiting them. Following this principle, only the Hanbalis allow a clause to be inserted in the marriage contract stipulating that the husband shall take no additional wives.

Today the Hanbali school is followed in the Kingdom of Saudi Arabia.

Happy, Healthy and Holy Organization (3HO). Another name for the California-based **Sikh Dharma of the Western Hemisphere.**

Hare Krishna Movement. This is a popular designation of members of the **International Society for Krishna Consciousness (ISKCON)**.

Haredi (Haredim). (See also **Hasidism; Orthodox Judaism.**) Haredim (Hebrew, those that "tremble" before the word of God, taken from Isaiah 66:5) refers to the Ultra-Orthodox Jewish communities in Israel and in the diaspora. They number approximately 300,000 in Israel, mainly in Jerusalem and Bene Berak. Referred to also by the Hebrew term *dati* ("observant"), they live in Haredi neighbourhoods and distinguish themselves from the modern Orthodox and Neo-Orthodox in terms of their conscious refusal to compromise with the modern world. Their own perception is of continuing the ways of traditional **Judaism**, unchanged, living lives fully within the framework of the commandments and customs as Yidn or erlicher Yidn (Yiddish (true) Jews or virtuous Jews). The Holocaust and the horrendous losses of the centres of Ultra-Orthodox Jewish life loom large and are reflected in their programmes of renewal and development. Their particular form of Judaism arose in the late 18th and early 19th centuries largely as a reaction to the *haskalah* and the collapse of *shethl* (Jewish town or townlet) and ghetto life in Europe. Their leaders, such as Rabbi Naftali Tzvi Yehuda Berlin (1817–93); Rabbi Moses Sofer (1762–1839); and Rabbi Shlomo Halberstam of Bobova (1848–1906) rejected secular studies and developed *Yeshivot* (institutes of higher education) in order to educate Jews in traditional Torah-learning.

The Haredi community is made up of two distinct strands—the groups of Hasidim and the Lithuanian-dominated Mitnaggdim. The former are divided into a number of different movements each led by its charismatic leader or Rebbe (*see* **Hasidism**). The latter often refer to themselves as Bene Torah (the sons or followers of Torah) or Bene Yeshivah (the sons or followers of the *Yeshivah*) and are based on groups affiliated to a particular *Yeshivah* (e.g. Mir and Kamenitz in Jerusalem and Ponievezh in Bene Berak). There is considerable variety in both groups. By the late 19th and early 20th centuries Hasidim and Litvaks (Lithuanians) found themselves no longer arch-enemies but sharing a concern for the defence of traditional Jewish life and learning. Tensions, however, are still evident between the two groups. For example, the Hasidic-dominated **Agudat Israel** stands against the Lithuanian Degel Hatorah, although they joined forces for the 1992 Israel general election. The Haredi community as a whole is non-**Zionist** but there are different levels of involvement, ranging from total rejection (**Neturei Karta,** Reb Arelah) to more moderate positions.

Yiddish is the vernacular for both groups and Hebrew is pronounced in an Eastern European fashion. In a number of ways the two groups have grown alike, for example, the Hasidim have also developed the *Yeshivah* as a central institution. Likewise in terms of leadership, although the Hasidic Rebbe derives his authority from piety and spirituality and not from his scholarship as in the case of the Lithuanian *Rosh Yeshivah* (the principal or head of a Talmudic academy); often the *Rosh Yeshivah* is a hereditary position.

Smaller groups of **Sephardim** have also in recent years adopted Haredi lifestyles and are part of this community. Many of these attend Lithuanian (and in some cases Hasidic) *Yeshivot.* In 1984 the Sephardi Torah Guardian Party (**Shas**) was established with the blessing of the leading Litvak authority, Rabbi Eliezer Schach (Rosh Yeshivah of Ponievezh) to gain political representation for Ultra-Orthodox Sephardi communities. Sephardim, however, tend to remain separate and follow their own traditions, although in recent years there is evidence of some intermarriage between them and other Haredim.

There are Haredi communities in New York (with Litvak Yeshivot in Lakewood, New Jersey; Telz in Cleveland, Ohio), Antwerp, London (with a Litvak *Yeshivah* in Gateshead near Newcastle) and in other Jewish centres worldwide.

The Haredi community, in Israel and the diaspora, continues to grow, mainly due to its large birthrate and to develop greater involvement with the politics of the wider Jewish community.

Harris Movement. The Harris (or Harrist) churches originated with a Grebo catechist from Liberia, William Wade Harris (c 1850–1929), who received his calling from the Angel Gabriel in a vision. Between 1913 and 1915, Harris baptized some 120,000 people in the Ivory Coast and Ghana, before being deported back to Liberia. In 1924 British **Methodist** missionaries came across Harris' converts and many became Methodists, but independent Harrist churches have continued to expand under prophetic leaders and healers such as John Ahue and Albert Atcho, and to found new offshoots, such as the Church of the Twelve Apostles in Ghana. Followers of Harrist churches are now numbered in the 100,000s and in the Ivory Coast enjoy official recognition.

Harvestime Group. *See* **House Churches.**

Hasidism. (*See also* **Haredi; Orthodox Judaism.**) Hasidism refers to the movement that began in the 18th century, consisting of various groups of Jewish pietists (*Hasidim*, pious ones), each centred around the "court" of its own *Rebbe* or *Tzaddik* (charismatic leader and spiritual and behavioural guide for his followers). There are currently tens of thousands of Hasidim throughout the Jewish world living close to their Rebbe, attending, if they can, his court for the Sabbath and festivals, eager to listen to his "Torah" (exegesis; teaching). Major groups include: **Lubavich; Satmar; Belz; Bratslav; Ger; Vizhitz;** and **Karlin-Stolin.**

The movement founded by the healer and visionary, Israel ben Eliezer (1699–1760, usually known by the acronym BeShT—Baal Shem Tov, Master of the Good Name) in Podolia (south-east Poland–Lithuania), was one of a number of groups notable for their ecstatic prayer and pious observance of the commandments. Besht's teaching attracted both the unlearned Jewish masses and a number of distinguished scholars, and although the notion developed only later, he can be seen as the first Rebbe. A collection of his sayings was published in 1780.

Dov Ber of Mezhirech, Besht's disciple, ensured the development of the movement when many of his followers founded their own Hasidic communities. In most cases these became hereditary dynasties. This decentralization was a significant factor in the rapid spread of Hasidism and by the beginning of the 19th century the majority of Eastern European Jews were Hasidim, creating a new and alternative Jewish social structure. Disputes between different Hasidic groups were common. Hasidism was initially opposed by the rabbinical authorities (*Mitnaggdim*, opponents)—and still is in some quarters—but by the middle of the last century Hasidim and Mitnaggdim found themselves facing the shared enemies of the modern challenges to traditional **Judaism.**

In spite of the plethora of different teachings and styles that developed, there are common threads. For example, there are disparate notions of the Rebbe, ranging from spiritual teacher to miracle-worker. Most, however, draw on the **Kabbalistic** view of the upper and lower worlds affecting each other. In Hasidism, this idea was taken to mean that the Rebbe was the link between the worlds and the conduit of divine grace (flow; power). The Rebbe is held to be free of all evil but has the capacity to raise his followers' evil and to "correct" it and transform it to the good. A second Kabbalistic teaching incorporated into Hasidism was that "there was no place empty of him" (God) and this was interpreted to denote that every aspect of the Rebbe's life and behaviour (including eating and drinking) was of vital significance to the Hasid. The related concept of *devekut* (attachment to God, constant God-consciousness in all activities—*avodah be-gashmiyut*, bodily worship), whilst a Hasidic ideal, was utilized to define the position of the Rebbe. Only he was capable of *devekut* and only through him could the Hasid attach himself to God. The Hasid is to live with burning enthusiasm (*hitlahavat*) and to experience and express joy (*simha*) in his life, particularly in prayer. All actions must be performed with the right intention (*kavanah*).

Hasidism operated, and continues to do so, at two levels. For the vast majority of Hasidim the message is veneration of the Rebbe and simple faith coupled with assiduous performance of the commandments. For a learned minority the Rebbe offers "advanced" spiritual development via the Hasidic interpretations of Kabbalah.

Post-Holocaust Hasidism lives in the shadow of the destruction of its European heartland, but has shown remarkable resilience in its attempts to re-establish its courts in Israel and America. What began as a radical movement within Judaism has become a distinctive but integral part of the contemporary Ultra-Orthodox Jewish world.

Havurat Judaism. (*See also* **Jewish New Agers.**) *Havurot* (fellowships) are small Jewish worship and study and/or communal groups that create intimate communities and stress active participation and the creative and spiritual dimensions of Jewish life. Many *havurot* have collectively produced their own prayerbooks and distinctive patterns of worship, including Sabbath observance, communal meals and often **Hasidic** stories, music and dance. A significant number of *havurot* have been connected with university campuses. Havurot Judaism is closely linked to the development of New Age Judaism. Many of the New Age communal groups were established as *havurot* and leading Jewish New Age figures have been associated with *havurot*. Influences include: Rabbi Zalman Schachter-Shalomi's 1960s Jewish renewal groups; articles in *The Reconstructionist* by Ira Eisenstein, Jacob Neusner and others; *The Jewish Catalogs* (a series of books on "Do-It-Yourself Judaism"); and Rabbi Arthur Green's founding of Havurat Shalom in Boston in 1968. A number of national organizations exist including: Schachter-Shalomi's P'nai Or ("Faces of Light") Religious Fellowship; The Network of Jewish Renewal Communities and The National *Havurot* Co-ordinating Committee (now aligned to the Federation of Reconstructionist congregations, see **Reconstructionist Judaism**). In addition, many "mainstream" congregations (especially **Reform** and **Conservative**) contain smaller *havurot* which serve to increase members' interaction and level of participation.

Heavenly Virtue Church. (Also known as **De Jiao.**) This is a new religious movement found in Hong Kong and Malaysia. It stresses ethics, virtue and wisdom, bringing together elements of five major traditions—**Confucianism, Taoism, Buddhism, Islam** and **Christianity**—which it claims to complete. Adherents, numbering perhaps over 200,000, are drawn overwhelmingly from the Chinese community, as its original name, Tien Te Sheng Hui, would lead one to expect.

Hebrew Christianity. *See* **Messianic Judaism.**

Hinduism. Hinduism refers to the plethora of religious systems and sects to be found in, or that originate in, India. The term, originally coined and used by the British colonial rulers, has come to be used more and more by Indians themselves. Defined in this way, there are more than 600 million Hindus in India and millions of others in Indian communities around the globe. In this century new forms of Hinduism and new religious movements that arose in India, or have incorporated Hindu elements, have attracted Westerners and centres have been established worldwide (for example, **International Society for Krishna Consciousness (ISKON).**

To view Hinduism as the "religion" of the Hindus is misleading, as it includes a bewildering diversity of gods and goddesses, scriptures, doctrines, beliefs, rituals and social forms. In addition there is an immense array of regional variations and local customs and practices. Indologists have offered various basic models to help grasp this complexity of religious forms.

While none of these models proves to be universally applicable, it is reasonable to suggest that one notion central to almost every Hindu group is the distinction drawn between the everyday world of the senses and the realm of the divine. This is not just a version of the more familiar contrast between the sacred and the profane. Hindus maintain that the divine realm is not really separate at all but rather that it penetrates and influences every aspect of the mundane world. There are many approaches to the securing of access to this divine domain. One of the most characteristic is that of the renunciation of the sensual world and the rejection of social norms. Becoming a *samnyasin* (world renouncer), or devoted to one, or under the guidance of a renouncer becoming devoted to a particular deity, is a common form of such access.

There is no single Hindu hierarchy and Hinduism is perhaps best seen as a loose collection of *sampradayas* (sects). Unlike **Christianity,** there appear to be sects without churches or denominations. The usual model is a loose community engaged in devotional practices to a particular god or goddess centred around a specific founding renouncer-teacher (*guru*), or the lineage of his disciples. In some cases, the structure is more formalized and an order of renouncers develops, usually with a lay following. In addition, there are literally tens of thousands of temples in India, each based around the image of the dominant deity (also present are almost always images of other deities). Temples serve as centres of pilgrimage and play a number of complex religious and what we might call social and economic functions.

Scholars often distinguish the "great tradition" from the "little traditions". The former refers to the Sanskrit scriptural tradition beginning with the *Vedas*, and the latter to its local forms. The original Vedic religion of the Aryan invaders, based on sacrifice, is recorded in their sacred texts, which serve as one of the principal foundations for the development of the Hindu religious tradition. These Sanskrit texts comprise the four *Vedas* (*Rig, Yajur, Sama, Atharva*); each of which divides into four sections (hymns, ritual codes, forest books, meditation/renunciation texts). They are classified as *shruti* (that which is heard) and held to be of non-human origin. Some sources insist that the acceptance of the authority of *shruti* is a defining characteristic of Hinduism (thus excluding **Buddhists** and **Jainas**). The Sanskrit language itself is called the "speech of the gods" and is seen as a bridge between the ordinary and divine worlds. Versions of these vedic rituals are still performed by priests (*brahmins*) and provide the basis for Hindu daily domestic ritual. It might be argued that the great tradition exists only as it is manifested locally.

A second textual category is *Smriti* (that which is remembered), comprising the two great epics, the ancient texts (*puranas*) and guides to *dharma*. These are central to much Hindu belief and practice. *Dharma* refers to the universal order and is discussed at the social, ethical and legal levels. Four stages are distinguished in the life-cycle (*ashramas*—student, householder, forest dweller, renouncer). There are also four ends of life, correlated with the life-cycle. While all four stages entail a concern with *dharma*, householders should pursue *artha* (worldly goods) and *kama* (pleasure), and renouncers should focus on *moksha* (liberation from the world).

There are also four levels of social status (*varna*—priest, warrior, worker, serf), each with a different *dharma* (in the sense of duty). This allows for the prescribed schedule of obligations incumbent on every Hindu to be clearly discerned based on gender, life-cycle stage, and status. Some sources also include character (*guna*) in the calculations of *dharma*. Beyond the four *varnas* are the untouchables (and non-Hindus).

The literary tradition also includes systematic philosophical treatises, traditionally divided into six schools, which are normally arranged into three pairs—*Samkhya*—Yoga, *Nyaya-Vaisheshika*, and *Mimamsa*-**Vedanta.**

This system of *dharma* (status and life-cycle) is the basis for the best known of Hindu institutions, its distinctive caste system. Within the broad framework of the four *varnas*, Hindus live as members of tens of thousands of *jatis* (hereditary occupational groups). A degree of separation between the caste groupings (*varna-jati*) is to be found, this is particularly evident in the case of the priestly caste (*brahmins*) who make great efforts to maintain purity and safeguard against pollution by contact with lower castes. Although the *Smriti* text presents the *varna* structure as rigid and fixed, in practice the *jati* system demonstrates considerable flexibility.

Whether or not one can actually locate the traditionally claimed 33 million gods of Hinduism, large numbers of deities and superhuman beings inhabit the divine world. The Christian, Jewish and Muslim debates about the dangers of polytheism have little resonance in Indian religious literature where the stress is on the character of the particular deity as link between the divine and everyday orders. A number of gods and goddesses are mentioned in Vedic literature, but the principal deities, Vishnu (see **Vaishnavas**) and Shiva (see **Shaivas**), are central in the *Puranas* and later literature. Both are worshipped in a huge variety of forms. Vishnu is held to have "incarnated" himself in a series of *avatars* (god-humans), the best known of which are Rama and Krishna. Shiva is characteristically worshipped in the form of the phallas (*linga*).

There are also female deities, who operate independently or as divine consorts to the male gods (e.g. Lakshmi, the consort of Vishnu). These are a number of major forms of the goddess (Devi), including Kali (the dark one); Durga and Parvati. The destructive character of the goddess is often stressed. In some of the **Tantric** traditions, the goddess is central in the form of *Shakti*, the feminine cosmic force.

All three of the major deities (Vishnu, Shiva and the goddess) are held to become "incarnated" in particular human beings (*avatars*) and are usually worshipped in their abundant local variant forms.

Central to Hindu religious ritual is the image (*murti*). These are found in every Hindu home and in temples. The god or goddess is called to invest the image during worship. It is more important to be "seen" by the deity than to see the *murti*. Daily *puja* (worshipful activity) is the norm, with gifts (food and flowers) being offered. *Bhakti* (devotion) is the most popular form of worship; in many cases the adherents' devotion alone being held sufficient to transcend the mundane world and participate in the life of the divinity. Meditative and yogic practices also play a major part in bridging the human–divine divide.

The integrity of Hinduism was first called into question by the Muslim invasions that began in the 8th century. This resulted both in open hostility and a series of attempts at synthesizing the Hindu and Muslim religious traditions. The Sant devotional and **Sikh** traditions are examples of such synthesis. The challenges of the modern world arrived with the coming of the Europeans. The two centuries of British rule transformed the transport, communications and administrative structures of India. The 19th century saw the development of a new Hindu ideology that presented Hinduism as a universal world religion (see, for example, **Ramakrishna Mission**). Since 1947 and Indian independence, modernization and industrial development are much in evidence. More recently, the tensions between different religious groups, particularly between Hindus and Muslims, have led to an increased radicalization of explicitly Hindu political groups and the development of what some scholars refer to as "Hindu fundamentalism" (see **Bharatiya Janata Party**). Caste discrimination is now outlawed and there are programmes of positive discrimination for scheduled castes. In spite of the evident forces of secularization, Hinduism has shown remarkable resilience, and it often seems that modernity and Hinduism are curiously compatible.

Hizb al-Da'wa. The Hizb al-Da'wa al-Islamiya, to give it its full name, is one of the most important **Shi'ite** fundamentalist groups in Iraq: *see* **Da'wa Party**.

Hizb al-Nahda. The Hizb al-Nahda, or Renaissance Party, was known as the Islamic Tendency Movement (Mouvement de la Tendance Islamique—MTI, Harakat al-Ittijah al-Islami) until November 1988 when it formally declared itself a political party under the new name. Official recognition was, however, denied it, both then and subsequently.

The Nahda is the largest of the **Islamist** movements in Tunisia. Its origins lie in a movement of Islamic renewal radiating out from Tunisia's traditional centre of learning, the Grand Mosque of Zaytouna, in the 1970s. This movement included the Association for the Preservation of the Quran founded in 1970, and a loose number of study groups established to discuss Islamic topics, including matters of doctrine and of individual and social ethics.

In 1981 the MTI was sufficiently well established to seek official recognition as a political party, but action by Islamists to enforce the fast of Ramadan by using threats to induce cafés and shops to close after they had chosen to remain open, and to close the bar in a Club Méditerranée centre, led to arrests and the imprisonment of significant numbers of MTI members, including 61 identified as MTI leaders. Although most were released in 1984, the state cracked down again in 1987: seven members were sentenced to death, and two were indeed hanged. Leader Rashid Ghanouchi was sentenced to life imprisonment. However, following the 1987 *coup* against President Bourguiba, the state's policy changed again, and many MTI members, including Ghanouchi himself, benefited from an amnesty. The change from MTI to Nahda occurred soon afterwards.

Nahda policies differ from those of many Islamist groups. The Nahda rejects violence (in contrast to the Islamic Liberation Party), accepts political and confessional pluralism, and advocates a modern interpretation of the Shari'a (Islamic law) according to general Quranic principles. The establishment of an Islamic state in Tunisia must be preceded by an active process of Islamic renewal so that the state will emerge democratically and not be imposed dictatorially.

Critics have contended that Nahda's commitment to democracy and tolerance is a façade, and point to the existence, admitted by the party, of an extensive underground network alongside the public organization.

Appealing mainly to students, the Nahda nevertheless has a broader constituency. In elections in 1989, candidates sympathetic to its policies (it was not accorded official recognition as a political party and so could not field official candidates of its own) gained 15 per cent of the national vote, and up to 30 per cent in some of the towns. Rashid Ghanouchi retired to Paris and was replaced as president by Ali Laaridh. Along with the six legal opposition parties, however, al-Nahda boycotted the June 1990 parliamentary elections.

The 1990 Iraqi invasion of Kuwait was supported by Ghanouchi, and received wide popular support in Tunisia. Al-Nahda's leaders, on the other hand, remained mindful of the need to support the Saudis in order to secure continued financial support. During the Gulf War of January–February 1991, significant anti-government disturbances led to violent clashes and the arrest of many leaders and hundreds of members of al-Nahda. The party officially suspended all activity in March 1991, although its members have remained active unofficially. Ghanouchi, meanwhile, has found asylum in the UK.

Hizbollah. (In Arabic *Hizb Alláh,* the Party of God.) Hizbollah was founded in 1983 with the direct involvement and support of the Islamic Republic of Iran. The name had been earlier used in Iran and applied to participants in popular demonstrations and paramilitary groups which worked to counter the influence of any dissident movements in the wake of the Iranian Revolution. Hizbollah remains closely linked to the Iranian government. The movement is concerned with morality within the **Shi'ite** community as much as with politics and has adopted a number of measures to try to enforce Islamic dress for women and to prevent the consumption of alcohol. Its goal is the establishment of an Islamic state in Lebanon, but its leaders have often shown a willingness to compromise. Shaikh Fadlallah, who often serves as unofficial spokesman for the organization, has spoken of an Islamic state developing out of the free choice of Lebanese Muslims rather than being imposed upon them. In order for this to happen, however, Lebanese Muslims must be in a political position which makes such self-determination possible. Hizbollah is committed to the cause of creating such a political situation in Lebanon.

Together with Islamic Amal it represents a religiously militant strand of the Lebanese Shi'ite community which stands in marked contrast to the (by Western standards) more moderate position of **Amal** and the Supreme Shi'ite Council of Lebanon. Hizbollah and Amal came to armed conflict with each other, not least over the question of the taking of hostages. Hizbollah is believed to be involved in a number of activities which have been undertaken in the name of the **Islamic Jihad**. These range from the taking of hostages to a number of suicide attacks on various foreign (principally American) institutions in Lebanon. Hizbollah co-operates with the **Sunni** group *Harakat al-Tawhid al-Islami* (Islamic Unity Movement) which shares its puritanical moral views and commitment to an Islamic state in Lebanon.

In May 1991 the leadership of Hizbollah fell to Abbas Mousawi. Hizbollah was the only militia to refuse to be disarmed in accordance with the Taif agreement, and it has been permitted by the Lebanese government to continue guerrilla warfare against the Israeli troops occupying southern Lebanon (and their proxy, the South Lebanon Army). In February 1992 the Israelis responded by bombing the car in which Mousawi and his family were travelling, killing all its occupants. The future direction of Hizbollah policy is now likely to become all the more uncompromising (symbolized perhaps by its recent self-designation as the Islamic Resistance). Following the assassination of Sheikh Mousawi, the leadership has been taken up by the 31-year old Sheikh Hassan

Nasrallah, who is a Sayid (i.e. someone claiming descent from the Prophet Muhammad).

Hoa Hao. A millenarian tradition known, in the Mekong delta of Vietnam, as Buo Son Ky Huong. Hoa Hao was founded by Huynh Phu So, who revealed the principles of a new "Buddhism of Great Peace" in 1939. Hoa Hao is similar in some respects to **Cao Dai,** but more orthodox in relation to **Buddhism**, and less syncretistic. Its adherents believe that Huynh Phu So is the Emergent Buddha.

Hoa Hao, named after the spiritual centre in south Vietnam where it was founded, does not attempt to unite religions and is opposed to elaborate rituals. During the 1940s it was strongly anti-Communist, and Huynh Phu So was murdered by the Viet Minh in 1946. During the Vietnam War Hoa Hao attracted thousands of anti-communist followers who wore amulets bearing the inscription "Buo Son Ky Huong", the first of these having been distributed in the 19th century by a mystic called Buddha Master of Western Peace. Buddha Master claimed to be a messenger from heaven who came to warn mankind of the imminence of apocalypse. Only those who took refuge in the Seven Mountains (where Maitreya would descend after the world had been purified) and practised true religion would be spared. Healing was the most common skill claimed by the early apostles.

Its current membership is large in certain traditional areas. Hoa Hao and Cao Dai both tried to attract Japanese assistance during World War II.

Hooppha Sawan. Hooppha Sawan (the Religious Land), 80 miles south of Bangkok, was founded in the early 1970s by Suchart Kosolkitiwong, a Thai Buddhist novice in search of a place for meditation, who subsequently established the site as headquarters of the International Federation of Religions to promote world peace and fraternity in 1975.

Hossoshu. One of the six Nara sects of Japanese **Buddhism**. It propounds an idealistic philosophy and has approximately 40 temples and 600,000 adherents at the present time. Hosso is a philosophical school which views consciousness as the basis for the appearance of the phenomenal world. Its head temples are the Kofukuji and the Yakushiji. The **Shotokushu** seceded from Hossoshu in 1950.

House Churches. A movement amongst **Protestants** which in Britain began in the 1970s, and grew from the feeling that the existing denominations were dormant. Strongly influenced by the Charismatic Movement, house churches are in part a rejection of traditional church buildings, formal liturgies, and a separate, trained ministry. Meetings, often called Christian Fellowships, may be held in private homes or hired public buildings. Chains of house churches exist in various groupings like the Harvestime Group, in which Bryn Jones, Goos Vedder, Terry Virgo and Arthur Wallis have played key roles and which is particularly strong in West Yorkshire. Harvestime has acquired a permanent home by buying the **Anglican** Diocesan offices in Bradford. A high point in their annual calendar is the Dales Bible Week which attracts 8,000 residents for prayer, praise, Bible study, and ministry. Other groups include Pioneers led by Gerald Coates in London, followers of G. Wally North, who exercises an itinerant international ministry from

near Prestwick airport in Scotland, and the Ichthus Movement led by Roger
Forster.

House of Growth. *See* **Seicho no Ie.**

Howling Dervishes. A colloquial label sometimes given to members of the
Rifa'iya Sufi order, and also to the **Halveti-Cerrahis.**

Hua Yen. The Chinese name of the Japanese Buddhist **Kegonshu.**

Human Potential Movement. Regarded by many as the psychological wing of
the **New Age** movement, it typically involves the development of emotional
competence, perhaps through a prior restructuring of one's concepts. Methods
involved may include **Primal Therapy,** Rebirthing, and **Psychosynthesis.**

Hussite Church. *See* **Reformed Catholic Churches.**

Hutterites. A group of Anabaptists which has kept separate from the
Mennonites, although sharing most of their beliefs. They were formed in
Moravia and were followers of Jakob Hutter who was martyred by burning in
1536. They developed as groups of agricultural collectives "holding everything
in common" as the early disciples had done (Acts 4, v32). These collectives are
known as "Bruderhofs". This group also migrated to both North America and
Russia. They are also known as the Hutterian Brethren.

I

I Kuan Tao. *See* **Unity Sect.**

Ibadiya. The Ibadis (hence, sometimes, "Ibadism") are a small group of
Muslims, the origins of whose movement antedate the **Sunni-Shi'ite** split.
The Ibadis are in a line of descent from the original "secessionists" from
(what became) mainstream **Islam**, the Khawarij or Kharijites. The latter were
involved in early religio-political disputes and civil war. They took the view
that believers who committed a grave sin should be expelled from the Muslim
community; and they resisted the trend towards making the leadership of the
umma in some sense hereditary in the family of the Prophet. Both features
have been retained among the Ibadis, whose traditions have evolved from this
source.
   Ibadi communities choose as their leader, or imam, the person whom they
regard as best qualified in terms of the two criteria of religious knowledge and
political (including military but also administrative) skills. Should the imam
commit a crime, he must repent or abdicate. Members of the group who
commit a serious sin may be excommunicated, or suffer imposed isolation
until they repent publicly after the Friday prayers. The particular penalty is

decided upon by a council (*mutawa'a* or *azzaba*) of perhaps a dozen people, and it is from this circle that a new imam is generally drawn. The council also acts as arbiter in tribal disputes.

As these features perhaps indicate, the Ibadi movement has remained confined to relatively isolated tribal groups who have preserved an ancient way of life. Some Ibadi communities are found today in the Mzab area of southern Algeria and in Tunisia, but their main centre is in Oman, where, however, the traditional fusion of religious and political leadership gave way in the 18th century to a separation of powers, the imam retaining religious leadership in the traditional Ibadi centres in the mountains, and the political leadership being relocated in the Sultan of Muscat on the coast. As a result of civil strife in the 1960s, the present imam, Imam Ghalib, went into exile in Saudi Arabia.

Ichthus Movement. *See* **House Churches**.

Iglesia ni Cristo. The Church of Christ is by far the largest of over 300 indigenous denominations in the Philippines which jointly constitute some 20 per cent of the population. It is sometimes known as the Church of Manalo, and members may be known as Manalistas—after the name of its founder, Félix Manalo (1886–1963).

Manalo was converted in 1904 to **Protestantism** through the **Methodist** Church, and began to study for the ministry. Part-way through this training he shifted to the **Presbyterian** Ellinwood Bible School. The **Disciples of Christ** next received his attention because he was attracted to their view of believers' baptism, and he was appointed one of their first evangelists in the Philippines. In 1912 the Seventh Day **Adventists** received him into membership and he worked for them.

Two years later, disillusioned with all the groups in which he had been involved, Manalo moved out on his own, believing himself specially called by God to this new responsibility. On July 27, 1914 the Iglesia ni Cristo was founded and incorporated as a church. The church grew fast in the first five years, with members drawn mainly from the Disciples. It also attracted attention for its very public debates over baptism, use of icons/statues in worship and its forbidding of the eating of blood-red meat.

Initially, growth was slow, but after the independence of the Philippines, membership rapidly expanded as the church adopted a strong, nationalistic stance. It spread throughout the Philippines and overseas with Philippino emigrants and workers. The wealth and power of the church can be judged from the many churches (known as chapels) which have been built on a grand scale. This church's success is due largely to the way in which it has indigenized Protestant **Christianity**. It uses Tagalog as its official language, and encourages the use of regional and local languages in services—it is *the* church for the Philippino, and is in touch with ordinary people, seeking to mobilize their support and encouragement.

The church fosters strong bonds with the community, and is highly organized with a centralized authority and power structure. Leaders exert considerable power, especially at election time, often dictating the outcome of local elections by the use of a block vote. The membership is thus highly disciplined—its Sunday and Thursday meetings are obligatory, and members are required to give a specific amount of their income (decided by the leaders) to the Church.

The church has a strong influence on business and social life. Members employ one another and support one another in business. The church also aids members in their businesses. The church is strongly anti-Catholic and anti-American, and trains its members to defend their own beliefs and to attack the beliefs of those with whom it disagrees.

Theologically, the Trinity is vigorously denied. Jesus, though Saviour, is truly human in all respects. Baptism is by immersion upon joining the church. It is a sin against the Holy Spirit to eat blood or meat cooked in blood. Salvation is only to be found by joining the true church. It is held as a cardinal belief that the true church disappeared in history (Romans 16:16), only to re-appear in the Philippines according to the prophecy of Isaiah 43:5–6. Manalo's leadership is affirmed by the prophecy in Revelation 7:2–3.

The church has an influential magazine, *Pasugo,* roughly translated as "God's Message", and operates a network of radio stations.

Iharaira. A Maori religious movement. Te Kooti, founder of the **Ringatu** Church in New Zealand, died in 1893. He designated no successor, but one of the influential people who was to follow in his footsteps was Rua Kenana. Rua was born in 1869 and, in 1904, heard the voice of God and Jesus appeared to him. When word spread of these experiences, many people came to consult him and to seek healing. Rua established his "New Jerusalem" in 1906. This became the centre of his activities and a place of pilgrimage for Maori people. He identified himself with Moses and drew a parallel between himself and the exiled people.

An astute leader, he established a community of apostles and councillors who enabled him to lead in a constructive and positive way.

In 1906 Rua was baptized as the Messiah and selected 12 disciples—more on the Old Testament model than the Christian—and followed the practices of Saturday sabbath. When he died in 1937 this prophet of charisma left behind a major influence amongst the Maori of the East Coast of New Zealand's North Island. Over recent years this influence has been increasingly Christianized.

Ikhwan. Ikhwan (or al-Ikhwan) means the Brothers. Some care is needed, though, in that it is a term with three possible referents.

First, it may refer to fiercely dedicated (some would say fanatical) Bedouin **Wahhabi** Muslims instrumental, through their military prowess, in the gradual establishment of the Kingdom of Saudi Arabia (completed in 1934).

Second, it may refer to their modern successors, the followers of the charismatic Juhayman al-Utaybi, who seized the famous mosque in Mecca in 1979 in an attempt to launch an insurrection against the ruling royal family whom they saw as a corrupt élite who had betrayed the Wahhabi ideals they claimed to uphold. The rebels were eventually overpowered, and al-Utaybi was killed.

Third, it may refer to the Ikhwan al-Muslimin, the members of the **Muslim Brotherhood**.

Imamis. The term Imamis is a more formal designation of the branch of **Islam** which is known more generally in the West as the **Twelver Shi'ites** (Ithna 'Asharis).

Integral Yoga. *See* **Aurobindo Ashram.**

International Network of Engaged Buddhists (INEB). Founded in Thailand in 1989 at a conference of monks and laity from 11 different countries, the Network had Buddhadasa Bhikkhu, Thich Nhat Hanh and Dalai Lama as its patrons. Affiliated groups may be found in 26 countries including France, Japan, USA, and the UK. The INEB aims to promote understanding between differing **Buddhist** traditions and is concerned with articulating authentic Buddhist responses to a wide range of issues such as alternative education and spiritual training, women's rights, the environment and development. It also serves as a clearing house for information on other engaged Buddhist groups and from time to time operates with spiritual activists from other religious traditions. The greatest concern of the Network is to empower Buddhists in areas under great duress such as Bangladesh, Burma, Cambodia and Sri Lanka. The Network publishes a tri-annual magazine, *Seeds of Peace*, in conjunction with the Thai Interreligious Commission for Development and has sponsored a variety of conflict resolution seminars for monks in the SE Asian region.

International Society for Krishna Consciousness (ISKCON). Popularly known as the Hare Krishna Movement, ISKCON was founded in New York by Swami Bhaktivedanta Prabhupada (1896–1977) in 1966 on the orders of his *guru*, who was at that time the leader of the Gaudiya Vaishnava Mission, a Bengali devotional society. ISKCON first attracted media attention through its saffron-robed devotees' exuberant chanting of the Hare Krishna *mantra* on street corners across the USA and Europe. The movement then gained an influential disciple in George Harrison, who made the *mantra* a chart hit and donated a large house, Bhaktivedanta Manor, as the British headquarters. Devotees understand Krishna as "the supreme personality of the Godhead" who may be most fully worshipped through the repetition of his holy name, hence the continuous chanting of the *mantra*, a practice derived from the 16th-century teacher, Shri Chaitanya. Initiated members live a disciplined lifestyle as celibate students or married householders, rising early, taking a daily cold shower and adopting a vegetarian diet. Alcohol and drugs are forbidden and sexual intercourse is held to be for procreation alone. Western devotees adopt Hindu styles of dress and names. Their chanting and missionary activities are a common sight in many Western towns and cities. There are over 100 temples, centres and schools worldwide, including an important presence in and around Vrndavan, the north Indian centre of Krishna worship. ISKCON has an estimated 3,000 full-time devotees, with an additional 200,000 congregational members, plus many sympathizers within the wider Hindu community. Soon after Swami Bhaktivedanta's death controversy fell upon the heads of some of his 11 appointed guru successors. Some of the 11 were later expelled from the movement and ISKCON is now guided by a Governing Body Commission meeting annually.

Inuit Religion. The Inuit (Eskimo) inhabit an enormous area of the arctic and sub-arctic, from Alaska to Greenland. They traditionally lived by hunting in a severe and dangerous environment and much of Inuit religion centred around animals and hunting rituals. Each animal was believed to have a spirit owner and the availability of animals was profoundly affected by the behaviour of humans. Animals were treated with great respect and many rituals surrounded their hunting. In Canada and Greenland the Inuit believed that all sea animals were under the control of a female Sea deity, who would hold back the animals when humans transgressed taboos. This then necessitated the trance journey of the Shaman to her home at the bottom of the sea to placate her and release the animals. Shamans played a central role in Inuit life in their capacities as game magicians and healers of the sick. **Shamanism** has declined along with traditional culture, but hunting still forms a major part of many Inuit communities and a respectful attitude towards animals persists.

Irani Zoroastrians. The **Zoroastrians** who preserved their tradition in Iran after the rise of **Islam**, as opposed to those who migrated to India (the **Parsis**). Forced by persecution and social pressures to retreat, with their two most sacred fires, into remote villages (notably, near the desert cities of Yazd and Kerman), most Zoroastrians subsisted in Islamic Iran in obscurity and poverty.

Between the 15th and 17th centuries, Irani Zoroastrian priests were in contact by correspondence with the Indian Parsis and, from the late 19th century onwards, Parsi reform movements influenced Zoroastrian city dwellers in Iran. The rural population has, however, remained "orthodox" in its isolation. During the Pahlavi dynasty (1925–1979) Zoroastrians enjoyed greater freedom because of their historical association with the pre-Islamic past. That association once again became a disadvantage with the Islamic revolution of 1979. At present there are approximately 30,000 Irani Zoroastrians.

Irvingites. An informal label for members of the **Catholic Apostolic Church**.

ISKCON. *See* **International Society for Krishna Consciousness,** commonly known as the Hare Krishna movement.

Islam. Islam is the worldwide religion of Muslims. Central to the faith is the Quran, the sacred text (or, orally, recitation) which for Muslims is the word of God revealed miraculously to Muhammad (570–623 CE) in the Arabic language. "Islam" means submission or surrender, in this case to God (Arabic: *Allah*), while a "Muslim" is "one who surrenders".

During his life Muhammad was associated with two main locations in Arabia; Mecca and Medina. Born in Mecca, Muhammad was based there until the year 622. During this time he emerged as an honest, trustworthy and successful merchant.

At the same time he became disturbed by the way in which Mecca's recent commercial success had led to disregard for moral values which he regarded as important. Merchants could all too readily be deceitful and unscrupulous, while the hardships experienced by the less fortunate Meccans could be disregarded.

Mecca was also a religious centre. It contained an important shrine, the Ka'ba, which was a centre of pilgrimage and contained figures symbolizing various gods worshipped by Meccans and the numerous pilgrims.

Troubled as he had become, Muhammad took to spending time on Mount Hira, a prominent hill outside Mecca. Here, at the age of about 40, he began to have an overwhelming sense of God communicating messages to him which he was to repeat to his fellow-Meccans. This was to continue for the remainder of his life. Hence for Muslims Muhammad is above all God's Messenger (*rasul Allah*). Moreover, this message constitutes perfect revelation (construed traditionally as consisting of God's actual words), and correcting the distorted accounts of earlier revelations to be found in the Jewish and Christian scriptures. It is complete and final. Hence the further designation of Muhammad as the Seal of the Prophets. The messages were collected to form the Quran—the Word of God.

Modern Western scholars sometimes argue that this collection took place gradually, over the years or perhaps even a couple of centuries following Muhammad's death. Others agree with Muslim scholars that the process of collection began during Muhammad's own lifetime and was completed shortly after his death at the latest. In the traditional view, inaccurate versions were destroyed, and the Quran as we know it (in its original Arabic, though not in translation, for here approximations and inaccuracies occur) is God's message as Muhammad received it.

A useful Muslim summary of the central thrust of this message is in terms of six beliefs: in the one God, the Compassionate, the Merciful; in resurrection to the Day of Judgement, followed by Paradise or Hell according to one's deserts; in angels; in scriptures, e.g. those of Jews and Christians, though only the Quran remains uncorrupt; in prophets, including Moses and Jesus, though Muhammad is the final and supreme figure; and in predestination. In addition, we find moral teachings about the importance of honesty, justice, compassion, and concern for the poor, the widow and the orphan. In passages which are believed to have been revealed later in Muhammad's life we find more detailed teaching about topics such as marriage, divorce, inheritance, and the division of booty.

Overcoming his initial reluctance, Muhammad proceeded to preach the messages as they came to him. They evoked considerable hostility, and accounts have come down to us of hardships and outright persecution experienced by the first Muslims. Numbered among these were his first wife Khadija, Abu Bakr (who was to be his immediate successor), and his cousin 'Ali (later also a successor as leader).

Relative failure in Mecca was followed by a crisis which resulted in the removal of Muhammad and many followers to Medina, an oasis settlement 200 miles to the north. This occurred in 620 CE and is known as the *Hijra* or Emigration. It marked a turning-point between failure and success, and the Muslim calendar is based on it—as the Christian calendar is based on the (supposed) birth date of Jesus.

There followed a period of conflict in which Meccan forces were finally defeated and Muhammad was able to enter Mecca at the head of a large army in 630. The Ka'ba became the centre of pilgrimage (*Hajj*) for Muslims that it remains to this day, while from the early Medinan period Muhammad had changed the direction of prayer from Jerusalem to Mecca.

From a non-Muslim perspective some controversy surrounds aspects of Muhammad's career, including some of his marriages following the death of Khadija in 620, and his treatment of three important Jewish groups in Medina. For Muslims, however, he remains an ideal figure, and Muslim theology developed the doctrine of his sinlessness. Hence, in part, the outrage occasioned by what Muslims could only construe as the scurrilous references to him in Salman Rushdie's novel *The Satanic Verses*.

Muhammad died unexpectedly in 632. Accounts of his words and actions, known as *hadith*, were preserved orally, and subsequently those deemed authentic were gathered together in a number of authoritative collections which have become normative for Muslims alongside (though not, strictly, on a par with) the Quran. They embody the Prophet's example, his *sunna*, which Muslims should seek to imitate. Non-Muslim scholars tend to be sceptical about the historical reliability of the *hadith*, and some Muslim scholars share some of these doubts. A group like the **Ahl-i Quran** which repudiates them is, however, very much the exception.

Islam has crystallized to a considerable extent around the famous "five pillars": the *shahada* or profession of faith that there is no god but God and Muhammad is His Messenger; formal prayers five times daily—*salat*; almsgiving—*zakat*; observance of the annual fast of Ramadan, involving abstinence from food, drink and sex from sunrise to sunset for a month; and pilgrimage to Mecca at least once in a lifetime, circumstances permitting, to participate in the annual *Hajj*.

In addition Islam has developed as a religion which lays great emphasis on its religious law, the Shari'a, which has its roots in the Quran and *Sunna*. Most Muslims adhere to one of four legal schools or rites, the **Maliki, Hanafi, Shafi'i** or **Hanbali. Twelver Shi'ites** have a comparable law school or tradition, the **Ja'fari.**

The broad distinction between **Sunnis** and **Shi'ites** derives from disputes concerning Muhammad's proper successor, and the proper nature of leadership in the Muslim world. These are referred to in the entries just mentioned, from which further cross-reference can be pursued. Sunnis form the numerical majority—over 80 per cent. (One tiny group whose origins antedate the Sunni–Shi'ite split are the **Ibadis.**)

Islam does not have a priesthood, but religious leadership is provided by religious scholars known collectively as the *ulama*. These are men who have completed a traditional Islamic education, usually specializing in religious law. This equips them to function as a judge (*qadi*) in a court of religious law, for example, or as a jurisconsult (*mufti*). Many others become prayer leaders (*imams*) and preachers in local mosques. In Sunni Islam there is no structured hierarchy of *ulama*, but in Twelver Shi'ism there is, with a number of *ayatollahs* at the top.

The mosque is the visible focus of the faith locally. Essentially a place of prayer, this is particularly apparent at the time of the weekly noonday prayer on Fridays. Mosques also function as community centres and the location of Quran schools. In some places, women are prohibited from entering the mosque, but this reflects patriarchal custom among some Muslim communities and not Islamic law. On the other hand, the area traditionally set apart for women, often at the back, is always much smaller than the main area for men. In its public ritual Islam, like **Orthodox Judaism,** assigns a more active role to men.

The issue of the position of women in Islam arouses considerable controversy today. The ideal advocated is typically one of having a different role but equal status. Both feminism and chauvinism are seen as deviations from this proper norm. There are, however, some Muslim feminists too.

Among both Sunnis and Shi'ites are to be found a number of Sufi organizations—in the Sunni case, a large number. Sufis are often referred to as mystics but, as is made clear in the entry on **Sufism,** this is somewhat misleading.

In Islam as elsewhere, movements of renewal and reform have arisen with the aim of purifying and reinvigorating the faith. Examples include the **Wahhabis,** the **Deobandis,** the **Muhammadiyah** and the **Tablighi Jama'at.** Sometimes a conscious effort has been made to incorporate modern Western thinking, as in the case of the **Islamic Modernists.** Political activism has been encouraged by organizations like the **Muslim Brotherhood** and the **Jama'at-i Islami,** while groups like **Hizbollah, Hamas,** the **Jihad Organization** and **al-Takfir wa'l-Hijra** resort to violence and are revolutionary in ideology: an Islamic theory of holy war is a resource on which they can draw (although like the Christian "just war" theory it can be abused). The term "Islamic fundamentalism" has come to be applied somewhat indiscriminately to several of these significantly different types of organization.

Popular media images notwithstanding, Islam remains an extremely varied phenomenon, as is illustrated by the considerable range of entries included here.

Islamic Call Society. The Islamic Call Society (Jam'iyat al-Da'wa al-Islamiya), established in 1970 and based in Tripoli, seeks in many ways to emulate the Saudi-based **Muslim World League**, whose structure as an international Muslim organization—general conference, world council, and regional meetings—it has increasingly imitated since its restructuring in 1982. The crucial difference, however, lies in the fact that it promotes the atypical interpretation of **Islam** developed by Libya's Qaddafi.

It established its own Islamic college in Libya in 1974, followed by branches in Damascus (1982) and London (1986), the first two in particular training quite large numbers of preachers and teachers. Other Islamic schools and centres have been sponsored in a dozen African countries, as have "Islamic hospitals" further afield in Bangladesh and the Philippines: Black Africa and South-East Asia are the focus of a great deal of the Society's activities.

As well as its religious educational and medical care work, the Society organizes a variety of conferences, including, every four years, the major meeting of its International Council. Like its publications, these serve among other things as a channel for presenting Qaddafi's religio–political interpretation of the USA, Britain, France and other Western nations as latter-day Crusaders intent on battle against Islam, and against whom in turn *jihad* is necessary.

In connection with its claim to international significance, the Society has begun to call itself the World Islamic Call Society (Jam'iyat al-Da'wa al-Islami al-'Alamiya), but its shorter original title remains in common use.

Islamic Council of Europe. This London-based organization was set up in 1973 with encouragement and support from the Saudi government, and with the aim of co-ordinating the activities and efforts of the numerous Muslim organizations in Europe. It has organized major conferences, and funded a number of research projects. The provision of **Islamic** literature to meet the needs of European Muslim communities has been an important task. Co-operation between the Islamic world and Europe, and the breaking down of prejudices and misunderstandings, has also been a prominent goal.

Islamic Foundation. Based in Leicester (UK), this organization publishes an attractive range of literature on **Islam**. Prominent on its lists are works by the late Saiyid Abul A'la Maududi (1903–1979), founder of the **Jama'at-i Islami**, as well as works on Islamic economics. The Islamic Foundation has personal links to this organization and to the **UK Islamic Mission**.

Islamic Groups. This vague title is sometimes used in relation to the situation in Egypt in order to refer to the rather ill-defined, but increasingly prominent, cluster of organizations known as **al-Jama'at al-Islamiya**.

Islamic Jihad. The Islamic Jihad (*al-Jihad al-Islami*) has been described as a loose association of particularly dedicated and daring members from other Islamic militant organizations. It is not known for sure whether the Islamic Jihad exists as a specific organization with its own structures and leadership. It is possible that the name refers to various *ad hoc* groups which come together for a specific purpose. Alternatively, it might be a cover name used to preserve the anonymity of other more visible organizations such as **Hizbollah,** Islamic Amal, the PLO and others. A number of suicide commandos have acted in the name of the Islamic Jihad and the organization has claimed responsibility for explosions at various foreign embassies, including the American Embassy in Beirut in 1983. Following the assassination of Sheikh Mousawi, the leadership has been taken up by Sheikh Hassan Nasrallah, who is a Sayid (i.e. someone claiming descent from the Prophet Muhammad). Most recently it claimed responsibility for the suicide bombing of the Israeli Embassy in Buenos Aires in March 1992 in retaliation for the assassination, along with his wife and 5-year old son, of the Hizbollah leader Sheikh Abbas Mousawi by the Israelis.

Islamic Leagues. This is a label sometimes used instead of Islamic Groups to refer to the increasingly important **al-Jama'at al-Islamiya** in Egypt.

Islamic Modernists (South Asia). The Modernists formed an élite stream of Islamic thought, but one of great importance in 19th and 20th-century South Asia. It flowed from the movements of revival and reform in early 19th-century Delhi; its source was Saiyid Ahmad Khan (1817–98), the descendant of high-ranking Muslim service families.

After the Mutiny uprising of 1857, Saiyid Ahmad decided that the answer to the problem of how Muslims should survive without power was to reconcile them to British rule. His method was to demonstrate that there was nothing in Western civilization that intrinsically undermined **Islam**. Like the **Ahl-i Hadith** and **Salafiya** he circumvented the medieval law schools and went straight to the Quran and Hadith for guidance. The basis of his exegetical principles was that the laws of Creation were the work of God, and the Quran was the word of God, and they just could not be contradictory. If they seemed so, it was because men failed to understand them correctly. As Saiyid Ahmad tested this basis in such areas as *jihad,* slavery and polygamy, he developed the dynamic principle of modernist thought, which is to distinguish between what is central to revelation and what is merely the historical wrapping in which it came. His concern was to translate that central purpose into modern circumstances.

This dynamic principle has been developed in modernist thought down to the present. It is there in Muhammad Iqbal's (1877?–1938) bridging of the gulf between Islamic universalism and the modern national state; it is there too in his bridging of the gulf between the sovereignty of God and that of the people in his transference of the main support of the shari'a from the consensus of the *ulama* to that of the people. It is most clearly worked out by the leading modernist thinker of recent times, and one-time head of Pakistan's constitutionally established Institute of Islamic Research, Fazlur Rahman (d. 1988), in his explanation of the reasoning behind the most important piece of modernist legislation, Pakistan's Muslim Family Laws Ordinance of 1961. Key institutions in carrying forward modernist ideas have been the Muhammadan Anglo-Oriental College at Aligarh (1877), the All-India Muslim Educational Conference (1886) and the All-India Muslim League (1906). Once Pakistan was won, Modernists hoped that it would be a laboratory in which their thought could be developed. In fact it came to be an arena in which they had to defend their corner against other heirs of South Asian Islamic responses to the West, most notably the **Deobandis**, the **Barelvis** and supporters of the **Jama'at-i Islami**.

Islamic Renaissance Party. This is a relatively recent Islamist organization with a presence in the Muslim states of the former USSR in Central Asia. However, it is still forced to operate underground or unofficially in most states. Only in one, Tajikstan, has it been allowed to register legally, and in some towns in the Ferghana Valley it has achieved some success in entering local government: an immediate effect is that alcohol is forbidden. It advocates the establishment of a series of Islamic republics, and its leaders have close links with the **Muslim Brotherhood** in Egypt and the **Jama'at-i Islami** in Pakistan. Its current strength is unclear, but its proposals that women be veiled and prevented from going to work do not exercise an obvious widespread appeal.

Islamic Resistance Movement. This important Islamic group in the West Bank and Gaza Strip is better known as **Hamas** (the acronym of its Arabic title, Harakat al-Muqawama al-Islamiya).

Islamic Revolutionary Guards. The Sipah-i Pasdaran-i Inquilabi Islami, to give the full title, or Corps of the Guardians of the Islamic Revolution—more simply, the Islamic Revolutionary Guards, are one of the mainstays of the Islamic state in Iran. As an institution, they had their origins in some of the street fighter groups active against the army in the closing days of the rule of the Shah. Following the revolution, on Khomeini's orders, they became organized by the new Islamic Republican Party, which had been founded as the political arm of the *ulama,* and used against the two guerrilla opposition groups, the Fidayin-i Khalq and the Mujahidin-i Khalq.

Subsequently the guards (*pasdars*) were built up as a military force loyal to the *ulama* and ready to protect the Islamic state against any attempted *coup* by the army. The protracted Iran–Iraq war of 1980–1988 facilitated this process, the guards eventually being accorded a ministry in their own right (although it was dissolved at the end of the war). Following the Israeli invasion of Lebanon in 1982, three thousand Pasdaran were sent to that country, where their presence contributed to the relative decline of **Amal**, and the growing influence of **Hizbollah**. They remain a significant power base for the radicals against the pragmatists in the country's leadership, although the latter are currently dominant under Ayatollah Rafsanjani, the President.

Under the Pasdaran organization, a further movement, of "boy warriors", emerged (the **Bassij**).

Islamic Salvation Front. This Algerian Islamist movement is better known by its name in French, **Front Islamique du Salut (FIS)**.

Isma'ilis. With a modern following of several million dispersed through India, Pakistan, East Africa and the Middle East, the Isma'ilis represent the largest branch of **Shi'ite** Islam after the Imamis or **Twelvers**. The sect emerged after the death of the sixth of the Shi'ite Imams, Ja'far al-Sadiq, in 765. Ja'far had originally intended his eldest son, Isma'il, to succeed him, but the latter died prematurely and the imamate passed to his brother Musa instead, in the line of Imams which went on to form the basis of Twelver Shi'ism. However, various factions dissented, some claiming that Isma'il was still alive, others that the imamate rightfully belonged to his son Muhammad. They are all commonly referred to as Isma'ilis (collectively Isma'iliya), or sometimes Seveners, since they diverge from the Twelvers in recognizing Isma'il as the seventh Imam.

In various guises, Isma'ili Shi'ism rapidly became the most militant alternative to **Sunni** orthodoxy and the political control of the dominant Abbasid dynasty. An efficient propaganda system developed under the first Isma'ili Imams, and in 909 the North African branch of the sect established the powerful Fatimid dynasty in Egypt, which flourished until 1171. Sub-branches such as the Qaramita (Carmathians) caused political upheaval in Arabia, the Yemen, and elsewhere.

Following a split in 1094, the Fatimid Isma'ilis divided into two main branches: **Musta'lis** and **Nizaris**. It is this latter branch which today represents the majority of the world's Isma'ili population, and which has become well known through the activities of its imams, who have used the title Agha Khan since the 19th century (hence the label **Aga Khanis**). The most radical group to break away from the Fatimid Isma'ilis was that of the **Druzes**.

Isma'ili doctrine emphasizes the esoteric interpretation of religious belief, distinguishing outward (*zahir*) from inward (*batin*) truths—hence the widespread use of the alternative name Batiniya for the sect. Outward Isma'ili thought and practice is essentially orthodox in structure, with little divergence from either Sunni or Twelver Shi'ite norms. The esoteric doctrine presents Islamic ideas within a perspective influenced by Greek philosophy, particularly Neoplatonism, to which alchemical, **kabbalistic**, and astrological ideas have been grafted. A cyclical theory of revelation divides history into seven periods, each initiated by a prophet, followed by six imams.

Italian Catholic Reformed Church. *See* **Reformed Catholic Churches.**

Ithna 'Asharis. The "Ithna 'Asharis" are the "Twelvers" within **Shi'ism**, and thus the **Twelver Shi'ites**.

J

Ja'faris. The term derives from the concept of **Twelver Shi'ism** as a fifth law school within **Islam**, with its origins in the legal teachings of the sixth Imam, Ja'far al-Sadiq (d. 765). The other four law schools—**Maliki, Hanafi, Shafi'i, Hanbali**—are found in **Sunnism**.

Jainas. Followers of the ancient and unbroken Indian religious tradition of Jainism, named after the *Jinas* or "Victors". According to traditional accounts, there are 24 such *Jinas* or *Tirthankaras* (Ford Builders) in each half-cycle of cosmic time. Mahavira (The Great Hero, c.599– 527 BCE) is the most recent as well as the last in the current half-cycle. For historical purposes, he is considered the founder of Jainism, and many of the earliest surviving texts claim to record his teaching. After his death, Jainism flourished, especially in north-east India, with many groups of wandering ascetics relying upon a substantial lay following to provide them both with begged food and new recruits. The majority of these ascetics, as appears to have been the case throughout Jaina history, were nuns.

According to traditional accounts, a famine (c.300 BCE) caused part of the community to migrate south, a geographical redistribution that apparently led to a religious dispute when the two groups resumed contact. Starting as an argument about accurate memory of the oral tradition (and thus about what constitutes the scriptural canon), this eventually (79 CE) engendered a major schism in the ascetic community, dividing it into **Svetambaras** (the white-clad) and **Digambaras** (the sky-clad), a division maintained to the present day. The names used reflect what became the chief point at issue: does the renunciation of all possessions, which is one of the prerequisites for becoming a true monk, require the complete abandonment of clothing?

In doctrinal terms, little divides the two major Jaina sects. Early practice was conditioned by three beliefs: (i) that nearly all matter, including the elements, is alive (in the sense of containing living beings or souls); (ii) that doing harm to these beings is wrong; and (iii) that such wrong action will have a deleterious effect upon the future condition and births of the actor. This effect is produced through the mechanism of *karma,* which, according to Jaina doctrine, consists of subtle matter that invades the soul of the passionate agent and literally weighs it down. Through the operation of diligent care and dispassionate restraint in all circumstances, and the cultivation of rigorous ascetic practice, accumulated *karma* can be shed and fresh accumulations prevented. The object is to attain complete liberation from the bonds of matter, a state of omniscient and blissful isolation at the apex of the inhabited universe.

The key element in Jaina practice is strict adherence to the principle of non-violence (*ahimsa*). Given that souls are ubiquitous, it is particularly important to restrict one's range and consumption of food. All Jainas are therefore strictly vegetarian, and fasting plays a central role in both ascetic and lay practice. The ideal death is one of ritually controlled starvation.

The development of a technical philosophy which stresses the manifold nature of reality and the relative nature of any possible statement about it has helped to check potential threats to ascetic practice from theoretical speculation about such matters as, for example, the reality of karmic bondage. Asceticism, through the living example of the monks and nuns, as well as through extensive and precisely formulated lay practices such as fasting has always been a focal point for the Jaina community's sense of its own identity.

Ascetics have a pedagogical and exemplary rather than a priestly function. For the majority of the laity, however, the practice of religion has been concentrated in temple worship (*puja*). Devotion to the *Tirthankaras*, who have gone beyond human contact, is considered fundamentally reflexive and meditative in nature; there are, however, numerous attendant deities who can be influenced on the **Hindu** pattern.

Both of the main Jaina sects enjoyed substantial royal patronage at various times. By the 12th century, however, the Muslim invasions in north India, and the increasing strength of Hindu sectarianism in the south, ensured a decline in both numbers and political influence. Further divisions took place within the two main sects, mainly concerning the use of images in temple worship.

Today there are concentrations of Svetambaras in north-east India and Digambaras in the south, and all main cities have Jain communities. Although there are perhaps fewer than 3,000,000 Jainas in India (including 6,150 ascetics, nearly three-quarters of whom are nuns), their economic and ethical influence is disproportionately great. Much of their prosperity is channelled into temple building and other religious activities. In the second half of the 20th century, Jainas have migrated, largely via East Africa, to establish small communities throughout the world. The first Jain temple in Europe was opened in Leicester in 1988.

The Jains have built many temples and produced outstanding examples of religious art and architecture throughout the subcontinent. As well as preserving Prakrit and Sanskrit classical religious texts in their temple libraries, they have also played a major role in the production of narrative literature of all kinds in various vernaculars. The pervasive influence of their cardinal doctrine of *ahimsa* on Indian thought and culture has been highlighted again in the 20th century by Mahatma Gandhi's espousal of non-violence under the influence of the Jaina layman, Shrimad Rajchandra (Raychandbai Mehta) the founder of the **Kavi Panth.**

Jainism. *See* **Jainas.**

al-Jama'at al-Islamiya. Although described in some press accounts as a particular organization, the designation al-Jama'at al-Islamiya is better understood as referring to a cluster of militant Islamist groups that have become a feature of Egyptian society in the last two decades. The labels Islamic Groups and Islamic Leagues have both been used to refer to the organizations in question. They recruit among university students and also in deprived suburbs e.g. of Cairo, especially among new arrivals from the countryside. Links are thought to exist between various of these groups and al-Jihad (the **Jihad Organization**)—responsibility has been variously attributed to both for the assassination in Cairo in May 1992 of a prominent critic of Islamist movements, Farag Fouda.

Membership of the Islamic Groups is believed to have swollen into thousands in recent years, and in some villages of Upper Egypt they have virtually replaced the forces of the state in the provision of various services including law and order. The government has responded from time to time with attempted crackdowns, particularly in the wake of incidents such as the shooting of 13 villagers, mostly **Copts**, in the volatile governorate of Asyut in June 1992, and also revenge attacks on the police in the same area.

Meanwhile the banned but tolerated **Muslim Brotherhood** distances itself from violence, but failed to condemn the murder of Dr Fouda, leading to surmises that there may have developed at least a tacit alliance between the Brotherhood and the Jama'at.

Jama'at-i Islami. The Jama'at-i Islami is a leading part of what has come to be called the "Islamic movement" in the second half of the 20th century. It is at the same time a prime example of "Muslim fundamentalism", which may be defined as a concern to return to what Muslims feel is the original form and intent of Islamic doctrine, but one which is much influenced by its 20th-century context. As such it shares similarities of concern and of approach with the leaders of the Iranian revolution, and with the **Muslim Brotherhood** and its more recent offshoots in Egypt. Indeed, its ideas played a significant role in the second stage in the ideological development of the Brotherhood from the 1950s onwards. Unlike other movements from South Asia, which were primarily concerned to develop ways of surviving as Muslims under colonial rule, the Jama'at has been concerned to answer the larger question of how to be Muslim in the face of the dominance of Western civilization. Power, it argues, is essential to the preservation of Islamic civilization. The Jama'at is an élite party of the righteous which is concerned to unite **Islam** with that prime expression of 20th century power, the modern state.

The origins of the Jama'at lie in the ideas of Saiyid Abul A'la Maududi (1903–1979), who was a journalist and a theologian but not a man with the training of a traditional Islamic scholar. By the 1930s, when he became editor of *Tarjuman al-Quran,* which was to be the vehicle of his ideas for the rest of his life, Maududi knew that his life's mission was, as he wrote, to "break the hold which Western culture and ideas had come to acquire over the Muslim intelligentsia, and to instill in them the fact that Islam has a code of life of its own". He opposed the movement for Pakistan on the grounds that what was needed was not a nation-state of Muslims but an Islamic state. In 1941 he founded the Jama'at to put this idea into practice.

Maududi's political vision may be expressed thus. Central is the belief that God alone is sovereign; man has gone astray because he has accepted sovereigns other than God—for instance, kings, nation-states or custom. All the guidance which man needs can be found in the Islamic Holy Law (Shari'a) which offers a complete scheme of life where nothing is superfluous and nothing lacking. Political power is essential to put this divinely ordained pattern into effect; the Islamic state has a missionary purpose. Moreover, because God's guidance extends to all human activity, this state must be universal and all-embracing, and because the state's purpose is to establish Islamic ideology it must be run by those who believe in it and comprehend its spirit—those who do not may just live within the confines of the state as non-Muslim citizens (*zimmis*). Naturally this state recognizes that God, not man, is the source of all law. The state is merely God's vice-regent (*khalifa*) on earth.

The Jama'at is highly organized, from the head of the organization, or Amir (Maududi held this position until 1970), to its provincial and district branches. The central organization is based in Lahore—despite his original opposition to the creation of Pakistan, Maududi moved there after its founding in 1947. Normal membership is restricted: often an applicant is kept under observation for months to see whether his behaviour meets the Jama'at's standards. Thus in 1971 the organization had only 2,500 members, but several hundred thousand postulants. Finance comes mainly from donations, and from the royalties derived from Maududi's many books.

Despite its small numbers the Jama'at has had a considerable impact on the politics of Pakistan. It campaigned successfully for the introduction of Islamic clauses to the Pakistani constitution of 1956, it consistently opposed the martial law régime of Ayub Khan, played an important role in the overthrow of Mr Bhutto in 1977, and had significant influence in the first few years of Zia ul-Haq's régime when Shariat (Shari'a) courts—operative still today—were established. The December 1991 Lahore High Court decision upholding the supremacy of Islamic law over all other laws in Pakistan demonstrates its influence. Its members constantly seek positions of influence from which they can advance their Islamic purpose, and up to May 1992 the Jama'at constituted the second most powerful part of Pakistan's ruling Islamic Democratic Alliance: it walked out in protest against the Prime Minister's refusal to continue backing its long-standing ally among the Afghan mujahadeen leader, Gulbaddin Hekmatyar. It subsequently launched a new party as a vehicle of its aspirations: the Pakistan Islamic Front.

In Bangladesh the Jama'at has considerable organizational strength, deriving support in particular from the younger generation who have been through higher education. In recent elections it has managed to win up to 20 seats in the Bangladesh parliament. In India, on the other hand, the Jama'at is of little political significance. In Britain it is represented by the **UK Islamic Mission** based in Leicester, its publications being produced by the associated **Islamic Foundation**, also in Leicester.

Jama'at Tabligh. Jama'at Tabligh is the Arabic name for the important Islamic reform movement more often known by its Urdu name, **Tablighi Jama'at**.

Jehovah's Witnesses. An **Adventist** sect founded by Charles Taze Russell who in 1872 started the International Bible Students' Association in Pittsburgh, USA. Soon he became the pastor of his own independent church and in 1879 began publishing a magazine *The Watchtower* to publicize his beliefs.

Having rejected his **Presbyterian** background, he was influenced by Adventists who believed the Bible could be used to predict the time and manner of the end of the world. Russell's studies led him to believe that Christ's coming took place invisibly in 1874 and that the Second Coming would be in 1914. He also concluded that the correct name for God is Jehovah and that Jesus was not one person of the divine Trinity but was originally the Archangel Michael, one of the sons of Jehovah (the other being Satan). His followers took the name Jehovah's Witnesses and called their meeting places "Kingdom Halls".

Their study of the Bible has led them to reject blood transfusions, participation in politics (on the grounds that since the Second Coming, national governments are in conflict with the rule of Christ) and the celebrating of festivals such as Christmas, Easter and birthdays. Their meetings focus on Bible study and methods of winning converts, mainly through home visits.

The organization has always been authoritarian and is now controlled by a Governing Body in Brooklyn, USA. All members are assigned an area to evangelize, and are required to report on their activities. Members may be disciplined by being expelled from the fellowship of believers. There is an intense antipathy to the established churches whose beliefs are misrepresented and abused.

There are believed to be about 6,000,000 Jehovah's Witnesses worldwide, a high proportion of these being in Africa. **Kitawala** is a related African movement.

Jesuits. A **Roman Catholic** religious order founded by Ignatius Loyola, who was born in 1491 in the Spanish Basque country. His new Order, the Jesuits, or Society of Jesus (S.J.), won Papal recognition in 1540. The Society was intended to combat **Protestantism**, to convert unbelievers and to educate the young. It has retained, especially, the latter aim. Its arsenal has been Ignatius's *Spiritual Exercises*—imaginative meditations on the life of Christ—arduous intellectual training, and military discipline. During the religious conflicts of the 16th century, many Jesuits were trained to undergo martyrdom; some achieved it. By the time of Ignatius's death in 1556, Jesuit missionaries had taken the gospel to China and to India. From 1609, in the virgin territory of South America, they created the "Reductions of Paraguay". These were self-supporting settlements, governed by the Indians under Jesuit supervision. The Jesuits' watchful gaze also deterred Portuguese slave traders. By 1767 the Jesuits had been driven from Spain, Portugal and South America. Political pressure compelled Pope Clement XIV to dissolve their Order in 1773. The Society was recalled to life in 1814 by Pius VII. Much as the **Benedictines** had illumined pre-Reformation **Christianity**, so the Jesuits' heroism and theatricality, with a strong suggestion of political intrigue, influenced the Catholicism of the baroque age.

Having been the engineers of the Counter-Reformation Church, the Jesuits were also its creatures. Vatican II brought revision. At the Society's 31st General Congregation in 1965–1966, Pope Paul VI intimated that their new enterprise must be the struggle against "atheism". The new General, Fr Pedro Arrupe, interpreted the fresh direction in what became a characteristic manner: "The battle against atheism is identical in part with the battle against poverty . . .". The 32nd and 33rd General Congregations stated that the primary aim of the Society is the propagation of justice. Some of the young Jesuits of South America, where the Society is once more concentrated, took this to entail the overthrow of established régimes. Fr Peter-Hans Kolvenbach, the Dutchman who was elected General in 1983, forbids members to be government ministers or to indulge in "negative criticism" of the Church. He is committed to the Jesuits' identification with "the poorest of the poor", considering that this must be woven into the curricula of their 2,000 universities, colleges and schools.

In addition to the three vows taken in all Orders, of poverty, chastity and obedience, some (currently 63 per cent) Jesuits take a fourth vow: to be loyal to the Pope. There were 36,000 Jesuits in 1965; there are now about 24,000, including students and lay brothers.

Jewish Feminist Groups. Jewish feminist groups are united by their desire for active participation in Jewish ritual, whether they are composed of observant or non-observant women. Group activities vary from religious retreats organized by B'not Ash ("daughters of fire" (annually)) and Nishmat Nashim ("Women's Soul" (bi-annually)) to organized prayer groups, in cities such as Baltimore, Chicago, Houston, and New York City.

Some groups, such as the Washington Heights Women's Service, use the traditional prayerbook; others rewrite traditional ceremonies, as shown by the various "women's *haggadot*" (prayerbook used for the festive evening meal(s) of Passover). Many women's groups gather once a month to celebrate *Rosh Hodesh* (New Moon), a holiday that was generally ignored until discussion of it in *The Jewish Catalog* prompted new interest in it, especially by women, who according to tradition, do not work on that day as a reward for not participating in the worship of the Golden Calf. *Rosh Hodesh* groups exist in a number of cities, including Boston, Montreal, and New York City. Additionally, many groups, including those that use the traditional prayerbook, have written new naming services for their daughters. In the late 1980s, a group of women who wished to read from the Torah on the women's side of the Western Wall, aroused great controversy, despite the group's leaders being Orthodox women. The Israeli Supreme Court (August 1989) ruled that the "women of the wall" must pray "in accordance with the custom of the site". At the end of 1988 the "First International Conference on the Empowerment of Jewish Women" was held in Jerusalem, co-sponsored by the American Jewish Congress, the World Jewish Congress and the Israeli Women's Network. Jewish lesbians, in addition to being part of larger groups, also have their own separate synagogues and prayer groups.

Jewish New Agers. (*See also* **Havurat Judaism.**) Jewish New Age movements are part of the wider emergence of New Age groups in the contemporary world, especially Europe and the USA. While these Jewish groups share interests in spiritual, experiential, therapeutic and meditative practices, and mystical theologies with other New Agers, they draw on specifically Jewish sources and traditions, particularly **Kabbalah** and **Hasidism.** New Age Judaism is made up of a number of diverse groups. Leaders include Rabbis Shlomo Carlebach (born 1926), Zalman Schachter-Shalomi (born 1924), Joseph H. Gelberman (born 1912) and Dr. Philip S. Berg.

Carlebach ("the singing rabbi"), an **Orthodox** rabbi and well-known composer and singer of Hasidic songs and teller of Hasidic tales, travelled in the late 1960s, teaching of the coming New Age of universal oneness; the life of celebration; methods for the transformation of consciousness, and outlining the crucial part that Jews are to play in this process. Carlebach teaches not only the ways of Jewish life but its "innerness" (*Pnimiyyut*). Influenced by many of ideas of the counterculture, he was the inspiration behind the establishment of a number of communal houses—for example, The House of Love and Prayer (San Francisco) and Or Chadash ("New Light", in Los Angeles). Approximately 40 families currently live in Moshav Me'or Mod'in, a communal settlement in Israel, involved in the production of organic and other health foods, founded by Carlebach in the 1970s. The Network for Conscious Judaism, founded by David Zeller, serves to disseminate Carlebach's form of New Age Judaism.

Schachter-Shalomi, a **Lubavich** Hasidic rabbi and Religious Studies professor, found his life changing after "dropping acid" with Timothy Leary in 1959. This experience both re-affirmed his commitment to his Jewish tradition (although he later cut his ties with the Lubavich Hasidim) and created an openness to other spiritual teachings. He was involved in Havurat Shalom (*see* **Havurat Judaism**) and in 1962 began formulating his plans for a centre to promote "Jewish renewal". This centre was to be a forum for experiments in prayer, the study of Jewish sources, the development of spirituality and the exploration of other forms of creativity. In 1975 he founded the B'nai Or ("Sons of Light") spiritual community in Philadelphia (renamed less chauvinistically as the P'nai Or ("Faces of Light") Religious Fellowship in 1985). Practices at the centre include Jungian psychotherapy, Hindu and Buddhist meditative techniques, Kabbalistic and Hasidic study and contemporary music and dance. Schachter-Sholomi became the leading "guru" for Jewish New Agers and groups across the USA and Canada affiliated to B'nai Or. He was influential in the setting up of one of the best known Jewish New Age groups, the Aquarian *Minyan* in Berkeley, California. There were seven P'Nai Or fellowships in the USA and Canada and two in Europe. Schachter-Sholomi is the author of many influential articles and books on New Age Judaism, including the guidebooks, *The First Step: A Guide for the New Jewish Spirituality* (1975; 1983, with D. Gropman) and *Fragments of a Future Scroll: Hasidism for the Aquarian Age* (1975). Recently, the Aquarian Minyan and a number of fellowships that have broken away from Schachter-Sholomi's organization together with other groups have formed The Network Renewal Communities.

Gelberman is an Orthodox rabbi who has developed a New Age Judaism, that brings together Kabbalah and Hasidic teachings (particularly as mediated by Martin Buber) with psychotherapy and New Age metaphysics. He has founded a number of institutions, including The Little Synagogue (New York); The Mid-Way Counseling Center; The Foundation for Spiritual Living; The Kabbalah Centre, and two inter-faith organizations, The Metaphysical Centre and The New Seminary.

Yehudah Ashlag (1886–1955) founded a *Yeshivah* in Bene Berak in Israel where particular attention is given to the study of the *Zohar* (a 13th-century mystical commentary on the Hebrew Bible and the foundational text of the *Kabbalah*). The translator of sections of the *Zohar* from Aramaic to Hebrew and the author of *Ha-Sullam (The Ladder),* a commentary on this text, he also established the Research Centre of Kabbalah in Jerusalem. Dr Berg, the current head of the Centre, is the author of a number of books on *Kabbalah* which stress its use as a source of knowledge about astrology, reincarnation, energy and other New Age concerns. The Centre has branches in New York, Los Angeles, Chicago, Tel Aviv, Paris, Mexico City, London, Antwerp and Hong Kong.

Other figures include Rabbi Joel DeKoven who teaches **yoga** and Rabbi Alvin Boboff, the co-founder of Dynamic Judaism, who practises psychic healing. Jewish New Age groups continue to grow and to network with each other as they develop new forms of the Jewish tradition that integrate New Age teachings.

Jews for Jesus. *See* **Messianic Judaism**.

Jihad Organization. The Jihad Organization (Tanzim al-Jihad) is the deadliest of the Egyptian Islamist groups committed to the use of violence. It was responsible for the assassination of President Sadat in 1981. Despite widespread arrests, and the imposition of death sentences or varying terms of imprisonment in trials in 1981–82 and again in 1984, further outbreaks of violence and, in 1987, assassination attempts on two former government ministers have been the responsibility of al-Jihad (as it is often known) and its splinter groups.

Violent clashes with the police have continued, and in 1988 there were also clashes with members of the **Muslim Brotherhood**. In contrast to the latter, al-Jihad regards its country's Muslim leaders as guilty of apostasy from **Islam**, and as ruling the state by heathen laws. These laws should be replaced by the Shari'a (Islamic law), and the means to this end is to fight to overthrow the heretical and despotic rulers. Muslims have neglected the *jihad,* a duty they must rediscover. Should it cost them their lives—whether in battle or as a result of state execution—paradise will be their martyr's reward.

Al-Jihad is among the groups believed to have sent members to fight with the Islamic resistance in Afghanistan. It refrained from calling for *jihad* on behalf of Iraq in the Gulf War of 1991, while at the same time warning against America's alleged objective of conditioning Muslims to accept their continued humiliation and the supremacy of the West.

Jihad-i Sazandigi. Jihad-i Sazandigi, or Reconstruction Crusade, is an organization formed in Iran in 1979, immediately after the revolution that brought Ayatollah Khomeini to power, for the purpose (among others) of taking the Islamic Revolution to the countryside. It became an important channel through which the new Islamic Republican Party, the political arm of the *ulama,* was able to extend its influence throughout the country.

Originally intended as a mass organization, it has become rather more exclusive—some would say narrow and doctrinaire—through insisting on purging itself of members regarded as being insufficiently committed to the cause of the Islamic Republic. Unlike the Pasdaran (**Islamic Revolutionary Guards**) or **Bassij**, the Jihad has a non-military character, and has been very active, especially in parts of the country ravaged during the war with Iraq, in rural development projects and reconstruction. Its members have built and staffed clinics and schools, as well as labouring on roads and other infrastructural projects such as bringing water and electricity to the villages. Membership falls predominantly in the 20–30 years age range.

Jinja Shinto or **Shrine Shinto.** Until the end of World War II **Shinto** was intimately related to the state. Emperors were seen as descendants of the Sun goddess Amaterasu O Mikami (venerated at the Grand Ise Shrine, Mie Prefecture). The sacrality of state galvanized Japanese national identity and facilitated political change at different points in history. Before the Meiji Restoration in 1867 it was quite possible to be Buddhist and still participate in Shinto activities, as Shintoism was perceived more as a cultural expression, than as a religion. To a certain extent this still holds true.

During the anti-Buddhist purging of the Meiji era (1867–1912), however, Shinto once again stood alone as the unifier of the Japanese consciousness and carried the country through various wars, culminating in World War II. After the war, in December 1945, under the American Shinto Directive, State Shinto was abolished; constitutional separation of religion and state was promulgated, and the Emperor was called upon to renounce his divinity. The new situation of religious freedom provided the basis for the establishment in February 1946 of the Association of Shinto Shrines (*Jinja Honcho*), a voluntary liaison body which now oversees the affairs of Shrine Shinto. Jinja Shinto claims around 62,000,000 adherents, but this figure must be qualified by the fact that Shinto membership is in no way binding or exclusivist. The priesthood number around 26,000 and are trained at seminaries, or the Universities of Kokugakuin and Kogakkan.

Jodoshinshu. A form of Japanese Pure Land **Buddhism**, founded by Shinran (1173– 1262), a trained **Tendai** priest who sought inspiration from the Pure Land scriptures. He followed his master Honen until 1202 when he was exiled as a result of the disapproval of the authorities over the rising interest in Pure Land devotion amongst the masses, who had hitherto had little contact with Buddhist teachings. During and after his exile Shinran wrote commentaries on the scriptures, the most famous of which is the *Kyogyoshinsho,* and hundreds of hymns in a vernacular style.

After his death, Jodoshinshu, the True Pure Land School (as differentiated from Honen's **Jodoshu** or Pure Land School) was disseminated variously by Shinran's descendants and disciples. The largest denominations today are those headed by direct descendants of Shinran, a continuing reminder of the founder's revolutionary marriage, which symbolically brought Buddhism into the realm of the previously secular Japanese family.

Shinran believed that during this age of degeneracy the individual has no choice but to rely completely on the grace of the Buddha Amida to bring him to salvation. Through the power of Amida, even an individual deeply bound by *karma* may, if the grace of Amida is invoked, achieve rebirth in the Pure Land.

Although Shinran claimed only to be continuing the work of his master, certain clear differences arose between Jodoshinshu and Jodoshu, due mainly to Shinran's insistence upon the worthlessness of self-effort. For Shinran the fulcrum of the relationship between Amida and humanity is faith in Amida's boundless compassion, which arises from the realization of the individual's *karma*-bound and spiritually destitute nature.

Institutional Jodoshinshu is organized around a sense of gratitude to Amida, to the exclusion of all other Buddhas and Bodhisattvas. The veneration of Shinran is also important. The most significant festival on the Jodoshinshu calendar is *Ho-on-ko,* the yearly memorial of Shinran's death. As a distinctly Japanese form of Buddhism (one of the few that did not arrive in a package from China) institutional Jodoshinshu also embraces such aspects of Japanese ritual life as funerals and ancestor memorial services, which provide its financial basis.

Historically there are 10 sects of Jodoshinshu, the largest of which are the Takadaha, and two headed by Shinran's descendants who were originally caretakers of his mausoleum, Shinshu Honganjiha and Shinshu Otaniha. In these groups temple mastership frequently passes from father to son. In recent years however Otaniha has been torn by internal disputes and more than 400 disaffected temples have seceded.

As with all Japanese religions statistical status is inconclusive, partly because a whole household registers with a temple, regardless of the religious tendencies of individuals concerned. However, Jodoshinshu is one of the biggest single Buddhist sects in Japan, and claims 14,000,000 adherents.

Jodoshu. Jodoshu was the first major Buddhist Pure Land movement to gain firm foundations in Japanese society in the Kamakura era. The founder was Honen (1133–1212) who had practised **Tendai** meditation on Mount Hiei, which he ultimately rejected in favour of *nembutsu* repetition based on faith in the saving power of Amida. The *nembutsu* ("*Namu Amida Butsu*"—"I take refuge in Amida Buddha") was regarded by Honen to be the only operable vehicle to Enlightenment in this age of degeneracy and was seen as a means of purification. Jodoshu stresses the believer's own power to influence rebirth, a factor later to be eliminated by Honen's disciple Shinran, the founder of the **Jodoshinshu** movement.

The Chionin in Kyoto is the head temple of this sect, which claims around 3,000,000 adherents.

John Frum Movement. This is an example of the phenomena known as **cargo cults**. It is found in Vanuatu in the Pacific. "Frum" means "broom", and John Frum was thought of as someone in the tradition of John the Baptist who would sweep away the inequalities between New Hebrideans and Europeans, and usher in a new age of justice, happiness and prosperity.

During World War II, 300,000 Americans suddenly arrived to set up, in a matter of months, their biggest base in the Pacific—complete with eight hospitals and 19 cinemas. The islanders were struck by the way in which blacks and whites worked together, and by their generosity and openness. In contrast to the British and French, who expected deference, the Americans treated people equally, restoring a sense of dignity. Yet they had wealth and power—their God was clearly pleased with them.

Missionaries had already introduced the idea of John the Baptist. This was now in effect combined with the idea of the mysterious, invisible generous benefactor "Uncle Sam" who provided the Americans with all their cargo, plus perhaps the equally mysterious Santa Claus who brought presents at Christmas for Europeans, to produce the messianic figure of John Frum.

He allegedly appeared on a beach of the island Tanna at sundown, dressed in white man's clothes but speaking the native language, and with a shining walking stick. He always went and stood in the same place, and people went to the beach to listen. (According to other accounts, it was a villager who stood up claiming to be a manifestation of John Frum, whom he described in the preceding terms.) His face remained invisible, but he urged people to have faith in America. People would come from America again to help them, and provide roads and proper houses. He urged them to leave the missionary churches, and they did. His promises were the same as the Bible's, and he was the road to Jesus. If they were patient, they would get money.

And they did: tourists came! Such is the current belief among adherents of the movement today. Their numbers are not known, and the movement appears to have splintered into several smaller groups, but it has not disappeared. Members perform a Volcano Dance to John, who said that he controlled the volcano, and that a road leads there from America. His army is believed to live inside it. Members also believe that if they are faithful to the memory of John Frum, then one day he will return.

Judaism. Judaism is the usual modern designation for the religion adhered to by Jews. World Jewry numbers approximately 14 million, six million of whom live in America and four million in Israel. Major communities are also to be found in Russia (over one million), France (600,000) and Great Britain (310,000).

One of the central ideas in Judaism is that Jews are a particular people, a community defined by an unbroken biological and cultural continuity from biblical times. Whilst descent via the maternal line has been the norm, in almost all forms of Judaism conversion to Judaism by gentiles has taken place, and continues to do so, converts becoming part of the lines of genealogy. As reflected in the literary sources of Judaism (the Torah—Hebrew Bible—and its authoritative commentaries), this idea of peoplehood is based on the certainty that the ancient Israelites entered a covenant with God. This covenant entailed certain obligations and responsibilities binding on them and their descendants, the Jewish people. Traditionally, every aspect of Jewish life has been governed by the *Halakhah* (law), the systematic elaboration of these covenantal obligations. Thus every Jew is duty bound to fulfil the commandments (*mitzvot*) that pertain to him or her.

Jewish communities, until the modern age, were largely separate and self-governing, with their own legal and educational codes and systems of authority. Each Jewish community, although to an extent independent, lived basically in the same recognizably distinctive fashion, following the same sacred pattern and calendar of rituals. These include a daily round of prayers; a week consisting of six days of work and the Sabbath day of rest (no work, riding, writing or business transactions); an annual series of festivities, remembrances, and fast days; and life-cycle rituals (such as male circumcision). There are also dietary laws, the best known of which is the ban on the flesh of the pig. Other commandments are concerned with dress codes, health measures, familial and social relations, charity, business, and ethics.

Modern Jewish history is usually held to have begun with the French Revolution and the granting of the rights of citizenship to the Jews of France. Modernity has proved to be something of a two-edged sword for Jews. On the one hand it offered, for the first time, full participation in the cultural, political and social life of the modern nation-states, promising the end of the marginality and persecution which had characterized Jewish life as a minority under Christian or Muslim rule. On the other, the communal forces that had historically preserved the integrity of the community were undermined.

Contemporary Jewry still lives in the shadow of the *Shoah* (Holocaust), the systematic murder of a third of their number by the Nazis during the years 1941–45. The Holocaust has led many Jews to reassess their confidence in the security offered by the legal and other protections of the modern (non-Jewish) state, and for some to question their acceptance of a God who rules over a world in which an Auschwitz can take place. The threat of the destruction of the Jewish people (and thus of Judaism) has led to Jewish survival in the modern world becoming a discrete and central value.

From the 18th century Jews became exposed to modern learning (history and science) and new social and political forms. Novel concerns were raised about the historicity of biblical claims, the national and religious aspects of Jewish identity, the rationality of Judaism and its structures of authority, and the part that it was to play in a radically transformed world. Traditionalists expressed their extreme opposition to these changes. Some Jews responded by leaving

the Jewish for the wider gentile community. Others attempted to create new
forms of Judaism compatible with modern times.

In a sense, all current forms of Judaism are a reaction or response to
these modern challenges. Outside of Israel, there are a sizeable number
of Jews who are not members of a synagogue or any Jewish organizations.
Those who are synagogue members are often identified by their particular
synagogue movements. **Reform Judaism** attempts to offer a Judaism suitable
for modernity. It places great stress on human autonomy in the individual
appropriation of the traditional laws and customs of Judaism. There is some
recent evidence for increasing levels of observance by Reform Jews and this
is, of course, quite compatible with the exercise of choice. **Conservative
Judaism** understands the *Halakhah* as authoritative but capable of adjustment
appropriate to meet changing conditions (see also **Masorti, Reconstructionist
Judaism**). The Reform and Conservative movements are most prominent in
America and account for the majority of Jews there.

Orthodox Judaism is made up of a wide variety of different groups that share
a belief in the divine origin of the commandments and that they are, therefore,
binding on all Jews. In practice, however, there is a broad range of levels of
actual observance (see also **Hasidism**). The Orthodox reflect the traditional
emphasis on the study of the *Talmud* (a text-book of Halakhic debates) and
its commentaries, and their communities are often centred around the *Yeshivah*
(institute of learning). The more Orthodox groups have maintained the Yiddish
language and see themselves living essentially unchanged traditional lives. In
the last two decades and in a quite unanticipated way, Orthodox numbers have
been growing for the first time in the last century and a half, their ranks swelled
by high birth rates and Jews who were not brought up in traditionally observant
families.

One of the Jewish responses to the emergent nationalism of the 19th century
was the growth of **Zionism** (Jewish nationalism). Originally opposed by both
Reform and Orthodox Judaism, Zionism, in the sense of support for the State
of Israel, now has almost universal backing among the different Jewish groups.
Particularly since the Holocaust, Israel plays a major role in the consciousness
and identity of the majority of Jews. The establishment in 1948 of the
first Jewish state for nearly two millennia raised a series of unprecedented
theological, Halakhic and political questions. For example, is the "ingathering
of the exiles" correctly interpreted as the "stirrings of the redemption"? Why
are there still Jews who are able to live in Israel and yet do not do so? Is a
Jew to be defined by traditional religious definitions or as a Jewish citizen of
Israel? And what has the Jewish tradition to teach Jews about modern politics
and statecraft?

Orthodox Judaism has played a particular part in the life of the "Jewish"
state due to influence of the religious parties in a political system based on
proportional representation (see **Mafdal, Shas, Degel Torah**) and the partial
incorporation of religious law (family and identity) into the state legal system.

After half a century of stress on physical survival following the Holocaust,
there is a heightened concern among an increasing number of Jews about the
survival of Jewish religious culture. Currently, half the marriages outside of
Israel are to non-Jews and the levels of Jewish learning, both in Israel and
outside, are diminishing. There is a growing polarization between Orthodox
and other forms of Judaism and between the non-religious and Orthodox in

Israel. At the same time, it can be argued that the number of *Yeshivah* students is at an unprecedented level, the main institutions of Jewish life are vigorous and the trends for the future are promising.

K

Kabbalah (Qabbalah, Cabalah). (*Also see* **Hasidism; Occultism**) Kabbalah (*Hebrew*, "that which is received", reception, tradition) formerly referred to the authoritative tradition of Rabbinic teachings and rulings, and now usually designates the Jewish esoteric traditions of the 12th and 13th century and their subsequent study, practice and interpretation.

The principal text of Kabbalah, *Sefer Hazohar* (The Book of Splendour), outlines a dynamic symbol system which serves to portray reality on a number of levels (the "created" universe, the "internal" structure of divinity and the mystical path). The *Zohar* offers a mystical commentary on the Torah (Five Books of Moses) utilizing this symbolic system. Hermeneutically there are mystical methods of exegesis for discerning the esoteric meanings of scripture. The *Zohar* accounts for diverse reality by means of an emanatory doctrine

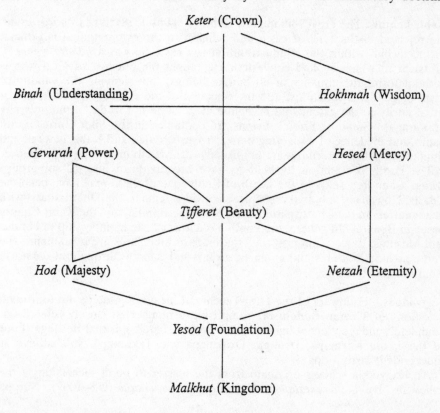

Keter (Crown)

Binah (Understanding)   *Hokhmah* (Wisdom)

Gevurah (Power)   *Hesed* (Mercy)

Tifferet (Beauty)

Hod (Majesty)   *Netzah* (Eternity)

Yesod (Foundation)

Malkhut (Kingdom)

rather than the traditional creation narrative. The process begins with *Ein Sof* (Hebrew, Without End), a potentiality beyond all experience and distinctions and through a series of stages (*Sefirot*, "potentialities", "vessels of divinity") of the emanation of the divine flow gives rise to the Upper and Lower worlds. The 10 *Sefirot*, referred to as the Tree of Life, given various diagramatic representations, offer a chart or map of the divine processes (see chart).

These *Sefirot* exist in dynamic relationships with each other (Left vs. Right side, Upper vs. Lower, etc.) and contemplation on these relationships gives access to the divine realms.

Sefer Ha-Zohar not only became one of the major influences on Jewish religious thinking but through its Latin translation gave rise to a Christian "Kabbalah".

After the expulsion of Jewish people from the Spanish peninsula at the end of the 15th century, a major Kabbalistic centre developed in Safed in northern Israel.

There were a number of significant developments, the most important of which was the work of Issac Luria. Lurianic Kabbalah came to be the dominant Kabbalistic system and influenced the **Sabbatean** movement and Hasidism.

Currently, in addition to the study of Kabbalistic texts by many of the Hasidic groups, there are a number of study groups and communities dedicated to the study of mythical literature (*see* **Jewish New Agers**). Many Kabbalistic practices have been incorporated into mainstream Orthodox Jewish life but are particularly evident among the Hasidim.

Kabir Panthis. The great Indian *guru* Kabir (c. 1440–1518) lived in north India. He rejected distinctions of caste and religion to the extent that it is difficult to locate him within the **Hindu** tradition (by caste he was a *jullaha* weaver), or **Islam** to which he had converted. He taught the oneness of God who is without form, the equality of all human beings, thus denying the validity of caste or gender distinctions, and the rejection of the efficacy of rituals and of ritual purity to the extent that he deliberately chose not to die in the holy city of Varanasi. Some of Kabir's hymns are contained in the **Sikh** Guru Granth Sahib, but evidence of a meeting between Guru Nanak and Kabir is weak and similarities in their teachings are not usually regarded as indicating dependence.

The Panth is traditionally held to have broken down into 12 sub-groups within a hundred years of the death of Kabir; one of these may have been the **Udasis.** Nowadays only two recognizable groups remain, the Dharmadasis with headquarters in the Chattisgarh district of northern India, and the Kabir Chaura based in Benares. In general the Panth has a lower caste membership of Hindus and Muslims, though amongst the Dharmadasis merchants are prominent. The Panth includes both lay and monastic groups and is found throughout the north from Gujarat to Bihar.

Kagyudpas. "Followers of the Oral Teaching Lineages." One of the four main traditions of **Tibetan Buddhism**, comprising a number of closely related but completely independent religious orders with a shared spiritual heritage. Four of these, the **Karmapa**, **Drukpa**, Drigungpa and Taklungpa, still survive as independent institutions.

All Kagyudpa schools originate from the master to pupil succession of the following five great exemplary founding saints: Tilopa (988–1069); Naropa

(1016–1100), Marpa the Translator (1012–1097), Tibet's first Kagyudpa; his student Milarepa (1052–1135), Tibet's most popular saint; and Gampopa (1075–1139), the systematizer of Milarepa's teachings. He created the organizational basis that served all subsequent Kagyudpa monastic and scholastic institutions.

Kagyudpas are Tibet's leading **yoga** experts, practitioners of the famous "Six Doctrines of Naropa". Renowned for their devotion, *Mahamudra* meditation, and spiritual songs, their emphasis on prolonged meditational retreats has earned them the sobriquet "Practice Lineage". Kagyudpas have from early times been intimately associated with the **Nyingmapas**, whose tantras and *termas* they continue to practise. For several centuries Tibet's largest tradition, they are now successfully spreading internationally. This is particularly so for the **Karma Kagyud** branch.

Kanji Panth. A 20th-century **Jaina** reform movement based on the charismatic personality of Kanji Swami. The Panth is a sub-group within **Digambara Jainism.**

Kapalikas. A defunct and highly unorthodox Hindu **Shaivite** ascetic tradition now largely subsumed by the **Aghoris.**

Karaites. The Karaites (literally "scripturalists"), a Jewish sectarian movement, accept only scripture (the Hebrew Bible or written Torah) as authoritative and reject the rabbinic traditions of interpretation (oral Torah). While the name appears in the 9th century CE, the movement's origins are to be found in the previous century when Anan ben David lost his bid for the leadership of the Babylonian Jewish community due to his heterodox views and began his own movement. The Karaite movement initially grew rapidly and the Karaite–Rabbinite (the **Judaism** of the rabbis) schism divided the Jewish world. By the end of the 11th century, however, and after a Rabbinic "counter-attack", the issue became resolved with the complete separation of the Karaites as a small schismatic group outside of "mainstream" Judaism.

Karaism developed its own traditions and rituals (characterized by a literalism in interpretation), calendar, order of services and did not permit intermarriage with non-Karaites. Currently, there are a number of communities in Russia; 1,500 in the USA (mainly in the Bay Area in California), and some 100 families in Istanbul. The majority of Karaites now live in Israel (20,000) under the leadership of Haim Hallevi of Ashdod, the Karaite Chief Rabbi.

Karakash. *See* **Donmeh.**

Kardecismo. Allan Kardec (1804–1869) was a French codifier of spiritism/ **spiritualism,** which he regarded more as a scientific philosophy than as a religion. Spirits of the deceased can communicate with the living through mediums—but in contrast to British spiritism, Kardec's system incorporated belief in reincarnation, also claiming that out of the hierarchy of spirits that inhabit the invisible spirit world, Christ was the highest ever to become incarnate.

It is in Brazil that Kardecismo has taken on the character of a religion, appealing to significant numbers of the urban middle classes. Perhaps more importantly, it has interacted with movements of African spiritism which have developed from **African traditional religions** brought across by slaves, leading to the syncretic and currently more widespread and influential **Umbanda** religious movement.

Karlin–Stolin Hasidism. Karlin and Stolin are the Lithuanian towns associated with the beginnings of the Perlov Hasidic dynasty, whose followers are referred to as Karlin–Stolin Hasidim. The first Rebbe and founder of this Hasidic movement, Rabbi Aaron ben Jacob (1736–1772), a disciple of Dov Ber the Maggid of Mezhirech, exercised great influence on the development of Lithuanian Hasidism. Renowned for their Hasidic melodies; their stress on joy; Talmudic study and strict observance of the commandments; the purificatory value of ritual immersion; fervour and solitary self-surrender in prayer and the education of women, the Karlin–Stolin established centres in the land of Israel (Tiberias and Jerusalem) in the 19th century and in America in the 20th. The Lithuanian dynastic leaders, the great-grandsons of Aaron, together with many of their followers were killed in the Holocaust. Currently, the movement has centres in America and Israel.

Karma Kagyudpas. Also known as the Karmapas, this is the largest of the surviving **Kagyudpa** schools of **Tibetan Buddhism**, founded by Karmapa Dusum Khyenpa (1110– 1193), a student of Gampopa. His reincarnation Karma Pakshi (1206–1283) is often believed to be the first incarnate lama (*tulku*) to be recognized in Tibet, and ever since then the Karma Kagyudpa school has been headed by successive serial Karmapa reincarnations, who are always the objects of intense devotion from their followers. Regarded as emanations of the celestial bodhisattva Avalokitesvara, the Karmapas remained Tibet's foremost incarnations until the coming of the Dalai Lamas some centuries later. The Karmapas are famous for their unique black hat, said to be a material replica of a spiritual crown woven from the hair of 100,000 goddesses, and the Karma Kagyudpas, heirs to Gampopa, specialize in combining monastic discipline and scholarship with advanced *tantric* practice and intensive meditation. The charismatic 16th Karmapa, Rangjung Rigpay Dorje, died in Chicago in 1981, after establishing over 100 centres in the West, and the activities of other Karma Kagyudpa lamas, such as Chogyam Trungpa, the founder of Samye Ling in the Scottish borders and the Naropa Institute in Boulder, Colorado, and Kalu Rinpoche, have helped give this school exceptionally sound foundations in exile. The current headquarters of the Karma Kagyudpas is at Rumtek in Sikkim.

Karmapas. *See* **Karma Kagyudpa.**

Kashmir Shaivism. Kashmir Shaivism is a form of Hinduism which developed in the Kashmir valley from the ninth to 11th centuries, supplanting **Buddhism** and **Shaiva Siddhanta.** This tradition maintains the identity of the individual self and the absolute, and forms the basis of the contemporary, popular religion of Hindus remaining in the valley, as well as an esoteric tradition which has been transplanted to the West.

A number of schools comprise Kashmir Shaivism, but three traditions are especially important, namely the Trika ("Threefold"), Spanda ("Vibration") and Pratyabhijna ("Recognition"). They recognize a group of Sanskrit texts called **Tantras** as their revealed source of authority, as opposed to the Vedas of orthodox **Hinduism**. The Trika tradition, so called due to its veneration of the three goddesses Para, Parapara and Apara, is mainly concerned with initiation, ritual and cosmology. The Spanda reveres the revelations of Shiva to Vasugupta (c. 875–925). In a dream Shiva revealed to Vasugupta a group of verses inscribed on a rock at the top of a mountain, which Vasugupta wrote down as the *Shiva Sutras*. Lastly the monistic Shaiva theology of the Pratyabhijna is represented in the works of Abhinavagupta (c. 975–1025), particularly in his *Tantraloka*. The Tantric Krama tradition should be noted as having a significant influence on Kashmir Shaivism. Apart from this esoteric tradition, the popular cult among Hindus in the valley has been that of the god Svacchanda Bhairava.

The central philosophy of monistic Shaivism is that there is only one reality identified as consciousness (*caitanya, samvit*), but also referred to in more personal terms as the god Shiva or by some other synonym. Shakti is the consort of Shiva, the female force in the universe which is its material cause. To realize the identity of the self with the supreme Shiva is to wake up to our pure subjectivity and to be liberated from the cycle of reincarnation (*samsara*).

Although providing the ideological backdrop, the sophistication and complexity of the teachings are not particularly in evidence in the daily lives of the remaining Shaiva brahmins of Kashmir or Kashmiri *pandits*, although Svacchanda Bhairava is worshipped. Their main concerns are the fulfilling of moral law (*dharma*) and social obligations with respect to their caste or *zat* (from the Sanskrit *jati*). The more esoteric aspects of Kashmir Shaivism have been preserved in an oral tradition, finding expression in the teachings of the *guru* Swami Lakshman Jee (d. 1992) who retained many of the ideas of Abhinavagupta. Lakshman Jee taught the awakening of an energy (*shakti*) within the body called Kundalini. Once awakened by **yoga** practices such as breath control, Kundalini rises through a central channel of the body, piercing various centres of power (*cakras*) as she rises, until she unites with Shiva at or above the crown of the head. The practitioner then experiences the bliss of union with Shiva.

Contemporary versions of Kashmir Shaivism now exist in the West. The Universal Shaiva Trust based in California propagates the teachings of Swami Lakshman Jee; Swami Cetanananda, the American abbot of the Nityananda Institute in Massachusetts, teaches a form of the Trika tradition; and the **Siddha Yoga** of the late Swami Muktananda claims to be based on the teachings of Kashmir Shaivism.

Kasogatan. Derived from Sugato (the well-gone), one of the nine epithets of the Buddha. A popular form of Javanese **Buddhism** of obscure origin but which claims to be related to the Majapahit kingdom—the last pre-Islamic Buddhist kingdom in Java c. 1500AD. Its adherents currently number several thousand. Leading figures have included Oka Diputera, a Balinese government official who served for a time as Director of Buddhist Affairs in the Ministry of Religious Affairs, and General Suraji.

Kavi Panth. A modern **Jain** lay reform movement established in 1924 to reconcile **Svetambara** and **Digambara** beliefs. The movement (*panth*) takes its name from its founders, the poet (*kavi*) Raychandrabai Mehta and his wife Devabhai. Kavipanthis have one sacred text, which is a collection of letters from the founder to various correspondents. Devotees worship the image of their founder along with images of other Jain *Tirthankaras*. The Panth is particularly influential in the cities of Gujarat and Kathiawar with perhaps 10,000 members overall. The movement is also known as Shrimad Rajchandra.

Kegonshu or **Flower Garland School.** One of the surviving Nara Sects of Japanese **Buddhism**. The teachings of the sect are based on the Mahayanist *Avatamsaka* (Flower Garland) *Sutra* which holds the mutual interpenetration and unity of all things. The great Buddha Dainichi is central to the ritual of the school, which approximates closely to the Chinese Buddhist Hua Yen school and has its headquarters at Todaiji, founded in Nara by Emperor Shomu in 749. There are about 60 temples and 900 clergy—over two-thirds of whom are women, and 45,000 adherents in Japan today.

Khalsa Sikhs. In 1699 the tenth **Sikh** Guru Gobind Singh created a new body within the **Sikh Panth**, the *Khalsa* or Pure Ones, Membership was by a new form of initiation (*amritsankar*). Besides keeping the outward form of the five Ks, certain moral regulations must be observed. These *kurahts*, intended to lead to purity of living, are; not to smoke, use drugs, drink alcohol, or commit adultery. These are in addition to the general precepts which require Sikhs to be honest, trustworthy, hard working, and to observe the equality of all people regardless of caste, class, or gender. The **Nihangs** are a sub-group of warriors within the *khalsa*, believed to have been created by Gobind Singh as a fighting force.

Khoja Ithna'Asharis. According to many of the Muslims who describe themselves as **Khojas**, the term means businessman, or professional, and should be considered as a caste (the Khojas are an Indian group by origin) or ethnic term rather than a sectarian one. However, the addition of the label **Ithna'Ashari** clearly introduces a "sectarian" factor. For unlike the majority of Khojas, who are **Isma'ili Shi'ites**, the Khoja Ithna'Asharis are **Twelver Shi'ites**. As followers of the twelfth Imam, who they believe to be in occultation, these members of the Khoja community share the religious beliefs and practices of many Iranian and Pakistani Shi'ites, and are known to intermarry with these communities, and also with European Twelvers. One can in fact achieve Khoja status by marrying a Khoja.

Unlike the Isma'ili Khojas, the Twelver Khojas do not seek to incorporate, or adapt, elements of **Hinduism** into **Shi'ism**, but the observer cannot help but draw similarities between the five revered persons of Muhammad, 'Ali, Fatima, Hassan and Hussain, with the five major divinities of **Smarta** Hinduism.

Like the Isma'ilis, the Khoja Twelvers are mostly prosperous traders and professionals, and outside India have been prominent in the economy of East Africa. The community now present in countries such as Canada and the United Kingdom have mostly come from Africa, and maintain close networks through their World Centre based in Stanmore, Middlesex (UK).

Khojas. The Khojas are an Indian community who mostly adhere to the **Nizari** sect of **Isma'ili Shi'ism** within Islam. Their name derives from the Persian word

Khwaja (Lord). A 14th–15th century Nizari missionary converted a caste, the Lohanas, and bestowed upon them the name of Khojas. Subsequently some Khojas transferred their allegiance to **Sunni** Islam, others to **Twelver Shi'ism** (a group now known as **Khoja Ithna 'Asharis**), and a few even reverted to **Hinduism**. Thus not all Khojas are Nizaris, although the identification is commonly made. (A similar qualification applies to the common identification of the Khojas with the **Aga Khanis**.)

The Khojas are not themselves an Islamic sect—they belong (mostly) to the Nizari sect. In many ways they retain characteristics of caste: one is born a Khoja, and caste rules of marriage and inheritance have obtained until quite recently (when customs associated with Hinduism have begun to lapse). They have a distinctive body of religious literature known as *Sat Panth* (True Path), and this incorporates and adapts certain elements from Hinduism: for example, 'Ali is regarded as an avatar of Vishnu, the Quran as the last of the *Vedas,* and the Prophet Muhammad is identified with Brahma.

Also characteristic of the Khojas are their *jama'at khanas*, or assembly and prayer halls, which form a focus of their community activities and function as mosques. Their communities are well organized under a religious community leader (*mukhi*) and an account keeper (*kamadiya*).

Khojas have a reputation as prosperous traders which they have consolidated under the leadership of the Aga Khans. In India they are located mainly in Sind, Gujarat and Bombay, although communities are to be found scattered throughout the country. Outside India they are particularly important in East Africa, although there are groups elsewhere, including Europe and America. A split which occurred in the 16th century resulted in the formation of a sub-group known as the Imam-Shahis (Imamshahis) or Satpanthis. As the latter name implies, they share much of the religious literature of the Nizari Khojas.

Kibbutz. (*See also* **Zionism.**) (Pl. *kibbutzim*)—one of a number of Israeli socialist collective settlements in which all property is communally owned and all members' needs are provided for. The movement has its roots in the attempt of secular Russian immigrants to the Land of Israel in the 1904–1906 immigration wave to "return" the Jews to their original condition by making them into communal farmers in their ancestral home. The first agricultural settlement, then called a *kevutzah* ("group") was founded in Deganyah in 1909. After World War I, the farms added industrial components, calling themselves *kibbutzim*. *Kibbutz* members saw themselves as the elite of the new Jewish society and provided many leaders for the new state of Israel.

Ideological always, the movement branched into four groups, three secular organizations; *Ha-kibbutz ha-Artzi ha-Shomir ha-Tza'ir* ("The National Young Guard *Kibbutz*"), *ha-Kibbutz ha-Me'uhed* ("The United *Kibbutz*"), *Ihud ha-Kevuzot ve-ha-Kibbutzim* ("the Union of *Kevutzot* and *Kibbutzim*"), all of which differ somewhat in their approach to socialism and Zionism, and a smaller religious group, *Kibbutz ha-Dati* ("The Religious *Kibbutz*"), which rejects the secular *kibbutz* members' claim that traditional **Judaism** was an inauthentic product of diaspora conditions. Approximately 4 per cent of the Jewish population in Israel live in *Kibbutzim*.

Kimbanguist Church. The church, officially known as L'Eglise de Jésus Christ par le Prophète Simon Kimbangu, was founded in 1921 by a **Baptist** catechist,

Simon Kimbangu (1889–1951), in the Lower Congo (Zaire), and it is one of the most important **African New Religious Movements**. Kimbangu, a prophet and healer, was imprisoned on a charge of sedition and his followers persecuted. Despite such pressures the church, now led by Kimbangu's three sons, has transformed itself from a revivalist movement with political overtones into an established church with over 4,000,000 members, official recognition and affiliation to the **World Council of Churches**.

Kitawala. The Church of the Watchtower or Kitawala is a widespread **African New Religious Movement** in central Africa influenced by the American Watch-tower and Bible Tract Society (**Jehovah's Witnesses**). African versions of the parent organization have arisen in Malawi, Zambia and Zaire, dating from around 1907, under leaders such as Elliott Kamwana in northern Nyasaland (Malawi), Nyirenda in the Belgian Congo (Zaire) and Jeremiah Gondwe in Zambia. Refusal to swear allegiance to secular authorities has led to widespread persecution (Kamwana was deported in 1909 and Nyirenda executed in 1926: Jehovah's Witnesses are also currently banned in Malawi), but Kitawala churches continue to attract adherents. Gondwe's Independent Watchtower Church, for example, was estimated to have 4,000 members in 1971, rising to 19,000 by 1976.

Kizilbash. *See* **Qizilbash.**

Komeito. The Clean Government Party (CGP) or Komeito, began as the political wing of **Soka Gakkai** and is now a substantial Japanese opposition party in its own right (it was officially separated from Soka Gakkai in 1970). Its official ideology is "humanitarian socialism", and reflecting the spirit of **Nichirenshu**, it promotes peace and social equality from a pragmatic rather than idealistic orientation. The present chairman is Koshiro Ishida and the party currently holds 9 per cent of the seats in the bicameral parliament.

Krishnamurti Foundation. The young Krishnamurti (1895–1985) was "dis-covered" on an Indian beach by the Theosophists C. W. Leadbeater and Annie Besant, and brought up to be the new World Teacher. In 1929 he repudiated this role, and denounced organized religion, ritual, dogma and gurus. The Theosophy movement (see **Theosophical Society**) then split in two, half of the members following him. For the rest of his life he travelled the world, teaching informally. His spiritual vision is close to **Buddhism** in its insistence that truth is formless and timeless and cannot be known by the conditioned mind, but only by direct perception.

The main centres of the Krishnamurti Foundation are in England, Swit-zerland, America and India. These function mainly as study centres, though there are also 11 schools; many pupils go on to university. Although he had no formal disciples, he influenced many people, and along with Gurdieff (*see* **Gurdieffian Groups**) is the most highly regarded Eastern teacher among the Western *intelligentsia*, acknowledged by leading scientists and philosophers.

Kriya Yoga. *See* **Self-Realization Fellowship.**

Kukas. An alternative name for the **Sikh**-derived, **Namdhari** movement.

Kumina. A small ancestor cult of African origin which is similar in some respects to **Convince,** and still found in parts of Jamaica. There are three ranks of spirits, known as zombies: sky gods, earthbound gods, and ancestors. They are invoked through drumming and singing. The ritual ends with the sacrifice of a goat. The most common rationale of ritual dances is the paying of respect to the dead ancestors of the people present.

Kyo Chong. A sect of Korean **Buddhism** amalgamated with **Son** in 1935 to form the **Chogye Chong,** the first distinctively Korean version of **Zen.**

Kyoha Shinto. Traditionally, there are 13 sects of Kyoha or Shuha (Sect) **Shinto**. These originated either with a charismatic founder or out of an amalgam of Traditional and Restoration Shinto and various non-Shinto's influences (**Buddhism, Confucianism, Taoism, Shugendo** folk beliefs and so on.) Common characteristics include founder veneration, worship of tutelary and national *kami,* purification, supplication and appeasement rituals and prayers, and the promotion of a virtuous life. Most of the sects have sacred scriptures written or revealed by their founder.

The sects are loosely classified into five types:

1. Mountain worship sects: Fusokyo and Jikokyo (Mount Fuji), and Ontakekyo (Mount Ontake);
2. Faith healing sects: Kurozumikyo, Konkokyo and **Tenrikyo**;
3. Purification sects: Misogikyo and Shinshukyo;
4. Confucian sects: Shinto Shuseiha and Shinto Taiseikyo;
5. Revival Shinto sects: Izumo Oyashirokyo, Shinrikyo and Shinto Taikyo.

Tenrikyo, the largest of the traditional 13 sects, now has independent status, and is dealt with separately as is **Omotokyo,** a new sect which is sometimes included under the Kyoha Shinto umbrella. Almost all the above have spawned splinter sects which have gained legal recognition since government controls over religion were lifted after World War II. As a whole Sect Shinto claims around 6,000,000 adherents, and a further 2,000,000 claim to belong to New Sect Shinto. Sect Shinto has no shrines. Its meeting places are commonly called churches. Its affairs are overseen by the Association of Sect Shinto, directorship of which rotates annually amongst the member sects.

L

Lahoris. *See* **Ahmadiya (Lahoris).**

Lao United Buddhists' Association. The LUBA was founded in the late 1970s, under the supervision of the Lao People's Revolutionary Party (LPRP), in an attempt to abolish the traditional hierarchical structure of the Laotian **Theravada** *sangha* and to subordinate Buddhist teachings to the ideology of the party. Monks were urged to propagate socialism, though on a theoretical level the party accepts that socialism and **Buddhism** are compatible. Since the early '80s the status of monks has improved and many, who had previously fled to Thailand, have now returned. *Sangha* membership is improving, popular festivals are being revived (despite official party disapproval of superstition), *wats* (monasteries) are receiving government money for refurbishment, and Pali studies and meditation courses are becoming widespread. The President of the LUBA, Maha Thongkhoune Anantasounthone, estimated (August 1985) that 6,897 fully ordained monks and 9,415 novices, in 2,812 *wats,* are spread throughout the country, with 20 per cent of that number in and around Vientiane. The morning alms round is becoming an increasing feature of Lao life once again and the hostility of the authorities has eased a good deal. Since 1985 Party members may temporarily enter the *Sangha* and several monks participate in the Lao Front for National Construction at the highest level.

Laotian Theravada. Laotian Theravada **Buddhism** followed much the same history as that of Cambodia and Thailand. Laos became independent of French rule in 1954. Prior to the Communist takeover in 1975 Buddhism was the state religion under royal patronage with no divisions into "orders" (as in Thailand and Cambodia), and a single patriarch. In 1975 virtually all 3,000,000 Laotians were Buddhists.

Prior to Communist rule Laotian Buddhism was at an earlier stage of modernization than its neighbours. The monks enjoyed a high degree of public respect and played a major role in public education. In 1965, the Institute of Buddhist Studies was established under the Ministry of Education, subsequently being transferred to the Ministry of Religious Affairs in 1975. Many monks continued their studies in Thailand and India, returning to important ecclesiastical and lay positions on their return.

Following the protracted civil war between the Laotian government forces and the Laotian People's Revolutionary Party (or Pathet Lao), the 600-year-old monarchy was abolished in 1975. Many monks fled to Thailand, Europe and the USA. Little is known with any degree of accuracy about the current state of the Laotian Sangha though leadership is provided by the **Lao United Buddhists' Association (LUBA).**

Latin-rite Catholics. *See* **Roman Catholics**.

Latter-day Saints. An alternative name for the **Mormons**.

Liberal Judaism. *See* **Reform Judaism.**

Lingayats. Lingayats or Virashaivas are the dominant religious community in Karnataka in South India, who worship Shiva in the phallic form of the *linga*. This is worn around the neck and is worshipped daily. Rather than performing the usual Hindu rites of passage, the Lingayats initiate their children into the tradition soon after birth. Part of the wider *bhakti* movement, the tradition traces its origin to Basava (d.c1167), who rejected the orthodox values of **Hinduism**, saying that knowledge of God (i.e. Shiva) is available to all, regardless of caste or gender. Basava and other poets composed free-verse devotional poems in the Kannada language which criticized ritual as being useless and praised the body as the true temple of Shiva. Lingayat doctrine is not dissimilar to that of **Kashmir Shaivism.**

There is a Lingayat order of ascetics, the *jangama*, though most members are householders. The Lingayats are free of many of the social restrictions of orthodox Hinduism: for example, the women participate in the choice of marriage partner and can re-marry upon the death of a husband.

London Church of Christ. This is a major UK base of the **Church of Christ** movement which is anchored in the Boston Church of Christ. Similar bases exist in Birmingham and Manchester.

Lubavich (Lubavitch) Hasidism. (*See also* **Agudat Israel; Hasidism.**) Habad was founded as a new movement in Hasidism by Rabbi Schneur Zalman of Lyady (1745–1812). The word Habad is an acronym of Hokhmah (Wisdom), Binah (Understanding) and Daat (Knowledge). These are the three highest ("intellectual") emanations of the divine mind (*sefirot*) which according to the Kabbalistic microcosm–macrocosm doctrine are to be found also in man. Schneur Zalman taught that the true basis of religious life was the intellectual meditation on God (the awakening of the higher potentialities ("Habad") and only on this secure foundation could the emotional sphere, so highly stressed in Hasidism, be properly developed. Habad, thus, represents a particular stress on the priority of the intellect compared with other Hasidic groups.

Schneur Zalman's *Collected Writings* (*Likutei Amarim,* 1796), normally referred to as (the) *Tanya,* is the first systematic work of Hasidic "theology" and remains the core Habad text. He taught a two-fold "perspectivism" concerning the nature of reality. From one perspective there is a process of the "going out" of divinity (the realm of emanation) and this divine creativity serves to invest all "creation" with the divinity (that constitutes "reality"). This notion led to the charge of pantheism, levelled against Habad, by its opponents. From the second (and divine) viewpoint there are no emanations of divinity only the appearance of the (many) emanations, which merely conceals the (One) divinity. The world is thus "nothing", that is, there is no "creation" at all—there is only God. The Hasid participates in this divine process in two ways. Firstly, the physical performance of the commandments reflects, and is reflected in, the outward movement of divinity. Secondly, by intellectual meditation on the *sefirot,* as manifest in the mind, the individual Hasid can re-unify the *sefirot* in their source (En Sof).

He was also opposed to the growing tendency among Hasidim to venerate the *Tzaddik* (Rebbe) as miracle-worker and understood the Rebbe as the intellectual and spiritual leader of his Hasidim.

His son and the second Habad Rebbe, Rabbi Dov Ber (1773–1827), established a centre in Lubavich in Belroussia, and Habad Hasidism is also commonly referred to Lubavich Hasidism. Dov Ber developed his father's teachings and was the author of *Tract on Ecstasy,* in which he sought to distinguish the spurious levels of emotional ecstasy from the "real thing". Lubavich became the largest and most prominent Hasidic movement in northern Russia.

Habad teaches that a portion of divinity (En Sof) is to be found in every Jew but that this "spark" is obscured by the "ego" and only when this is transcended can the spark be awoken. This awakening is the result of intellectual insight but can be fostered by ritual practice.

Rabbi Joseph Isaac Schneerson (1880–1950), the 6th Rebbe in the line of succession, was the leader of Orthodox Jewry in the Russia and after 1917 devoted his considerable energies to working for the preservation of traditional Jewish life under Soviet rule. He was exiled by the Soviet government in 1927 for his activities and with many of his followers moved to Brooklyn (New York) where he established his headquarters in 1941. J. I. Schneersohn was a major figure in the general and widespread post-War revival of Orthodoxy in America. Under his leadership, Lubavich developed its "outreach" programme to non-Lubavich Jews and offered many the opportunity to return to a traditional form of Jewish life (*see* **Orthodox Judaism**).

The present Lubavich Rebbe, Rabbi Menahem Mendel Schneersohn (1902), the son-in-law of Joseph Isaac Schneersohn (7th in the dynastic line), presides over the largest contemporary Hasidic group and a veritable international empire of educational facilities (high schools and *Yeshivot*), publishing ventures (Kehot publishing company) and media services (radio and television stations and channels).

As the absolute authoritative and venerated Rebbe for his tens of thousands of Hasidim and the even larger number of sympathizers, he is one of the most significant figures in the contemporary Jewish world. His immediate followers live in close proximity to the Lubavich headquarters in Brooklyn and live lives centred around their Rebbe. Many Lubavich are engaged in a life-long programme of the study of Habad and other Jewish sources with specialists teaching the Habad interpretation of *Kabbalah*. They will often carry a copy of *Tanya* and can be seen studying around the city. Many spend an hour a day or more reciting the Shema (a particular prayer) in order to focus their energy on unifying the upper and lower forces in their minds. Usual Hasidic practices, including song and dance, also feature prominently in the Lubavich path. In addition, thousands regularly visit the Rebbe for a personal audience in order to ask for advice and guidance on all aspects of their existence.

The current Rebbe has continued to develop his father's "outreach" programme and many thousands of Jews from a non-Orthodox programme have become Lubavich Hasidim or have adopted to some degree a more traditional, observant, Orthodox lifestyle. At Jewish centres around the world Lubavich Hasidim encourage and sometimes cajole Jews into performing the commandments. They have a fleet of trucks and buses ("(Commandment) Mitvah-tanks") which offer instruction and the opportunity to fulfil commandments. On Friday nights, all over Israel and in New York, they encourage Jewish women to light Sabbath candles and they are particularly evident at Jewish festival times attempting to persuade Jews to follow the patterns of traditional observance. The Lubavich strive for a high public profile, for example, they light Hannukah candles in Times Square and in other centres. They have also focused attention on Jewish students at university campuses around the world. The Rebbe has forged an "army" who work tirelessly for their perception of the good of Jewry.

A theological position underlies these practical efforts at reviving traditional Jewish practice. Habad holds that each Jew possesses, however apparently hidden, a portion of the divine spark. This spark, when awoken, will move towards others and they attempt to create a "critical mass" of such sparks in order to hasten the redemption. Often the analogy of the human body is utilized to talk of Jewry, with each limb and cell necessary for the healthy functioning of the whole. Every Jew, thus, is of "supreme" value and, in general, Habad is more open to gentile converts than is usual among Orthodox Jewish groups. These efforts have been highly successful.

Habad has an ambiguous relationship to the modern world. They see little, or no, value in secular education and yet have a Rebbe who was a one-time university student. They rail against the evils of the modern world and yet have a most positive, albeit selective, "instrumental" attitude to modern technology (videos, films, facsimiles, satellite broadcasting, etc.).

Again, and much more importantly, they have an uneasy relationship with the reality of the State of Israel. They supported the establishment of the Jewish state in 1948 but the Rebbe has never visited the country. Since 1967, however, Habad has been heavily involved in Israeli party politics. Lubavich (along with **Ger Hasidism**) have come to dominate Agudat Israel and play a dominant role in the political activities of the Ultra-Orthodox community. The Rebbe has consistently taken a hard line on the "occupied territories" and has rejected the "land for peace" option. Lubavich involvement in Haredi politics was a significant factor in the fragmentation of Haredi parties. The Rebbe and Rabbi Eliezer Schach have challenged each other for the Haredi vote.

Before the recent collapse of the USSR, Lubavich worked clandestinely in the Soviet Union and since the collapse of state socialism have been active throughout the countries of eastern and central Europe. Radiating out from the Brooklyn centre, there are Lubavich centres in North Africa, Israel (Kfar Habad, Jerusalem and Tel Aviv); France, Britain, Canada, Italy, Australia and other Jewish communities.

Most recently (1992) there have been rumours and newspaper and magazine articles claiming that the Rebbe (who is without an heir) is the messiah and that the redemption is at hand and will be marked by the Rebbe's triumphant arrival in Israel.

Lusitanian Church. *See* **Reformed Catholic Churches.**

Lutherans. Martin Luther (1483–1546), often regarded as the founder of the **Protestant** Reformation, was a monk, priest and theological lecturer at the University of Wittenberg, Germany. His studies led him to the belief that, through the grace of God, faith alone is necessary for salvation, churches, priests and even good works are not essential. These beliefs were summarized in the 95 *Theses* which he is said to have nailed to the door of Wittenberg Church in 1517. Later he deduced there were only two true sacraments, Baptism and the Eucharist, rather than the seven defined by the **Roman Catholic Church**. In 1521 he was excommunicated.

He continued to teach and his views spread through Europe. Within 20 years the Lutheran Church had become the state church of Germany, Scandinavia and much of Eastern Europe. Luther translated the Bible into German, wrote a number of hymns and married a former nun, Katherine von Bora.

The Lutheran Church is still the state church in most Scandinavian countries. In Sweden membership is automatic, one must choose to opt out. In Germany some Lutheran churches have joined with **Presbyterian (Reformed)** churches to form a united church. Lutherans believe that the Bible is the sole rule of faith, to which creeds and tradition are subservient. For this reason much modern biblical criticism has been led by Lutherans. The *Book of Concord,* first published in 1580 collects together the beliefs of Lutherans in the words of the creeds, of Luther, and in an agreed statement of faith drawn up in 1577. There is a single order of priesthood, although oversight is given by a "General Superintendent" of an area, who in some countries is known as a bishop. However methods of church government vary from country to country. Services are liturgical and will normally include a sermon based on the Bible. Celebration of the Eucharist has, as in other denominations, become more frequent in recent years. Hymns are still an important part of worship.

In many countries (as in the case of the United Kingdom) there are small Lutheran churches ministering primarily to ethnic groups, particularly former refugees from Eastern Europe such as Latvia or Estonia. Most Lutheran churches belong to the Lutheran World Federation whose headquarters are in Geneva, Switzerland. The Lutheran Church is one of the largest denominations in the world with global membership estimated at over 60,000,000.

M

Macumba. An Afro–Brazilian spirit possession cult which is similar in its syncretism and in other respects to **Candomblé, Voodoo** and **Shango.** It has gradually passed from religion to magic, and is often associated with immorality and wrong-doing.

Mafdal (Mizrahi, National Religious Party). (*See also* **Orthodox Judaism; Zionism.**) Mizrahi was founded in 1904 as a religious, Orthodox party joining the Zionist Organization with "The land of Israel for the people of Israel according to the Torah of Israel" as its motto. Mizrahi developed into an international organization of religious Jews who support the State of Israel. In the land of Israel, two independent groups were formed—the Mizrahi party and the Mizrahi Workers' Party. These two joined together to form Mafdal (National Religious Party) in 1956. Mafdal (and earlier as its component parts) has been a coalition partner in every Israeli government (Labour and Likud) and have been a major factor in Israel's political stability since 1948.

Traditionally, under pressure from both its non-religious coalition partners (seeking to limit its proposed religious legislation) and from the more separatist Orthodox parties, Mafdal has sought a pragmatic accommodation of the religious sector in Israel's mainly non-religious society, while maintaining its long-term aim of the establishment of a Torah-state. It has defended religious interests against secular pressures and worked for co-operation between the non-religious and religious in the building of the Jewish state, the establishment of which Mafdal considers to be of religious–messianic significance.

Mafdal followers have been ardent supporters of the state and have generally accepted their national service, unlike the non-Zionist Orthodox, and this has often been combined with *Yeshivah* study. Mafdal institutions, where there is an attempted synthesis between religious and "secular" values, include the state–religious schools, Bar Ilan University, and the religious *Kibbutzim* and Moshavim, with their practical synthesis of Zionist labour and Orthodox values.

Mafdal's strategy of co-operation with the ruling non-religious parties has ensured its almost continuous control of the Ministry of Religious Affairs. This has allowed Mafdal to wield great influence over the Chief Rabbinate and religious courts and councils and to operate an extensive system of patronage.

After holding between 10 and 12 Knesset seats from 1949 until 1977, Mafdal's electoral support fell dramatically to only five seats in the 1988 election (the six seats won in 1981 were reduced to four in 1984).

Significant factors in this decline include the radicalism of its younger members—many of the ultra-nationalist groups have their origins in Mafdal—and the ethnic/**Sephardi** factor. Mafdal's view that the 1967 victory has "messianic" import and that the occupied territories are "God given" run counter to much current thinking and in the 1992 general election Mafdal secured six seats. It appears as if its reduced status might be permanent.

Mahanikay. The largest fraternity of **Theravada** Buddhist monks in Thailand. Of the over 28,000 monasteries presently operating in the country, 26,694 belong to the Mahanikay. The order escaped the monastic reforms imposed by the kings of the late 19th century and it remains more closely aligned with the common people. In the 1930s the order became imbued with a democratic spirit and as a result the mid-century saw fairly intense conflict with the other, more aristocratic fraternity, the **Thammayut.** Disagreements are primarily organizational and political but do not affect the doctrinal domain, in which there is virtual accord. In the mid-'70s some, mostly well-educated, monks of peasant stock formed the Federation of Buddhists of Thailand (FBT) to press for a less autocratic system of *Sangha* government. The fraternity has been prominent in the popular democracy movement which led to the downfall of Prime Minister General Kraprayoon in May 1992. The Mahanikay was also found in Cambodia, though it was merged with its rival fraternity, the **Thomayat,** by the Heng Samrin government in 1975.

Mahanubhavs. An Indian **Vaishnava** devotional movement particularly strong in Maharashtra state. Adherents focus their devotions on a group of five historical figures known as the "five Krishnas" who are believed to be manifestations (*avatara*) of the Supreme Being. The most prominent of the five, Chakradhar (1194–1276), is held to be the founder of the group. Although their devotion to Krishna links them to the mainstream **Hindu** tradition, the Mahanubhavs reject caste and pollution laws and the authority of the Vedas. The main text of the movement is a collection of Chakradhar's sayings, the *Sutrapatha,* and devotees tend to adopt a fairly ascetic lifestyle. Also known as the Manbhavs, or Manbhaus, the group show family resemblances to their larger Marathi rival, the **Warkaris.**

Mahayana Buddhism. *See* **Buddhism.**

Mahdiya. Mahdism is a generic term for Mahdi-led messianic movements in **Islam**. More particularly it refers to a movement in the Sudan that has continued to be influential down to today.

Muhammad Ahmad (1848–1885), a member of the Sammaniya **Sufi** order, proclaimed himself Mahdi in 1881, and with the capture of Khartoum in 1885 (and the death of General Gordon and his garrison) established an Islamic state in the Sudan. Drawing a parallel between himself and the Prophet Muhammad, he called his movement the **Ansar**—the Helpers—as Muhammad called those who assisted his move from Mecca to Medina. After his death six months later, leadership of the movement fell to a deputy, and the Islamic state lasted 14 years until defeated by an Anglo–Egyptian army under General Kitchener in 1899.

Despite initial British attempts to suppress the movement, the Ansar continued and eventually revived and regained legitimacy under the Mahdi's charismatic posthumous son Abd al-Rahman al-Mahdi (who retained the leadership until his death in 1959). Yet it had now changed character considerably, entering into limited co-operation with its former foes, the British (and also the Sufi orders). Following independence in 1956, it has been influential through its support for its own political organization, the Umma Party.

In elections scheduled for June 1969, two Ansar leaders, Sadiq al-Mahdi, a great grandson of the Mahdi, and al-Hadi al-Mahdi (Sadiq's uncle), were widely expected to come to power as Prime Minister and President respectively. They represented two wings that had emerged in the Ansar movement, the pragmatic modernism of Sadiq and the religious conservatism of al-Hadi. Sadiq exercised political control of the Umma Party, while al-Hadi exercised spiritual leadership of the Ansar with the title *imam*.

In the event, Colonel Nimeiri's military *coup* intervened. In 1970 the Ansar stronghold on Aba Island was bombarded, and thousands of Ansar, including their *imam* al-Hadi al-Mahdi, were killed. This was not, however, the end of their influence. Sadiq al-Mahdi, with traditional Ansar support, remained a leading political figure throughout Nimeiri's rule (running the gamut from leader of an attempted *coup*, exile, prime ministerial office, and imprisonment). After Nimeiri's deposition in 1985 he emerged yet again, following the elections in 1986, as Prime Minister, until the further military *coup* of 1989.

A long-time supporter, with the **Muslim Brotherhood**, of introducing Islamic law in the Sudan (Sadiq al-Mahdi has at times been quite close to Hassan Turabi, the gifted leader of the country's Muslim Brotherhood), al-Mahdi nevertheless, in marked contrast to Turabi, strongly opposed the autocratic imposition of Shari'a by President Nimeiri in 1983. He had led a commission to develop a modern interpretation of Shari'a based on the Quran and Sunna but, unlike Nimeiri's policy, side-stepping the medieval law manuals. Also unlike Nimeiri, he opposed the imposition of Shari'a on the non-Muslim peoples of the southern Sudan. In the post-Nimeiri period the Islamic laws were frozen, but the Shari'a issue remains a live one.

Maitatsine. This Hausa word meaning "he who curses" was applied to the leader of a millenarian Muslim sect in Nigeria, Alhaji Muhammadu Marwa, and is sometimes used as a label for the sect itself. The more widely used name for the latter, however, is **'Yan Tatsine**. Marwa was killed in an attempted takeover of the city of Kano in 1980, but the sect has survived.

Malabar Christians. *See* **Syro-Indian Churches**.

Malangs. Malangs are male religious mendicants who belong to the bi-shar' (without the Shari'a) group of **Sufi** orders. They are mainly to be found in northern India (especially the Punjab) and the Deccan. Other Muslims consider them to be unorthodox. The difference between the bi-shar' and the ba-shar' (with the shari'a) orders lies in the concept of inner and outer world. Like other Sufis, the Malangs believe in the existence of both worlds. The ba-shar' Sufis, however, live in the outer world and attempt to purify this outer world to bring it on the same level as the inner world. They have to make a transition from one world to the other. The Malangs totally disregard the outer world and concentrate only on the inner one. Henceforth, they have no need for the Shari'a which is used for regulating the outer world. The Malang communicates directly with God without mediation by external prescriptions. This communication takes place in a state of intoxication through hashish or other narcotics. In this state the Malang can also disregard his body, the only connection with the outer world.

A characteristic of the Malang is his particular style of dress. He sees himself to be the bride of God and thus to be subservient to God. Malangs wear female ornaments, bangles and rings to emphasise this position. An iron bangle is often found, indicating that their tie with God cannot be broken. They wander from shrine to shrine but might also, on the command of God or a living saint, attach themselves to a particular shrine. In spite of their emphasis on equality, theirs is a hierarchically structured community.

Malikis. The Maliki rite or school of Islamic law (*madhhab*) was founded by Malik b. Anas (d. 795), a lawyer of Medina and pupil of Abu Hanifa, founder of the **Hanafi** school. Malik's main views are contained in *al-Muwatta* (*The Beaten Path*), which outlines the practice followed in Medina, supported by numerous Traditions (sayings and deeds of the Prophet and his close companions). It represents one of the earliest collections of such material, and Malik is also highly regarded as a traditionist.

Malikis, one of four **Sunni** schools of law alongside the Hanafis, the **Shafi'is**, and the **Hanbalis**, are currently predominant in North and West Africa and Upper Egypt. They are generally thought to be more tradition-conscious and conservative than the Hanafis or Shafi'is, and are opposed to the strategems (*hiyal*) used by Hanafis to circumvent Shari'a rulings that appear to be inconvenient or unsuited to new situations, for example the ban on taking interest. They also oppose the excessive use of analogy (*qiyas*), particularly as practised by the Hanafis. In common with other schools they accept the consensus of religious scholars (*ijma'*) as a source of Law. They base their acceptance of this consensus on consideration of the public interest.

In modern times Maliki interpretation of law has shown signs of greater flexibility than the classical theory seems to allow. In Morocco from the 15th century onwards Maliki jurists developed a practical approach to formulating law to suit actual conditions, recognizing that this might not meet the requirements of strict Maliki doctrine. In Egypt the famous modernist Muhammad 'Abduh (1845–1905), so influential for the **Salafiya**, was himself a Maliki. Working from the Maliki view that a jurist should assume God's desire for human welfare in choosing between Quranic and Prophetic texts, he held that in framing laws a jurist should always seek to promote the general welfare and should do this by the use of human reason, working from general **Islamic** moral principles. 'Abduh's views are consistent with the generally moralistic outlook of the Malikis regarding the purpose of Holy Law.

Manalistas. Members of the **Iglesia ni Cristo** in the Philippines may be referred to as Manalistas after the movement's founder, Felix Manalo (1886–1963).

Mandaeans. An extremely small, virtually extinct religious community concentrated in south-western Iran and southern Iraq, once erroneously referred to as "Christians of St John the Baptist", in allusion to their baptismal rituals. They are possibly of Palestinian or Syrian origin and were identified by some Muslims with the Sabaeans (*Sabi'in*), a scriptural group referred to in the Quran. A large body of religious literature, written in a form of Aramaic in the Mandaean language, has been studied, and some of it published. Their beliefs, which involve a system of emanations from the Godhead, suggest a Gnostic influence or origin.

Maori Religion. The Maori comprise 10 per cent of New Zealand's population and are closely related to other Polynesian groups in language, culture and religion (*see* **Polynesian Religions**). Maori religion today is a reflex of traditional Polynesian beliefs seen through the perspective of more than a century and a half of Christian conversion, some developing towards nativistic cults (*see* **Ringatu**) and others towards more recent trends in post-colonialist, nationalistic discourse.

There is some debate over whether traditional Maori religion has a god similar to the Christian deity. What is clear is that during the last century this claim became firmly established. This supreme being, Io, resides in the highest of 12 heavens, and acts through a hierarchy of gods, spirits, guardians and ancestors. Creation occurred when Rangi, the sky god, mated with Papa-tua-Nuku, the earth mother, to generate numerous gods such as Tane, Tangaroa and Rongo to rule over nature and human activity. The realm of gods also includes the *wairua* (spirits), the *tipuna* ("ancestors"), the *kaitiaki* ("guardians") as well as the *kehu* ("ghosts") and the *taniwha* ("monsters").

There are no strictly maintained barriers between the realm of the gods and that of humans. The *tipuna*, for example, the remembered ancestors or the living dead, belong to both realms. Community is what binds the living and the dead—the latter live on because they are remembered by the former, and if appropriately recognized and regarded, can bring blessing to the former. The people, the nobility (*rangatira*) and the high chiefs (*ariki*) are bound together by loyalties in the extended family (*whanau*), the sub-tribe (*hapu*) and the tribe (*iwi*).

The religious practitioners (*tohunga*) are specialists in maintaining equilibrium in the community, and assuring its quality. Some are experts in magic and others in the sacred. The realm of the dead, which also inter-penetrates the human sphere, is presided over by the guardian of the third realm, the underworld (*hinenuiotepo*). This is where death, disease and evil have their origin. All three realms are infused with *mana* (undifferentiated "holy power") which can erupt in people or places or be found in certain objects such as the greenstone tiki. Caution is essential when humans approach places or people endowed with such power. Before normality can return, the *tapu* (the sacredness) must be lifted. But even in the course of ordinary life, a person is special. Each has, within the life principle (*mauri*), a soul, and one's *mana* (status, prestige or "face") endowed at birth must be protected at all costs.

The Maori is conscious of the sacredness of the whole of creation. Kinship with nature and the land was essential for human well-being. In approaching the sacred there was a set form of words to use (*karakia*)—the words once uttered were said to release power, and thus bring about change in a particular situation or achieve a certain purpose.

Sickness and disease were thought to have their origin in an evil force, and were taken seriously, not only with a prescription of herbal medicine, but in the choice of *karakia*: there was a *karakia* for the lifting of *tapu* and a different *karakia* for the lifting of *makutu* (curse) laid by someone with evil intent. The tohunga were experts not only with words and herbal remedies, but were also aware of what we would call the psychology of sickness.

Death is a time of intense sensitivity. It is essential for the family and tribe that the appropriate *karakia* are used to release the spirit of the person (*wairua*) which waits until the rituals have been completed before it begins its journey to Cape Reinga at the northernmost tip of New Zealand. From there it descends to the floor of the ocean to travel on to the abode of the dead (*hinenuitepo*). The funeral ceremonies (*tangi*) around an open casket are conducted in the meeting house on the *marae*. Visitors are received with a *karanga* and conduct themselves with solemnity, acknowledging first the ancestors of the *marae* and its family, then addressing the deceased person and the family in mourning, before receiving the visitors into the community with a handshake and "hongi"—the pressing of noses and the sharing of living breath—the most delicate of all personal contacts. The visitors are then asked to eat and drink. At an announced time, the final funeral rites are performed, the casket sealed and burial in the tribal area then takes place.

The *marae*, the grass area in front of the meeting house, is where speeches are delivered and visitors received. The Maori is a skilful orator: all who speak demonstrate an extensive knowledge of tribal traditions and mythologies. The *whare tupuna* (meeting house) is where the community meets, sleeps and conducts its affairs. A visit to a *marae* is an essential part of a young person's education; tertiary institutions have a *marae* on campus. A Maori university has been founded and Maori studies are readily available at all other New Zealand universities.

The Maori in recent years are open about their beliefs, values and traditions. A bicultural relationship is being forged with difficulty, but with measurable success, between the Maori and the European New Zealander. There has been considerable Maori influence on the mainline **Anglican** and **Roman Catholic** churches in New Zealand in the last quarter century. This is evident in liturgical language and practice as well as in theological discourse.

Thus, the ancient form of Maori religion is experiencing an open renaissance in the latter part of the 20th century, going a long way to restore dignity to the Maori people of New Zealand.

Maori Religious Movements. The Maori response to the missionary movement and the European colonization of early New Zealand was to protect their identity and their traditions. An affinity with the Jews and the Old Testament was the cornerstone of the Maori defence against **Christianity**. Between 1830 and 1850 there were 10 major religious movements which arose with this background.

The 1850s was the decade of healers with nine main movements identified. The colonial struggle culminated in the Land Wars of the 1860s which saw the Maori increasingly defranchized of land, and thus of their spiritual identity. Prophetic movements arose during this period of which 16 were of major importance, with many more of minor or local significance. By the turn of the century the struggle over land had concluded, with the Maori defeated.

During the Land Wars, Maori were increasingly disillusioned with Christianity, seeing it as the vehicle of colonization. Reform movements were thus often a direct response to oppression and disillusionment. In the 20th century Maori have increasingly sought spiritual roots in Maori churches (**Ringatu** and **Ratana**) and, in many cases, *tohungas* (Maori religious specialists) have kept alive the values and ideals of pre- (Christian) European religion, and have passed on their knowledge and skill to successive generations.

In the 1980s, after a century of quiet struggle, the Treaty of Waitangi, signed in 1840 between Queen Victoria and the Maori tribal chiefs, was given an important place in New Zealand law. A tribunal was established to attempt to unravel and resolve problems arising out of the early colonial history of New Zealand and the clash between the European and the Maori.

Mar Thoma. *See* **Syro-Indian Churches.**

Maraboutism. The French term *"marabout"* (from Arabic *murabit*) originally meant a warrior for **Islam** living in a *ribat* (frontier-post) but later came to be applied in North and West Africa to an adept of **Sufism**, or quite generally to a holy man in a loose sense. Thus maraboutism is used to refer to the range of Islamic beliefs and practices associated with the *marabouts*, including aspects of popular Islam frowned upon by stricter believers, such as reliance on talismans and amulets.

The *marabout* is thought by those who venerate him to possess *baraka* (sacred power) which "rubs off" on to believers through physical contact during his life, and through contact with his tomb-shrine after his death. Such shrines are very numerous in North and West Africa. The *baraka* may also be thought to be passed down through the *marabout*'s living descendants. In cases where he is—or is thought to be—descended from Muhammad, the *baraka* is of exceptional importance as that of the Prophet himself.

Maraboutism was a major target of Muslim reformers inspired by the **Salafiya** and also by **Wahhabism**, but it continues to exercise a powerful appeal.

Maria Legio. Founded by two Luo Catholics, Gaudencia Aoko and Simon Ondeto, in western Kenya in 1963 and named after a **Roman Catholic** organization, the Legion of Mary, Aoko was a charismatic figure who sought to combine RC and **Pentecostal** elements in worship. The movement, which in the 1970s claimed over 90,000 members (mainly among the Luo), emphasizes healing, exorcism, community and morality. Numbers declined with the departure of Aoko, but Maria Legio remains the largest African Instituted Church (*see* **African New Religious Movements**) to spring from a Roman Catholic background.

Maria Lionza. Maria Lionza is an Afro–Catholic cult found in Venezuela. Like **Shango** and **Santería,** both of which have now spread to Venezuela, it is a syncretic mix of **African traditional religions** and elements drawn from **Roman Catholicism.**

Mariavites. *See* **Old Catholic Mariavite Church**.

Maronites. The various branches of the Maronite Church chose affiliation to the **Roman Catholic Church** between the 14th and 16th centuries, thereby engendering one of the largest Catholic **Uniate** communities in the Middle East. In 1985, the Church numbered 1,576,462 members. A high proportion live in Syria and in Lebanon, although many have emigrated in recent years. Maronites have been deeply affected by the civil strife which has been endemic to these regions in the last half century. Most of the Maronites of Syria are concentrated in the west. Here they practise conservative forms of Catholicism. Survival takes priority over innovation. They are also relatively open-minded. The situation entails pragmatic co-operation amongst Christians of different traditions, and with moderate Muslims.

Twenty-nine per cent of the Lebanese people are Maronite. In 1926, when France made Lebanon an independent State, it was thought that Maronites would constitute a majority. By 1943, there was in fact a ratio of six Maronites to five Muslims. The Maronite ascendancy has now collapsed, under the pressure of massive Palestinian immigration, in the wake of the 1967 Arab–Israeli War, and Maronites now support Israel's war against the Palestinian Liberation Organization, to which Lebanon gives shelter. In 1975, civil war broke out between Muslims and Christians, after gunmen fired upon Pierre Gemayel, then leader of the Maronite Phalange Party; Maronite gunmen responded in kind. Gemayel became President from 1982–1988 and was, as a Maronite figurehead, a target for Muslim ill-feeling. The Maronites have proposed, first, in 1977, in a statement entitled "The Lebanon We Want", that each religious community should form a separate federal entity within the state of Lebanon; second, in 1984, after the Lausanne Conference, that Lebanese politics be secularized (both proposals are equally unacceptable to the Muslims).

The most important Maronite groups today, usually divided among themselves, are the religious leadership in Bkirki, centred on the Patriarch Nasrallah Sfair, those attached to Gemayel, those following the Phalange Party Leader George Saadeh, and those engaged in the Christian Brigades of the Lebanese Army, led by General Michael Aoun. Any long-term solution to the Middle Eastern crisis depends partly upon the Maronites.

Maruyamakyo. A popular Japanese new religious movement which draws heavily on the mountain worship traditions of **Shugendo.** Pilgrimage to Mt Fuji is the central feature of the movement which recognizes the existence of a universal parent deity. Members must observe the major spring and autumn festivals.

Masorti (Masorati). *See* **Conservative Judaism.**

Mawlawiya. The Mawlawiya is a **Sufi** order associated in particular with Turkey, and popularly known as the Whirling Dervishes. Members of the order are known as Mawlawis (from the Arabic) or Mevlevis (from the Turkish).

Taking its name from the great mystical poet Mawlana ("Our Master") Jalal al-din Rumi (1207–73), the Mawlawiya was one of the earliest orders to attract European interest, largely due to the distinctive dance which gave rise to the label Whirling Dervishes. Born in Khurasan, an area of north-east Iran known for its ecstatic Sufis, Rumi moved during the Mongol invasion to settle in the Turkish town of Konya, which was to become the centre of his order. Under the influence of a wandering dervish, Shams al-din of Tabriz, in whom he recognized "the perfect man", he turned increasingly from sober to ecstatic Sufism, composing a vast quantity of Persian mystical verse. Rumi's famous work, the *Mathnawi,* in about 25,000 rhyming couplets, is regarded by the Mawlawis as revealing the inner meaning of the Quran. The Mawlawiya developed into a major urban, aristocratic and wealthy organization in the Ottoman Empire (in contrast to the **Bektashiya** which retained a more popular rural base). It spread from Turkey into Eastern Europe, but its centres in the Arab world remained almost entirely Turkish in membership.

Mawlawi initiates face a demanding period of preparation, totalling almost three years (1,001 days), before being admitted to full rank in the order. After performing a prayer of repentance they must devote themselves to a series of menial tasks, such as sweeping floors, cleaning latrines, shopping and working in the kitchens, with the aim of fostering humility. In addition to regular prayers, they have to attend for training in the symbolic ritual dance of the Mawlawiya and, like the Khalwatiya, to undergo times of retreat. Only when they have completed the novitiate can they participate in the famous whirling dance to achieve a controlled, highly disciplined ecstasy. The dance is full of symbolic significance, alluded to in the poetry of Rumi, the turning of the dancers being said to represent the circling movement of the spirit, culminating in leaping up to a state of union with the Divine. Mawlawis emphasize the importance of love and the need to respect everything of use to humanity, including the inanimate. In the past they have been noted for their tolerance towards other faiths, despite their poor relations at times with other orders. Their chief rivals have been the Bektashiya, and they have been condemnatory of the more extravagant practices of the **Rifa'iya**.

Today the Mawlawiya is in decline and confined to Turkey, where the ecstatic dance is performed annually in Konya, the site of Rumi's tomb, from Dec. 11–17, the anniversary of his death. A once major order has become in danger of being relegated to a tourist attraction. The order appears to have died out in Greece since the 1920s, and in Yugoslavia since World War II. In the Arab lands the Mawlawi centres have been closing down since the 1950s. One of the best known at Tripoli in northern Lebanon survived into the 1970s, and in Beirut the last shaikh of the Mawlawiya was killed in May 1982 during the Israeli bombardment of the city. The decline appears to be due to a number of factors, the most important being official suppression, the close association of the order with Turkish aristocracy, and the difficulty of reconciling the Mawlawi Way with a modern working lifestyle.

Mayan Religion. Mayan Indians in Guatemala and southern Mexico retain elements of their traditional religion, which is an example of **Mesoamerican Traditional Religions (Mayan)**.

Mazdaism. *See* **Zoroastrians.**

MBI. *See* **Buddhayana**.

Melanesian Religions. Melanesia comprises a number of different island cultures. They are situated north-east and east of Australia and comprise Iriyan Jaya (which is part of Indonesia), Papua New Guinea, the breakaway island of Bouganville, the Solomon Islands, Vanuatu, the Loyalty Islands, Wallis and Futuna, and Fiji. The phosphate island of Nauru in the mid-Pacific is also related to this area. The inhabitants of these island groups are dark skinned (hence the name), and the area is particularly rich in religious practices which have attracted the attention of anthropologists and interpreters of religious traditions.

Since **Christianity** came to this area, it has largely overshadowed the primal religious traditions. However, in more recent times, as independence has come to these island groups, attention has been given to the primal religions of each island group, as Christians have begun to rethink Christianity, whether **Roman Catholic** or **Protestant**, in the context of a new, emergent Pacific identity. A considerable lead has been given to the task of finding suitable expressions for indigenous theologies by the Pacific Council of Churches, and at the centre of this thrust is the Pacific Theological College situated in Fiji, and its Catholic counterpart. A pivotal role has been played in the gathering of Pacific histories and interpreting cultures by the University of the South Pacific which is also situated in Fiji. The University of Papua New Guinea, situated in Port Moresby, is also playing a major role in gathering together the traditions of the past, and in interpreting the varieties of cultures emergent in these areas.

The tradition of male cults is particularly strong in Melanesia. The initiation cults in particular guarantee entrance into the stages of adulthood and through the difficult passages of life, from birth, adolescence, marriage and death. Often the rituals of the male cults involve elements of mutilation, including circumcision, blood letting, tattooing and strengthening the males in their relations with females. There are different cults that specialize in equipping their members with various qualities which are deemed to be necessary for tribal life. Initiations take place in special "spirit houses" called "haus tambaran". An important part of Melanesian religion are the frequent "Sing Sings": elaborate festivals of song and dance in which the entire community becomes involved, and which follow a seasonal rhythm. These festivals are interconnected with the economic life of the community since such festivals often lead to complex trading arrangements. "Sing Sings" often involve the use of masks which comprise the most important artefact of Melanesian religion, central to the male cults. They embody various spiritual beings and spirits from the Melanesian pantheon of deities. Bull roarers are used to create sound effects and to generate an atmosphere of the extra-ordinary.

Among the most interesting new religious movements, particularly in Vanuatu, are the **cargo cults.** They also occur in the Solomon Islands and are intimately connected with the coming-of-age of these island communities.

Fiji's spirituality is also very complex. Fire-walking ceremonies are a particular feature of island life, demonstrating the mastery of spiritual consciousness over physical pain. The **Methodist** Church has played an important role in Fiji politics and, over more recent years, with the rise in nationalism, there has been a recovery of Fijian primal religious identity. This identity has begun to find its way into expressions of Christianity, particularly at the edges of culture. A striking feature of Fijian life is also the development of Indian religions, **Hinduism** and **Islam** in particular, but also some **Buddhism**. Although the Indian and the Fijian communities have a tense relationship, there is a growing awareness of the religious strands of the peoples of these islands.

The rich heritage of primal religion in this area has drawn attention to the characteristics described by the terms *Mana* and *Taboo*. R. H. Codrington brought the attention of the scholarly world to these concepts, and his study of the way in which *Mana* and *Taboo* operated has been refined in more recent studies. They are explained briefly in relation to **Polynesian religion.** The religious world is rich with gods, spirits (good and bad) and ghosts. The living have strong relationships with the dead as communities seek to balance their lives. In this the use of religious practitioners is essential. This concern with primal religion is often overlaid with the Christian tradition, Roman Catholic or Protestant. As these island communities rediscover their primal religious traditions, a rich heritage is being revealed, and this will be increasingly used in the search for viable and authentic expressions of religious faith.

Melkites. Syria is home to six Catholic rite communions (Melkite, **Armenian**, Syrian, **Maronite, Latin** and **Chaldean**), of whom the Melkites are the most numerous. There are currently officially 924,202 Melkite believers. Melkites follow the Byzantine rite. They are drawn from the most highly cultured echelons of Syrian society. Their Patriarch lives in Damascus. During the 1960s, they suffered under the Baathist government, which closed Melkite schools and proscribed Melkite youth organizations. Since then, the cultivation of adult catechetics has been essential. Accordingly, Melkite clergy, already in receipt of a sophisticated theological education, are also well versed in pastoral skills. The Congress of Melkite Catholic Clergy was established in 1969. Its annual assemblies provide a forum for ecumenical dialogue. Most Melkites live in Syria, but they are also to be found in Lebanon, Jordan, Egypt, America, Australia, Europe and Africa.

Mellusians. *See* **Syro-Indian Churches**.

Mennonites (Anabaptists). The Mennonites get their name from Menno Simons, a former **Roman Catholic** priest who in 1537 became the leader of the Anabaptist community in Holland. The Anabaptists' distinctive doctrine was that the Bible taught that Christians are a community of believers and that therefore baptism, the sign of membership of the Christian community, could only be given to believers. At that time all babies were baptized as infants, so a mature person being baptized as a sign of commitment was, said the Anabaptists' opponents, being "re-baptized". The Anabaptists, however, denied that infant baptism had any effect and did not have their infants baptized.

Their views brought them into conflict with the church and the state: they were severely persecuted and attempts were made to suppress their teaching. As a result many Mennonites emigrated to North America from the middle of the 17th century. In Europe the Mennonite flair for agriculture and a capacity for hard work led in 1788 to an invitation from Catherine the Great for them to settle in the Ukraine and teach local farmers their methods.

There are Mennonites in the Ukraine and other ex-Socialist Republics to this day.

The Mennonite desire to follow Bible teaching as closely as possible led to their refusal to accept military service, refusal to take oaths and refusal of public office. In 1693 an extreme group formed the first of the **Amish** communities, which survive today as closed, primarily agricultural communities, rejecting all forms of modern technology.

Another group of 16th century Anabaptists were centred on Zurich in Switzerland. They were initially known as the Swiss Brethren, but their beliefs were the same as those in Northern Europe. Menno worked successfully to unite these two groups into a single movement.

One group of Anabaptists which has kept separate from the Mennonites, although sharing most of their beliefs, is the **Hutterites**.

The Mennonites also travelled to South America and set up communities in such places as Mexico and Paraguay. Today they are strongest in America and Canada, although there are many internal divisions based on minor differences of doctrine or ethnic origin. The worldwide membership is about 1,250,000.

Mesoamerican Traditional Religions (Mayan). The ferocity of the Spanish invasion in northern and central Mexico meant that the Aztecan religion was all but obliterated in the wake of advancing Christian armies. The same cannot be said for the Mayan area to the south, where traditional religious beliefs and practices continue in a dynamic form. At present, some 8,000,000 descendants of the Maya live in Southern Mexico and Guatemala, still adhering to many aspects of the world view of their more famous ancestors.

The religion of the modern Maya is not exactly equivalent to that of the Maya of the Classic period since the high priests' theocratic centres such as Tikal and Chichén Itzà have long since been deposed. In addition, the last 500 years have seen much syncretism with **Roman Catholic** orthodoxy. Yet the majority of Mayas still work the land on isolated small-holdings and maintain a profound link with the old gods of agricultural fertility. The Earth Lord provides the creative energy to successfully cultivate the staples of maize, beans and squash. The Earth Lord is often represented as a fat *ladino* (non-Indian) who jealously guards his treasures, but can be tempted into a fruitful relationship of reciprocity by sacrifices of candles and incense on the mountain tops and in the caves. Other lesser deities play a role in the agricultural enterprise, such as Catholic saints who each protect a particular crop, and the fertile Mother Moon who is often linked with the Virgin Mary. The Father Sun, unlike during the times of the Mayan empire, plays only a supporting role, as does the Morning Star, who was the warrior god of the ancient Maya.

In southern Mexico and western Guatemala, Mayan peasants believe that each person has an animal spirit (or *nagual*). The animal spirit is like an *alter ego*, which lives with the Earth Lord deep inside the mountain. A powerful person may have a strong animal spirit such as a jaguar or hummingbird, and a meek person may have a butterfly or deer as their *nagual*. The animal spirit has an ethical dimension, since if the person breaks moral codes, the Earth Lord will release the animal spirit into the forest, thus exposing the person to grave physical danger. If the animal spirit were killed, the person will die also. Many **shamanic** healing practices are concerned with returning the animal spirit to its corral inside the mountain. This set of beliefs, however, is not shared by the Maya of eastern and central Guatemala. We must be careful, then, not to over-generalize about the Maya, since there is a great deal of variation at the level of both the village and 20-odd linguistic groups.

The community structure which has served as the vessel for traditional Mayan beliefs is the religious brotherhood (or *cofradía*). Catholic priests formed the brotherhoods in the 16th century in order to better evangelize the indigenous groups, but the villagers have made them all their own. The religious brotherhoods still organize fiestas for the village saint, as was originally intended, but they also became the whole social structure of the community, the fora for political decisions, economic strategies and Mayan and Catholic religious practices. During a man's life, he moves up the hierarchy, each time taking on a greater civil or religious duty. One year he may be mayor, the next year in charge of the saint's feast-day and the following year responsible for feeding the Earth Lord. Ultimately, he becomes an elder, responsible for the material and spiritual well-being of the community.

In recent years, the religious brotherhoods have ceased to be the main structure of local religious life. The unity of the community has been undermined by economic differentiation, migration, an intervening state and civil war (in Guatemala). In addition there have been a number of massive changes within orthodox religions. **Protestantism** has been very successful in converting Mayan peoples, and it is estimated that evangelicals now represent 35 per cent of the Guatemalan population and the majority of active churchgoers. There have now been two Protestant presidents of Guatemala in the space of the last 10 years. The Catholic church has also gone through profound changes, and from the 1970s on began forming base groups in each community. These Bible-based groups displaced the traditional religious brotherhoods in many areas and are now the main force in local Catholic life. The leaders of the base groups, or catechists, have waged a campaign against what was seen as the idolatry of Mayan beliefs. The Christ-centred religious ethic of the catechists has resulted in the demise of the Earth Lord and the importance of saints.

Yet the old gods have not left the scene completely. There are at present many ethnic revivalist movements throughout the Mayan area, seeking to renovate the ancient agricultural rituals. They seek to construct a new Mayan identity, incorporating many traditional religious practices. This revivalism is a prominent feature of Mayan religion, and played an important role in historical political movements such as the Tzeltal rebellion in 1712 and the War of the Castes in the 1860s. The latter rebellion was centred around a Talking Cross, expressing a Mayan content in a Christian form, and to this day armed Mayan guards protect the Talking Cross in a church in the Yucatán.

Messianic Judaism. This Christian mission, active across the English-speaking world, in Israel and most recently in the post-Socialist states of eastern Europe, aims to convert Jews to an evangelical form of **Christianity** with the retention of elements of Jewish identity and practice. Its origins are to be found in the 19th-century Hebrew Christianity missions to Jewish immigrants to America and western Europe and to Jewish communities in eastern and central Europe. Messianic Judaism, however, evidences the 1970s' concern with ethnic identity and encourages Jews to accept Jesus as their messiah and to establish separate messianic Jewish communities rather than assimilate within the existing Protestant churches.

Many of the earlier Hebrew Christian groups have been renamed to reflect these new emphases (e.g. from the American Board of Mission to the Jews to the Chosen People Ministries). There are a number of independent movements (including the Union of Messianic Jewish Congregations and Messianic Jewish Alliance of America) and congregations, all of which stress the Jewishness of Jesus who is referred to as Yeshua. One of the best known is Jews for Jesus (formerly known as the Hineni Ministries), founded in 1984.

Methodists. A **Protestant** denomination which owes its origins to the preaching and organizational skill of John Wesley. On Monday April 2, 1739 Wesley, a high church **Anglican** clergyman "submitted to be more vile" (as he says in his journal) and preached to a crowd of 3,000 people on land outside the city of Bristol. It was the start of a life of preaching all over the country, frequently outdoors, often to people who through poverty or despair would never enter a church, but always calling people to repentance from sin, and a faith in Jesus Christ leading to justification with God and the inner assurance of salvation. Banned from many Anglican pulpits he said "The world is my parish" and travelled the length and breadth of the country on horseback.

John Wesley encouraged his followers to go to their local church for worship and the sacraments. However he organized them into "classes", groups of believers who met together each week to learn and encourage each other in the Christian faith. The system may have been based on his contacts with the **Moravians**. They became known as "Methodists"—a name originally applied to a similar group which John and his brother Charles had belonged to whilst at university. Charles wrote hymns which were set to inspiring tunes (often the popular songs of the times by such composers as Handel and Mozart which were a means of teaching the Arminian theology of universal grace which the Wesleys espoused). In 1784 John Wesley ordained two men as presbyters (or priests) and another as a Superintendent (or bishop) prior to their travelling to work in America where there was a desperate shortage of Anglican clergy. This act, which denied the doctrine of the Apostolic Succession, caused an inevitable split between the Anglicans and Methodists, although it did not take place until after Wesley's death in 1791.

Methodism spread rapidly outside Britain as a result of emigration and missionary activity. American Methodists early became independent of the British Methodist Conference. In the USA most of them belong to the United Methodist Church. In the 19th century splits occurred in the British Methodist body caused by differences between those who emphasized lay (i.e. non-priestly) ministry, and worship led by the inspiration and style of the preacher (Primitive Methodists) and those who preferred a liturgy very similar to that of the Church of England (Wesleyan Methodists). The Primitive Methodists were active in social reform, particularly trade unionism.

In the 20th century the various Methodist denominations in Britain have mostly come together to form a single Methodist Church. Both ministers and local preachers have been retained, but it has become normal for only ministers to administer communion, though this right may be given to lay people in exceptional circumstances. Each Methodist society belongs to a circuit, in which the senior minister is called a superintendent. Circuits are part of a District (comparable to an Anglican diocese) led by a Chairman of District. Each level has a representative body and at national level there is the annual Methodist Conference. The President of the Methodist Conference is elected annually. In 1992 Kathleen Richardson became the first woman President.

Most Methodist Churches belong to the World Methodist Council. Many churches overseas, brought into being through missionary work, are now autonomous bodies. Estimated worldwide membership is 26,000,000.

Mevlevis. Members of the **Mawlawiya Sufi** order are sometimes referred to as Mevlevis (from the Turkish) rather than Mawlawis (from the Arabic). They are also popularly known as the Whirling Dervishes.

Mikkyo. *See* **Shingonshu.**

Milli Görüs. Milli Görüs—"national view"—is a conservative Turkish religio–political grouping which promotes a particular synthesis of **Islam** and nationalism. It was closely associated with the religious National Salvation Party in the 1970s, but was banned in the wake of the 1980 military *coup*. Currently it supports the National Salvation Party's successor, the Welfare Party. It is particularly active among the Turkish community in Germany (where, however, it is overshadowed by the **Süleymancis**).

Minzoku Shinto. Folk **Shinto**. Japanese folk religion has been mainly preserved through Shinto. It is basically magico–religious in character, and emphasis is on ritual and taboos, not doctrine or ideas. The calendar year is dotted with festivals, mostly thanksgivings and purifications, which relate to ancient totemistic beliefs. Divination plays a major part in folk belief, and even today palmistry, astrology, fortune-telling the setting of auspicious and inauspicious days and so on are commonplace. The petitioning of *kami* for mundane benefits or protection, ancestor veneration, worship at family altars, and so on have all been embraced by the various religious institutions, but are basically rooted in folk belief.

Many new religious movements take their inspiration from these deep-rooted aspects of the Japanese psyche, and **shamanism**, possession and mediumship proliferate, especially among founder figures.

Mission Covenant Churches. *See* **Congregationalists.**

Mizrahi. *See* **Mafdal.**

Mobilization of the Oppressed. *See* **Bassij-i Mostazafin.**

Mongolian Buddhism. Following their 13th century conquest of Tibet, some of the Mongol élite, notably Khubilai Khan, were converted to **Tibetan Buddhism** by their erstwhile hostage, the **Sakyapa** hierarch Phagpa (1235–1280). But it was the third Dalai Lama, Sonam Gyamtsho (1543–88), who brought the process of converting the Mongols to completion by devoting the last 10 years of his life to missionary work in Mongolia. When his reincarnation, the fourth Dalai Lama, was recognized in Altan Khan's great grandson, the "Golden Descendants" of Genghis Khan became firmly identified with **Gelugpa** Buddhism, and soon all Mongolia adopted the Gelugpa religion.

Yet the deep sincerity and faith so characteristic of Mongolian Buddhism was quickly exploited by China's Manchu emperors, who ingeniously established institutions to control and use Gelugpa Buddhism as a means of eroding Mongolian political and military power. Thus by the early 20th century, even many deeply religious Mongolians perceived a conflict between their religious institutions and their national aspirations for independence from Manchu China.

After 1948, Inner Mongolia remained under Communist China, with the result that Mongolian Buddhism and culture as a whole have been virtually eradicated throughout that region through the permanent resettlement there of a vast preponderance of Chinese immigrants. But Outer Mongolia survived as an independent state under Soviet control, and Mongolian culture and **Buddhism** have fared much better there, despite Communist persecution. With the demise of Soviet Communism, a Buddhist revival is beginning in Outer Mongolia, although political threats from China remain strong enough to prevent the Dalai Lama from visiting. A large quantity of Tibetan-language Buddhist books have survived in Ulan Bator.

Some Mongolian peoples such as the Buryats live in territories now part of Russia, and practise the Gelugpa tradition of Tibetan Buddhism. At the time of writing their future remains unclear, although hopeful. A Gelugpa monastery founded in Tsarist times in St Petersburg has been re-opened, but the full extent of European Russian participation in Tibeto–Mongolian Buddhism is not yet clear.

Moonies. The followers of the Reverend Sun Myung Moon are popularly known as the Moonies. Their organization is more formally known as the **Unification Church.**

Moorish (–American) Science Temple of America. This organization originated in Newark, New Jersey, in 1913 in the preaching of Noble Drew Ali (born Timothy Drew: 1886–1929). Its name was based on Drew's claim that black people were descended from the Moabites of Biblical fame, with Morocco as their true homeland. Moreover, **Islam** was their (and the) true religion.

Following its founder's death in 1929, the movement's leadership was assumed by a young member, R. German Ali, who supervised the steady growth of the movement during the 1940s and 1950s. Since then, however, it has been eclipsed by a rival organization founded by one of Drew Ali's followers, Wallace Fard Muhammad: the Nation of Islam, more popularly known as the **Black Muslims**.

Nevertheless, it still exists in much reduced form, with its particular version of the message of black superiority as contained in its small sacred book, compiled by Drew, entitled *The Holy Koran of the Moorish Science Temple of America*.

Moral Re-armament (MRA). This international movement was founded by an American **Lutheran** minister, Dr Frank Buchman (1878–1961). It began shortly after World War I when Buchman began a tour of European universities holding house-parties and recommending the idea of a "quiet time" in which divine guidance was to be sought. Stress was placed on the four "absolutes": absolute purity, absolute honesty, absolute love, and absolute unselfishness. In the 1920s, groups were set up in more than 60 countries, and in South Africa the name "The Oxford Group" was mistakenly used but came to be adopted with pride. The group was always anxious to secure the good will of important and famous people, which led to suspicions that it had been too uncritical in its attempts to court Hitler.

In 1938, the name "Moral Re-Armament" was adopted and the emphasis shifted from individuals to nations. The aim now was to strengthen national morale, create a better spirit in industry, and provide whole-hearted opposition to Communism. From 1946, MRA world assemblies began to be held at Caux-sur-Montreux, Switzerland.

There are signs that the collapse of Communism could bring a shift to the movement's original emphases.

Moravians. In 1722 a Moravian lay preacher, Christian David, visited Count Zinzendorf of Saxony and persuaded him to allow a group of Moravian religious exiles to settle on the Count's estate. This group belonged to the pietist Unitas Fratrum (Unity of the Brethren), who believed in simple, holy living, closely based on biblical principles, and in sharing faith with unbelievers. They had been exiled from Moravia (now part of Czechoslovakia) following the victory of the Catholics at the Battle of White Mountain in 1620.

These Moravians built a community which they called Herrnhut ("In the Lord's care"). Their communal life was very disciplined: single men lived together in households separate from single women and married couples lived separately from single persons. These separate groups were known as choirs. Soon the Moravians began to travel abroad to share their beliefs. They went to the rest of Europe, North America (where they first settled in Pennsylvania), Greenland, the West Indies and parts of South and East Africa. In England a community was founded in Fetter Lane, London and was attended by John Wesley, the founder of **Methodism**. He first met Moravians on board ship when he was travelling to America in 1735, and was greatly impressed by the depth of their faith. In 1738 he visited and stayed at Herrnhut.

Moravian worship emphasizes Christ and his suffering. The Church has its own hymnbook (Unitas Fratrum produced the first Protestant hymnbook in 1501) and liturgy. Central is the Easter Litany (1749) used at the Easter Dawn service, which is a statement of the Moravian's faith. Moravians have the three traditional orders of ministry—deacon, priest and bishop; only bishops may ordain.

Membership is about 500,000 worldwide, with the largest communities in USA, South Africa and Tanzania. The headquarters is still at Herrnhut in Germany.

Mormons (Church of Latter Day Saints). In 1830 Joseph Smith (1805–1844) from New York, USA published *The Book of Mormon*, a history of a group of Israelites who emigrated from Jerusalem to America in Biblical times. He claimed that the book had been written by the prophet Mormon on gold plates buried in the ground. The prophet's son, Moroni, had appeared to Joseph Smith in 1827, telling him where to find the plates. Using special crystal spectacles (called Urim and Thummim) Joseph was able to translate the plates, and said the *Book of Mormon* was a supplement to the Bible. He said that in 1829 he had been given authority by John the Baptist and the apostles to found a new Church.

Joseph Smith attracted many followers—and enemies. He was murdered while in prison in 1844. His successor, Brigham Young, led a trek across America to Utah, where Salt Lake City became the headquarters of the movement. From 1843 till 1890 Mormons accepted the practice of polygamy which brought them into conflict with neighbouring states. However Mormons also believe in tithing (giving up one-tenth of your income to the church) and many young Mormons go overseas for two years at the age of 18 as missionaries—at their parents' expense.

Mormons believe that God has a body of flesh and has evolved from man. By his own efforts man may become divine. Membership of the Mormon community is essential for salvation. For this reason they are very active in the study of family history, almost every church having its own genealogical library. Dead ancestors who are identified by Mormons are baptized by proxy in a special service.

Mormons have clear standards of behaviour, they avoid tobacco, tea, coffee and alcohol (the communion service is celebrated with water, not wine). There is a strong emphasis on family and on community involvement. Worldwide membership is estimated at about 5,000,000.

Mouvement Croix-Koma. An indigenous new African Christian movement (literally, the Nailed to the Cross movement) in the Congo. It originated in 1964 when a Roman Catholic layman, Ta Malanda, began to attract massive followings in a campaign against witchcraft. Malanda regarded his campaign as a movement within the **Roman Catholic Church** rather than as a separate church. He organized week-long courses, or retreats, at his headquarters in Kankata during which participants learnt to renounce their fetishes (which were then placed on public display). By the time of his death in 1971, an estimated 20 per cent of the population of the Congo—and virtually the entire population of some regions or tribes—had visited Kankata, which became something of a centre of pilgrimage. Subsequently the movement gradually severed its links with the Roman Catholic Church, becoming an independent organization.

Movement of Islamic Resistance. This is a translation of Harakat al-Muqawama al-Islamiya, better known by its acronym of **Hamas**. It is the main Islamic group in the West Bank and Gaza Strip.

Muhammadiyah. The Muhammadiyah (Followers of Muhammad) is a major Muslim socio-religious organization in Indonesia, with several million members. Founded in 1912 by H. Achmad Dahlan and some fellow *ulama* at the traditional Javanese court in Jogjakarta, its origins reflect the influence on South-East Asian Islam of the Islamic modernist **Salafiya** movement in the Middle East.

With increased steamship travel consequent upon the opening of the Suez Canal in 1870, the number of Muslims embarking on the pilgrimage to Mecca also increased, with many of them staying on to study for a while before returning to South East Asia. Having themselves absorbed the reforming modernist ideals, they sought to propagate and implement them through their publications and new schools and organizations in Singapore, Malaysia and Indonesia, coming to be known collectively as the Kaum Muda, or "new faction", in contrast to the "old faction", Kaum Tua.

Focusing on the Quran and *Hadith* at the expense both of medieval tradition and the syncretistic beliefs and practices of local folk **Islam**, the Kaum Muda sought to develop a form of faith which combined fidelity to the teaching and example of Muhammad with clear relevance to the circumstances of the modern world. The Muhammadiyah was founded in Java to pursue these twin aims through establishing a new system of Islamic education to rival—and ideally, perhaps, to replace—the traditional Indonesian *pesantren* system.

Pesantren are a centuries-old institution consisting of local, often rural, centres of Muslim education run by *kiai* (*kiyayi*), the traditional religious leaders. The content of their teaching lacked, from an Islamic modernist's perspective, both doctrinal purity and contemporary relevance. The new schools and boarding schools (*madrasas*), often urban, set up by the Muhammadiyah sought to remedy these defects, and with considerable success, establishing a strong reputation for a good modern education which has incorporated technologies and new methods imported from the West. Such has been the growth and development of the Muhammadiyah education system that it today virtually rivals that of the state, from infant school level right through to university level.

Moreover, in addition to its impressive record in education, Muhammadiyah has been active in welfare work, and now runs a range of orphanages, clinics and hospitals. Also its women's movement, Aisiah, has been noted for its vigour. As an organization, however, Muhammadiyah no longer stands out for creative reformist religious thinking, and young Indonesians inspired by the Islamic renewal of the 1980s have tended to gravitate to local mosque-based associations and Usroh groups outside the older organizations like Muhammadiyah and its traditional rival, **Nahdatul Ulama**.

Unlike Nahdatul Ulama, Muhammadiyah has by and large eschewed political activity, and does not evoke government hostility today under President Suharto any more than previously under Sukarno, or indeed during wartime Japanese or earlier colonial Dutch rule.

Finding its support originally among merchants and traders, the Muhammadiyah has successfully broadened its appeal and now draws widely on members of the state bureaucracy as well as on the rural population.

Muridiya. This 20th century **Sufi** order was founded by Amadu Bamba Mbacke (c1850–1927). The establishment of the order is sometimes seen as an adjustment to the new circumstances of occupation in Senegal after the final defeat of the Wolof by the French in 1886. Amadu Bamba was a member of the **Qadiriya** for a number of years, noted for his personal piety, his unworldliness, learning and poetic skills. In 1891, or thereabouts, he claimed to have seen the angel Gabriel in a vision, calling on him to spread the faith. The site of this experience was later called Touba ("repentance"). The French, concerned that he might lead a *jihad* against them, exiled him to Gabon (1895–1902) and Mauritania (1903–7), during which time he built up a reputation for miracles, such as spreading his prayer mat on the ocean and surviving a fiery furnace and an island of snakes and devils. He is thought to have left the Qadiriya while in Mauritania, teaching the rituals of his own new order. His relations with the French later improved, as he counselled his followers against *jihad,* urging them to "go and work". Before his death in 1927 the Muridiya built a great mosque at

Touba, where he was buried, and which was to become the object of annual pilgrimages.

The Murids venerated their founder as a saint in his lifetime and some even regarded him as God on earth and openly addressed him as such. Crowds gathered around him in the hope of receiving blessing (*baraka*) transmitted in his saliva. The Muridiya has built up a strong economic base in Senegal through taking their founder's advice on work seriously and cultivating peanuts as a major cash crop. Murids are also very active in Senegalese politics, building on the foundations laid between 1920 and 1960 when, it has been said, France governed the economically and politically crucial peanut basin in conjunction with the Murid hierarchy in a kind of indirect rule; a tradition largely continued in independent Senegal under Leopold Senghor and Abdou Diouf.

Musar Movement. (*See also* **Orthodox Judaism.**) Musar (Hebrew, instruction) in its general sense refers to Jewish ethical literature, more narrowly it refers the late 19th century ethical movement founded in Lithuania by Rabbi Israel (Lipkin) Salanter (1810–83). He created a system of vigorous self-examination that he insisted was a vital part of religious and spiritual development alongside Torah study and observance of the commandments. Its aim was not merely a formal intellectual study of ethical literature but the development of the emotions and the spiritual virtues, such as humility. It involved directed meditation on ethical literature and practical exercises. The Musar *shmooz* (or *shmues*—ethical discourse and associated practices) as directed by the *Masgiah Ruhani* (Hebrew, spiritual supervisor) are now part of the curriculum in Lithuanian-type *Yeshivot* (institutes of higher education).

Muslim Brotherhood. The Muslim Brotherhood (Ikhwan al-Muslimin) is the most visibly successful of the 20th-century Islamic reformist organizations in the Arab world. It was founded in 1928 or 1929 by Hasan al-Banna (1906–49), a primary schoolteacher in the Suez Canal port of Ismailiyya, Egypt. His father had studied under the great modernist scholar Muhammad 'Abduh at al-Azhar, and he himself came under the influence of 'Abduh's disciple, Rashid Rida, while training in Cairo to be a teacher. He was strongly affected by the reformist ideas of the **Salafiya**, but was also an active member of a minor **Sufi** order, the Hasafiya, into which he was initiated by the son of its founder. The new movement clearly bore the marks of both these tendencies in al-Banna's thought and he described it as "a Salafi message, a **Sunni** way, a Sufi truth, a political organization, an athletic group, a scientific and cultural union, an economic enterprise and a social idea".

The Brotherhood may be seen as arising out of the frustration of Egyptian Muslims with the unwillingness, or inability, of the official religious scholars and Sufi orders to confront the actualities of occupation by the unbelieving British, and corruption and growing secularism in the upper *échelons* of Egyptian society. It may be seen as no accident that the Brotherhood should have thrived in Ismailiyya, the town housing the headquarters of the Suez Canal Company and the British forces stationed in Egypt. Al-Banna became the first Supreme Guide of the Brothers, providing a leadership not unlike that of a Sufi shaikh to his disciples. Below him the movement was organized in a strict hierarchy under a Guidance Council with several committees. Members belonged to "families", cells of five to 10 Brothers, families then being formed into clans, clans into groups and groups into battalions, the largest units. From 1942 a special section was established, devoted to the *jihad* against both foreign occupiers and the decadent society within.

The early membership of the Brotherhood was drawn largely from the rural working class in the 1930s. By the 1940s it was becoming more firmly based among the urban lower middle class, and subsequently gaining support among university students and staff, civil servants and professionals. The Brotherhood operated as a highly successful propaganda machine through its publishing ventures, schools, athletics clubs, and campaigns to promote literacy and hygiene, in addition to more traditional-style mosque addresses. The message was essentially of the need to break away from the blind imitation of past authorities, to accept only the Quran and the most reliable *hadith*s as sources of the Holy Law (Shari'a), to work towards a totally just Islamic society. Brothers were to perform their religious duties strictly and lead good moral lives, abstaining from alcohol, gambling and fornication, avoiding usury and not playing or listening to music, dancing or watching corrupting entertainments. Their womenfolk were to be educated to become good wives and mothers, to wear "legal" dress, not to work alongside men or attend mixed gatherings. Despite al-Banna's personal commitment to Sufism, most Brothers came to oppose it as no true part of **Islam**. The movement had from its beginnings been anti-imperialist and became also anti-**Zionist**, anti-Communist and frequently hostile to Christians viewed as the new Crusaders threatening the Islamic world.

On the death of al-Banna, murdered by the secret police in 1949, the number of Muslim Brothers in Egypt was estimated at around 500,000. The leadership of the movement was assumed by Hasan al-Hudaybi, a judge, who was anxious to promote the image of the Brotherhood as a respectable, moderate organization that renounced terrorism. Nevertheless, the Brothers continued to be involved in anti-British agitation and took an active part in the riots of January 1952, allying themselves with the Free Officers who took over in the July coup. Yet relations soured between Nasser and the Brothers, since the new régime's brand of socialism and nationalism conflicted with their desire for an Islamic state and allegiance to a wider Islamic community. In November 1954 a Brotherhood plot against Nasser was uncovered, leading to the arrest of many members, including al-Hudaybi, and the official dissolution of the movement.

Among those arrested was Sayyid Qutb (1906–66), the radical ideologue of the Muslim Brothers. During his 10 years in gaol he became ever more convinced of the need for a tougher approach to seeking the reformation of Egyptian society, sunk so far in corruption and decadence as to constitute a society that was no longer Islamic but *jahili*, "ignorant" of the true religion in the same way as the society of pre-Islamic Arabia. The best known expression of his revolutionary position is contained in *Signposts*, a book written mainly in prison and published around the time of his release in 1964, but banned by the government not long after its publication. Shortly afterwards Qutb was again arrested, implicated in a new plot against Nasser, sentenced to death, and hanged on Aug. 29, 1966. His ideas and example inspired a number of members to leave the mainstream Brotherhood and form their own militant groups, such as **al-Takfir wa'l-Hijrah**. Meanwhile the more moderate leadership was later accommodated by Presidents Sadat and Mubarak and, although prevented from operating as a separate political organization, the Muslim Brothers participated in the April 1987 parliamentary elections by putting up candidates in alliance with the Liberals and Socialist Labour Party, and succeeded in gaining a number of seats. However, in an atmosphere of souring relations with the government, the Brothers boycotted the elections of November 1990.

Outside Egypt the Muslim Brotherhood has spread to other Arab countries, sometimes existing under other names, for instance in Algeria as Ahl al-Da'wa (People of the Call) and in Tunisia as al-Hizb al-Islami (the Islamic Party). In Jordan it achieved notable successes in the November 1989 parliamentary elections and Brotherhood candidates have been appointed to key ministries. In Algeria Brothers were very active in 1991 in organizing Islamic opposition to the socialist régime and demanding an Islamic state. However, in Syria they were suppressed and forced underground after violent struggles with the Baathist régime of Hafiz al-Asad from the mid-1970s to early 1980s. Since July 1980 membership in the Syrian Brotherhood has been illegal and punishable by death.

Muslim Parliament of Great Britain. Established in the UK in 1991, this organization has made claims that it will become a truly representative expression of British Muslims. This seems unlikely, not least because its main protagonist, Dr Kalim Siddiqui, is also the Director of the Muslim Institute, and an ardent advocate of the current Iranian form of **Islam**. Initial concerns of the Muslim Parliament have included Muslim education in Britain, economic conditions of Muslims in Britain, and discrimination arising out of *The Satanic Verses* affair. It has also called for volunteers to fight (in defence of Muslims) in the former Yugoslavia.

Muslim World League. The Muslim World League (Rabitat al-'Alam al-Islami) was established in 1962 in Mecca, where it continues to be based. Founded partly to establish Saudi leadership against the leadership claims of President Nasser and his Arab nationalist cause, the League has come to assume many of the activities of the Pakistan-based **World Muslim Congress**, and currently reflects Saudi determination to appear as the chief spokesperson of normative (**Sunni**, even **Wahhabi**) **Islam** in order to counter Iran's (**Shi'ite**) claim to a comparable role.

The organization promotes the dissemination of the faith, and supports Muslims worldwide, including those in minority situations: its permanent Secretariat in Mecca includes Departments of Islamic Culture, of Publicity and Publications, of Muslim Minorities, and of Islamic Law and Jurisprudence. By its own admission, 99 per cent of its finances come from the Saudi government, and critics—not only the Iranians—regard it as a tool of the Saudi régime.

It has encouraged the formation of regional councils of Islamic organizations, for instance the Islamic Co-ordinating Council of North America, and the European Council of Mosques, and has sponsored a variety of Islamic associations, mosques (through its subsidiary, the Mecca-based Supreme World Council of Mosques) and conferences around the world. It employs approximately 1,000 missionaries worldwide (one third of these in Africa and another third in Indonesia), and trains imams, preachers and missionaries in its training centre in Mecca. It also sponsors the World Assembly of Muslim Youth, and publishes the informative English-language version of its monthly journal, *The Muslim World League Journal*. In 1974 it became a member of the non-governmental organizations of the UN. It has on occasion been referred to as the religious counterpart to the more political **Organization of the Islamic Conference**.

Musta'lis. The Musta'lis are the smaller of the two main surviving branches of **Isma'ili Shi'ism**. They are sometimes also known as the Tayibis. When the Fatimid Caliph al-Mustansir died in 1094, followers of his younger son al-Musta'li distinguished themselves from the **Nizaris**. The sect originally transferred its centre from Egypt to the Yemen, where it still exists under the name of Sulaymanis. In the early 17th century, a distinct line of leaders (*da'is*) emerged, whose followers are known as Daudis (or in India commonly **Bohoras**). Apart from their main centre in Gujarat, there are also numbers of Daudis in East Africa, Mauritius, Myanmar (Burma), and elsewhere. They probably number about 300,000.

N

Nagas. Nagas are a semi-military ascetic order in **Hinduism**, venerating Shiva as their deity. The Nagas go naked or "sky-clad", covering their bodies with ashes, bearing tridents, and wearing their hair long and matted in imitation of their god. As part of the **Dashanami** monastic order, philosophically they adopt the monism of Shankara's Advaita **Vedanta**. Nagas live in monasteries or can be peripatetic ascetics. Every 12 years at the great Kumbha Mela festival, the Nagas are among the first to enter and bathe in the holy Ganges, indicating their high esteem in the hierarchy of Hindu monastic orders. The name *naga* probably comes from *nagna* or "naked", rather than from the name for the snake-deities of Indian mythology.

Nahda Movement/Party. These terms are used somewhat loosely to refer to one of two groups. One is the Mouvement de la Nahda Islamique, or Islamic Renaissance Movement (**Hamas**), in Algeria; the other is the currently more influential **Hizb al-Nahda,** or Renaissance Party, in Tunisia. The latter was known until 1988 as the Mouvement de la Tendance Islamique, or Islamic Tendency Movement.

Nahdatul Ulama. The Nahdatul Ulama (NU)—Union of Muslim Teachers—is perhaps the largest Muslim organization in Indonesia. It was founded in 1926 by traditionalist *ulama* disturbed by the rapidly growing appeal of the Islamic modernist organization, **Muhammadiyah**, founded 14 years earlier in 1912. Against the reformist challenge of the system of more modern education being established by the Muhammadiyah, the Nahdatul Ulama sought to safeguard the position of the traditional, largely rural, centres of learning known as *pesantren* or *pondoks*. These were in effect the power base of the *ulama*, or *kyai* (*kiyayi*) as they are known in Java, the religious leaders who taught in them and indeed often owned them.

The continued flourishing of the *pesantren*, with the families of the *ulama*, staff and students all living together on the premises, would be seen by the Nahdatul Ulama as a sign of its success, yet although it is today a larger organization than the Muhammadiyah, the latter's record in education and welfare work is stronger. Moreover, while committed originally to preserving a very traditionalist curriculum of Islamic education in the face of the Salafiya-inspired reforms advocated by the Muhammadiyah, over the years the NU-run *pesantren* too have adopted a broader outlook, and subjects such as science, technology, modern languages, economics and business studies are now widely accepted. In that sense it would be misleading today to present the difference between the NU and the Muhammadiyah in terms of a simple traditionalist-modernist dichotomy despite continuing major differences in theology.

In 1953 the NU became a political party, with a concentration of electoral support in East Java, and under Sukarno it held responsibility for the Ministry of Religious Affairs. In the 1970s it emerged as the dominant party in the federation of four Muslim political parties imposed by the Suharto régime and deliberately given a non-Muslim label, Partai Persatuan Pembangunan (PPP), Unity Development Party. The government's policy of undermining specifically Muslim parties culminated in the PPP's adoption, in 1984, under intense pressure, of the state Pancasila ideology as its sole ideological foundation. The Five Tenets include belief in one God, but deliberately refrain both from specifying this in Muslim terms and also from including a clause specifying that Muslims are bound by the *syaria* (Shari'a).

The intense pressures to which the NU was subject during the government's Pancasila campaign were a prime cause of the factionalism to which it succumbed in the early 1980s, and since 1984 it has withdrawn from politics with the aim of reverting to being the sort of socio–religious organization it was before 1953. One effect of this has been to weaken dramatically the power of *ulama* to deal with local grievances, because there are no longer NU politicians whose support they can enlist. Electoral support for the PPP has declined dramatically too.

Although the NU's abdication of political involvement derives from a declared aim of "returning to its 1926 roots", the current climate of Islamic resurgence is very different from that prevalent when the NU was founded. It remains to be seen how it will adapt to the changed circumstances. Now as then, though, the *pesantren* constitute its indispensable base.

Nakali Nirankaris. Literally, false **Nirankaris.** A Sikh-derived splinter group more regularly called the **Sant Nirankari Mandal.**

Namdharis. A **Sikh** reform movement. Baba Balak Singh, 1799–1861, protested against moral laxity in the Panth, especially the use of drugs and alcohol, lavish weddings and the giving of dowries. He also condemned meat-eating though this was never proscribed by the *Gurus*. Namdharis believe that Guru Gobind Singh did not die in 1708 or end the line of human guruship but appointed Balak Singh in his stead. The present Guru has his headquarters at Baini Sahib in the Punjab.

Khalsa Sikhs often lump Namdharis and **Nirankaris** together as heretical movements. In fact Namdharis differ significantly from the latter by their insistence on a reformed and restored *khalsa*, rather than a return to the pristine teachings of Nanak. Nevertheless they are more obviously wayward, from the khalsa perspective, than the Nirankaris because of their continuing belief in a living guru. Namdhari men are distinguished by their white homespun cotton clothing and turbans tied horizontally across the forehead. They are also known as Kukas.

Nanak Panth. The community of followers of Guru Nanak (1469–1539). A name applied to the early **Sikh** community, for whom Nanak is the first guru in a sequence of 10, and more latterly to those Sahajdhari Sikhs who disregard the discipline of the *khalsa* as established by the final Guru, Gobind Singh in 1699. The central practice of Panthis is the remembrance of the Divine Name (*nam simaran*), though Nanak himself may also be venerated. The **Nirankaris** are, in essence, part of the Panth.

Nañiguismo. This is a Cuban Afro–American spiritist cult about which, due to its secretive nature, relatively little is known. It appears to involve secret societies which practise certain rituals derived ultimately from **African traditional religion** in Nigeria: apparently it originated in Calabar and was taken to Cuba in the 19th century.

Naqshabandiya. This great **Sufi** order is probably the most widespread after the **Qadiriya**, frequently associated with reform and with resistance to attacks on **Islam**. Originating in Central Asia in the 12th–13th centuries, the first Naqshabandi masters traced their spiritual line of descent back to the early caliphs of Islam, Abu Bakr and 'Ali, and are said to have followed in the tradition of the Malamatis ("Blameworthy ones"), who sought to attract blame by disguising their true inner piety by outwardly impious behaviour. 'Abd al-Khaliq al-Ghujdawani (d. 1220) is credited with laying down the basic rules of the order and developing the practice of the silent recollection of God (*dhikr khafi*) as against the vocal *dhikr* of other orders. The name of the order derives from Baha al-din al-Naqshabandi (1318–89), himself a Tajik from a village near Bokhara, whose famous mausoleum became one of the major places of pilgrimage in Central Asia. Probably his best known saying, and one which epitomizes the Naqshabandi outlook, is that "the exterior is for this world, the interior for God".

Naqshabandis believe in seeking spiritual communication with the holy dead, especially past masters of the order, who may make contact in dreams and visions, sometimes in the vicinity of their tombs or shrines. Thus some Naqshabandi shaikhs have claimed to be initiated by dead predecessors. Outwardly the Naqshabandis live fully in the world, at times associating with temporal rulers, at times active in opposing them, but always journeying inwardly with God and aspiring to replace base with virtuous qualities. They concentrate on God in their characteristic silent remembrance, seeking to form a mental image of the heart with God's name inscribed on it, and practising techniques of breath control as an aid to constant consciousness of God. They may also meet for gatherings with vocal remembrance, but in times of persecution this has not always been possible and is not essential.

The Naqshabandiya spread southwards into India in the 16th century, where it developed new directions under the inspiration of Ahmad Sirhindi (1563–1603), often known as the "renewer (*mujaddid*) of the second millennium". His branch of the order was therefore called the Mujaddidiya ("renewerist"). It was strongly **Sunni**, concerned with the strict application of Holy Law (Shari'a) and assertion of a purified Islam in the face of any attempts at accommodation with **Hinduism**. Probably the most celebrated among reforming Naqshabandi shaikhs in India was Shah Wali Allah of Delhi (1702–62), who pioneered the translation of the Quran, urged a fresh examination of the Quran and Traditions and the need to compare them with the views of all four Sunni legal schools in order to overhaul the system of Islamic law. He also wished to see a range of social and economic reforms, and his ideas have had a continuing influence among Muslims of the Indian subcontinent far beyond Naqshabandi circles.

The Mujaddidi branch of the Naqshabandiya was introduced into the Ottoman Empire in the 17th century, where it flourished in Turkey and Syria, enjoying special popularity among religious scholars. In Damascus it gained yet another new sub-order at the hands of the Kurdish Shaikh Khalid al-Shahrazuri (1776–1827), who, like Sirhindi, emphasized strict uncompromising Sunnism and adherence to the Holy Law, and was notably hostile to Christians and Jews. The Khalidi influence extended to Turkey and Iraq (where it became linked to Kurdish nationalism) and into South East Asia, where it remains active in rural communities in Sumatra and Java. In Turkey the Naqshabandiya was officially suppressed by Ataturk in 1925 along with other orders, following a rebellion by Kurdish Naqshabandis. Although still banned, it has resumed its activities in recent years and appears to have a large, politically conscious membership opposed to the Turkish secular state.

In its homeland in Central Asia the Naqshabandiya was in the forefront of resistance to 19th-century Russian imperialism. Under the Soviet state it managed to survive in secret with very wide support. It seems to have been helped by its ability to infiltrate the ranks of the Communist Party and KGB in line with the traditional Naqshabandi policy of seeking to influence rulers. It was also well-designed not to attract attention by its practices of silent *dhikr* and inconspicuous small group meetings. It can be expected to flourish in the present atmosphere.

At the peripheries the Naqshabandiya was introduced into China in the 18th century, where it gave rise to the New Sect marked by its militancy and involvement in rebellions in the 19th century. In Western Europe Naqshabandis are reported as active in Germany, France and Britain, with groups meeting in a number of cities, including Birmingham and Oxford.

Naths. Naths or Kanphatas are an order of **Hindu** yogis, recognizable by their split ears (*kan-phata*) and large earrings given them at initiation. Naths either shave their heads or grow their hair long, wear ochre robes, apply ashes from their fires to themselves and carry a begging bowl and a staff. They have a number of monasteries throughout India, some of which belong to the sub-sects of the order. Naths are generally **Shaivas,** though in western India they tend to be **Vaishnavas** and in Nepal they can be **Buddhists.**

Theoretically only higher castes are initiated, though there are exceptions to this rule and sometimes women are admitted. At initiation the yogi takes a vow of celibacy and vows not to engage in paid employment thus ensuring poverty and reliance on the laity. The tradition's founders are said to have been the legendary figure Matsyendranath and his disciple Gorakhnath (c1200 CE) who wrote one of the tradition's major texts. Naths teach that liberation from the cycle of reincarnation is possible in life by developing a perfected or divine body. Such a body is created through the practice of hatha yoga and by awakening the dormant energy within the body called the "snake-power" or *Kundalini Shakti.* Another practice of the Naths is turning the tongue, after cutting the frenum, back into the throat in order to catch the drops of the nectar of immortality (*amrta*) dripping from the crown of the head.

Nation of Islam. This was the name originally given to the US movement which later became famous as the **Black Muslims.** This movement subsequently changed its name twice, in 1976 to World Community of Islam in the West, and in 1980 to American Muslim Mission.

These changes were accompanied by major doctrinal shifts which were not to everyone's taste within the movement. The original name has been retained by two or three different groups which sought to perpetuate the original Black Muslim ideology. Easily the largest of these is that led by Louis Farrakhan, with an estimated 5,000 to 10,000 members, but there is also a small splinter group led by the self-styled Caliph, Emmanuel Abdullah Muhammad, and another led by John Muhammad, brother of the founder Elijah Muhammad.

National Religious Party. *See* **Mafdal.**

Native American Church. This is a loose umbrella organization drawing members from over 50 different tribes, and best understood as an expression of **Peyotism.**

Native American Religions. The native tribes of the North American continent have developed, over thousands of years, an enormous variety of religious beliefs and practices. Each tribe effectively has its own unique religious configuration, thus making it essential that we speak of religions and making it difficult to make generalizations. Although much has been lost and/or destroyed following European contact, much still survives, necessitating the use of the ethnographic present tense in describing Native American beliefs and practices.

Underlying all these religions are nonetheless some common core concerns: the first has to do with a world view based around origin myths which speak of a time when humans and other beings were not differentiated as they are today. This forms the basis of the widespread native American concern with the essential cosmic harmony in the universe—a harmony in which humans, animals, trees and plants, natural phenomena and supernatural powers each play a role. It is often difficult to distinguish "natural" and "supernatural" in native American thought, since the natural world is imbued with the sacred. This is not to suggest that the whole universe is sacred, since native Americans distinguish certain places, objects and phenomena as sacred. Nonetheless, the natural world is of prime concern since sacred power manifests commonly through natural phenomena. Relationships to the sacred are of central concern, particularly to animal aspects of the sacred and in most of North America it is common for individuals to seek a "guardian spirit", often through a "vision quest".

The acquisition of a guardian spirit is widespread among native Americans, except in the south-west. One acquires a guardian spirit through a vision or dream, or in some cases through inheritance or purchase. Guardian spirits are usually animal in form, though they can take virtually any form. Guardian spirits give power and help to their owners and the latter often carry amulets, medicine bundles or other outward representations of their spirit. Powerful spirits can give an individual the power to cure others and he or she usually becomes a *shaman* or medicine man (*see* **Shamanism**).

Most typical is the acquisition of a guardian spirit through "vision quest". One of the most distinguishing features of many native American tribes, the vision quest reflects the importance of a personal relationship to, and experience of, the sacred. Typically associated with a rite of passage as well as the acquisition of a guardian spirit, the practice involves the supplicant retiring, after a period of purification through fasting, praying and use of sweat lodge (see below), to an isolated place where he continues to fast and pray until granted a vision or dream where a spirit appears, which will then grant a song and bestow certain powers. The individual then assembles a medicine bundle comprised of objects associated with the spirit. If the vision so indicates, the individual may embark on a career as a *shaman*, or medicine man. Repetition of the experience is seen as a way of renewing power.

The sweat lodge is a widespread native American rite of purification involving the construction of a domed lodge made from saplings and covered with blankets or skins. A pit in the centre holds heated rocks on to which water is poured, making the dark interior hot. Individuals pray and smoke. The rite serves both as a means of renewing a close relationship with the sacred as well as purifying oneself in preparation for further rites, such as the vision quest. The sweat lodge has undergone a considerable revival, and is one of the central rites to be found in the movement called **Pan-Indianism**.

Native Americans traditionally perceive time in cyclical terms, not linear ones; some Indian languages lack terms of past and future, consequently everything is potentially in the present, including the time of myth, which is why myth and the world of the sacred are so potent and accessible. This cyclical view is represented symbolically in the widespread use of circles to denote the universe. Each tribe generally has established a close and intimate link to the territory they inhabit, and particular landforms and sites can have great religious significance.

A broad differentiation can be made between hunting tribes and agricultural ones in terms of religious orientation. Hunting tribes generally place strong emphasis on individualism and individual relationships to the sacred. There is much animal ceremonialism and crisis rituals mediated by a *shaman* or medicine man who uses helping spirits to cure the sick, locate game and lead other rituals, including an annual ceremony of cosmic rejuvenation such as the Sun Dance.

One of the best-known ceremonies of the native Americans of the Plains, the Sun Dance is at heart an annual renewal ceremony, taking place during the summer and involving the construction of a lodge, having cosmological significance. At its centre is the Sun Dance pole, representative of the world pillar. Typically individuals made a pledge to perform a rite, involving purification and dancing facing the sun. Among the Lakota, there is the piercing of the supplicants' skin with skewers which are then fastened by rope to the pole. The supplicant dances and prays whilst attempting to tear himself free of his bonds, representing both sacrifice of flesh and freeing from ignorance. This activity is a means of achieving individual power, as well as cosmic renewal and reaffirming the well-being of the tribe as a whole. Suppressed at the end of the 19th century, this ceremony was practised clandestinely until the 1950s, and has undergone a significant revival since then.

Agricultural societies, on the other hand, in contrast to the hunting tribes, tend to have more anthropomorphic spirits, stress rain and fertility ceremonies, which occur regularly at the same time each year, and are usually under the direction of medicine societies, rather than individual specialists. Clearly the more settled peoples can develop more permanent shrines, temples and material artifacts than the more nomadic hunters. Some of the most elaborate ceremonialism was found on the north-west coast, where ample food supplies and large permanent settlements allowed the development of an enormously rich culture, with animal masks, totem poles (a form of family heraldic denoting spirits with which the family had a close relationship) and a sacred half of the year when individuals were initiated over a period of months into religious societies.

Much of this latter culture and many others were lost due to the destructive effects of European culture, in particular the deliberate suppression of native religious practices in the late 19th century. Resistance to White encroachment was mainly military, but there were some religious responses, notably the millenarian movement known as the Ghost Dance, which flourished at the end of the 19th century under its founder, a Paiute Indian called Wovoka.

Most syncretic religious responses tended to be either short-lived or very localized, the most notable exception being the widespread Peyote Cult, or **Peyotism**. Many native Americans became Christians, whilst trying to maintain a distinctly Indian identity. In recent years on a tribal level there have been increased efforts to maintain and revitalize traditional practices, and to regain possession of, or access to, sacred sites lost under earlier unjust treaties. On a national level, certain religious practices, including "sweat lodge" have been utilized by younger Indians from different tribes in Pan-Indianism.

All tribes have been affected, in varying degrees, by the coming of the Europeans. Hunting tribes particularly have suffered enormously from loss of territory and game, as well as the universal effects of disease and cultural suppression, but traditional religious practices continue to flourish, particularly in the south-west.

Nazarenes. This was an early name for Christians (Acts 24, 5) and later an early sect of **Christianity**.

The Church of the Nazarene is the largest of the Holiness (Perfectionist) churches. It was formed early in the 20th century through a number of mergers and came to Britain in 1906 through the work of George Sharpe in Scotland. Its headquarters are in Kansas, USA and it is believed to have over 800,000 adherents. Church government is democratic, and similar to the **Methodists**. The Nazarenes administer colleges, hospitals and schools and are active in missionary work.

Neo-Buddhism. A term coined to denote the **Buddhism** of social protest established in India, more specifically in Maharashtra state, by Dr B. R. Ambedkar in the early 1950s. Neo-Buddhist ideals are represented today by the **Buddhist Society of India** and the **TBMSG**.

Neo-Catechumenal Way. *See* **Roman Catholic Church**.

Neo-Hasidism. (*See also* **Hasidism; Jewish New Agers.**) The name given to the diffuse and wide-scale interest in Hasidic literature and teachings among contemporary non-Hasidic Jews. Whereas Hasidim follow the Rebbe of their particular Hasidic dynasty, the neo-Hasid is not bound in this way. Also, Hasidim live completely within a social and religious framework centred on their Rebbe, while the neo-Hasid utilizes Hasidic materials as one of the sources and resources for his/her Jewish spiritual life. Neo-Hasidism is often associated with Martin Buber, whose translations and romantic renderings of Hasidic tales and interpretative writings on Hasidic themes were the main vehicle for the transmission of Hasidic teachings to the non-Hasidic world.

Neo-Orthodoxy. *See* **Orthodox Judaism**.

Neo-Paganism. This label is often used to refer to the modern revival of **Paganism**: the two terms are not infrequently used interchangeably.

Nestorians. The Nestorian Church represents an ancient form of Eastern **Christianity** separate both from the **Orthodox Church (Byzantine tradition)** and from the **Oriental Orthodox Churches,** though sometimes loosely grouped with the latter. Also known as the "Assyrian" or "East Syrian" Church, the Nestorian Church dates back to the fifth century, taking its name from bishop Nestorius, Patriarch of Constantinople, whose teachings were condemned by the Council of Ephesus (431). Nestorius taught that in Christ were two separate persons, the human and the divine, in opposition to the prevailing view that Christ was a single person with two natures. For Nestorius, Mary the mother of the human Jesus could not be venerated as "Mother of God" (Theotokos), as she was by those who accepted the decrees of the Council.

The original stronghold of Nestorianism was Mesopotamia (Iraq and Iran), and there were also Nestorian missions to India and the Far East. Nestorian missionaries probably established the original Malabar community of South India (*see* **Syro–Indian Churches**). The influence and population of Nestorianism in the Middle East and Asia were dramatically reduced during the Mongol invasions of the 14th century, and the surviving remnant was further reduced and dispersed during World War I.

The Nestorians worship in ancient Syriac, mainly using the Liturgy of Addai and Mari. The patriarch of the Church is known as the Catholicos of the East, which is a hereditary office, passing from uncle to nephew. Baghdad in Iraq was the main centre of the Nestorian Church for most of its history, but in recent decades the Catholicos has for political reasons lived outside Iraq, first (from 1940) in the United States, where there is a small Nestorian diasporate, and more recently (since 1976) in Tehran (Iran). A schismatic Nestorian Church also exists; its rival Catholicos was in 1972 officially recognized by Iraq as the true patriarch of the Nestorians. Today the Nestorians number roughly 100,000 worldwide.

Neturei Karta. (*See also* **Haredi; Orthodox Judaism; Zionism.**) The Neturei Karta (Aramaic, "Guardians of the City") are one of the groups that make up the Haredi (Ultra-Orthodox) community of Israel (Edah Haredi. NB.

sometimes this term is used more narrowly to refer to the "hard" separatist communities). Neturei Karta is the most vocal of the **Ashkenazi,** anti-Zionist groups who do not recognize the legitimacy of the State of Israel, and maintain a campaign throughout the diaspora protesting at the "desecration" of Jewish life in the "unbeliever" state of Israel. Originally part of the communities that were represented by **Agudat Israel,** the Neturei broke away in the 1930s, rejecting what they saw as Agudat compromises with the secularists and breaches in the separatist Ultra-Orthodox life established in pre-state Palestine. They are still stridently anti-Agudat Israel.

Like other Haredi groups they live *Yeshivah*-centred lives, strictly observe the commandments, follow their rabbinic leaders and refuse to use Hebrew as their daily vernacular and speak Yiddish. In addition, they also refuse any activity that could be deemed as co-operation or recognition of the Zionists. Thus, they refuse to use Israeli currency; would prefer to live "in exile" under Palestinian Arab rule, and "celebrate" Israel's Independence Day as a day of mourning.

The ranks of the Neturei Karta are filled with the Reb Arelah (a Hungarian "sect" that follows the teachings of Rabbi Aaron (Reb Arelah) Roth, and broke away from the **Satmar Hasidim,** distinguished by their gold-braided frockcoats) and other extreme Ultra-Orthodox groups.

The Neturei Karta, although small in numbers, have been reasonably effective at limiting the activities of the "compromisers", such as Agudat Israel, by their constant programme of pressure and propaganda.

New Age. On the surface, the New Age looks as though it provides a bewildering and conflictual array of beliefs and activities. Virtually all forms of religious life are utilized, from eastern mysticism to "**pagan**" traditions of Europe and North America. New Agers work with crystals; serve as channels in order to receive messages from spiritual agencies; practise holistic healing; or tap into the energy provided by the earth Goddess. Some favour hallucinogenic drugs (ecstasy is currently in vogue); others go on enlightenment intensives, or practice meditation.

Beneath this apparent diversity, however, there lies a distinctive account of what it is to be human. Essentially, the New Age is all about self-religiosity. The self, itself, is held to be perfect, the source of truth, wisdom, energy, creativity and tranquility. Indeed, the Self is often called "God" or the "Goddess".

New Agers are able to engage in an apparently heterogeneous set of activities, drawn from many religious traditions, because they believe that these are all means to the same end: discovering the perfection that lies within. These paths—enlightenment seminars of the **est** variety, finding "attunement" with nature (for the Self-God is typically held to exist within the natural order as a whole as well as in the human body), or (even) hard and conventionally futile manual labour—are all held to serve to liberate the self from the contaminating effects of life in contemporary society. The New Age will dawn when people discover their true nature, casting off the destructive effects of having been socialized to perform in the unnatural constructs of mainstream life: the nuclear family; the capitalist enterprise; or the competitive educational system.

New Agers have a major problem: what should be done about the unenlightened mainstream of society? Some, following that earlier eruption of the New Age, namely the spiritual wing of the counter-culture of the later 1960s, have chosen to ignore this difficulty. They reject the mainstream as much as possible—in the UK, for example, living on the dole in squats, retreating to small-holdings in the Celtic fringe, or joining the bands of travellers who roam from free festival to free festival (at least during summer months)—of which Glastonbury is perhaps the most well known. In contrast, others are hard at work aiming to "transform" mainstream institutions. They run management trainings for large companies, attempt to influence the political process (as with the Natural Law Party in Britain and the New Age wing of the environmentalist movement), or seek to find ways of interfusing New Age experiences with **Christianity** and the health profession.

Overall, the New Age is best regarded as a highly celebratory form of spiritual humanism. As such, it is rooted in deep-seated cultural trajectories: the Western Romantic tradition; the American evolution of New Thought-cum-**Positive Thinking**; the progressive introduction of Eastern spirituality to the West; and, more generally, the ever-increasing tendency for us to ascribe value to the self.

Conventionally dated from the 19th century, when the East significantly impacted on religiosity in the West (cf. the founding of the **Theosophical Society** in New York in 1875), New Age retreats, programmes, "seminars" and disciplines have proliferated. This is not to say that there are commensurate numbers of full-time New Agers.

The New Age is best seen as comprising a diverse range of (oft-competing) means to the common end of self-sacralization, which is now firmly established as a significant "how to change your life" complex, pronounced by the spiritually informed experts of the field. There might not be many fully-fledged New Agers, but there are plenty of people who tap into New Age cultural resources—the bookshops, the spiritual therapy centres, the New Age holiday facilities, the management training courses and the health provision outlets—when the occasion demands. A recent Gallup Poll reports that 12,000,000 are New Age inclined in the USA.

The future of the New Age seems assured. Here is a universalized spirituality grounded in a global scheme/vision. It claims authority from a wide range of traditions. Here is a development which chimes in with the celebratory individualism of so much of our time. Hence it is much more appealing than the "fallen man, listen to God out there" dynamic characteristic of traditional Christianity. And here is a development which appeals to all those who feel anxious about the effects of modernity: from the impact on the environment (Mother Earth) to humankind itself. The New Age might not be an organized and conspiratorial "movement" (as it has been described), but it is a movement in the sense of having a dynamic career.

Counting against this optimistic scenario of the future, the New Age is controversial. A number of key figures have disgraced themselves. Accusations of psychological coercion are not unknown. And leading New Agers have a habit (so it might seem) of going over the top with their promises: and so estranging those who might be looking in their direction to "unlock potential".

The New Age exemplifies strands of "late" modernity—in particular, some argue, exaggerating the authority and value of the self—and in so doing it is almost certainly paving the way for its own "transformation", or day of reckoning, in the future. As some commentators suppose, the New Age is an Age too far. According to this account, its future appeal could well be undermined by the probability that faith in human-kindness will have to face the fact that there will be competition for ever-increasing scarcity of resources.

New Church of Jerusalem. The name of the formal organization in **Swedenborgianism.**

New Sect Shinto. A name used to denote various modern groups within **Kyoha Shinto**, such as **Omotokyo**.

New Testament Church of God. This is a West Indian **Pentecostal** church which is one of the black churches which have become well established in the UK with a national headquarters and regional organizations.

New Thought. This movement, originally of 19th century origin, is currently known as **Positive Thinking.**

Nichirenshoshu. A form of Japanese **Buddhism** derived from the teachings of Nichiren, although often classified as a new religion with its origins in the early 20th century.

Nichirenshoshu (the True Nichiren School) claims Nichiren (1222–1282), who has *bodhisattva* status in some circles, as its religious source, and Nichiko his disciple, as sectarian founder. The movement has become distinctly international, attracting the young, pop stars and entertainers. This is often accounted for by the "this-worldly" nature of Nichiren Buddhism, which in its modern milieu has become notable for advocating chanting (*daimoku*) for mundane and material ends, based on Nichiren's teaching that the benefits of practice are attainable here and now. Nichirenshoshu claims that Nichiren Buddhism should be established as the state religion and that Japan should be the platform from which the truth introduced to the rest of the world.

The Daisekiji on Mt Fuji is the head temple of this denomination. Membership is difficult to quantify because **Soka Gakkai** (the lay movement affiliated to Nichirenshoshu) numbers are often included in statistical reports, though 16,000,000 seems a reasonable estimate. Nichiren Buddhism appeals predominantly to the working class, partly because of its emphasis on a strong sense of membership, which appeals to the modern Japanese alienated by their overwhelmingly industrial environment.

Nichirenshoshu of the UK (NSUK). The British section of **Soka Gakkai International (SGI).**

Nichirenshu. A form of Japanese Mahayana **Buddhism** which originated in the Kamakura period. Nichiren (1222–1282), a vociferous and prophetic nationalist, trained as a Tendai priest, and studied **Zen** and Pure Land Buddhism on Mt Hiei. Ultimately he left the mountain, in order to propagate the doctrine of absolute faith in the Lotus Sutra, an early Indian text. To Nichiren, the most important part of this sutra is its second half, the *honmon*. This stand was later to become the source of dissension amongst disciples. Nichiren vehemently opposed all other Buddhist sects on the grounds that the fate of Japan rested on there being one true sect, and he utilized a method of conversion called *shakubuku* (break and subdue), a practice that deliberately provoked a decisive response, whether positive or negative. Nichiren was exiled twice, and his movement was persecuted. This he interpreted positively; this rejection by the misguided state confirmed his mission.

Nichirenshu advocates the chanting of the *daimoku, Namu Myohorengekyo* "Adoration to the Lotus Sutra", the five Chinese characters of which embody Absolute Truth in its essential form. Also venerated is the *daimandara*, a mandala depicting the *daimoku* surrounded by Sakyamuni, *bodhisattvas, kami*, etc.; an abstract representation of the cosmos with Sakyamuni at its centre. The final element of Nichiren's thought, the *Kaidan,* represents the place of ordination also understood as a secret place within the believer's heart.

Nichirenshu itself claims nearly 2,000,000 devotees, although there are larger denominations e.g. **Nichirenshoshu, Reiyukai** and **Soka Gakkai,** which also claim Nichiren as founder. The head temple, the Kuonji, is on Mt Minobu in Yamanashi Prefecture, at the site of Nichiren's tomb.

Nihangs. A warrior sub-group of **Khalsa Sikhs.** believed to have been created by the 10th Guru, Gobind Singh, in 1699.

It is said that the idea was inspired by the suicide squads of the Mughal army who first used the name. They are formed into four armies (*dals*), each with a *jathedar* (captain). They live in encampments (*deras*), and are easily recognized by their blue clothes, and turbans, and their weapons which often consist of spears and swords but also modern rifles and automatic weapons.

Ni'matullahiya. One of the very small number of **Shi'ite Sufi** orders, the Ni'matullahiya traces its origins to Shah Ni'mat Allah Vali (1329–1431), a Syrian-born **Sunni** teacher of Iranian origin who spent the last part of his life in Mahan near Kerman, in south-east Iran. After Ni'mat Allah Vali's death, leadership of the order moved to India. In the 18th and 19th centuries, however, there was a significant Ni'matullahi revival in Iraq and Iran. In the 20th century, many educated and middle-class Iranians belonged to the order. There are three main branches of the Ni'matullahiyya in modern Iran: Gunabadi, Dhu'l-Riyasatayn, and Safi 'Ali Shahi. Estimates of membership range from 50,000 to 350,000. Recently, Ni'matullahi missions have been established in Europe and America under the tutelage of the leader of the Dhu'l-Riyasatayn branch, Dr Javad Nurbakhsh (Nur'Ali Shah).

Nippon Kirisuto Kyodan. The United Church of Christ in Japan has almost 200,000 members, and is the largest **Protestant** Church in the country. Founded by American **Presbyterian** and **Reformed Church** missionaries in 1858, it was forced by Government decree to unite with other Protestant bodies in 1941. After the war, it reaffirmed its distinctiveness and several churches withdrew. It has accepted its share of war guilt, and is increasingly concerned about the revival of nationalist currents, such as the Theocratic emperor system.

Nippon Sei Ko Kai. The **Anglican** Church in Japan came into existence in 1859 when missionaries arrived from the American Episcopal Church. It was recognized in law in 1887. In 1930 a province of the Anglican Church was formed. Its bishops and other church leaders are all Japanese and it is financially independent. It has 55,000 members.

Nipponzan Myohoji. Founded by Nichidatsu Fujii early this century, this sect, one of the overwhelming number that trace their lineage back to Nichiren (1212–1282), promotes radical pacifism. Although a small denomination in Japan (about 1,500 celibate ascetics) Nipponzan Myohoji is famous worldwide for its "peace pagodas" as well as drum beating and chanting the *daimoku* at peace demonstrations.

Nirankaris. Baba Dayal Das (1783–1855), a shopkeeper from Rawalpindi, is the founder of this **Sikh**-derived movement. Though not a **Khalsa Sikh,** he grew up in an environment in which marriages were conducted by **Hindu** priests and images of Hindu gods were often found in *gurdwaras*. He taught a return to the pristine teachings of Guru Nanak and in particular the discipline of meditating on the Divine Name (*nam simaran*). He also attempted to eliminate alien accretions from Sikh practice and to affirm the nature of God as formless (*nirankar*). The present character of ceremonies, especially marriage, owes much to his efforts. A belief emerged amongst some of his followers that he was a successor to Guru Gobind Singh and since his death there has been a succession of gurus to whom authority is given, rather than to the Guru Granth Sahib. After the partition of India, the Nirankaris abandoned their base in Rawalpindi and are now found centred on Chandigarh. Khalsa Sikhs often, misleadingly, lump the Nirankaris together with the **Namdharis** as heretics. In fact the two groups are quite distinct. The Nirankaris are essentially part of the **Nanak Panth** in that they wish to return to the pristine simplicity at the root of the Sikh tradition. In the beginning members did not join the *khalsa*, though nowadays many adopt *khalsa* insignia. Many non-Khalsa Sikhs and Hindus are also attracted to Nirankari teachings.

Nizaris. The Nizaris are the larger of the two chief branches of **Isma'ili Shi'ism**. They are also commonly known as the **Aga Khanis.** The sect emerged on the death of the Fatimid Caliph al-Mustansir in 1094, giving its allegiance to his displaced elder son Nizar. They established communities in Syria and in Iran, where their chief centre was at the fortress of Alamut. Known as "Assassins" (*Hashishiyyin* or *Hashshashin*), they represented a powerful political presence until the destruction of their strongholds by the Mongols in the 13th century. The Iranian line of Imams remained quietist until the mid-19th century, when the first Aga Khan (as their Imam now began to be called) rebelled and subsequently fled to India, where he and his successors allied themselves to the British.

A Nizari community had already existed in India from the 14th century. They are generally known as **Khojas**, although the term strictly applies to individuals born into an Indian caste grouping, and some Indian Nizaris belong to quite different groupings. Under the leadership of the Aga Khans, the Isma'ili Khojas have become a wealthy and widely distributed community, with a major presence in East Africa.

Nuer and Dinka Religion. The Nuer and Dinka are closely related Nilotic peoples mainly living in the southern Sudan. Traditionally pastoralists, the economic and religious life of the Nuer and Dinka have been greatly affected by recent civil war and famine, as well as earlier mission influence and colonialism. Their religion is an example of **African traditional religions**.

Both the Nuer and Dinka live in patrilineal clans, with no centralized authorities. A supreme deity, *Kwoth*, ("spirit"/"breath") among the Nuer, and *Nhialic*, ("sky") among the Dinka, is distant but concerned with the world and its affairs. Myths of origin speak of separation from the sky, the dwelling place of the deity, who is petitioned with prayers, hymns and offerings, an activity which forms an integral part of an individual's everyday life. Lesser spirits, classified by the Nuer as spirits of the air and spirits of the below, and divided by the Dinka into sky spirits and those associated with clan groups or ancestors, are closer to human affairs, and may form relationships with particular groups or individuals. Sickness is often caused by spirit possession. Ritual specialists belonging to particular lineages, (Leopard-skin priests—Nuer; Masters of the Fishing Spear—Dinka) are capable of interceding on behalf of the people and of performing efficacious sacrifices. Prophetic leaders have also been active in the 19th and 20th centuries, possibly as a response to colonial pressures and subsequent political turmoil, although they may have much older roots in Nuer and Dinka society.

Nurcus. The "Followers of Divine Light"—a movement also sometimes known as Nurcular Camaati (Jama'at al-Nur), Association of Light, or simply as the Nur movement—is a movement of renewal within Turkish **Islam** based on the ideas of the religious leader "Bediüzzaman" ("without equal in his times") Said Nursi (1876–1960).

Born in Nurs in the Eastern, Kurdish, part of Turkey, Said made somewhat rebellious progress through the education system established in that region by the **Naqshabandiya Sufi** order, but also studied some secular, modern Western science, and the theme of the compatibility of the Quran with modern science (he went so far as to claim that the Quran predicted the aeroplane, the railway, the radio, electricity) is prominent in his writings and amongst his followers, the Nurcular.

Although indebted to the Naqshabandiya (Turkish: Nakşibendiler) in various ways, he was also highly critical of the Naqshabandi establishment, and defiantly adopted as his patron the figure of the founder of their great rivals, the **Qadiriya.** A notable theme of his later thinking is that all the Sufi orders have a contribution to make to Islam, and one should not display exclusive allegiance to any single one. (The Nur movement has been described on occasion, incorrectly, as a Sufi order itself.)

Having been to some extent supportive of the Ottoman state's appeal to Islam as a means of mobilizing popular support, Said Nursi fell foul of the Turkish Republic established in 1923, being exiled to a village in Western Turkey for alleged involvement in the Kurdish revolt of 1925. Convinced of a divine calling as mucedded (*mujaddid*), he gained a sizeable and growing number of disciples and followers, to the alarm of the authorities who imprisoned him for a period as a potential threat to the state. Further jail terms were to follow in 1943 and 1948. Yet throughout this period of state-enforced secularization, his influence spread as he conveyed his message of revitalizing Islam through a renewal of faith in the heart of the ordinary believer. Said Nursi also had political influence at the highest level.

Said Nursi's main work, the *Risale-i Nur* (Discourses on Divine Light), is revered almost as a sacred book, and adherence to the Nur movement (and Nur philosophy—Nurculuk) involves group study of this text. The publication of his writings in Turkey has been permitted since the 1950s, and they are now being translated into several languages—including German, since the Nurcular have a significant following in what was formerly West Germany. There are also small Nurcu groups elsewhere in Western Europe, as also in North America.

Nurcus oppose the Kemalist notion of a secular state, but advocate peaceful persuasion rather than violence. Consistently with this, they have disparaged the Iranian revolution. Their apparent success in gaining some support amongst cadets in a Turkish military school—where normally Kemalist principles are presupposed—caused the authorities considerable concern. They also oppose the "Turkish-Islamic Synthesis" propounded by some right-wing intellectuals and officials, being emphatic that Islam is a universal religion and not a nationalist creed.

Both in Turkey and in Germany, one way in which they gain followers is through the support they offer students (and in Germany, workers) living away from home—often by providing friendly accommodation. (In this respect they resemble the **Süleymancis**.) In their basically non-political approach to Muslim renewal, they bear comparison with another missionary movement, of South Asian origin, the **Tablighi Jama'at**, rather than with organizations such as the **Muslim Brotherhood** or the **Jama'at-i Islami**. From within Islam, nevertheless, critics might claim with some justification that direct study of the Quran has been unduly neglected by the Nurcus in their enthusiasm for the *Risale-i Nur*.

Nusayris. A quasi-Muslim sect, also known as **'Alawis** ('Alawiyun), mainly found in Syria. The name is taken from Abu Shu'ayb Muhammad ibn Nusayr, a representative (*bab*) of the tenth **Shi'ite** Imam (d. 868), but the sect was first organized in Iraq by a certain Abu 'Abd Allah al-Khasibi (d. 968). By the 12th century, however, the Nusayris were firmly established in Syria. Nusayri doctrine, like that of other extremist Shi'ite sects, is a complex mixture of **Islamic**, gnostic, **Christian**, and local elements. The Imam 'Ali is raised to the status of the divinity, figuring in a Trinity alongside Muhammad and the early Shi'ite saint Salman. In contrast to Muslim belief, they regard women as lacking a soul. Conventional Islamic practices are discarded in favour of an allegorized interpretation and a range of distinct festivals and ceremonies. Their meeting places are closed to outsiders.

In recent years, the Nusayris have exercised disproportionate political power in Syria, through their control of the Baathist party and the army. They have sometimes sought greater religious legitimacy by claiming to be a community within **Twelver Shi'ism**. Several million Nusayris live in the region between Latakia in Syria and Antakya in Turkey.

Nyingmapas. "Followers of the Ancient Teachings". Tibet's oldest Buddhist tradition, famed for its emphasis on the first Buddhist *tantras* to reach Tibet. After defeating his mainly Buddhist neighbours in China, Bengal, Nepal, Kashmir, Uddiyana, and Central Asia, Tibet's Emperor Trisongdetsen (756–797) nevertheless felt shamed by Tibet's simpler culture; so inducing, possibly as tribute, many famous Buddhist teachers to visit Tibet, he commanded a translation of the Buddhist canon, a process his successors continued for nearly a century. The Nyingmapa tradition is based upon these first translations; hence they follow the *Mahayanist* philosophy of Bengal's monk-logicians, Santaraksita and Kamalasila, the formless Atiyoga meditation of

Western India, and the **tantric** yogas of Padmasambhava. Padmasambhava's royal descent and spiritual powers earned him the role of imperial *guru* and the gift of an imperial wife, Yeshe Tsogyal, later his leading disciple. His prestige established, devotion to Padmasambhava as founding guru for the whole Tibetan nation remains central for Nyingmapas and other Tibetans alike.

Nyingmapas have three unique features; mystical revelations called *Termas*, a decentralised cellular structure and minimal political involvement. Nevertheless invading Mongols, Manchus, and their Tibetan puppets occasionally attacked Nyingmapas, apparently through fear of their occult powers.

The Nyingmapa tradition specializes in integrating **Buddhism** into real-life situations, accommodating married lamas as well as monks and hermits. Since China's destruction of Tibet, the Nyingmapa tradition has begun attracting many new converts worldwide. In particular, the work of the incarnate lama, Tarthang Tulku, who in 1969 established the Nyingmapa Centre in Berkeley, California, has done much to bring western attention to these teachings.

O

Obaku Zen. The smallest school of Japanese **Zen Buddhism** with approximately 460 temples and 340,000 followers at this time. Doctrinally not dissimilar to the much larger **Rinzai** school, the Obaku was brought to Japan by Chinese missionary monks in the mid-17th century as a response to religious stagnation during the early Tokugawa Shogunate. Shortly after establishing itself on Japanese territory, it published a staggering 6,956-volume canon of Buddhist writing which represented the doctrines of all Buddhist schools in operation at that time.

Obeah. A secretive Jamaican cult of African origin—the name probably derives from the Ashanti word *obayifo,* meaning "witch". The term is used more generally for conjuring and magic, in particular harmful magic. The spirits of deceased practitioners of obeah are used by devotees of **Convince** to assist them in their divination practices.

Occultism. Western Occultism ("occult" literally means "hidden") encompasses various methods of developing latent powers ("psychic"/"magical") through extensive training in order to discipline the will. An occultist's training takes many years and involves the balanced development of intellectual, emotional and physical potential. The highest ideal of the occultist is to "work for the sake of the work" (or for the sake of mankind), with no personal benefit. The history of occultism shows many who have fallen short of this.

Many occultists pursue their work within a mystery tradition. One or more central mysteries are understood by the novitiate to the best of his/her ability, and through ritual, meditation and long periods of study the meaning of the mystery is deepened. Schools of occultism and mystery schools have an exoteric (outer) and esoteric (inner) teaching, and the school is structured to reflect this.

Common to most Western traditions of Knowledge is the study, in both theory and practice, of **Kabbalah** (also Cabala or Qabalah). It is best known as the ancient and inner teaching of **Judaism**, and is also central to the mystical teaching of the Abrahamic religions. Kabbalah is a living tradition in its own right, and is periodically reformulated to meet the needs of the time. One of its foremost exponents today is Z'ev Ben Shimon Halevi, author and teacher of groups in a number of countries. Kabbalah, in Hebrew, means to receive. Kabbalists use a key symbol of the tree of life, a structure which sets out the macro- and microcosmic order and, through awareness of these different subtler levels of reality, knowledge (not information) is received. It is variously practised as a key to mysticism, meditation and magic. Gareth Knight is one of the most widely known teachers of Kabbalah as a magical training system and his work on archetypal symbolism is highly regarded.

The most significant group in the late 19th-century occult revival was The Golden Dawn, a magical order whose origins were a mixture of **Freemasonry, Rosicrucianism** and, indirectly, **Theosophy**. One of today's direct descendants is The Servants of the Light, a school of occult science whose director of studies, Dolores Ashcroft-Norwicki, was herself trained by Dion Fortune's Society of the Inner Light. The Servants of the Light offer a Kabbalistic training into the mysteries of the tree of life and the symbolism of the Grail.

Old Catholic Churches. The Old Catholic Church numbers about 400,000 members worldwide and compromises those churches belonging to the Union of Utrecht. These churches accept the doctrines of the Church prior to 1054 (the year of the Great Schism which divided the Eastern and Western churches) and reject more modern doctrines such as the infallibility of the pope. Clergy may marry and services are in the vernacular. The doctrines were stated in the Declaration of Utrecht made in 1889 by the then five Old Catholic bishops of Holland, Germany and Switzerland.

The Church falls into two distinct groups, West European (German, Austrian, Swiss, Dutch) and, a larger group, East European (Polish, ex-Yugoslavian, American Polish). The earliest of these was the Church of Utrecht founded in 1724 after Dutch Roman Catholics were accused of the heresy of Jansenism (a belief in the necessity and irresistibility of the grace of God). After the First Vatican Council in 1870 some Roman Catholics in Germany, Austria and Switzerland rejected the doctrine of papal infallibility and joined the Western grouping.

The Polish National Catholic Church was founded in Pennsylvania, USA in 1897 by Polish Catholics, after conflicts with the Roman hierarchy over Church property and ecclesiastical control. The first bishop of this church was consecrated by Old Catholic bishops in Utrecht in 1907. It now has over 250,000 members in the USA and Poland. The Old Catholic Church in ex-Yugoslavia is much smaller and began with the Croatian Old Catholic Church in the early 1920s. It has since united with other small ethnic Old Catholic churches in the region.

Since 1932 Old Catholic Churches have been in full communion with the **Anglican** Church.

Old Catholic Mariavite Church. The Mariavite movement began in Poland with Feliksa Kozlowska, an impoverished gentlewoman, after she claimed to see visions in the 1890s. She believed that she was called to the Third Order of **Franciscans,** and later to create a new exemplary order of priests to replace the corrupt **Roman Catholic** clergy. She depended on the spiritual support of the Virgin Mary and especially Our Lady of Perpetual Succour, focus of a late medieval **Orthodox** cult. She found little support before 1900 when a Catholic priest, Jan Kowalski, turned to her for spiritual and sexual satisfaction. Kowalski provided leadership for the tiny sect and recruited a few young priests. But he also drew it to the attention of the Inquisition in Rome, which ruled that Kozlowska's visions were bogus. The sect would probably have been suppressed at that point had not the Russian Tsar who ruled over Poland issued a decree on religious toleration in 1905 which provided some legal cover.

Mariavite priests followed Franciscan ascetic ideals, addressed popular spiritual needs, and shunned politics. By 1907 about 250,000 people supported the movement particularly in the rural areas of central Poland. Despite the opposition of the Catholic hierarchy, the Mariavites were protected by the Russian government because they were apolitical and diverted the energies of priests and people away from subversive activities. They also called for the fusion of Catholicism and Orthodoxy. In 1909 Kowalski was consecrated bishop by the **Old Catholic** Bishop of Utrecht, but when the Polish state was created after World War I, numbers declined and in 1924 the Old Catholics withdrew their recognition. During World War I the Church was the target for severe persecution.

Today the Church is reduced to 24,000 members in 41 parishes, who are urged to make an annual pilgrimage to Plock.

Olive Tree Church. Like the **Unification Church** of the Moonies, this is a new religious movement originating in South Korea, where it has developed extremely large property holdings, and major urban-industrial complexes. It was founded in 1955 by Pak T'ae-son, who is regarded as the immortal Olive Tree of Revelation 11.4, and an oracle of God who has magical powers of healing. Membership has increased rapidly in recent years with estimates of members reaching 1.5 million. The headquarters of this millennial movement are at the Castle of the Millennium, near Seoul.

Omotokyo. A relatively new Japanese **Shinto**-oriented sect. Omotokyo was founded in 1892 by the widow Deguchi Nao after revelatory visions of the god Ushitora no Konjin. The sect is essentially messianic, calling for the establishment of the kingdom of heaven upon earth. Deguchi's son-in-law, Deguchi Onisaburo, famed for his healing and **shamanistic** powers, systematized the religion, and was seen by many as the predicted messiah. Omotokyo proclaims itself an international religion, and advocates world peace and social reform in accordance with its tenets. Membership has recently waned, and is reckoned at about 150,000.

Open Brethren. In 1829 a group of Christians from various denominations met privately in a Dublin room to share in a Communion service. These early "ecumenical" meetings gradually attracted more people who were concerned that the communion service should be an act of unity between Christians, regardless of denomination. One member of the group was Francis Newman, younger brother of John Henry Newman. Others included J. N. Darby (*see*

Exclusive Brethren), A. N. Groves, Lord Congleton and Edward Cronin (a converted Roman Catholic).

Francis Newman's friend Benjamin Newton became convinced that this view of scripture was correct. Newton lived in Plymouth and a strong congregation preaching these doctrines was established there, leading to the present tendency to refer to Plymouth Brethren, a name not used by the Brethren themselves. A similar situation arose in Bristol. Gradually the movement spread across the country.

After the split with the Exclusive Brethren in 1849 the Open Brethren continued to expand both through missionary work and writing. Many Brethren were involved in innovative social work and included people with influence in national politics. Dr Barnado is perhaps the most famous. Missionaries went to Europe, to Australia and New Zealand (where they are still strong today) to Persia, India, Africa and America. Churches today still have the Breaking of Bread as their central weekly service. Open Brethren (unlike Exclusive Brethren) observe believer's baptism, and continue to assert the importance of preaching and the Bible, and the need for total commitment to Christ. Worldwide membership is about 1,500,000.

Opus Dei. Opus Dei, a **Roman Catholic** religious order, was founded in 1928 as a right-wing student movement. Its founder was the Spanish priest Jose María Escriva de Balaguer (1902–1975), who was beatified by the Pope in 1992. Its aim is to sanctify everyday life, particularly professional work. Opus Dei is a personal prelature of the Roman Catholic Church. A personal prelature is the equivalent of a bishopric: just as all Catholics within a diocese fall under their Bishop's authority, so all members of this worldwide prelature answer to their Prelate, in matters relating to Opus Dei. The current Prelate is Bishop Alvaro del Portillo. Opus Dei has more than a thousand priests, and 75,000 lay members in more than 80 countries. It is the Roman Catholic church's fastest growing, wealthiest, and most controversial society. Criticism has arisen over allegations of secrecy about membership and involvement in the worlds of politics, high finance and academia.

Orange People. A popular designation for adherents of **Rajneeshism** because of their distinctively coloured clothes.

Order of Friars Minor. *See* **Franciscans.**

Order of Preachers. *See* **Dominicans.**

Organization of the Islamic Conference (OIC). The OIC (al-Mu'tamar al-Islami) was established in 1971 and is based in Saudi Arabia. It is an international organization whose declared aims include promoting **Islamic** solidarity among member states, of which there are currently 45. Its supreme body is the Conference of Heads of State which is scheduled to meet every three years: the sixth such summit meeting took place in Dakar, the capital of Senegal, at the end of 1991. There is also an annual conference of member countries' foreign ministers.

The OIC supports education in Muslim communities worldwide, and through its Islamic Solidarity Fund, established at the second summit conference in

Lahore, Pakistan, in 1974, it has helped to establish Islamic universities in Niger, Uganda and Malaysia. Humanitarian assistance to Muslim communities affected by wars and natural disasters is also given. Politically the OIC opposes Israel and seeks to play a constructive role in troublespots involving Muslims, e.g. in Afghanistan, Chad, Lebanon, and the Iran-Iraq and Gulf wars.

Following the break-up of the USSR, Azerbaijan has joined the OIC, Kazakhstan sent a delegation to the 1991 summit, and all six predominantly Muslim republics are expected to join in due course. Albania was also represented at the Dakar summit, having been granted observer status.

The organization suffers, however, from tensions between its Arab and non-Arab members, and is weakened in many people's eyes by its identification with Saudi interests. Moreover, the hostility between many Muslim states (as in the Iran–Iraq and Gulf wars) has also very often been a major factor in preventing the OIC from moving beyond passing resolutions to developing a strong, united and effective stance in world affairs. It remains to be seen whether current, tentative exploration of the basis for an Islamic Common Market will eventually yield positive results.

The OIC is seen as complementing the other major Saudi-based organization, the **Muslim World League.**

Oriental Orthodox Churches. The term "Oriental Orthodox" identifies an important but often neglected group of Churches of the Middle East which represent some of the oldest traditions of **Christianity**. They include the **Armenian Church**, the **Coptic Church,** the **Ethiopian Orthodox Church** and the **Syrian Jacobite Church**. The **Nestorian** Church, sometimes loosely counted among them, strictly belongs in a group of its own.

The identity of these Churches is defined positively by their fidelity to the Council of Ephesus (431) and negatively by their repudiation of the decrees, or at least the authority, of the Council of Chalcedon (451). The latter affirmed that Christ united two natures, human and divine, within a single person; the opposing monophysite view, that Christ's humanity was a function of his single divine nature, was condemned as undermining the reality of the incarnation. But these non-Chalcedonian Churches are not necessarily accurately described as monophysite: their rejection of Chalcedon owed something to ecclesio–political factors and something to theological misunderstandings, and the extent to which their adherents still affirm the more extreme forms of monophysitism is open to question.

The Oriental Orthodox Churches, ethnically and geographically separate in the past, have in modern times established close ties with one another, as was demonstrated at a conference of their heads and representatives held in 1965 in Addis Ababa, where intentions were formulated to work for greater understanding between themselves and other Churches. Moreover, despite their undoubted monophysite emphasis, the Oriental Orthodox are very close to the **Orthodox Church (Byzantine)** in their general theology, style of worship and ecclesiastical customs.

Orthodox Church (Byzantine). The Orthodox Church is a family, or federation, of independent and in most cases national Churches bound together by common traditions of worship and theology which were developed within the Greek-speaking, Byzantine culture of the eastern Mediterranean. Officially defining itself as the "Orthodox Catholic Church", it claims to be the true representative of the original undivided Church with over 150,000,000 baptized members. It should not be confused with the **Oriental Orthodox Churches**.

In the 5th century, **Syrian, Armenian** and Egyptian sections of the hitherto undivided Church became separated from the mainstream Church, which now consisted of a Greek-dominated eastern half with its centre at Constaninople (Byzantium) and a Latin-dominated western half with its centre at Rome. Religious disputes and misunderstandings, exacerbated by cultural and political differences, eventually led to open schism (1054), and thence to the emergence of two separate institutions; the Byzantine Orthodox Church and the **Roman Catholic Church**. Despite their many differences (most crucially about ecclesiastical authority) these two Churches affirm fundamentally the same doctrines and recognize the validity of each other's sacraments. A symbolically significant event was the meeting in 1964 between Pope Paul VI and Patriarch Athenagoras I at which they withdrew the mutual excommunications of 1054.

For the Orthodox Church, authority is exercised collectively. This "decentralized" view of ecclesiastical authority is expressed through the tradition of **Autocephalous Churches**. Although no Church or bishop has overall authority, the Church of Constantinople, known as the "Ecumenical Patriarchate" and headed by the Ecumenical Patriarch, is traditionally accorded primacy of honour and certain rights of initiative on account of its historical role as the mother Church of Byzantium. Thus the Ecumenical Patriarch may be called upon to mediate in disputes and to express the whole Church's official recognition of an individual Church's claim to autocephalous status.

Although the distinction between one Church and another is in theory territorial, in practice the complexities of history have produced national or ethnic Churches without coherent geographical boundaries. The main dividing factor is language, since Orthodox worship is meant to be conducted in the local vernacular (which in practice is often a language now become archaic). This close identification of each individual Church with the language and culture of a particular national or ethnic group has proved a source both of strength and of weakness. On the one hand it has helped preserve national identity, especially during the long periods of foreign occupation suffered by most Orthodox countries. On the other hand believers from one group may not readily recognize those of other nationalities or cultures as co-religionists.

The various Churches can be conveniently described under five main headings; (1) the four ancient patriarchates; (2) the principal Greek-speaking Churches; (3) the Churches which are neither Greek nor Slavonic; (4) the principal Slavonic Churches; and (5) the newer Churches of Slavonic origin.

(1) The *four ancient patriarchal Churches* are surviving outposts of Orthodox **Christianity** in what for centuries have been predominantly **Islamic** countries. The Church of Constantinople (in Istanbul in Turkey) is all that is left of the once powerful and extensive Church that formed the spiritual and cultural centre of the Byzantine Empire. Its original heartland was Greek Asia Minor and what is now modern Greece (where the Church eventually became autocephalous). Today it has jurisdiction over a number of disparate groups: a dwindling community of Greek Orthodox Christians in Turkey; the Greek and Slavonic monastic communities of the semi-independent republic of Mount Athos; Greek Orthodox dioceses on Crete, Patmos and the Dodecanese islands;

and emigrant communities in Western Europe, North America and Australia, including autonomous Slavonic communities wishing to be independent of the jurisdiction of Churches in communist countries. Turkey continues to impose restrictions on the Patriarchate: for example, the Patriarch himself must be a Turkish citizen. Worldwide the Church numbers around 5,000,000 members.

The Churches of Alexandria and Antioch are Byzantine versions of the original patriarchates which split off from the mainstream Church in the 5th century to become, respectively, the **Coptic Church** and the **Syrian Jacobite Church.** The Church of Alexandria (in Egypt) has jurisdiction over Orthodox Christians throughout Africa, but its members are mainly Greeks and Arabs living in Egypt, Ethiopia, the Sudan, Kenya, Uganda and Tanzania (about 250,000 in all). Its ecclesiastical traditions and language of worship are Greek. The Church of Antioch preserves traditions of Syriac Christianity and worships in Arabic. It has jurisdiction over Arab Orthodox communities in Syria, Lebanon, Iraq and various emigrant communities in the United States (around 500,000 in all). The patriarch, since 1899 an Arab rather than a Greek, now resides in Damascus. The Church of Jerusalem (until 451 part of Antioch) is dominated by Greek senior clergy, while the vast majority of its members are Palestinian Arabs living in Israel and Jordan (about 75,000 in all). It is this Church which has custodianship of most of the Christian holy places in Israel and Jerusalem. It also has responsibility for the tiny autonomous Church of Sinai (St Catherine's monastery).

(2) The main *Greek-speaking Churches* are those of Cyprus and of Greece. These, despite their shared language and customs, are administratively quite separate. The Orthodox Church of Cyprus is one of the oldest independent Churches, established by the apostles Paul and Barnabus and autocephalous since 431. The primate is the archbishop of Constantia, resident in Nicosia. His traditional role as ethnarch, or national leader, of Cypriot Christians is a legacy of the Ottoman system of governing the Christians through their Church leaders. It has nearly 500,000 members. The Orthodox Church of Greece was originally part of the Church of Constantinople, but assumed autocephalous status in 1833, following the creation of modern Greece after four centuries of Turkish occupation. The archbishop of Athens is primate.

The Church of Greece is now the only Orthodox Church officially recognized as a State Church, though formal ties between Church and State, often a source of tension in the past, are gradually being loosened. Even so, national and religious identity still go hand in hand. The membership of the Church is four-fifths of the population of Greece itself: namely 8,000,000.

(3) *Churches neither Greek nor Slavonic.* The ancient kingdom of Georgia, in the Caucasus, was converted to Christianity in the 4th century. The Church of Georgia, headed by a Catholicos-Patriarch, became independent of the Patriarchate of Antioch in the 8th century. In the 19th century it was incorporated into the Church of Russia, and from 1917 until the collapse of communism remained under the control of Moscow. Always one of the smallest Churches, today it numbers roughly 1,000,000 members. The Church of Romania, by contrast, is the second largest Orthodox community in the world, numbering at least 15,000,000. Though much influenced by their Byzantine and Slav neighbours, and during Turkish rule dominated by Greek clergy, the Romanians have remained basically a Latin people. An

autocephalous Romanian Church was established in 1864, but the present Church, a much larger entity brought into being with modern Romania, dates from around 1925.

(4) *Principal Slavonic Churches.* Byzantine missionaries established Orthodoxy in Serbia and Bulgaria during the 9th century, and autocephalous Churches existed in the mediaeval period. A **Serbian Orthodox Church** was recognized in 1879, but the modern Church, uniting a number of originally separate dioceses, dates from 1922, following the creation of Yugoslavia after World War I. Serbian nationalism and Serbian Orthodoxy have always gone hand in hand. During World War II the Serbs suffered heavily from their Croatian compatriots, many of whom were Nazi supporters as well as Catholics. Bitter and violent conflict between Orthodox Serbs and Catholic Croats were resumed following the post-communist division of Yugoslavia into independent states. Today the Church numbers about 8,000,000. The modern Church of Bulgaria proclaimed its autocephalous status in 1870, against the wishes of the Ecumenical Patriarchate. Today it numbers about 6,000,000 members.

Russia officially became Orthodox at the end of the 10th century, remaining dependent on Constantinople until 1448, when it claimed autocephalous status. The Patriarchate of Moscow, until the end of the 20th century the centre of the greater Russian Church, was officially established in 1589. While other Orthodox countries passed through a period of Ottoman rule, Russia alone remained a free Orthodox country. The Church grew into a powerful institution, extending its domain both as result of Russian expansionism and through its own missionary effort (in Japan and Alaska). The history of **Russian Orthodoxy** is complex and contentious, especially in relation to the rival Roman Catholic **Uniate Churches** established among Orthodox populations in territories along Russia's shifting western frontiers, e.g. the **Ukrainian Uniate Catholic Church**. The Patriarchal Church of Moscow and all Russia has for centuries been the largest single Orthodox Church, numbering just under 100,000,000 in 1917, though only around half that number by the end of the communist era. This number has now been reduced further by the independence of Churches formerly part of or dependent upon the Moscow Patriarchate (see 5 below). Under seven decades of communist oppression, Church leaders in response evolved various strategies of co-existence and co-operation, not always compatible with their professed Christian principles, and even when compatible not always sympathetically understood by those living in the free world.

(5) *Newer Churches of Slavonic origin.* The political upheavals of the 20th century resulted in the emergence, or re-emergence, of new independent Churches among the Slavs and other clients of the old Russian Empire. In 1923 the small Church of Finland, founded in the 12th century, placed itself under the jurisdiction of the Ecumenical Patriarchate. In 1924 the Ecumenical Patriarchate granted autocephalous status to the Church of Poland, a status recognized by Moscow only after World War II. In 1951 Moscow itself recognized the independence of the small Church of Czechoslovakia, made up of a small minority of ex-Uniate Carpatho–Russians. The Church of Albania was granted autocephalous status in 1937; but, in a country populated mainly by Muslims and ruled by a repressive régime which in 1967 declared Albania the world's first officially atheist state, it had at one time virtually ceased to exist.

The "Orthodox Church in America", which traces its origins to Russian missions in Alaska in the 19th century and which was previously called the "Russian Orthodox Greek Catholic Church of America", gained independence from Moscow in 1970 and has had aspirations, never fully realized, to bring together the Orthodox of all national groups living in the United States. The Orthodox Church of Australia, an autonomous body based on the large Greek emigrant community, has corresponding aspirations.

With the disintegration of the communist bloc national Churches again began to proclaim in their newly independent homelands the independence from Moscow they had long proclaimed as diasporate groups: these include the Estonian, Latvian, Lithuanian, Belorussian and Ukrainian Orthodox Churches. Likewise, with the break-up of Yugoslavia, the Macedonian Orthodox Church reasserted a long-standing claim to autocephalous status persistently refused by the Serbian Orthodox Church.

The teachings of the Orthodox Church are defined by the decisions of the seven ecumenical councils (325–787), and given philosophical and mystical expression in the writings of the Church fathers. In theory further ecumenical councils might be convened, though it is difficult to imagine under what circumstances. The Orthodox Church does not accept the authority of any of the subsequent councils recognized as enumenical by the Roman Catholic Church, nor have the basic teachings of the Orthodox Church been subject to the kind of doctrinal elaborations and scholastic definitions characteristic of Latin Christianity. Orthodox Christianity tends to emphasize prayer and worship rather than doctrine and its worship and theology are strongly Trinitarian. Great devotion is paid to the saints and especially to Mary, who is venerated not in her own right but as Mother of God (*Theotokos*). As in Roman Catholicism, seven sacraments are recognized: baptism, chrismation, eucharist, confession, anointing of the sick, marriage and priesthood. Communicants receive by spoon a fragment of bread from a chalice of wine. Orthodoxy accepts the "real presence" of Christ in the sacrament, without attempting to define this doctrinally. There is a three-fold ministry of deacons, priests and bishops. Secular priests are always married, while the bishops are celibate, recruited from the monastic clergy. Monasticism has always been a vital part of Orthodox tradition: the monasteries helped keep the faith alive in difficult times, combating heresy and political interference alike. There are no separate "orders" such as exist in western monasticism. The main occupation of Orthodox monks and nuns is prayer and worship, though monasteries also attract lay visitors.

The most distinctive features of Orthodox Christianity are to be found in its rich tradition of worship and religious art. The long and elaborate services, sung or chanted by choir or cantor, are celebrated in churches richly decorated with lamps and images, the congregation standing throughout. The high point of the Church year is Holy Week (Easter), culminating in the feast of the Resurrection, which in Orthodox countries retains the importance it had in the early Church. The veneration of icons in churches and homes link all the main themes of Orthodox belief and practice: devotionally they provide a focus for prayer and worship and theologically they express the themes of divine incarnation and human salvation.

Most of the Orthodox Churches are now members of the **World Council of Churches**, and many are involved, in one way or another, in the ecumenical movement.

Orthodox Church in America. *See* **Orthodox Church (Byzantine).**

Orthodox Church of Australia. *See* **Orthodox Church (Byzantine).**

Orthodox Church of Cyprus. *See* **Orthodox Church (Byzantine).**

Orthodox Church of Greece. *See* **Orthodox Church (Byzantine).**

Orthodox Judaism (Orthodoxy). (*See also* **Haredi; Hasidism.**) Orthodox Judaism holds that the written Torah (the first five books of the Bible) was revealed verbatim to Moses by God and that the rabbinic commentary on it, the oral Torah, is divine in origin and is just as binding as the written version. (Although teaching the same beliefs, Hasidic Judaism is considered in a separate article due to differences in its ethos.) Some refer to it as "Orthopraxy" because it emphasizes correct practice, yet the term is useful as it locates the reasons for observance and hesitancy to change Jewish practice in theology, not just respect for tradition.

Orthodoxy, as well as its sub-divisions, stems from the beginning of the Jews' ability to participate in Europe's modern nation-states. Just as European Christians attempted to "modernize" their religion, so too did some Jews, particularly German **Reform** Jews. These efforts were vigorously opposed by Hungarian rabbi Moses Sofer (1762–1839), known as the Hatam Sofer ("the perfect scribe"), whose dictum "Novelty is forbidden by the Torah" became the watchword of those who considered modernity an enemy of traditional Jewish culture. In his eyes, all of Jewish tradition, whether from the *Mishnah* and *Talmud* or from later local *minhag* ("custom"), was equally valid and immutable.

At the other end of the traditionalist spectrum was German rabbi Samson Raphael Hirsch (1808–1888), the leader of "neo-" or "modern" Orthodoxy. He argued that one could be fully modern and fully traditional, although favouring some minor liturgical changes. Yet this support for combining **Judaism** and modernity, encapsulated in his interpreting the rabbinic phrase, *Torah im derekh Eretz* ("Torah and an occupation" [Avot 2:2]), to justify participation in the modern state, did not stop him from becoming the leader of a German Jewish group which broke from the Reform-dominated "official" Jewish community recognized by the government.

While issues of modernity and emancipation produced Hungarian and German forms of Orthodoxy, traditional Judaism in Russia, Lithuania and Poland was divided by Hasidism, a pietistic movement emphasizing prayer over Torah study, and in its second generation, teaching that certain men, *tzaddikim* ("righteous ones"), could intervene with God on behalf of their community. Hasidism's critics, the Mitnaggdim ("opponents"), led by Rabbi Elijah Shlomo Zalman, "the Gaon (Sage) of Vilna" (1720–1797), stressed the importance of diligent Torah study at its *yeshivot* ("seminaries"). Rabbi Israel Lipkin (Salanter (1810–1883)) began the **Musar** movement ("ethics") which stressed rigorous self-examination and fear of God. Later, the Hasidic–Mitnaggdic rift ended as they joined in opposition to non-traditional forms of Judaism originating in the West. Today, these two groups comprise the Haredim ("those who fear (God)") or as they are sometimes referred to, the "ultra-Orthodox."

The Orthodox communities of Britain, America, and Israel, traditionalism's main centres after the Holocaust, have been influenced by all these trends as well as by local conditions. Regardless of personal observance, most British Jews affiliate with Orthodox synagogues, which are divided into several organizations, the largest being the United Synagogue founded in 1870. Jews' College (London) established in 1856, is the principal institution for the training of Orthodox rabbis and cantors for Britain and the Commonwealth. It also offers academic degree courses in Jewish Studies. Other groups include the Federation of Synagogues, founded in 1887 by Lord Swaythling, which is oriented towards Eastern European Orthodoxy and the Union of Orthodox Hebrew Congregations, founded in 1926 by Rabbi Victor Schonfeld, to unite Western Orthodoxy. The latter group included Adat Israel, which was established to perpetuate German-style Orthodoxy.

In America, the Orthodox are a minority of the Jewish population, behind the Conservative and Reform branches of Judaism. Major Orthodox organizations include the Union of Orthodox Congregations of America (founded 1898, and representing more than 700 congregations) and the National Council of Young Israel (1912), a synagogue group founded by Americanized Orthodox laity and under lay leadership until after World War II. American Orthodox rabbis are organized in two major groups, the Union of Orthodox Rabbis of the United States and Canada (1902), comprising of Eastern European rabbis and the Rabbinical Council of America (1923, reorganized in 1935), comprising more than 800 American-trained rabbis, and supporting the institutions for their training. Orthodox educational institutions include the Torah Umesorah ("Torah and tradition"), the National Society for Hebrew Day Schools, founded in 1944 with 498 schools in 1985 and Yeshivah University (1928, with component units dating to 1897). Recent American Orthodox leaders include rabbis Joseph Dov Soloveitchik (1903) and Moshe Feinstein (1895–1986) whose *halakhic* ("Jewish legal") decisions were respected universally by Orthodox Jews.

In Israel, the Orthodox are also a minority, but comprise a majority of religious Jews. Institutionally, only Orthodox rabbis may perform marriages, divorces, and conversions; **Zionism** itself was originally controversial among Orthodox Jews with some calling for a return to Zion and others arguing that not only must Jews wait for God's messiah to restore Jewish sovereignty but also that traditional Jews could not co-operate with the secular Zionists. Today there are four main groups of Orthodox Jews in Israel: an anti-Zionist minority, comprised of **Neturei Karta** ("Guardians of the City") and the Edah Haredi ("Haredi community"); a number of haredi communities, hasidic and mitnagdic, who have limited contact with the state; **Sephardi** traditionalists, represented politically by the **Shas** party; and religious Zionism, which sees religious value in Zionism and the State of Israel, despite its secular leadership. One group of religious Zionists, the **Gush Emunim** ("the bloc of the faithful"), following the teachings of Rabbi Abraham Isaac Kook (1865–1935) as mediated by his son, Rabbi Tzvi Yehudah Kook (1891–1982), were instrumental in the establishment of the settlement movement, believing that Israeli history, especially the 1967 Six-Day War, was part of God's redemption of the Jews. They are opposed by the Orthodox peace groups, Oz V'Shalom ("Strength and Peace") and Netivot Shalom ("Paths of Peace"). In recent years, a number of religious Zionists have also tended towards greater rigour in observance.

Other important current trends in Orthodoxy are the Baalei Teshuvah ("masters of repentance") and the Hozrei be-Teshuvah ("returning in repentance") movement in which formally non-traditional Jews become Orthodox, generally, *haredi*. The movement, strongest among Israelis and travellers, rejects Western culture and has led to the creation of a unique Orthodox sub-culture.

Oxford Group. *See* **Moral Re-armament.**

P

Paganism. The word Pagan (from Latin *paganus*) means country dweller, and Paganism (or Neo-Paganism) uses ritual as a tool to end the alienation arising from a separation from nature. The terms "Paganism" and "Neo-Paganism" are often used interchangeably, and are sometimes also used as synonyms for **witchcraft.**

Pagan beliefs date back to early man, and aspects of the legacy handed on include working in stone circles, celebration of season festivals, worship of the old gods and especially the Goddess in her manifestations as maiden, mother and crone. Similar kinds of **shamanic** nature religion that worships a goddess are sometimes linked with modern political movements—green witches with the ecological movements, etc.

Important seasonal festivals include the Winter Solstice (adopted and adapted by Christians in the form of Christmas), Beltane (the Spring Festival of the first of May associated with maypole and Morris dancing), and the Summer Solstice (with Glastonbury and Stonehenge as favoured venues in the United Kingdom for this celebration of midsummer).

Pan-Indianism. "Pan-Indianism" is a term used to describe beliefs held by many young native Americans who hold that, at heart, all **Native American religions** and cultures are the same and present an integrated set of beliefs and rituals common to all tribes. This is a recent idea, formed in response to white domination, and would not find favour with many representatives of traditional tribal religions. Nonetheless, Pan-Indianism is an important feature of contemporary native American religious life, underlying such rituals as **Peyotism** and the increasing use of the sweat lodge, vision quest and other rites, as well as being an important impetus in asserting native American rights, particularly in regard to sacred sites and land disputes.

Parsis. Literally "the Persians", the **Zoroastrian** community in India, so-called because they migrated from Iran in the 10th century CE and settled in north-west India. Parsi fortunes improved early in the 19th century with a move from Gujarat into Bombay. This provided opportunities for business and professional activities, underpinned by education in Western-style schools.

Increased contact with other religions, the criticism of Christian missionaries, and western scholarship caused internal divisions over theological and doctrinal problems. These mostly concerned the question of whether dualism, some form of monotheism on the Semitic model, or even monism lay at the heart of their tradition. In particular, the inability of Parsi priests to rebut these criticisms satisfactorily engendered a new self-consciousness among lay people and signalled a decline in priestly influence. This crystallized into a number of reform movements, variously influenced by outside agencies, including the **Theosophists.**

Within the context of the wider Indian society Parsis operate as a caste, which helps to sustain both their religious exclusiveness and their economic strength as a group. Apart from the fire temples, Parsi institutions are controlled by a *panchayat*, or community organization. Among the properties they own are the *dakhmas* or "towers of silence", where corpses are placed to be consumed by vultures and other carrion-eaters in conditions that are minimally polluting. The fire temples, which are the concern of the priests, fall into two categories, on the basis of their grade of ritual fire. Among the eight holiest in India is one at Udvada, north of Bombay, where the fire is said to have been burning continuously for a thousand years; consequently it is a special place of pilgrimage for Parsis. Of the "ordinary" fire temples (*agiari*), there are 40 in Bombay alone.

Since Independence Parsi fortunes have faded; there has been a quickening of the outside influences working on the community, and the population (approximately 100,000) has continued to decline. This has led to a further attempts to define what constitutes Parsi identity. Their economic, political and cultural influence continues, nevertheless, to exceed massively their numerical strength.

Parti Islam Se-Malaysia (PAS). This is the main political organization representing resurgent fundamentalist **Islam** in Malaysia. It was established in 1951, prior to Independence, to promote radical reformist Islam in the polity of the emergent nation, its founding members having left UMNO (the United Malay National Organization), the Muslim–Malay party which has dominated the multi-racial government coalitions since Independence in 1957, because of its refusal to endorse the establishment of Malaysia as an Islamic state. PAS and UMNO have been rivals ever since.

PAS has achieved intermittent power in three states of the Federation, but has only a small but vocal group of members of parliament, despite an increasing share of the national vote (43 per cent in 1986). PAS is committed to the establishment of an Islamic state based on the Quran and *Sunna*, and the promotion of Islamic economics.

In the 1980s it sought to broaden its appeal by attacking religious–ethnic chauvinism and advocating Islam as the solution to problems of social injustice for all, not just Muslims. UMNO-led government repression has increased, however: in the "Memali incident" of 1985, 14 villagers died and many more were arrested in a police attack on a community of militant PAS supporters led by Ibrahim "Libya"—who was also killed. While that remains an extreme instance, tensions between PAS and UMNO supporters continue to grow: symbolic of this is the way in which they may now well meet separately in the mosques for prayer, or indeed build entirely separate mosques.

In the October 1990 election PAS gained control of the northern state of Kelantan, and now faces the challenge of living up to its supporters' hopes in practice.

Pasdaran. The Pasdaran organization in Iran is the corps of the **Islamic Revolutionary Guards.**

Patriarchal Church of Moscow and All Russia. *See* **Orthodox Church (Byzantine).**

Pax Christi. Pax Christi is a **Roman Catholic** peace organization. It was founded in 1946 by the French Bishop Theas. Its immediate aim was to bring about "reconciliation between the French and German peoples". As the Cold War escalated, it broadened its purpose to include healing the rift between Soviet Russia and the West. In the 1970s and 1980s the group was vocal in its opposition to nuclear weapons.

Pax Christi continues to campaign against the "poverty and the arms trade", which it perceives as "the root cause of war". The English section seeks to put an end to world religious conflict and, closer to home, to curtail the deployment of Trident missiles. Since the conclusion of hostilities between East and West, Pax Christi has turned its attention to the North/South axis.

Pax Christi publishes the journal *Justpeace*. It has 2,000 members, in 22 sections, worldwide.

Pentecostal Churches (Charismatic). Pentecostalism is not so much a doctrine as an experience. Members of pentecostal churches believe that all the gifts of the Holy Spirit mentioned in 1 Corinthians 12 are available to Christians today; in particular, the gifts of speaking in tongues, healing and prophecy.

Although there are suggestions that in previous revivals (for instance that of the 18th century leading to the foundation of **Methodism**) these experiences occurred, the historical evidence is ambiguous. Pentecostalism is usually regarded as having begun in America at the turn of the 20th century, when meetings at the Azusa Street church in Los Angeles became the springboard for the movement. The flamboyant preaching of Aimee Semple MacPherson based at the Angelus Temple made the movement more widely known. In 1907 it reached Britain through the preaching of T. B. Barrett at All Saints Church in Sunderland.

There are many pentecostal denominations. The two main ones in Britain are the **Assemblies of God** and the Elim Pentecostal Church. The former are linked with the Worldwide Assemblies of God Church, one of the largest international pentecostal denominations which has its roots in the Azusa Street revival. The Elim Pentecostal Church grew out of the ministry of George Jeffreys in Ireland in 1915. It has a more central organization, being governed by a conference and having its own ministerial training college. A third strand of Pentecostalism is the **House Church** movement.

Within the established churches, particularly the **Anglican** and **Roman Catholic** churches, the charismatic movement has become a significant influence on worship and liturgy. The distinctive style of pentecostal worship, worship songs with simple words and music (often sung with raised hands), times of silence giving any member of the congregation the opportunity to pray or give a prophecy, services of healing; all these are now an accepted part of mainstream church life in many places. The Pentecostalists (named after the Jewish feast of Pentecost when, according to Acts 2 the church first received the Holy Spirit) or Charismatics (from Charism—"Gift") are acknowledged to be the fastest growing movement in the church, with worldwide membership (excluding those within existing other denominations) estimated as over 25,000,000.

Peyotism. (*See also* **Native American Religions.**) A syncretic ritual of the Native Americans, peyotism, or the peyote cult is a ritual which spread across much of the Plains area at the end of the 19th century. Involving the use of the hallucinogenic cactus *Lophophora Williamsii*, it combines traditional elements with Christian ones, centred round the central ethics of the "Peyote Road", a life of responsibility to family and tribe, avoidance of alcohol and curing of illness. Ceremonies, usually lasting one night, involve drumming, singing and visions under the direction of a "Road Chief". It has attracted significant numbers of followers among many tribes, notably the Navajo.

Most adherents belong to the Native American Church, originally the Native American Church of Oklahoma, incorporated in Oklahoma in 1918 at the instigation of James Mooney, an anthropologist sent from Washington to investigate peyote use. In 1945 it became the Native American Church of the United States. Peyotists from over 50 different tribes belong to this loose inter-tribal organization, which allows much individual tribal variation in ritual. In 1978 the *American Indian Religious Freedom Act* protected the sacramental use of peyote by members of the Church. In 1990 the Supreme Court challenged the law and the legality of peyote use is now decided on a state-by-state basis.

Peyotism is also a feature of some Mesoamerican traditional religions, notably in Mexico.

Pioneer. *See* **House Churches.**

PL Kyodan. A new religious movement in Japan, PL Kyodan (Church of Perfect Liberty) is a synthesis of Tokumitsukyo with **Buddhist** and **Shinto** elements. It was originally called Hito no Michi Kyodan whose second leader, Miki Tokuchika, regrouped the faithful in 1946 under the new name PL Kyodan. The central teaching of PL is "life is art". Humanity is essentially divine, and this nature must be developed creatively. PL has a high public profile and is involved with social programmes. It claims over 2,000,000 adherents, with headquarters in Osaka.

Plymouth Brethren. This widely used label refers to the group known as the **Open Brethren**.

Pocomania. Meaning "little madness", Pocomania is an Afro–Protestant cult found in parts of Jamaica and similar in many ways to **Revival Zion**. Singing round a pole with a flag induces possession by ancestors or angel spirits. Full baptism by immersion is also a feature of the movement.

Polish National Catholic Church. *See* **Old Catholic Churches.**

Polynesian Religions. Polynesia is the largest of the island groupings of the Pacific, ranging all the way from the north central Hawaiian Island group, to the south-east where the statues of Easter Island continue to exert their fascination. The area includes the Line Islands, the Marquesas, Society and Austral Islands of French Polynesia, the Cook Islands, Kiribati, Tuvalu, Tokelau, Samoa (Western and American), Niue and Tonga. **Christianity** strongly influenced religious beliefs in the area with the epoch of European colonization, and very nearly destroyed the primal religious nature of the area. However, in more recent times, traditional spiritualities have emerged as stronger factors in the religious life of the people of these islands. Moreover, churches throughout the region have become interested in indigenous theologies related to the island cultures, and this has meant a renewed interest in the primal religions. A large number of anthropologists and religious specialists and historians of Christianity have become interested in this part of the world.

Hawaii occupies a position of particular significance in Polynesian spirituality, as its name is also given to the legendary homeland where the spirits of Polynesian people go after death. It is also seen as the distant ancestral home of the gods and chiefs of Polynesia. But this Hawaii of legend and myth is probably not to be associated with the island people themselves, but is best interpreted as the mythological point of origin of Polynesia. The religious structure of Hawaiian society was the most advanced in the region. There were 10 colleges of priests each specializing in different aspects of spirituality—sorcery, necromancy, divination, medicine, surgery and sacred architecture.

A chief characteristic of Polynesian spirituality is its concept of life as a journey or a pilgrimage across vast watery spaces, and here one sees the strong influence of the geographical characteristics of the region on the development of the religious life of the people. Polynesian creation mythology is similar to that of many other indigenous cultures worldwide, with the concept of primal emptiness (*Kore*) and primal darkness out of which the gods have given birth to all creation. *Tane*, one of the major deities, plays the role of trickster and cultural hero who pulls up land out of the oceans for human beings to live on. But he was also a tragic figure, for he dies trying to win immortality from the Goddess of Death.

Polynesian religion has given rise to two particular concepts of major significance. *Mana* is the name given to the sacred power which is believed to infuse the whole of creation. Wherever *Mana* erupts is a place of danger and that is represented by the concept of *Tabu* or *Taboo*. When a place or a person is Taboo, they might not be approached or touched by anyone who has not gone through the correct preparations. Chiefs and the dead were Taboo as were all who came in contact with them. During pregnancy and menstruation women are regarded as Taboo. Wherever the spirits are said to abide is also Taboo. The medicine man or medicine specialist and the priest are Taboo because they deal with sacred matters. In fact it is the priest who plays the major role in the community—educating, healing, exorcizing and enabling the people to keep in contact with the living dead. The Tohunga undertake rituals at key moments in a person's life: birth, death, marriage, and there are various initiation points in the human journey. Sanctuaries were set aside for worship, and as the place where the divine and the human realms touched each other. Tribal traditions and religious knowledge were all held in high esteem, and were believed to have been brought from Heaven by Tane in three baskets, and revealed to the people by the priests under strictly controlled circumstances in their houses of sacred learning. Beside the priests there were other specialists of the sacred who concentrated, for example, on divination. Others were specialists in black magic. A sorcerer was someone who was believed to have particularly strong power which could be used to cause disaster in the lives of individuals and communities unless harmony was established between people in the tribal group and between the tribal group and nature.

Positive Thinking. Better known as New Thought which as a movement formed itself in the middle of the 19th century. In the 1820s the magnetic healing of Franz Anton Mesmer, an Austrian, was introduced to America. Mesmer claimed the existence of a magnetic cosmic fluid which could be focused in one person and transferred to another. In the transfer a hypnotic trance and the healing of the physical body occurred. Through the writings of Charles Poyen, these ideas were handed on to Phineas Pankhurst Quimby. Pupils of his, Warren Felt Evans, a **Swedenborgian** minister, philosopher and author, and Mary Patterson, later known as Mary Baker Eddy, founder of **Christian Science,** continued and promulgated Quimby's work. Dissenting Christian Scientists also contributed through their independent teachings and writings to shape New Thought ideas. These can be summarized as follows: while they accept the Scriptures as divine revelations, they deny their literal meaning by Spiritual Interpretation, a method which allows the discovery of new connotations. Although the Bible stands as Truth, its meanings stand at variance to those held by orthodox religion, sometimes to the point of constituting a complete repudiation of the latter, such as the Calvinist doctrines of sin, predestination, and damnation. New Thought emphasizes health, happiness and prosperity as legitimate religious concerns. Others proclaimed the principles of New Thought in a variety of ways: Ralph Waldo Trine, for example, by publishing books, Emma Curtis Hopkins by teaching, the Fillmores, Nona Brooks and Ernest Holmes by creating the bases for churches. Today the influence of New Thought extends well beyond the membership of its churches (Christian Science, Divine Science, Religious Science, Unity School of Christianity), with its literature reaching a wide audience and its ideas being promulgated by writers such as Norman Vincent Peale, Dale Carnegie and Maxwell Maltz.

Presbyterians (Reformed). The Presbyterians were, like the **Lutherans,** products of the European Protestant Reformation.

In 1533 John Calvin, a French legal and theological scholar, was expelled from the University of Paris for his reformist views. He found his way to Geneva, Switzerland, where he became the inspiration and leader of the reformed church over much of Europe.

Like Luther, Calvin believed that the Bible contains all that is needed for the Christian faith. Any doctrine or practice not supported by scripture should be rejected. But Calvin also had a deep sense of God's power and therefore believed that in all his dealings with people, God takes the initiative. This led to the doctrine of predestination, that God has chosen some people for salvation and others for damnation, and to belief in the compelling power of grace (that God's grace cannot be rejected by an individual). These doctrines were rejected by other **protestant** groups, notably **Methodists** who believed Christ died for all, but that Christians could fall away from their faith.

Calvin was a gifted administrator and his belief in the sovereignty of God led to a belief that the state, though a body separate from the church, should conform as far as possible to the will of God. In Geneva under Calvin laws reflected the teaching of the Bible, and education, which enabled people to read the Bible for themselves, was encouraged and expanded.

The movement spread and took root particularly in Holland and Scotland. From there it was taken overseas by emigrants to South Africa, India and Northern Ireland. Today the Presbyterian Church of Scotland is the state church of Scotland and is the largest presbyterian church in the world. Styles of worship vary, but churches are usually led by a Presbyter, responsible for preaching, sacraments and spiritual guidance, elders responsible for administration and church discipline and deacons who care for the poor and needy.

Calvin's emphasis on the importance of Christian principles in the life of the state has led many Presbyterians to take an active role in political life. In the 16th century John Knox preached in Scotland against both Mary Queen of Scots and Queen Elizabeth I (the "monstrous regiment of women"). Today in Northern Ireland most Unionists have Presbyterian backgrounds (the Rev. Ian Paisley is a minister of the independent **Free Presbyterian Church**) and in South Africa the **Dutch Reformed Church** has both conservative and liberal branches.

In many countries (including England) Presbyterian and **Congregational** churches have joined to form a United Reformed Church. Most Presbyterian and Reformed churches belong to the World Alliance of Reformed Churches. Worldwide membership is estimated at around 40,000,000.

Primal Therapy. Seen by many as belonging to the **Human Potential Movement,** or indeed to what has been labelled the "self religions", Primal Therapy has attracted considerable numbers of Americans and Europeans who have sought to process deep-seated emotions by acquiring the skill of emitting a primal scream.

Primitive Methodism. *See* **Methodists.**

Progressive Judaism. *See* **Reform Judaism.**

Protestantism. Protestantism arose in the 16th century as a protest against certain doctrines of the **Roman Catholic Church.** In 1517 Martin Luther nailed a statement of "95 Theses" of belief to the door of Wittenberg Church in Germany, and four years later he was excommunicated. Within 20 years, due in great part to the administrative gifts of John Calvin (*see* **Presbyterians**) the movement had spread throughout Europe and later, through emigration and missionary work, to every country in the world.

Protestants treasure their direct personal relationship with God, and reject the need for church or priest as an intermediary. The Christian who has sinned is made acceptable to ("justified") a wholly good God by faith through grace alone, not through the sacraments of the church nor through his own good works.

The understanding of this came to Martin Luther through his study of the Bible, particularly the Epistle to the Romans. Protestants give high priority to the individual study of the Bible, and therefore to preaching: though the object of both is to witness the Word of God i.e. Jesus Christ ("the Word was made flesh" John 1, 14). It is his dying which reconciles humanity to God, despite the estrangement of sin. Personal response to God's love and forgiveness, and to freedom from guilt is the gratitude of good works and love for others.

For many years the conflict of ideas centred around the meaning of the Eucharist. Roman Catholics believed that the "substance" (an abstract mediaeval philosophical concept) of the bread and the wine was changed when they were consecrated so that by "transubstantiation" they become the body and blood of Christ. Protestants dismissed this as superstition and insisted that Christ was present with the worshippers as they enacted a memorial of the Last Supper. Many of these arguments and much of the debate about justification by faith have been explored and reconciled through the work of ARCIC—the Anglican, Roman Catholic International Commission.

A central doctrine of Protestantism is the "universal priesthood of all believers". Certain people may be set aside for ministry (and most Protestant churches have a structure of authority) but it is recognized that every Christian may be a priest to every other. This is now the main area of conflict between the Roman Catholic and Protestant churches (and between **Anglo-Catholic** and Protestant wings of the **Anglican** Church) and affects the debate on such matters as the ordination of women, administration of the Eucharist and the authority of the Pope.

The emphasis on a personal relationship with God through individual Bible study and revelation has led to many splits in the Protestant church as individual Christians strive to live and worship to the glory and purpose of God. This trend has been, to some extent, reversed by the growth of the ecumenical movement which encourages denominations to work together and eventually to unite. The Charismatic Movement has also affected both Catholics and Protestants and may be a means of healing this 500-year-old schism.

Psychosynthesis. A method of spiritual awakening designed by Roberto Assagioli, an Italian psychiatrist. The goal is a euphoric state of joy and mental illumination and love in the realization that all life is one. There is an emphasis on the self as a centre of pure consciousness, and this has led to its being described as one of the "self religions" within the much larger complex of **New Age Movements**.

Pure Land School. Also known as the Japanese Buddhist **Jodoshu.**

Pushtimarga (Way of Grace). A branch of the **Hindu** *bhakti* tradition founded by Vallabhacarya (1479–1532). It flourishes chiefly in Bombay, Rajasthan and Gujarat, and its adherents belong mainly to the commercial castes. The most characteristic feature of its worship is *seva* (service), which consists of a dedicated attendance upon Krishna's image understood as the Lord's own true and living form. There are eight periods in each day when the Lord Krishna is believed to grant the sight of himself to his faithful and this means that the priests of the Pushtimarga spend most of their day in dressing the image and providing its meals. The key scripture of this *sampradaya* is the *Bhagavata-purana,* upon which Vallabhacarya wrote a commentary. According to this, the only true reality is the Lord Krishna, and liberation can be attained by his grace alone. He is to be worshipped in particular by recitation of the *mantra* "Shri Krishna is my refuge".

Renunciation plays little part in the movement for Vallabhacarya spent most of his life as a householder and believed that his Lord had commanded him to marry and have children. His followers today dedicate "mind, body and wealth" to Krishna. The leaders of the *sampradaya* are householders and have the title *maharaja*. Its places of worship are known by the name *haveli,* which means a private mansion, implying that the Lord Krishna lives there as an honoured guest of the *maharaja*.

Q

Qadianis. *See* **Ahmadiya (Qadianis).**

Qadiriya. The Qadiriya is one of the oldest and most widely spread **Sufi** orders, represented in most Islamic countries from West Africa to South East Asia, although in many areas there are other more popular orders. The name is taken from the great saint 'Abd al-Qadir al-Jilani (1077–1166), the details of whose life pose many contradictions and who does not seem to have intended the founding of any Sufi Way. He is known principally as a **Hanbali** preacher who, after a period of legal training in Baghdad, led a wandering ascetic life in Iraq for about 25 years before returning to preach in the city. Many stories are told about his piety, unworldiness and miracles, but their historicity is open to question. After his death (his tomb is in Baghdad) he became generally regarded as a saintly miracle-worker with many popular shrines. His intercession was often sought, and many followers claimed to have seen him in visions and dreams. However, some Qadiris tried to play down the miraculous aspects of al-Jilani's role, notably the famous Hanbali Ibn Taimiya (d. 1328), who considered such visions to be the work of demons. He was himself to have an important influence on the thought of the anti-Sufi **Wahhabis** as well as on the **Salafiya,** the **Muslim Brotherhood,** and recent radical Islamists.

The Qadiriya has not developed any rigid system of teachings and practices, which vary from country to country and among different Qadiri groups. At their communal gatherings Qadiris normally recite verses in praise of the Prophet, and other sacred songs, sometimes to the accompaniment of musical instruments and with various bodily movements designed to induce ecstasy, typically the slow turning from right to left, while uttering pious formulae. A 40-day retreat is also practiced by Qadiris, who reduce their consumption of food until they are fasting completely for the last three days. In some areas local pilgrimages are made to shrines of 'Abd al-Qadir al-Jilani, and festivals are celebrated in his honour, for example at Salé, Morocco, where the Jilali branch of Qadiris present sheep and oxen to his descendants during the third month of the Islamic lunar year.

In the early modern period the Qadiriya has at times been associated with reformist activities and also with *jihad* against lax and syncretist Muslims and against European colonialists. In Hausaland (northern Nigeria, Niger) Usuman dan Fodio (1754–1817) experienced a dream vision of 'Abd al-Qadir al-Jilani, who girded him with the Sword of Truth to use against the enemies of **Islam**. He then led a successful *jihad* to counter un-Islamic practices connected with **African traditional religion** and to enforce the Holy Law. In Algeria another Qadiri shaikh, 'Abd al-Qadir (1808–83), was a reformist Sufi anxious to establish the Law (Shari'a) and opposed to saint cults or **maraboutism**. He also fought a lengthy *jihad*, in this case against the French from 1832–47, but was finally vanquished and imprisoned in Paris until 1852, after which he was allowed to settle in Damascus. Other Qadiri jihadists fought against the Dutch in Indonesia in the late 19th and early 20th centuries. Like some **Naqshabandis, Sanusis** and Tijanis, they represent an activist strand of Sufism, but other Qadiris have continued in the older quietist pattern of the medieval Qadiriya.

Qalandars. The Qalandars are one of the better known "irregular" **Sufi** orders, of which numerous examples are to be found in the Indian subcontinent. To call them irregular is to refer to their being *bi-shar'*, or "outside the Islamic law", in contrast to mainstream orders like the **Chishtiya**. In this respect they resemble the **Malangs**. Their name is derived from the alleged founder of the order, a native of Spain called 'Ali Abu Yusuf Qalandar (known too as Bu 'Ali Qalandar, d. 1323) who settled in India. His tomb at Panipat near Delhi is venerated as a shrine. The Qalandars are mendicant beggars who have a reputation for calling down a curse on any household where their request for alms is refused.

Qimbanda. Practiced by a small minority in Brazil, this is a movement of the type known generally as Afro–American spiritist, but differing from the much more widely practiced **Umbanda** in that it involves the invocation of evil spirits rather than benevolent ones.

Qizilbash. Qizilbash (from Turkish—"red head") is a term applied in a broad sense to designate ethnically diverse heterodox Muslim communities whose origin can be traced back to the historical encounter between the **Sunni** Ottoman Empire and the **Shi'ite** Safawid dynasty during the 15th to 17th centuries. The name itself was given by the Ottomans to nomadic Turkic partisans of the Safawid dynasty who used to wear 12 red bands on their head-cover as a token that they worshipped the 12 imams.

The Qizilbash contributed a lot to the rise of the Safawids to power and after the establishment of the Safawid state in 1501 enjoyed the status of military aristocracy and high-ranking bureaucracy. Known to have been mighty warriors, they are the only troops in the Muslim world that could rival the Ottoman janissaries.

To the contrary, in the Ottoman Empire the Qizilbash were considered a religion of opposition and a threat to the established political order; therefore they were persecuted and scorned. The term Qizilbash itself had a pejorative meaning in the Turkish vernacular and their religious practices and beliefs were regarded as a counter-culture. The Qizilbash enjoyed the moral support and guidance of the **Bektashiya** which seems to have become a receptacle for all sorts of non-Sunni currents.

The faith of the Qizilbash is rather syncretic, comprising elements of **Islam, Zoroastrianism** and **Christianity**. It is marked by sometimes far-reaching disregard of Muslim ritual and worship. A central figure in their system of beliefs is Ali, the fourth caliph, who is not less revered than Muhammad himself. Therefore followers of the sect have also been called **Alevi,** Aliani, Ali-ilahi. The deification of Ali comes only next to pantheism—tiny particles of God, according to their doctrine, are to be found everywhere in nature and the universe. They also have elaborated a cult of fire and stone. The Qizilbash do not honour the Quran as a holy book or mosques as sites of worship and drink alcoholic drinks during their ceremonies, which usually take place at night. They usually live in esoteric communities practising extreme endogamy and their doctrine is kept a secret from strangers. Vertical linkages within each community are very strong, but contacts between Qizilbash groups in different countries seem to have been scarce. Because of so little exchange it is hard to speak of a uniform Qizilbash doctrine.

Qizilbash women in general are much less secluded than their orthodox Muslim counterparts. They do not cover their faces, speak freely to male relatives and neighbours and participate in all ceremonies side by side with men. Since the honour of women in Islam is often regarded as derivative from seclusion, this has given grounds for allegations (e.g. in Turkey) of immoral practices and even promiscuity.

Qizilbash communities are to be found today in Turkey, Iran, Azerbaijan, Afghanistan, in Kurdish-inhabited lands, and Bulgaria. In Afghanistan they constitute an important and politically influential social group; in Azerbaijan the name Qizilbash has sentimental overtones derived from the past glory of the Safawid dynasty; while in modern Turkey they are still considered to be an inferior group with stigmatized identity.

Quakers. This is the long-standing popular name applied to members of the **Society of Friends**.

R

Rabita. Taken from the Arabic name of the **Muslim World League**, this is sometimes used in an English-speaking context as an abbreviation for that organization.

Radhasoami Satsang. This Indian religious movement, which draws on both **Sikh** and **Hindu** traditions, was founded in 1861 by Shiv Dayal Sahib (1818–1878), later known as Soamiji Maraj, in Agra. After his death the group split into three separate movements led by different *gurus:* the original group; the Radhasoami Satsang (Beas), named after their centre in Beas, Punjab; and the Radhasoami Satsang (Dayalbagh). Other splinter movements have continued to develop and there are currently a number of active groups across India, Europe and America. Membership of groups is kept secret.

All groups share a belief in the Supreme Being (Radhasoami), who presides over the three-level universe, each of which contains six further subdivisions. Only the techniques and teachings of the Radhasoami movement can carry the soul to the highest levels, other religions providing only a partial ascent. The human soul comes into being through emanation from Radhasoami, but it is imprisoned in matter. Radhasoami became incarnated in Soamiji Mararaj, and in each subsequent guru, in order to teach the way to liberation. These gurus—each referred to as *Sant Satguru* or Supreme Master—play a crucial role as the object of worship and the sole source of salvific knowledge.

Radhasoami techniques include the repetition of the holy name "Radhasoami", the contemplation of the holy form, and "sound practice" which, through accessing the spiritual sound current, guides the soul back to Radhasoami. The gurus impart secret meditation techniques to their initiates, such as the closely guarded *surat-shabda-yoga* (spirit world **yoga**), and great stress is placed on the "scientific" nature of the teachings which are often expressed in terms of contemporary technological language. These techniques are related to those of the Hindu **Tantric** traditions.

There are many independent groups devoted to particular leaders. The largest of these is the Radhasoami Satsang (Beas), currently led by Charan Singh, the disciple of Baba Sawan Singh (1858–1948), who was the inspiration for the first American sect in 1911. Other groups include, Radhasoami Satsang (Soamibagh) and Sawan Kirpal Ruhani Mission (Science of Spirituality, named after Hazur Baba Sawan Singh and their guru, Kirpal Singh (1896–1974)). The latter's son, Sant Darshan Singh (1921–   ) is the present guru. There is also a centre in New Hampshire, Sant Bani Ashram, devoted to the teachings of Ajaib Singh, a disciple of Kirpal Singh.

Raja Yoga. *See* **Brahma Kumaris.**

Rajneeshism. The movement centred on Bhagwan Shree Rajneesh (born 1931), a former professor of philosophy who in 1974 founded a community in Poona: the Shree Rajneesh Ashram. With a permanent population of some 2,000 people, it attracted many thousands more visitors, but in 1981 Bhagwan suddenly disappeared, to reappear shortly afterwards in Oregon where a new base was established, known as Rajneeshpuram. An astonishingly wide variety of courses was available, making the identification of a common underlying philosophy virtually impossible. In broad terms, though, Rajneeshism has been identified as one of the self religions.

Followers were known as the Orange People because of the colour of the clothing they wore. They also took a new name, and wore a picture of Bhagwan on a necklace of wooden beads. In 1985, however, scandal occurred when Bhagwan's personal secretary, Ma Anand Sheela, was arrested and later imprisoned for various irregularities, and Bhagwan himself was expelled from the United States, leaving his followers in a state of confusion and upset.

Bhagwan was now known as Osho ("Friend") Rajneesh, and sought to re-establish himself in Poona. The distinctive orange colour for clothing disappeared, though during meditation followers were encouraged to wear white or maroon. However, before the movement could regain anything of its former strength Rajneesh died in 1990, rendering its future all the more uncertain.

Ramakrishna Mission. The Mission, one of the most successful of modern **Hindu** religious movements, has its roots in the life of the Bengali saint Ramakrishna. Born Gadadhar Chattopadhyaya in 1836, Ramakrishna began at an early age to experience religious ecstasies. After migrating to Calcutta, he became a priest of the temple of Kali at Daksineswar which had been constructed by a wealthy widow. Ramakrishna was particularly attached to the worship of Kali, and his devotion to that goddess, coupled with his religious ecstasies, began to attract disciples. As a result of pressure from his family, he married his wife when she was only five years old, but the marriage appears to never have been consummated. In fact, Ramakrishna saw in his wife the embodiment of the goddess he worshipped, giving her the name Sarada Devi.

Among the many disciples that Ramakrishna attracted from the intellectual, Europeanized upper classes of Calcutta was Narendranath Dutt, who is better known Swami Vivekananda. After Ramakrishna's death in 1886, his disciples decided to form an Order to perpetuate his ideals. Thus was born what one might characterize as the first Hindu missionary society, with Vivekananda carrying the message of Ramakrishna throughout India and, ultimately, to the West in 1893 when he spoke to the World Parliament of Religions in Chicago. Subsequently, a number of centres, under the aegis of the newly-formed **Vedanta Society,** were established in the United States. After his return to India in 1897, Vivekananda established the Ramakrishna Mission to ensure their continued success. This institution still functions to-day with its headquarters at Belur near Calcutta. It boasts over 100 centres in India itself and more than 50 others around the world. It also administers impressive medical and educational facilities throughout India, and has remained in the forefront of charitable institutions in that country.

Ramanandis. A sect perhaps founded by legendary teacher of Kabir, Rama-nanda, sometime in the 15th century. Today it is the largest **Hindu Vaishnava** ascetic order (*sampradaya*), regularly vying with **Shaiva** rivals, the **Dashanamis,** for the best site at the great pilgrimage grounds of India. There is a threefold membership of householders, non-renouncers and renouncers with the first group providing lay support for the other two categories. Non-renouncers dwell in monasteries and hermitages which are found in large numbers throughout western and central India, the Ganges basin and the Himalayan foothills as well as in Nepal. Renouncers, who hold pride of place in the order, are homeless but unlike other Indian *samnyasins*, who wander in solitude, the Ramanandi renouncers travel in small groups which constitute an itinerant monastery or *khalsa*. The wanderings of these groups are not aimless for they obey an annual cycle in which all the major Vaishnava pilgrimage centres are visited at the astrologically correct time. The Renouncer smears his body twice a day with ash from a sacred fire and, while he has no permanent place of residence, Ayodhya, in northern India, is traditionally considered to be the central focus of the order, as the birth-place of the god Rama. Today it is the focus of militant Hindu activity, and in particular since the demolition of a mosque held to occupy the actual site of Rama's birth (*Ramajanmabhumi*). Non-renouncer Ramanandis, together with members of other groups such as the **Bharatiya Janata Party** and the **Vishwa Hindu Parishad,** were prominent in this enterprise.

Ramdasis. A Hindu **Vaishnava** devotional movement based on the teachings of the Maharashtrian saint and poet, Ramdas (1608–1681). Ramdas' main work is the *Dasbodh*, in which he outlines a philosophy of monist **Vedanta**. He also stressed the supreme importance of the *guru* and devotion to Rama, hence his name which means "slave of Rama". In his lifetime he established a large number of monasteries (*math*) in the region of western India and is perhaps best known as the spiritual preceptor (*guru*) of Shivaji, the founder of the Maratha state. The Ramdasi movement went into decline after the fall of the Maratha kingdom in 1817, but since Indian independence the group has risen to prominence once again, partly on the back of the Maharashtrian nationalist cult of Shivaji. Ramdasis wear orange/brown clothing and may be celibate monks or laity. About 40 *maths* currently flourish and devotees concentrate their attentions on study of the *Dasbodh* and worship of Rama.

Rashtriya Swayamsevak Sangh (RSS). The Sangh (RSS) grows out of a tradition of Hindu communalism that stretches back to the beginning of the 20th century. The RSS itself was founded by Dr Keshav Hedgewar in 1925. The organization draws on earlier traditions of militant **Hinduism** and promotes the Hindu religion, Hindu society and Hindu culture. It opposed the pluralistic stance of Gandhi and Nehru, preferring instead to work for a governmental system that more accurately reflected the majority status of Hindus in India. Although it avoided involvement in the struggle for independence, the RSS came to public attention as a result of its activities in the Hindu-Muslim riots at Nagpur in September of 1927. It grew in influence during the communal disruptions that marked the last days of the British Raj, commanding some 10,000 cadres in 1945, but it was the assassination of Gandhi in 1948 by a Hindu sympathetic to its aims that thrust it into the front ranks of Indian politics. Banned until July 1949, it was subsequently allowed to resume functioning. It continued to forge bonds with non-Congress political parties and during the Emergency (1975–1977) it was again banned for a short period. The power base of the RSS is the urban middle class and particularly the petty bourgeoisie who have been most directly in economic competition with the Muslim minority. The RSS has close links with the **Bharatiya Janata Party (BJP)** and the **Vishwa Hindu Parishad (VHP)**.

Rastafarianism. The Rastafarian movement appeared in Jamaica during the 1930s. It was inspired by the Jamaican Marcus Garvey's Back to Africa movement, and his prophecy of a black messiah who would liberate black people. The accession of Ras ("Prince") Tafari to the imperial throne of Ethiopia in 1930 as the emperor Haile Selassie was seen by some as fulfilment both of Garvey's prophecy and of Psalm 68 with its alleged claim that the black race had been singled out by God for special attention.

Rastafarian beliefs are fluid and varied, but in general they regard themselves as one of the 12 tribes of ancient Israel, and some believed Haile Selassie to be the Messiah who would redeem them from white oppression—which they identify as due to the modern Babylon of Britain, the United States, and the Jamaican state (plus, for some, the church)—and return them to the homeland Africa. This last belief, in the return to the promised land, is today often interpreted symbolically rather than literally. Harmony with nature is important, and most Rastafarians are vegetarians (or, indeed, vegans).

In Dominica, Rastafarians are known as "Dreads", meaning simply the power that lies within every individual. Uncombed hair (dreadlocks) and beards are characteristic of male adherents, and hats and other garments may use typical Rastafarian colours: black for the race, red in memory of the blood of slaves, green for the promised land, and gold for a golden future. Strict moral standards are fostered, and members may renounce alcohol and tobacco, but there is widespread use of cannabis (ganja) which is considered to be sanctioned by the Bible.

Anti-white sentiment has been important but is not universal. **Christianity** has been rejected by many as the white man's religion, but some Rastafarians have been baptized into the **Ethiopian Orthodox Church**. The Bible is accepted as God's word—as interpreted by Rastafarians—and readings from it feature in their meetings, as does the singing of hymns, the words of which have been adapted to reflect Rastafarian beliefs. This is characteristic too of their other songs, which often combine social comment with praise of Ras Tafari (and ganja). Their influence on popular music through the development of reggae is well known.

It is estimated that Rastafarians in Jamaica number approximately 100,000. Numbers elsewhere in the Caribbean, in Britain, or in the United States are not known, but their cultural influence in terms of poetry, music or art is of still wider international significance.

Ratana. In 1918 as Tahupotiki Wiremu Ratana was standing on the verandah of his home, a small cloud arose out of the sea, then approached and swirled around him. To his astonishment a voice spoke in Maori: "Fear not, I am the Holy Ghost . . . . Ratana, I appoint you as the mouthpiece of God for the multitude of this land. Unite the Maori people, turning them to Jehovah of the thousands, for this is his compassion to all of you". His family thought him mad or drunk when he told them about this experience. Later, an angel appeared to him and repeated the message and commissioned him to preach the Gospel to the Maori people, and to heal their spirits and their bodies.

After Christmas 1918 he turned to ministry full-time, and soon his fame as a preacher and faith healer had spread. On Christmas Day 1920 an undenominational church was opened, built with Ratana's own funds. It was a great occasion with **Roman Catholic** and **Protestant** clergy taking part in the dedication, in the presence of more than 3,000 people. A religious revival spread throughout the Maori. By 1921 more than 19,000 had joined Ratana and his movement. Although the Catholic Church withdrew its support, the movement had strong backing from **Anglicans** and **Methodists.**

At Pentecost in 1925 the Ratana Church came into existence as a separate organization, and in July that year it was recognized by the Government when the Registrar General of Births, Deaths and Marriages gazetted the names of 38 representatives authorized by the state to conduct marriages. The break with the Anglican Church followed two years later, but the Methodists left relationships open.

According to the Ratana Church Creed deposited at the time of its registration with the Registrar General, the Church had a firm Christian basis— belief in Jehovah, Father, Son and Holy Ghost; Jesus Christ as the human form of God's son; the Holy Ghost, the breath of Jehovah; the Holy Christian Church; humans as co-workers with God; the Holy Bible as the record of

Jehovah's greatest revelation; the faithful agents who are God's workers and messengers, and finally Ratana as the mouthpiece of Jehovah.

As the movement grew in influence, a temple was opened in 1928, on the prophet's birthday. As the Labour Party emerged as a major force in New Zealand politics there were contacts with Ratana. Closer relationships were forged in 1928, and since 1936 the four political representatives of the Maori people who sit in Parliament have considered themselves part of the Labour Party and have served the country, when the Labour Party has been in government, with distinction. Ratana died in 1939, but his influence has continued in the Ratana Church, and has touched all of Maoridom as well as the political life of the nation. In recent years Ratana has shown a noticeable growth.

Ravidas Panthis. An Indian devotional movement. Ravidas (1414?–1526), also known as Rai Das, was a *chamar* (cobbler), and mystic of deep spirituality. At the end of the 19th century, *chamars*, in the hope of improving their social status, converted to **Sikhism** in large numbers, but religious acceptance did not result in them achieving this aim. Socially they remained untouchable. Some began to proclaim themselves to be neither **Hindu** nor Sikh but Ravidasi. The *Guru Granth Sahib*, which contains 41 of the hymns of Ravidas, continues to be the focus of worship and the word *gurdwara* is often used to describe the place of worship. Ravidasis tend to keep the *kesh*, i.e. uncut hair, and turban, and are frequently mistaken for Sikhs. Currently, however, a *granth* using only the hymns of Ravidas is being prepared and the time may come when it replaces the *Guru Granth Sahib*. The celebration of the birthday of Guru Ravidas in February/March is another development paving the way for this movement to become a separate tradition. Members of the Panth are mainly found in the Punjab.

Reconstructionist Judaism. Most recent of the Jewish "denominations", Reconstructionist Judaism is based on the teachings of Rabbi Mordecai Menahem Kaplan (1881–1983). Kaplan, an instructor in the Jewish Theological Seminary from 1909–1963, originally had no intention of forming a new movement, hoping instead that his understanding of **Judaism** as a religious civilization, as presented in his 1934 *Judaism as a Civilization,* would offer a new way to all branches of Judaism. He argued that Judaism is a culture whose primary aim is the perpetuation of the Jewish people. Thus, Judaism is to serve its people, not vice-versa. He defined the "God-idea" in Judaism to be the power that makes for salvation which, in this era, must be this-worldly.

In 1935 he and others founded *The Reconstructionist,* a monthly journal, and later issued a new Passover *Haggadah* (1941) and Sabbath Prayerbook (1945), changing prayers claiming Jewish exclusivity and challenging the belief that all Jews would return to the Land of Israel when the Messiah came, arguing that Israel must be restored but not all Jews must return to it. Despite his attempt to write liturgy for all Jews, his work was condemned by the Orthodox Union and he was "excommunicated".

In 1955, The Reconstructionist Foundation of Congregations was organized, requiring member congregations to belong either to the **Reform** or **Conservative** movements following Kaplan's opposition to creating a new movement. In 1968,

however, the movement became a separate organization, The Federation of
Reconstructionist Congregations (since 1982, The Federation of Reconstruct-
ionist Congregations and Havurot) with its own seminary, The Reconstructionist
Rabbinic College, open to both men and women and since 1975 having its
own rabbinic organization, The Reconstructionist Rabbinical Association.
Currently, Reconstructionist Judaism estimates a membership of 50,000 and
over 60 congregations worldwide with 40,000 members in America, 8,000 in
Canada, and 2,000 in Curacão, the Netherlands, and Israel.

Reform Judaism. Reform Judaism, also known as Liberal or Progressive
Judaism, is the denomination most concerned with creating a modern **Judaism**.
At times, quite radical in its jettisoning of older Jewish ideas and practices,
the movement has, in the past generation, become more receptive to certain
elements of tradition.

Reform rejects the traditional view that the written Torah (the five first books
of the Hebrew Bible) were revealed verbatim by God and that the oral Torah
(the Mishnah and the Palestinian and Babylonian *Talmudim*) is the sole basis
for interpreting the written Torah, while stressing Judaism's universalistic and
ethical qualities, and more recently participating in the American Civil Rights
movement, and similar causes.

Reform Judaism began in Germany and its development is related to
events and ideas both inside and outside the Jewish community. European
society, especially German society after Kant, was swept by the ideas of the
Enlightenment which demanded that religion be "reasonable" and modern
(even a major opponent of Reform Judaism, Rabbi Samuel Raphael Hirsch
(1808–1880) emphasized the concord between Judaism and modernity). This
was also the age of European Jewry's emancipation, which came with the
stipulation that Jews modify their religion in order to become "proper" citizens.
Many Jews also saw "modernization" as an ideal though they were less
enthusiastic about abandoning their Jewish identity. These Jews looked for
a way to become full citizens while still being committed to what they saw as
the rational and universal core of Judaism.

The first Reform institutions were Israel Jacobson's Seesen temple (1810),
with Jacob Herz Beer's temple in his Berlin house (1815), and the more
permanent temple in Hamburg (1818) following. At the time, the name
"temple" was used by some traditional Jews but Jacobson saw his as a
universalist replica of the ancient shrine and later Reformers considered
theirs replacements for it. Worship in these temples included organ music,
not only challenging prohibition using instruments during worship as a sign
of mourning for the Temple in Jerusalem and its instruments, but using an
instrument identified with **Christianity**. The liturgy was changed also, now
including the vernacular and rejecting the hope that the Messiah would appear
and lead the Jews back to the Land of Israel.

These changes were justified by the argument that Judaism had developed
historically and thus contemporary Jews could modify their religion and reject
what were considered to be rabbinic additions. These views were put forward
most strongly by Abraham Geiger (1810–1874), an early leader of German
Reform and scholar of *Wissenschaft des Judentums* ("the scientific study of
Judaism"). The movement drew traditionalist anathemization and was hindered
by Prussia's government which feared making a potentially more appealing

Judaism. The movement, however, spread throughout Germany, also having some impact in the rest of Europe.

In America, the absence of governmental control or interference with religion made it possible for Reform to grow rapidly. The first non-traditional synagogue was founded in Charleston, South Carolina (1825) but did not last long. German–Jewish immigrants in the mid- and later 19th century had had exposure to Reform and their children warmly embraced the Reform tradition. As in Germany, there were disputes between the more moderate and radical factions; the former being championed by men such as Isaac Meyer Wise (1819–1900), and the latter being led by David Einhorn (1809–1879). Wise hoped to find a way to both modernize and unify American Jewry but after some unity was achieved in Cincinnati, it soon became clear that Reform was to be a separate domination. By 1883, the institutions Wise founded, the Union of American Hebrew Congregations (1873) and the seminary, Hebrew Union College (1875, merged with the Jewish Institute of Religion in 1950) became exclusively Reform. The date marks the graduation of HUC's first students, an event celebrated by a banquet featuring shellfish, prohibited by traditional dietary laws.

Einhorn's son-in-law, Kaufman Kohler (1843–1926), re-established the supremacy of the radical wing by writing the "Pittsburgh Platform" which was considered at an 1885 Reform rabbinic conference and then adopted at the 1889 founding meeting of the Reform rabbinate, the Central Conference of American Rabbis. The platform, which defined Reform for 50 years, repudiated Jewish dietary laws, belief in Heaven and Hell, the messiah, and the return to Zion.

The ideas embedded in this document dominated American Reform Judaism until the 1930s when they were challenged by the rise of anti-Semitism in Europe and America as well as the long-term impact of waves of Russian immigrants (beginning in 1881) who were less assimilationist than German Reform Jews. Reform's change of attitude was shown in the 1937 Columbus (Ohio) Platform which implicitly supported Zionism while also affirming the importance of Jewish life in the diaspora, as well as universal social justice. Any doubts about Reform's stand on Zionism was eliminated in 1942 when it endorsed the *Biltmore Program* for the creation of a Jewish State.

Recent decades have seen Reform retrace its steps towards greater appreciation of tradition with the movement's 1976 "Reform Judaism—A Centenary Platform" (The "San Francisco Platform") listing of a number of ritual practices among Reform Jewish "obligations" being quite different from the Pittsburgh Platform's approach. The most recent series of prayerbooks *(Gates of Prayer* and *Gates of Repentance)* have much more Hebrew than their predecessors, *The New Union Prayerbooks*.

Yet Reform has also remained innovative, ordaining women rabbis since 1972. It also has changed its definition of Jewish identity to include as Jews those with Jewish fathers and non-Jewish mothers. This adoption of patrilineal descent in addition to matrilineal descent was opposed by Israel's Progressive Jews. Reform also officially tolerates its gay and lesbian rabbis though it urges them to consider the implications of "coming out of the closet" before doing so.

Despite the refusal of its Orthodox rabbinic establishment to recognize them as a *bona fide* Jewish movement, Reform has remained committed to

Israel. In 1963, HUC-JIR established a campus in Jerusalem and requires its rabbinic, cantorial and Jewish education students to study there for a year. The Association of Reform Zionists of America (ARZA) made significant inroads at the last World Zionist Organization conference and was instrumental in having that body call for plurality in Israeli Judaism. Reform has established two **kibbutzim** in Israel, Yahel and Lotan.

Reform Judaism is the largest component of the **World Union for Progressive Judaism,** founded in 1926. In addition to North America's 846 Reform congregations and 297,435 families, Progressive Judaism counts among its ranks at least 30,000 Liberal and Reform Jews in Great Britain, 5,000 families (six congregations) in Argentina and Brazil, 8,000 members (11 congregations) of the Australian and New Zealand Union for Progressive Judaism, 800 Israeli families (15 congregations) and smaller groups elsewhere in Europe and South America.

Reformed Catholic Churches. A number of churches owe their origin to schism from the **Roman Catholic Church** by a group of priests. Of these the largest is the Czechoslovak Hussite Church (membership mainly in Czechoslovakia but with branches in the USA). This was founded in 1920 after demands by a group of priests for a liturgy in the Czech language, the abolition of the celibacy of the priesthood and lay participation in church government had been rejected by Rome. The church does not believe in the Apostolic Succession (bishops are elected for seven years only) and rejects the doctrines of Original Sin and Purgatory.

Other such churches are the Italian Catholic Reformed Church (formed 1881 by a schism of 12 priests and six churches) and the Lusitanian Church in Portugal (formed 1871 by a schism of 11 priests). .

Reformed Church. *See* **Presbyterians (Reformed)**.

Reiyukai Kyodan. A Japanese new religious movement, the doctrine of Reiyukai Kyodan (Society for Companions of the Spirits) is rooted in **Nichiren-shu.** Rites include the recitation of an abridgement of the Lotus Sutra. This predominantly lay organization is based on the belief that salvation of one's ancestors will pre-empt one's own salvation. Interpreted on a national level, social discord and calamity in Japan are due to the ritual neglect of ancestral spirits.

Reiyukai was founded by Kubo Kakutaro (1892–1944) and his sister-in-law, Kotani Kimi, a charismatic and shamanic personality. The sect claims around 3,000,000 adherents, and is noted for its promotion of traditional values, especially relating to the family.

Religion of Heavenly Wisdom. A Japanese, **Shinto**-based, new religious movement more widely known as **Tenrikyo.**

Religion of the Heavenly Way. The English rendition of **Chondo-Gyo,** a Korean new religious movement.

Republican Brothers. The Republican Brothers, also known as the New Islamic Mission (or, until 1969, al-Hizb al-Jumhari, Republican Party) attracted attention during President Nimeiri's Islamization programme in the Sudan in 1983–1985 in particular. More of a religious movement than a political organization, its inspiration lay in its leader, Mahmud Muhammad Taha (b. 1911). Revered for his spirituality and learning, Taha developed a radical methodology for transforming and liberalizing the traditional shari'a, and for interpreting the Quran.

The Brothers distinguish between the First Message of Islam, found in the later, Medinan, suras of the Quran, and the Second Message, found in the earlier, Meccan, suras. In the First Message one finds teachings about spreading **Islam** by the sword, and alluding to the inequality of the sexes. These became incorporated in the shari'a. Yet this First Message, although it contained positive reforms such as banning female infanticide and introducing the alms tax in support of the poor, was intended to be transitional as part of a gradually applicable revelation. It was to be replaced by the Second Message, whose moral and spiritual teachings should now be allowed to transform the traditional shari'a, enabling inclusion of modern notions of human rights, democracy and socialism.

Taha's views were regarded with abhorrence by the mainstream Muslim leadership, to the extent that he could be reviled as a heretic. Whatever the merits or otherwise of his methodology, the fate of this 74-year-old non-violent reformist Muslim leader under Nimeiri evoked international criticism. He was widely regarded as a victim of internal politics when he was arrested, summarily tried, and then hanged in January 1985 for alleged sedition and apostasy. His followers, who number a few hundred committed members and several thousand sympathizers, continue to propagate his teachings: a prominent advocate is the Sudanese jurist Abdullahi Ahmed an-Na'im, author of *Toward an Islamic Reformation*.

Female members are known as **Republican Sisters.**

Republican Sisters. Female members of the Sudanese **Republican Brothers** movement. Many follow a communal way of life with disciplined routines of work, discussion and prayer. Dressed in white robes and working in pairs, they were in the habit of actively seeking converts by engaging people in conversation on the street, e.g. in Khartoum. This pattern was disrupted, however, following the execution of their leader for alleged sedition and apostasy in 1985.

Revival Zion. An Afro-Protestant cult found still in parts of Jamaica, and similar in many ways to **Pocomania.** Weekly services involve drumming, prayers and Bible readings as in **Convince,** but here the spirit possession that occurs involves the spirits of prominent Old Testament figures (for instance Moses, Joshua, Jeremiah), apostles and evangelists from the New Testament, archangels (for example Michael), Satan, and the dead. Possession by the Holy Spirit also occurs. The ritual of baptism is a further feature of the movement.

Rifa'iya. The Rifa'iya is one of the oldest **Sufi** orders, founded in the marshes of southern Iraq by Ahmad b. 'Ali al-Rifa'i (1106–82). Rifa'i gatherings are accompanied by the beating of drums and dancing, and by the accomplishment of extraordinary feats while in a state of ecstasy. Characteristic Rifa'i practices are dancing in fires and eating the flames until they are extinguished, putting heated iron into one's mouth, and biting the heads off live snakes. In India the Rifaʻis are often known as Gurzmar because of the practice of striking their bodies with a *gurz*, a sort of iron mace. All such acts are taken as exemplifying the ability of the spirit to overcome the base flesh. In modern times critics have sometimes accused Rifaʻis of resorting to jugglery.

The Rifaʻiya is well established in Iraq, Syria and Egypt, although in Syria it has been repressed since 1979 for allegedly harbouring anti-governmental members of the **Muslim Brotherhood.** Small communities of Rifaʻis have been documented in Yugoslavia and East Africa, and they are active in parts of the Indian sub-continent (Gujarat, the Deccan, Malabar, the Laccadives and Sri Lanka).

Ringatu. The founder of the Ringatu Church, Te Kooti, was educated at a mission school and read the Bible. During the Land Wars of the 1860s he was employed as an ammunition carrier by the Government, and five years later was arrested on a charge of spying, condemned without trial and exiled to the Chatman Islands off the coast of the South Island of New Zealand.

In 1867, following an illness, Te Kooti was called by God to be a prophet. In 1868 he escaped and returned to New Zealand where he was hunted by the Government for four years. On the basis of a number of religious experiences during this period, Te Kooti came to identify himself with Moses, and saw it as his vocation to deliver the Maori people from the oppression of foreigners. He saw the Maori people as the children of Israel and their experience as that of Hebrews in Egypt. His escape from exile was a parallel to the escape of Moses and the people of Israel from Egypt.

Ringatu attracted a strong following among the Maori people, and it was Te Kooti's rejection of **Christianity** that led him to base his church on Old Testament and Jewish ideas. The celebration of harvest festivals and the feast of the Passover were inaugurated, commemorating the deliverance of the escape of the exile from the Chatham Islands. Services were held on the 12th day of every month, and Saturday worship was instituted.

Ringatu is a Maori Christian Church today. Although it has a smaller following than **Ratana**, it still is widely respected throughout Maoridom.

Rinzai Zen. A form of Japanese **Buddhism.** The purpose of **Zen** adepts is to reproduce here and now the Enlightenment experience of the Buddha through meditation and related practice. Zen attempts to reach the absolute as simply and directly as possible, rejecting the rituals and formalism characteristic of the aristocratic Buddhism which was its predecessor in Japan.

Zen arrived in Japan from China. The most significant early transmitter was Eisai (1141–1215), a **Tendai** monk, like all the Kamakura era reformers, who studied in China and brought back the Rinzai branch of Zen. It seems that to some extent he retained his esoteric Tendai allegiances, and the Kenninji temple in Kyoto over which he presided some time after his return provided for Tendai and **Shingon** rituals, as well as being one of the great centres for the propagation of Rinzai Zen.

Rinzai, essentially a monastic school, places emphasis on the precepts, and on meditation. It is also characterized by the use of the *koan,* a type of riddle designed to expose human reason as severely limited. These are set by Rinzai masters to encourage disciples out of their habitual modes of thinking. The master–disciple relationship is crucial. Only a master can declare a disciple enlightened, and the onus is on the aspiring disciple to seek out the right master.

Rinzai achieved a strong early footing through the patronage of the *samurai* class, who were attracted by its simplicity and the aura of propriety and order of the neo-Confucian values which had accompanied Zen in its transmission from China. Unlike the rival **Soto** school, Rinzai was, from its inception, a strong advocate of Chinese literary and artistic traditions.

The sects of Rinzai are mainly based in the Kyoto area, displaying institutional rather than doctrinal differences; the largest of which is Rinzaishu Myoshinjiha. All have a large lay following, in total around 3,000,000 adherents, who meet not only in temples, but also in factories, offices, schools and universities for sitting meditation (*zazen*) sessions and discussions with masters. The Rinzai monk D. T. Suzuki (1870–1966) was influential in bringing Zen teachings to the West where they were popularized in the 1950s by the Beat poets of America.

Rissho Koseikai. A Japanese new religious movement founded in 1938 by former members of **Reiyukai Kyodan,** Niwano Nikkyo and housewife Naganuma Myoko, Rissho Koseikai (Society for the Establishment of Righteousness and Harmony) advocates a spiritual path in which specific individual and societal problems are examined in the light of a collection of **Buddhist** doctrines, predominantly **Nichiren**-influenced. Folk religious practices, such as divination and healing, have played a diminishing role since the war. The administrative set up is complex, and there is significant stress on strong member-leader relationships. Headquarters are in Tokyo, and the sect claims almost 5,000,000 members, making it the largest of those groups that have emerged from Reiyukai.

Risshu. One of the three surviving Nara sects of Japanese **Buddhism**. Emphasizing strict adherence to monastic discipline (*vinaya*), it has about 30,000 members. One of its affiliated schools is the **Shingon Risshu**.

Roman Catholic Church. More than 872,104,646 people call themselves Roman Catholic. This means that they were baptized by a Roman Catholic priest, who in turn has been ordained by a bishop believed to be bound both in an historical chain which leads in unbroken succession to the first Apostles, and in a hierarchical chain which binds his own episcopal authority to that of the Pope. The Pope is held to be both bishop of Rome and, as the successor of Peter, the guide of Christian doctrine and morals. When the Church draws on the unanimous voice of the ecumenical Councils, it is taken to be infallible Christian dogma. Roman Catholicism is thus hierarchical, traditional and sacramental. For Roman Catholics a sacramental act is one in which Christ is made effectively present. There are seven sacraments: baptism, confirmation, eucharist, ordination, anointing of the sick, confession, and marriage.

By the eighth century, the Popes had made a pact with the Frankish kings of the West. The latter supplied armed protection to Christian mission, whilst the former conferred a sacral charisma upon the Holy Roman Emperor. A transition has been made from Christian societies (c.100–300) to *Christendom* (312–1303), finally dissolved in the struggle between Pope and Emperor for the upper hand (the "higher sword"), and to the unstable fusion of

modern nationalism and Catholicism (c.1450–1789) created in France, the
Austro–Hungarian Empire and in Spain and its South American dominions.
Contemporary phenomena as diverse as the Charles Maurras's Action Française
(condemned at Rome in 1907 and 1926) in the first half of this century, and
the flourishing of Marxist theology in South America (if not condemned,
discouraged) in the second, pay tribute to the persistent refusal of Catholics
to acknowledge either an autonomous secular State or an autonomous market
economy.

The 19th century saw the retreat of **Christianity** from the claim either to
dominate public institutions or to explain external reality. In 1878, Pope
Leo XIII responded to the Christian need for an objective and rational
theology and to the secularization of European politics and social life with the
encyclical *Aeterni Patris*, which recalled Catholics to Thomism, the theology of
St Thomas Aquinas (1224–1274). In *Rerum Novarum* (1891) Leo castigated the
evil consequences of an economic liberalism uninhibited by objective morality.
The errors of the age were perceived as subjectivism, relativism and historicism.
Each was condemned during the "Modernist Crisis" of 1905–1908, during which
the Roman Curia invoked its full authority against a spectre partly projected by
itself. The influential mid-20th-century Catholic theologian, Bernard Lonergan
noted that the catholicism of 1905–1960 is summed up in the fact that it named
the worst of all heresies "modernism". For some, it was a time of the flowering
of Catholic thought: in Germany and Poland, Max Scheler, Ida Görres,
Edith Stein, Erich Przywara and Roman Ingarden invented an admixture of
Thomism and phenomenology; in France, Jacques Maritain and Gilson devised
neo-Thomistic philosophies, whilst their compatriots Charles Péguy, Bernanos,
and Claudel created Catholic novels and poetry; the "New French Theology" of
Henri de Lubac, Louis Bouyer, Yves Congar and Jean Danielou bloomed; as
did the "English Catholic Spring" of the 1920s and 1930s, and whose spokesmen
were Chesterton, Christopher Dawson, Belloc, Eric Gill, David Jones, Evelyn
Waugh, Martin D'Arcy and Ronald Knox. For others it was a fallow time, a
time of stifling conformism.

The Second Vatican Council (1962–1965), the Church's 21st Ecumenical
Council was convened by Pope John XXIII. After what seemed to some to have
been a century's confinement in a medievalist straitjacket, Catholics embraced
the new liberties which the Council enshrined: pluralism in theological method,
the encouragement of ecumenical contacts, the freedom of Biblical scholars to
practice historical criticism, the relaxation of the plethora of rules encircling
religious life, the devolution of episcopal control ("collegiality"), and the
translation of the old, beautiful Tridentine Mass from Latin into the vernacular
of the "New Mass".

The encyclical *Humanae Vitae* was published by Pope Paul VI in 1968 to a
roar of disapproval. It became a symbol of the chasm between Papal loyalists
and *refuseniks* which rent the Church for the next 20 years, and of which there
are few signs of repair. *Humanae Vitae* taught that artificial contraception is
contrary to the natural law. There followed an exodus from seminaries, and
the new phenomena of public dissent on the part of prominent theologians,
and private dissent from a central moral teaching on the part of perhaps
the majority of lay people and their local clergy. The novelty is that the
dissent refers, not only to the pastoral application of Catholic ethics, but
to their underlying principles. Sexual issues, such as contraception, abortion,

homosexuality, and the celibacy of the clergy, have become the storm-centre of the Church. The present Pope is John Paul II. His 1991 commemoration of *Rerum Novarum, Centesimus Annus* describes campaigns to enjoin Third World countries artificially to regulate births as a form of "chemical warfare". It is highly improbable that his successors will depart from his stand. The resulting friction has led both to the diminution of belief in Papal authority, and to its centralization. If, as some believe, there is an implicit schism in the Catholic Church, it is probable that it may at some date become explicit. In 1988, Cardinal Archbishop Lefebvre (see **Conservative Catholic Churches**) led numerous Catholics who had refused to countenance the New Mass into a breakaway Church.

Many divisions have been brought about by the alienation of middle-class Catholics from the social structures and paradigms of rationality on which Catholic doctrine is based. The Pope's pronouncements appear to these men and women to be the strident assertion of impracticable ideals. Catholics will remain within their Church only if convincing restatement(s) and practice(s) of Catholic thought and social life are found. Thus, the most significant growth areas of contemporary Catholicism are the new religious communities. Reflecting the emphasis of Vatican II, they are largely composed of lay people. These base communities thrive in varying forms from Central Europe to Brazil. They include, amongst others, the biblically-oriented Neo-Catechumenal Way, the intellectually reflective, Italian-based Communio è Liberazione, founded by Don Giovanni Giusseppe and attached to Henri de Lubac's theology, and the élitist and reactionary purism of **Opus Dei**. These new groups are significant for the Church because its ethic is fitted to members of a community, not to isolated individuals, and because any new Catholic theology will be grounded in the experience of Christian society, as was St Augustine's *City of God*. *Centesimus Annus* gives its support to "intermediary groups" and claims that the primary task of "a business firm is not . . . to make a profit but [to be] . . . a community of persons . . .".

Pope John Paul II appears as an authoritarian to many in the West, whilst demonstrating a open-mindedness unthinkable in his predecessors. Thus, *Mulieris Dignitatem* (1988, *On the Dignity of Women*) is neither acceptable to Christian liberals nor the rehash of conservative dogmas which both his opponents and his supporters might prefer. The encyclical disavows the notion of the ordination of women to the priesthood, though it recalls that in the Christian Bible " . . . God's love is presented . . . sometimes as the 'feminine' love of a mother". It states that motherhood is *not* merely physical but " . . . a *human fact* . . . linked to the personal structure of the woman . . . ", thereby lifting the argument about natural law out of the realm of biology. This is of a piece with the author's "Personalist" philosophy, drawn from Thomism, from Gabriel Marcel's existentialism, and from the realist phenomenology of Max Scheler. These may be the intellectual roots of the future re-statement of Catholic philosophy.

Romanian Uniate Catholic Church. *See* **Eastern Rite Romanian Catholic Church; Uniate Churches**.

Rosicrucianism. Rosicrucians follow the teachings of Christian Rosenkreutz (1378–1484?) whose life, possibly mythic, was recounted in documents that aroused considerable interest when published in Germany in the early 17th century. Rosicrucianism integrates esoteric **Christianity** with a mastery of the laws of nature through alchemy and other magical practices. Many **occult** groups claim a Rosicrucian origin—notably today the Ancient and Mystical Order Rosae Crucis (AMORC). AMORC was founded by the prolific writer H. Spencer-Lewis in 1915, and is now an international organization offering tuition by correspondence course.

Russian Orthodox Church. This term can refer either specifically to the Patriarchal Church of Moscow (*see* **Orthodox Church—Byzantine;** section 4) or, more broadly, to all the Churches of Russian language and culture, whether or not currently under the jurisdiction of Moscow.

Russia became a Christian province of the Byzantine Church of Constantinople at the end of the 10th century. Its first metropolitan see was at Kiev, but in the 14th century Moscow became the principal see and its metropolitans were thereafter Russians, not Greeks. The Church grew in power and influence, and in 1448 declared itself **autocephalous.** In 1589 Moscow was recognized as a Patriarchate, and henceforth regarded as the "Third Rome" (Constantinople being the second). **Roman Catholic** influence in territories Russia had formerly annexed or temporarily lost (Ukraine, Poland and Czechoslovakia) led to the formation of **Uniate Churches,** which retained Slavonic customs and forms of worship while acknowledging the authority of the Pope. Enmity between the Uniate and Orthodox Churches became a permanent feature of Russian religious life, especially in the Ukraine, where in later centuries many Uniates returned—some freely, others under coercion—to Russian Orthodoxy.

In 1721 Peter the Great abolished the patriarchate, replacing it with a Holy Synod of bishops. In 1917 the Patriarchate was restored, which distanced the Church somewhat from the doomed Tsarist régime. The Russian Church has been one of the few Orthodox Churches in recent centuries with the opportunity to undertake missionary work. A small autonomous Church in Finland was established by the 12th century, and in the 19th century Churches in Japan and Alaska (the latter eventually covering the whole of North America) took root.

During the long period of anti-religious communist rule, all Church activities except worship itself were suppressed, and thousands of Christians suffered imprisonment and martyrdom for their faith. During World War II, in recognition of the Church's patriotic support, Stalin granted the Church a number of substantial concessions. This led, in the post-war years, to an official *rapprochement* between Church and State, whereby the Church could enjoy a limited freedom in return for a measure of State control. But the ideological pressures and anti-religious propaganda continued, together with subtler forms of control, some of it now exercised from within the Church hierarchy. Many Russian Orthodox joined dissident and illicit "underground Churches", prominent among them the **True Orthodox Church;** their histories, as well as the full story of the official Church under communism, have yet to be written.

Russian expatriates in Europe and North America who chose to dissociate themselves from the Moscow Patriarchate placed themselves under alternative but still legitimate jurisdictions: the Russian Exarchate in Western Europe (based in Paris), the Russian (Orthodox) Church Abroad (also known as the Synodal Church), or the autocephalous **Orthodox Church in America.**

Members of other national groups, who in the Soviet Union were under the Moscow Patriarchate, formed independent administrations of uncertain status, typically appealing to the Ecumenical Patriarchate, in Istanbul, for recognition. These included the Ukrainian, Belorussian, Latvian, Lithuanian and Estonian Churches, all of which are, or have been, part of the Russian Church in the broader sense. Also deriving from the greater Russian Church are the small but now autocephalous Churches of Poland and Czechoslovakia.

The collapse of communism and the break-up of the Soviet Union left the Church uncertain how best to take up again its religious freedoms and social responsibilities. Judging by the numbers of eastern Europeans once more filling the churches and voicing their Orthodox faith, the communist attempt to eliminate organized religion has failed, and the potent mixture of religious fervour and patriotic nationalism in Russia and the newly independent republics helps explain why. What assessment will be made of the accommodations and compromises made by the Church hierarchy is likely to be a matter of debate for many years to come. One challenge faced by the hierarchy is the competition from other religious groups and especially other Christian denominations now possible in the new climate of religious freedom. Notable here is the hostility expressed towards moves made by Roman Catholic Church to renew its following in Russia, moves which have re-opened deep historic wounds.

Patriarch Aleksei, the present leader of the church, is Estonian by birth. It is reported that he is planning to build a memorial church in Yekatarinburg over the remains of the house in which Tsar Nicholas and his family are believed to have been shot in 1917.

Ruthenian Church. (*see also* **Orthodox Church (Byzantine); Uniate Churches.**) This is the local church of the Subcarpathian Ukraine. It has been allied to Rome since the Union of Uzhorod in 1646. In 1944, it had 461,555 members, using the Byzantine Rite. It was ingested by the **Russian Orthodox Church** in 1949. By the mid-seventies, it had just 290,170 members. The break-up, first of state-imposed Communism, and by the close of 1991, of the Soviet Union itself, may enable it to recover the modicum of self-government required for its survival.

S

Sabbateans. *See* **Donmeh.**

Sahaja Yoga. Sahaja Yoga is unusual among new religious movements originating in the East in being founded and run by a woman, Nirmala Devi (b. 1923), known as the Divine Mother. *Sahaja* means spontaneity, and she teaches spontaneous union with the divine within by awakening a powerful spiritual energy called *kundalini*. She has a large following in India, but only a few hundred British disciples, some of whom live in a communal ashram. Most continue with their normal lives, though all members are encouraged to make donations to the movement.

Sai Baba. *See* **Satya Sai Baba Satsang.**

Sakyapa. "Grey Earth School". One of the four major traditions of **Tibetan Buddhism**, named after the colour of the soil at the site in Central Tibet where its first monastery was built by Khon Konchog Gyalpo in 1073. Following an Indian tantric model, leadership of the Sakya school is the hereditary property of a single family, the Khon. The Khon hand down several **Nyingmapa** *tantras* bestowed on their ancestors directly by Padmasambhava in the eighth century, but the main body of Sakyapa doctrine comes from the newer *tantras* that Khon Konchog Gyalpo received from Drogmi, a Tibetan trained in Nepal and India. The Sakyapa are particularly renowned for their practice of the Hevajra Tantra and the related teachings of *Lamdre* ("Path and Fruit").

The Sakyapas are special devotees of Manjushri, Bodhisattva of Wisdom. Through the agency of Sakya Pandita (1181–1251) they exerted a major formative influence on Tibet's entire monastic higher education system. It was a Sakyapa, Khyentse Wangpo (1811–1892), who initiated and intellectually underpinned the Rimay movement.

A Sakyapa hierarch Phagpa (1234–1280) was made ruler of Tibet by Khubilai Khan, and Sakyapa rule in Tibet continued for a century. Always retaining their headquarters at the holy site of Sakya, the Sakyapas developed thousands of monasteries throughout Tibet, and produced the two sub-schools of Ngorpa and Tsharpa. Following the Chinese invasion of Tibet, the Sakyapa tradition continues in exile. The Phuntsok branch of the Khon has established a monastery in Seattle, USA, and the reigning hierarch from the Dolma branch, His Holiness the Sakya Trizin, is currently developing a Sakya College in Dehra Dun, India.

Salafiya. The Salafiya may be compared with the **Islamic Modernists (South Asia).** It owes its inspiration to the late 19th-century Islamic Modernists Jamal al-din al-Afghani (1839–97) and Muhammad 'Abduh (1845–1905). Both had called for a return to follow the example of the *salaf*, the elders or ancestors, i.e. the members of the earliest community of believers in 7th-century Medina, rejecting the blind imitation of later generations. In so doing, Muslims would be rediscovering the true **Islam**, a religion of reason not hostile to modern science and technology, but capable of meeting the needs of man in the modern world. At the hands of Muhammad Rashid Rida (1865–1935), 'Abduh's best known disciple, the Salafiya developed into a reform movement with a following from Morocco to Indonesia. Rida was interested in the creation of a just system of Islamic law and government suited to modern conditions. To achieve this, he stressed the importance of establishing as exactly as possible the actual practice of the *salaf*, and then relating it to current needs.

The Salafiya played an important role in Algeria and Morocco from the 1920s until independence, bolstering Muslims' awareness of their Arab and Islamic cultural identity in the face of French colonialism, and assuring them that Islam did not have to hold them back from social and economic progress. In Algeria the major figure associated with the movement was 'Abd al-Hamid b. Badis (1889–1940), who in 1931 founded the Association of Reformist Ulama to work for the reform of Algerian Islam in opposition to both **maraboutism** and French cultural influence. A major part of their programme involved the establishment of schools to teach Arabic and Islam alongside modern sciences, and the publication of journals to disseminate their ideas. In Morocco a parallel pattern marked the development of Salafi activities centred on the old capital of Fez.

The Salafiya continues to exist as a trend in reformist thought, but appears to have been largely overtaken by the new radicalism, to whose emergence it has made such a significant contribution.

Salvation Army. In the summer of 1865 a former Methodist minister preached to a crowd in a tent in a Quaker cemetery in the East End of London. His congregation was composed of the poor, the illiterate, the immoral, the dirty; the people who felt that society and certainly the Church had no place for them. William Booth spoke to them of the dangers of hell and the love of God and demanded that they turn away from their sins and be saved.

Many did come forward wanting to give their lives to God. Wealthy Christians who had taken an interest were so impressed that they supported William Booth financially and enabled him to start a "Christian Mission" in a former public house, with a reading room, hall and accommodation for eight missioners. At first William Booth encouraged the new Christians to join a church but soon found that they were not accepted.

In 1878 he gave the movement a new name "The Salvation Army". A book of *Orders and Regulations* soon appeared, the first brass band performed at an Army event and new Christian words were written to popular tunes of the day, in response to William Booth's often quoted words "Why should the devil have all the best tunes?" In 1880 the uniform was created including the famous bonnet for women which was specifically designed to protect the wearer from the rotten eggs, overripe tomatoes and even physical blows of the Army's opponents.

From the start women have had total equality in the Salvation Army. This was greatly due to the influence of William Booth's wife Catherine, who was a gifted preacher and practical administrator. As the movement spread rapidly worldwide her children became its first overseas leaders, with such success that today the Army is active in over 70 countries with more than 4,000,000 adherents.

The ordinary members are "soldiers", sign Articles of War and belong to a corps. Officers are the equivalent of ministers in other churches and are in command of a corps. Ranks of officers are similar to those in the secular army, the highest rank being General, of whom William Booth was the first. The Salvation Army concentrates on Christian action, running hostels for the homeless, a missing persons bureau, rehabilitation centres for alcoholics, hospitals, schools, food kitchens etc.

The Salvation Army still seeks for the conversion of people to a life of commitment to God and the experience of His love for them. Members are encouraged to give publicly their personal testimony. They believe that the Bible is divinely inspired, and preaching is central in their services. The decision was made by William Booth early in the Army's history that the movement would not celebrate the Lord's Supper. Two reasons were given; the problem that was created for reformed alcoholics who could not safely receive even a sip of wine, and the uneasiness in Victorian times on the part of both men and women at the possibility of women officers giving communion to male soldiers.

Samaritans. The Samaritans, sometimes labelled a Jewish sect, are a group which has its origins in northern Biblical Israel but which separated from the rest of the people today known as Jews. The precise history of this separation is debated but it appears to have been completed by Jesus's time if not 300 years prior. Like the Jews, their holy text is the Torah but unlike them, their holy site is Mt Gerizim, where they continue to offer a Paschal (Passover) sacrifice. Their current population is around 400, centred in Holon, a Tel Aviv suburb, and Shechem (Nablus).

Samkauw Hwee. Literally, "the three religions". An Indonesian new religious movement more widely known as **Tridharma.**

Samnak Paw Sawan. Literally "the Abode of Heavenly Fathers", this is an urban Thai movement which practises spirit exorcism. It was founded in the early 1970s by Professor Kloom Vajroban, a professor of zoology at Chulalongkorn University, Bangkok. Mediums have included a Vietnamese member of the **Cao Dai** sect.

Sant Nirankari Mandal. Also known as the Nakali Nirankaris (false Nirankaris) to distinguish them from the more established Asali Nirankaris. A modern **Sikh**-derived movement which enjoys profound hostility from **Khalsa Sikhs.** It may be traced back to Babu Buta Singh, a prominent **Nirankari** who, in the 1930s, was requested by his peers to cut back on his drinking. His disciple, Baba Avtar Singh, seems to have founded the movement a few years after his master's death in 1943. The canonical writings of the Mandal differ in a few minor respects from that of the Nirankaris. They rose to public prominence when Jarnail Singh Bhindranwale, an up-and-coming Khalsa militant, led a violent demonstration against a Mandal conference in Amritsar in 1978. Shortly after this, in 1980, the then leader of the movement, Baba Gurbachan Singh, was assassinated. Since that time the Mandal has kept a low profile.

Santería. This Spanish word meaning image-worship is the name given to the syncretic mix of **African traditional** and **Roman Catholic** religion in Cuba. It is also practised by Cuban immigrants and exiles in North America, and by some African Americans, in such cities as Miami, Los Angeles, New York, Chicago and Detroit. In Cuba itself, partly as a result of measures of control introduced by Castro, there is evidence of some decline.

In Santería, as in **Candomblé** in Brazil, most of the African elements—the names and functions of the gods, type of spirit possession and sacrifice—are derived from the Yoruba traditional religion. However, the Catholic counterparts of the Yoruba gods often differ in the two places, Shango the god of thunder and lightning being equated with St. Barbara in Cuba and with St Jerome in Bahia in north-eastern Brazil.

Stones hidden under the altar are believed to contain the life and power of the gods. They have to be baptized and fed with herbs and the blood of animal sacrifices. In return, some of the participants in the ceremonies become possessed by some of their spirits.

Santi Asok. A this-worldly Thai Buddhist movement founded in 1975 by former TV producer and singer Phra Photirak (1935–). Having received ordination in both Thai **Theravada** monastic fraternities, Photirak came in for hostile criticism from the ecclesiastical authorities after claiming to have achieved the highest level of spiritual perfection (*ariya*). His relation with the *Sangha* is now ambiguous but he has built up a considerable lay and monastic following. Santi Asok teaches an individualistic programme of "dhammic action" of a moral reformist kind. Emphasis is placed on diligence, moderation and a simple lifestyle and the traditional practice of meditation is repudiated. Followers meet together in discussion groups and a strong value is placed on reason. Superstitious practices, including many of the activities of the *Sangha,* are condemned. Lay and monastic members often live together in urban "Dhamma families" and the laity wear distinctive blue Thai peasant clothing. Males commonly sport military style haircuts. The Palang Dharma Party (PDP) of Maj.-Gen. Chamlong Siimeuang, Photirak's most prominent lay follower, though electorally ineffective, supports Santi Asok's "path of righteousness". Santi Asok has its origins in downtown Bangkok, but now has established itself in four Thai provinces. Unlike its companion movement, the **Thammakaai Religious Foundation,** it accepts donations only from proven followers.

Sanusiya. The Sanusiya is a **Sufi** order associated with Libya in particular, and which takes its name from its Algerian founder, Muhammad b. 'Ali al-Sanusi (1787–1859), known as the Grand Sanusi. After a period spent in Mecca as a disciple of the reformist Moroccan Sufi Ahmad b. Idris (1760–1838), along with his subsequent rival Muhammad 'Uthman al-Mirghani, who went on to found the Khatmiya, he set up his own Sufi centre (*zawiya*) there, but was forced to leave Mecca in 1840. He then settled in Cyrenaica (eastern Libya) before moving in 1856 to a new base at an oasis in the Libyan desert to the South, where he could avoid the interference of the Turkish authorities and build up the strength of his order among the nomadic tribes of the Sahara and beyond in Chad and further areas of West Africa. A network of Sanusi centres was established, each with its own mosque, school, accommodation for teachers and students and for passing caravans. Each had its own lands cultivated by the Ikhwan (brethren), a practice similar to that of the **Wahhabis** in early 20th-century Arabia.

During the later 19th century the Sanusiya spread peacefully, but from 1902 came under attack by the French in its bases south of the Sahara. From 1911 the order was then engaged in resistance to the Italian occupation of Libya, surviving despite the destruction of its centres and, with British support, enthroning the head of the Sanusiya as King Idris I of Libya on achieving independence in 1951. It remained the only Sufi order to create a modern state with its leaders as hereditary monarchs until their overthrow in September 1969 by Colonel Muammar al-Qaddafi. One of the first acts of the new régime was to bring the order under government control and prevent the opening of new Sanusi centres. The Sanusiya was declared to be responsible for allowing corruption and drunkenness, for spreading a perverted mystical conception of

Islam, and the monarchy itself was condemned as an un-Islamic institution. Sanusis have continued to provide one of the strands of religious opposition to the Qaddafi régime.

Sanusis are widely regarded as reformist neo-Sufis. Like the Tijaniya they are opposed to the noisy recollection of God (*dhikr*), emphasize the need to seek contact with the Prophet Muhammad and encourage their members to work rather than seeking charity. In a spirit of fostering reform they insist on the fresh examination of the Quran and Tradition, bypassing the early authorities of the four **Sunni** schools of jurisprudence, and making new interpretations of legal points through independent reasoning (*ijtihad*). However, unlike the Tijanis and the Arabian reform movement of the Wahhabis, they permit practices associated with the veneration of saints.

Sar cult. An alternative rendering of the more commonly used designation, **Zar cult.**

Sarvodaya Sramadana. A modern Sri Lankan Buddhist movement aiming to present a purely Buddhist model of social development. Established in 1958, following a spiritual transformation of a team of college-based missionaries working in a deprived community, its founder is A. T. Ariyaratna. Rooted in the teachings of Anagarika Dharmapala, instigator of the Maha Bodhi Society, its function is to promote village renewal through various collective–community projects. Work groups are based upon the concept of *sramadana* (selfless gift of labour) and draw on all members of the community irrespective of religious status. Praxis is seen as essential to the nature of **Buddhism** and consequently monks have been a target of recruitment and are encouraged to emerge from their monastic ghettos. Although Gandhi first used the term *sarvodaya* (welfare of all), Ariyaratna developed the concept into "the awakening of all", implying a moral awakening to self-sufficiency of villages in contrast to the Western non-Buddhist model of industrialization. The main emphasis is not upon an improved quality of life but on a full understanding, through praxis, of the nature of reality as defined by **Theravada** Buddhist tradition.

Although peasant-based, the ideological infrastructure originates with the Sinhala Buddhist urban upper-middle-class. On the governing body of Sarvodaya, all are educated, 24 per cent being professional educationalists with little personal experience of village life. To date, the Sarvodaya movement has been actively promoting its ideals in over 5,000 of the 25,000 villages of Sri Lanka and is the largest non-governmental organization in the country. This socially engaged Buddhism has also appealed to Western Buddhists.

Satanism. Satanism encompasses a number of practices, the essence of which is the profaning of Christian worship. Included in these are the Black Mass, reciting the Lord's Prayer backwards and the desecration of Christian sacred objects, including the symbolic replacement of symbols of light with those of dark.

Satanic themes have provided the basis of a number of well known films, plays and novels. The imagery used is often distorted in its meanings by the media to such an extent that the practices of true Satanists are lost. The Satanist's philosophy is a hedonistic one of living life to the full through gratification of physical, emotional and mental desires. As very little authoritative material has been published it is impossible accurately to gauge the size of membership, but numbers are small in comparison to those for **Paganism** and **Witchcraft**, and commitment tends to be short-lived.

The Church of Satan, founded in America by Anton Le Vey in 1966, has functioned largely as a movement teaching self-assertion.

Satmar Hasidism. Satmar is a Hungarian Hasidic movement, now based in Williamsburg (Brooklyn, New York), with followers in Israel and other Jewish centres. Although the Satmar is a comparatively recent development in **Hasidism,** it draws on older northern Hungarian Hasidic traditions. The current leader is Rabbi Joel Teitelbaum, whose father, Rabbi Moshe Teitelbaum (1888–1982) escaped from Hungary in 1944 and established his court in America. The centre in Brooklyn became a focal point for Hungarian Jews in the years immediately after the war and the Satmar made great efforts on behalf of refugees.

The Satmar are among the most rejectionist of all Jewish communities in terms of their encounter with the modern world. They do not attribute value to any form of secular studies, see themselves at war with modernity and have attempted to re-create a complete and perfect replica of pre-Holocaust Jewish life—in America. Moshe Teitelbaum, in his work, *Vayoel Moshe,* advocated a staunch anti-**Zionism** and the Satmar continue to be among the most vociferous opponents of all types of Jewish nationalism. They regularly publish and disseminate anti-Zionist materials and hold public anti-Israel rallies. Teitelbaum's opposition, utilizing an argument found in the *Talmud,* reflects what once was a dominant Orthodox rabbinic viewpoint. He also gained notoriety in the Jewish world for his claim that the Holocaust was divine punishment for the "sin" of Zionism.

The Satmar have been involved in a series of disputes (theological and legal) with other Hasidic and non-Hasidic groups. They have created a community almost totally closed to other Jews and the modern world. In many ways the Satmar represent the continuity of the 19th-century, Ultra-Orthodox (particularly Hungarian) life-style and theology once so much a feature of European Jewry.

Satya Sai Baba Satsang. Satya Sai Baba (b. 1926) claims to be the reincarnation of the 19th-century mystic Sai Baba, and also an *avatar* of the Indian god Vishnu. His teaching is traditionally Hindu. However, he is best known as a "miracle worker" or magician who regularly "materializes" sacred ash and other objects (including gold watches) at *darshans* in his Indian ashrams. He claims 10,000,000 followers, mostly in India, but also many Westerners, including about 10,000 British. The administrative and religious centre of the Satsang is Puttaparthi, Andra Pradesh. Sai Baba teaches a fairly traditional monist (*advaita*) form of **Vedanta**.

Satya Samaj. A modern Indian **Jain** sect, founded in the 1960s by Pandit Darabarilala, who is also known as Swami Satyabhakta. It has several hundred adherents and is primarily concerned with social, rather than religious matters. In particular, it opposes the caste system and welcomes Muslims as full members. Its main temple and headquarters are to be found at Wardha, Madhya Pradesh.

Sauras. The name applied to **Hindu** worshippers of the sun god, Surya, one of the five traditional deities of **Smarta** devotion. This style of devotion is thought to be extremely ancient though it has declined greatly since its peak in the 13th century CE. Numbers of devotees today are small and the majority of Surya temples are neglected. An exception to this rule is the Temple of the Sun at Konarak, in the eastern state of Orissa, which is well preserved and acts as the prime focus of the movement.

Scientology. A religio-therapeutic system founded in 1950 by L. Ron Hubbard, an American who once wrote science fiction novels. Hubbard called his system "Dianetics", but when it was attacked by doctors and psychiatrists, he buttressed it with a quasi-religious philosophy, based on transmigration, and an ecclesial structure. "The Church of Scientology", as it became, is instrumental in orientation, offering explanations for personal failure, mental and physical ill health. These ills and inadequacies are put down to "engrams", the physiologically or neurologically recorded experience of trauma in early life, the womb, or a past life. The aim of Scientology is to provide a technique to erase fully the "engrams", leaving the individual free to act unimpeded by time, space, mass, and energy, and capable of realizing effectively the reserves of superhuman powers. Achievement of this goal comes to those who complete expensive courses. For its core members, Scientology is often experienced as totalitarian.

Second Adventist Church. *See* **Adventists.**

Sect Shinto. *See* **Kyoha Shinto.**

Seicho no Ie. Founded in 1930 in Kobe by Taniguchi Masaharu, a former member of **Omotokyo**; Seicho no Ie (House of Growth) claims the doctrinal integration of all Japan's major religions, including **Christianity.** Emphasis is on positive thinking. Suffering is an illusion which arises from ignorance that mankind is essentially perfect. Realization of this "truth of life" through certain practices, such as chanting and meditation, will restore humanity's filial relationship with the divine. Seicho no Ie is characterized by a mainly middle-class, conservative membership, of well over 2,000,000, and by its championing of the Emperor, the military and patriotic causes.

Sekai Kyuseikyo. A Japanese new religious movement founded by **Omotokyo** member Okada Mokichi (1882–1955), Sekai Kyuseikyo (World Messianity) advocates healing through the laying on of hands using power derived from the deified founder, and advances the ideal of an earthly paradise through communion with divine beings. Membership is quoted at around 700,000.

Sekai Mahikari Bunmei Kyodan. The founder of this new religious movement, also known as the World True-Light Civilization, Okada Kotama, previously a member of **Sekai Kyuseikyo**, received a revelation from the creator god, Su, in 1959. It claimed Japan as the centre of the universe, and Okada as the mediator of divine rays of light from Su which would effect the purification of humankind, who had become polluted by restless spirits, often those of ancestors.

The central ritual, claimed by Mahikari as scientific, is a purification rite, *Mahikari-no-waza*, in which the performer, by virtue of his or her initiation (a three-day "seminar") and the amulet worn by all members, exorcises his or her restless spirits. On a larger scale *Mahikari-no-waza* is thought to prevent natural and political catastrophes. Its widespread practice is said to result in the return of humankind to divine stature.

The sacred centre of Mahikari is in Shizuoka, although it also has headquarters in Tokyo, and some international membership, predominantly in the United States. Membership is approaching 100,000, and though small the sect has a high public profile.

On the death of Okada in 1974 a succession dispute resulted in a schismatic movement named Sukyo Mahikari. Sekai Mahikari Bunmei Kyodan is presently led by Sekiguchi Sakae, a disciple of Okada. The doctrinal differences between the two groups are negligible.

Self-Realization Fellowship (SRF). One of the first **Hindu**-oriented movements to establish itself in the West. Founded by Paramahansa Yogananda (1893–1953), who is held to be the fourth in a line of Indian *gurus*, the distinctive teaching of the SRF is *kriya yoga*. In 1920, Yogananda was sent by his teacher, Sri Yukteswar, to the International Congress of Religious Liberals in Boston. Shortly after arriving in America he established the mother centre of the SRF in Los Angeles. It remains the headquarters of the movement. The SRF is noteworthy in having pioneered correspondence courses for its membership based on the writings and oral teachings of the founder. A six-month minimum initial study period is required before initiation into *kriya yoga* can take place. Initiation by a minister of the SRF, followed by sustained practice is said to result in a merging of consciousness with the *guru*. Monks and nuns belonging to the Self-Realization Order reside at the Los Angeles centre and the movement has active branches throughout the world. The SRF is perhaps best known through its founder's highly popular and classic exposition of the spiritual life, *The Autobiography of a Yogi*.

Sephardi. (From biblical "Sepharad" (Obadiah 1:20) later interpreted as Spain). Refers to Spanish and Portuguese Jews and their descendants, sometimes used to describe all Mediterranean Jews, although most Jews from North Africa and the Near East (excepting Turkey) are not Sephardim, rather they are members of the Edot ha-Mizrah ("Eastern Communities").

Spanish Jewry was the largest and most important medieval Jewish community until 1391 but its influences came to an end when Jews were expelled from Spain in 1491 and Portugal (1497). From 1391–1491, many Jews converted to **Roman Catholicism** but continued to practise **Judaism** secretly. These crypto-Jews, derogatorily referred to as *Marranos* ("swine"), were the target of the Spanish Inquisition (established in 1480). After 1492, the Sephardim and many *conversos* fled to Turkey, Italy, Holland and the Land of Israel and later England and the Americas. By the end of the 17th century, Sephardi Jewry had lost much of its influence in the Jewish world. Many European Sephardi communities were destroyed during the Holocaust. Current Sephardi centres include Latin America, the USA and Israel.

Sephardi Judaism differs from **Ashkenazi** (Central and Eastern European) Judaism in cultural, liturgical, and linguistic ways (differing pronunciation of Hebrew, as well as Sephardi use of Judeo–Spanish and Ladino). While both hold the written and oral Torahs to be the basis of Jewish law, later Sephardi and Ashkenazi legal codes differ in many areas, such as Sephardi law permitting certain foods during Passover, which the Ashkenazim forbid. The Sephardi community has its own Chief Rabbi in Israel and systems of courts and education.

Sephardi Torah Guardians' Party. *See* **Shas.**

Serbian Orthodox Church. An **Autocephalous Church** of the **Orthodox Church (Byzantine)** rite. Established by Byzantine missions in the 9th century, the church maintained strong links with Rome until the 13th century, reaching its zenith under Stephen Dushan (1331–1355). Becoming autocephalous in 1879, the original seat of the patriarch was Pec. This was transferred to Belgrade in 1920. The church hierarchy is strongly nationalistic and supports President Milosevic's dream of a greater Serbia. Montenegran church members have accordingly attempted to set up their own autocephalous patriarchate. There are c. 8.25 million adherents spread across Serbia, Montenegro, Bosnia and Herzegovina.

Sevener Shi'ites (Seveners). The label Sevener Shi'ites (or simply Seveners) is sometimes given to the **Isma'ilis** as a convenient way of distinguishing them from both the **Twelver Shi'ites** and the **Zaydis** (Fivers) within **Islam**.

Seventh Day Adventists. *See* **Adventists.**

Shafi'is. The Shafi'i rite or school of **Islamic** law (*madhhab*) traces its foundation to Muhammad al-Shafi'i (d. 820), a pupil of Malik b. Anas, the founder of the Medinan **Maliki** school. Al-Shafi'i is generally admired for his intellectual contribution to studying the principles of Islamic jurisprudence. He recognized four "roots" or sources of the Holy Law: the Quran, Prophetic Traditions, consensus of the religious scholars (*ijma*) and analogical reasoning (*qiyas*). He held that the Prophet was divinely inspired in all his acts and sayings, and that God had commanded men to obey the Prophet. Therefore, in common with the Malikis, he attached great importance to Traditions. There could be no disagreement with matters that were clearly decided by reference to the Quran, Traditions or consensus. However, in other cases he accepted the use of analogy subject to stricter rules than those employed by the **Hanafis.** For al-Shafi'i, it was not man's concern to work out laws for himself, but to discover God's laws by applying the methods of jurisprudence to the four sources of the Law. Unrestricted reasoning could not be allowed in order to deal with new situations, and the jurist should not question God's purposes if he found a law thus discovered to be inconvenient, or contrary to his wishes.

In Egypt, a cult of al-Shafi'i flourishes, centred on his tomb in Cairo, in a manner normally associated with **Sufi** shrines. By coincidence his name, Shafi'i, means "intercessor", and he is addressed as such in letters sent (or taken) to the shrine, a practice that has been going on for centuries. The letter-writers are normally concerned to seek help in having an injustice remedied. The mosque-tomb is a centre of international pilgrimage, visitors often rubbing the wooden screen surrounding the actual tomb in order to absorb the saint's *baraka* (sacred power). Once a year a colourful festival is celebrated in the mosque's immediate neighbourhood.

At present most Egyptians are Shafi'is, especially in Lower Egypt, and the Shafi'i school, which is **Sunni**, is to be found in South Arabia, the Gulf state of Bahrain, East Africa, along the western coast of India, and in Sri Lanka, South East Asia and some areas of Central Asia.

Shaiva Siddhantins. This tradition of **Hindu** thought originated in Kashmir, where it was supplanted by **Kashmir Shaivism**, but now exists only in South India, particularly in Tamil Nadu. It contains two strands, one derived from the Kashmiri tradition which used Sanskrit as its medium of expression, the other derived from Tamil devotionalism (*bhakti*) expressed in the poetry of the Nayanmars (4th–9th centuries CE). Among this collection of poetry is Tirumular's *Tiruvacakam* (5th century CE), about the soul's absolute dependence upon Shiva, which is sung daily in Shaiva temples and in the home. The most important text of theology is the *Civananapotam* by Meykantatevar (c. 1200). Here there are three eternal realities: Shiva the transcendent Lord who is also immanent in the world; the soul (or "beast") who is utterly dependent upon Shiva and caught in a cycle of transmigration; and the cosmos or that which binds. The soul, of which there are an infinite number, becomes omniscient and omnipotent upon liberation like Shiva. Liberation is through surrender to Shiva and his grace. Shaiva Siddhanta is the tradition behind the popular worship of Shiva in Tamil Nadu and is the philosophy of the Adishaiva priests who administer the South Indian Shaiva temples.

Shaivas. In **Hinduism** devotees of the god Shiva are known as Shaivas. The Shaiva religion possibly has its roots in the pre-Aryan Indus Valley Civilization (c. 2000 BCE) where a seal was found depicting a horned, phallic figure reminiscent of Shiva as Lord of animals and ascetics. Most Shaivas revere the Shaiva *Agamas* and *Tantras* as their scriptural authority, though other texts are held in esteem such as the Shaiva *Puranas,* which depict the mythology of Shiva, rituals and other aspects of Shaiva religion. While accepting the reality of other Hindu deities, Shaivas maintain that Shiva is the supreme God. For example, **Kashmir Shaivas** are monists, maintaining that Shiva is the ultimate reality with which all particular souls are identical, while **Shaiva Siddhantins** are dualists, maintaining that there is a plurality of souls eternally distinct from Shiva. Shaiva ascetics or renouncers adopt the insignia of their god, covering themselves in ashes, wearing their hair long and matted and bearing a trident. Some Shaiva ascetics practise **yoga** in order to attain liberation, while others smoke hashish in order to commune with their deity. Notable orders of Shaiva ascetics are the Nagas, **Naths** and **Aghoris**. The **Lingayats** or Virashaivas who worship Shiva in his phallic form as the *linga* are prominent in South India. Chidambaram, Tamil Nadu, the site of Shiva's dance, should be particularly noted as a centre of Shiva worship. Even if not dedicated to Shiva as their primary deity, most Hindu temples will have a shrine to Shiva, especially in his phallic form as the *linga*.

Shakers. The Shakers of Saint Vincent are an Afro–Protestant cult similar in many ways to the **Spiritual Baptists,** or Shakers, of Trinidad, with the main differences being that the order of worship is based on that of the **Methodists**

rather than the **Baptists**, and there is a hierarchy of offices. Proceedings may also be more informal.

Shaktas. Shaktas are **Hindu** devotees of the Goddess (*Devi*) in one of her forms as mother, ferocious destroyer or young virgin. Devi is also worshipped as the power (*shakti*) of Shiva manifested in his consorts such as Parvati and Sati and as the consorts of Vishnu such as Lakhsmi. At a popular level Devi is worshipped in regional forms throughout India and paid homage at many pilgrimage sites where, according to legend, parts of Sati's corpse fell, dismembered by Vishnu, as Shiva danced wildly with it. She is worshipped particularly in Bengal, Assam and Nepal, though Hindu temples throughout India will have a shrine to the Goddess as Durga, the slayer of the buffalo demon. Shaktas generally are concerned with the power manifestations of the absolute and are characterized by rituals involving actual or visualized sex, the worship of virgins as manifestations of the Goddess and by animal sacrifice.

A broad distinction can be made between those who follow orthodox worship of Devi and unorthodox **tantric** worship. Tantric devotees can be further divided into the Shri Vidya and the Kalikula traditions.

The *Shakta Tantras* categorize devotees according to three hierarchical and progressive dispositions: the condition of the "beast", of the "hero" and of the "divine". This classification is directly related to the use of five ritual ingredients called the five "m"s, which are regarded as an anathema to the orthodox, namely meat (*mamsa*), fish (*matsya*), wine (*madya*), parched grain (*mudra*) and sexual intercourse (*maithuna*). The "beast" worships in the "right-hand" mode using the five "m"s purely symbolically, whereas the "hero" uses the five "m"s as actual ritual ingredients; the ritual probably being performed within a circle of devotees. The heroic mode of worship with its emphasis on the erotic and the terrifying is described more in the Kalikula tradition than in the gentler Shri Vidya. The "divine" is a state of awareness which transcends different modes of worship, in which the devotee is identified with the Goddess.

Shaktas also practise *Kundalini yoga*, the awakening of *shakti* within the body. The body is visualized in a subtle form as having a central channel from the crown of the head to the region of the anus. Six or seven centres of power (*chakras*) are located along its axis, at the anus, genital organs, navel, heart, throat, between the eyebrows, and at the crown of the head. Either side of this are two further channels from the nostrils, joining the central channel at its base. The "snake power" Kundalini residing in the anal *chakra,* once awakened by yogic breathing exercises, rises up this central channel, piercing the *chakras* as she moves to finally unite with Shiva at the crown of the head. The practitioner is then filled with the bliss of divine union.

Shamanism. The word "shaman" originates among the Tungus tribe of Siberia where it refers to a religious specialist whose contact with the sacred rests on ecstatic abilities. In essence shamanism (the configuration of beliefs and practices surrounding the shaman) involves a tripartite cosmology—earth, heaven and underworld—linked by a central axis, the world tree or pole. By virtue of his or her special abilities, the shaman can, in trance, travel to the different parts of the cosmos in order to contact spirits. The aid of the spirits is solicited by the shaman to assist members of the tribe in his capacities as healer of the sick, diviner, hunting magician and spiritual guide. The shaman can induce trance at will, commonly with the aid of a drum, and his initiation into the profession involves an experience of death and rebirth. By extension, the term is used to describe comparable figures in cultures in other parts of the world, e.g. Northern Eurasia, North and South America, Australia, Japan, and Africa.

Shamanism may predominate in the society or be peripheral to it. Strictly speaking the terms shaman and shamanism should only be applied where the characteristics outlined above are present. Where certain elements are present, but not all, it may be more appropriate to speak of medicine men, sorcerers, mediums etc.

"Medicine man" is a general term used to describe a Native American sacred specialist who cures through the use of sacred power. Although the term is often used to describe all such specialists, strictly speaking a differentiation should be made between shamans, who use trance states to contact helping spirits to cure, and medicine men (or women) who will commonly use a combination of learned knowledge and helping spirits, or in some cases, learned knowledge solely. In certain areas, medicine men may form medicine societies. The term medicine refers to both physical artifacts—herbs, fetishes, etc.—and to sacred power and knowledge.

Also to be distinguished from shamanism is spirit-possession, such as occurs e.g. in various Afro-Brazilian or Afro-Caribbean cults such as **Candomblé, Convince, Pocomania** and **Shango.** In spirit-possession the spirits invade the practitioners, whereas in shamanism the specialist (shaman) seeks to enlist the aid of the spirits.

Shamanism is undoubtedly one of the oldest forms of religious practice and is mainly characteristic of hunting societies. As such it has declined along with traditional hunting cultures. Nonetheless it survives in many areas (indeed is being revitalized in some) and its influence can be detected in some form in most religions.

In addition, Shamanism has begun to exercise an appeal in modern western societies as part of the **New Age** movement, including the **Human Potential Movement.** The practice of urban shamanism is advocated, for example, as a means by which modern urban dwellers can rediscover the sanctity of Nature and tap into the energy of the universal life-force which underlies and interconnects all forms of animate and inanimate existence. Thus it is seen as a way in which people can expand their consciousness to embrace realities which transcend normal everyday experience, yet which should not be regarded as "supernatural" since they are part of Nature. From being the province of a limited number of specialists (shamans), shamanism is being changed, in this context, to become a spiritual technique open in principle to all.

Shango. Shango, the name of the Yoruba god of thunder and lightning, is also the name given to the syncretic mix of **African traditional** and **Roman Catholic** religion found in Trinidad and Grenada. In many respects it is similar to **Candomblé** in Brazil, one variant of which is also known as Shango (Portuguese: Xangô), to **Santería** in Cuba, and numerous other forms of African–Catholic syncretism found in the Caribbean and South America in particular.

African gods (not only Shango) are identified with Catholic saints, and a four-day ritual held annually is of central importance. Prayers, drumming,

dancing and singing conduce to the possession of a number of the participants
by the spirit of the god recognized in that particular cult centre. There follow
animal sacrifices involving for example doves, pigeons, chickens, turtles, goats
or sheep. Spirits of the dead are regarded with caution, as they can trouble
people. Cult leaders may be revered as healers.

Shas (Sephardi Torah Guardians' Party). (See also **Orthodox Judaism;
Zionism.**) Israeli non-Zionist, religious, **Sephardi** political party, created
to contest the 1984 general election. Shas is the largest (along with **Mafdal**)
religious party in Israel and highlights the strength of Sephardi religious
support and the significance of the ethnic factor in Israeli politics. Shas
was founded by former members of **Agudat Israel** and sponsored by Rabbi
Eliezer Schach and the former Sephardi Chief Rabbi, Obadiah Yosef. It
expressed Sephardi dissatisfaction at the way their interests were pursued
by the **Ashkenazi** Agudat. A major issue was the amount of government
funding being used for Ashkenazi projects; other concerns include the
marginalization of Sephardi concerns as reflected in that Yiddish is the
official language of the Council of Torah Sages. Separate Sephardi lists
had operated at the municipal level since 1983. Shas, although sharing many
positions with Agudat Israel, took a broader view of its potential constituency
and is less hawkish over the future of the occupied territories. Shas joined
the government of National Unity (1984–1988). Unexpectedly Shas doubled
its support by taking six Knesset (Israeli parliament) seats in 1988—Agudat
gained only five. Shas retained its six seats in the 1992 elections and is
part of the coalition government with control of the important Interior and
Absorption ministries.
  Although Shas has been beset with scandals and resignations it appears to
have become a stable electoral party on the Israeli political scene representing
the religious voice of the Sephardi community.

Shi'ism. Shi'ism is a generic term covering a variety of sectarian movements
in **Islam**, all of which have in common some principle of hereditary succession
from Muhammad's cousin and son-in-law 'Ali ibn Abi Talib (d. 661). The
largest groups are the **Twelvers** (Ithna 'Asharis, or Imamis), **Isma'ilis** (with
numerous sub-divisions), and **Zaydis.** There have also been numerous extremist
groups (*ghulat*), among which the most important survivors today are the
Nusayris, Druzes, and **Ahl-i Haqq.** There are a few Shi'ite **Sufi** orders, including
the **Ni'matullahiya** and Dhahabiya. Modern Twelver Shi'ism has spawned a
number of heterodox movements, some of which have passed outside Islam
entirely (for example Shaykhis, **Babis,** and **Bahais**). It has also given birth to
a number of religio–political movements, including **Hizbollah.**

Shin Buddhism. A name commonly applied to the Japanese True Pure Land
School or **Jodoshinshu** after its founder Shinran Shonen (1173–1262).

Shingonshu. The major form of **Tantric Buddhism** in Japan, Kukai (774–835)
was the founder of this school. Shingon is based on the premise that human
understanding cannot approach absolute truth. The only reliable practice,
are therefore symbolic rituals; in the case of Shingon, *mantra, mudra,* and
mandala. Dainichi Nyorai (Skt. *Mahavairocana*), from which all Buddhas and

bodhisattvas emerge, is the absolute and immanent Buddha-nature pervading all phenomenal reality. When this Buddha-nature is awakened through subtle changes in consciousness prompted by the complex matrix of Shingon ritual, "enlightenment in this body" (*sokushin jobutsu*) takes place.

Since access to advanced teaching requires initiation the school is sometimes called Mikkyo (secret) or Shingon Mikkyo. Despite this élitist attitude towards practice, Shingonshu has continued to prosper throughout the centuries. This must in part be due to the centrality of Kukai's personality. He is venerated in popular worship. Shingon has maintained a fairly passive stance toward other Japanese religions, which has doubtless aided its survival.

Central scriptures for the sect are the *Mahavairocana* and *Vajrasekhara sutras*. Shingon's centre almost since its inception has been Mt Koya on the Kii peninsula, still one of the most popular destinations for pilgrims in Japan. Including its current 18 sub-sects Shingon claims around 11,000,000 adherents, a priesthood of 16,000 and 11,000 temples. Shingon seems to have had a powerful influence over mountain worship sects, such as **Shugendo**.

Shinto. Also known as the way of the *kami* (gods), this is the indigenous religion of Japan, emerging with the mythic foundation of Japan and the world through sexual and spontaneous generation by *kami*, and developing into a complex structure of rituals and institutions which have served to underpin Japanese culture throughout the centuries.

Rather than being soteriological in character, Shinto is the outward signifier of the way the Japanese identify with their environment. *Kami* are not only mythological divinities, but include all aspects of nature, agricultural activities, and spirits of the dead. The early clans would venerate their own particular ancestor *kami*, and even now certain *kami* are believed to preside over particular localities, specific groups of people, and different aspects of human life. Often it is difficult to differentiate *kami*.

Early Shinto was never defined or systematized. In fact it was not until the arrival of **Buddhism** in the 6th century that the word Shinto was introduced to distinguish it from the newcomer. Whilst Shinto is institutionally organized now, it has never had a doctrine as such, no system of ethics and no theology. Ritual purification and the accurate execution of devotions to *kami* (who can be malevolent, but more commonly benign) in a total affirmation of the goodness of life and fertility, provide the contours of Shinto, and its here and now concerns. Shinto has a celebratory character. Most Japanese have Shinto weddings, children have special ceremonies, and shrine festivals often take to the streets. Portable shrines shouldered by young males, in which the local *kami* is believed to be temporarily enshrined, are paraded in an often ecstatic atmosphere. Shinto exists today in three main forms: Shrine or **Jinja Shinto,** Sect or **Kyoha Shinto,** and Folk or **Minzoku Shinto.**

Shiv Sena. Also known as the Army of Shiva, this is a Hindu communal party. Its immediate predecessor was the Sampoorn Maharashtra Samiti which transcended traditional political party lines to crystallize resistance to the perceived incursion of South Indians into Maharashtra. Founded in 1967 by Bal Thakare, Shiv Sena had a paramilitary cast which made it very useful to the Congress Party which wished to weaken the left-wing parties then on the ascendant in Bombay. Initially active only in Bombay proper, the party soon expanded into the suburbs and to Pune. It has recently formed *ad hoc* electoral alliances with the **Bharatiya Janata Party (BJP)**.

Shotokushu. A modern form of Japanese Mahayana **Buddhism**. Prince Shotoku (574–622CE) is considered the father of Japanese Buddhism, and is venerated as a cultural figure of great worth. In 1950 the Shotokushu seceded from the **Hossoshu**, claiming the oldest Buddhist temple, commissioned by the Prince himself, the Horyuji, as its head. Membership is around 12,000.

Shouters. This is a designation used for the **Spiritual Baptists** of Trinidad, although according to some accounts it refers to a particular variant of this in which places of worship include both an altar with a crucifix and a central pole (*poteau–mitau*), the latter being derived from African Fon religion. The Shouters of Trinidad are also similar in many ways to the **Shakers** of Saint Vincent.

Shri Shankaradeva Sangha. A **Hindu Vaishnava** reform movement in Assam, owing its origin to Shankaradeva (1449–1548), whom his followers believe to be an *avatara* of Vishnu. Founded in 1933, it claims to be Assam's largest religious organization. The reforms which it introduced involve the rejection of the role of the brahmin priest, especially in funeral rites, the prohibition of worshipping any deity other than Vishnu, the breaking down of caste rules within the Sangha, and the substitution of an initiation committee for the individual initiating *guru*. The key scripture of the Sangha is the *Bhagavata-purana*.

Shri Vaishnavas. One of the oldest **Vaishnava** orders (*sampradayas*). Its name is derived from the fact that its members worship not only Vishnu, but also his consorts, chiefly Sri/Lakshmi, the goddess of prosperity. The first teacher of the *sampradaya* was the South Indian Nathamuni (10th century), who collected together the hymns of the Alvars, earlier poet-saints of Tamil Nadu. The theology of the Shri Vaishnavas was given a philosophical basis by Ramanuja (c.1017–c.1137) and his philosophy is known as "qualified non-dualism", a form of **Vedanta**, because it posits Brahman alone (identified with Vishnu) as the supreme reality, yet gives to individual selves and the material world a sufficient degree of dependent reality to allow *bhakti* to take place.

There are two sub-sects, the Vatakalai (northern culture) and Tenkalai (southern culture), which are divided not only by their respective emphases upon Sanskrit or Tamil origins, but also by their theories regarding divine grace. Following their teacher Vedanta Deshika, the Vatakalai believe that human beings make some contribution to their salvation, whereas the Tenkalai teacher Pillai Lokacarya held that salvation depends entirely upon God. The Tenkalai call these two positions the "cat-hold" and the "monkey-hold" schools, for they say that the Vatakalai believe that the soul must cling to God as a baby monkey clings to its mother, whereas in their own view the soul is like a kitten which is picked up by its mother without making any effort of its own. The Shri Vaishnavas today are most numerous in Tamil Nadu, but are found in the other south Indian states also. They have 108 major temples, the most famous of which are those of Tirupati and Shrirangam.

Shrine Shinto. *See* **Jinja Shinto**.

Shugendo. Literally, the way (*do*) of controlling (*shu*) sacred power (*gen*), Shugendo is a Japanese religious tradition probably deriving from the life and teachings of its mysterious founder En no Gyoja (634–701?), also known as Shokaku. Master En is said to have led an ascetic life on Mt Katsuragi, Nara Prefecture, where he developed the capacity to fly through the air and command the powers of nature. The sect was first institutionalized in the 11th century and has always remained an essentially lay organization hostile to the priestly and monastic establishment. From the 13th century, Shugendo became influenced by the cosmological thought of the Buddhist **Shingonshu**, though it is now often classified as a denomination within **Tendaishu**. Strictly speaking, however, Shugendo is an amalgam of many traditions. In 1872 Shugendo was officially abolished by government decree, in an attempt to purify Shinto from extraneous elements, though since 1945 it has been rehabilitated. At present the sect has six main shrines, 180 temples and approximately 100,000 adherents. Initiated practitioners are expected to undergo a series of severe mountain retreats and for this reason are referred to as *yamabushi*—those who sleep in the mountains.

Shuha Shinto. *See* **Kyoha Shinto.**

Shwegyin Nikaya. The second largest monastic fraternity (*gaing*) within the **Burmese Theravada** Buddhist *Sangha*. Founded as a reform movement in the mid-19th century by the abbot of Shwegyin, the order now has around 50,000 ordained monks and differs from the other three fraternities mainly in its highly puritanical interpretation of monastic discipline (*vinaya*). Despite its size, in comparison with the **Thuddama Nikaya** which comprises about 90 per cent of the total monastic population of Burma, it has been historically influential, particularly in its support for the monarchy. Its political standpoint in present-day Burma is difficult to assess.

Siddha Yoga. An organization claiming great antiquity, though established in recent years to promote the **Kashmir Shaivite** teachings of the late Swami Muktananda. The present leader of the movement is Guru Mai, Muktananda's American translator, who succeeded him on his death in 1982. The headquarters are at Ganeshpuri, 60 miles from Bombay and there are approximately 40 centres (*ashrams*) worldwide. Siddha Yoga has established itself quite successfully in South America and there are thriving centres in Mexico, Japan and New York. The movement uses satellite links for communication between members.

Sikh Dharma of the Western Hemisphere. In 1969 Sant Harbhajan Singh Puri, also known as Yogi Bhajan, began to teach **yoga** in Los Angeles. Some Americans became attracted by his Sikh faith and within a few months the first conversions had taken place. Such western Sikhs are Amritdhari and, besides keeping the five Ks, both men and women wear the turban. They can be distinguished from other Sikhs by their clothing which is Punjabi and white in colour. Yogi Bhajan also teaches *kundalini yoga* at a secular university and is co-president of the World Fellowship of Religions. The movement is also known as the Happy, Healthy and Holy Organization (3HO).

Sikhism (Sikh Panth). Sikhism originated in the Punjab region of north-west India in the early years of the 16th century CE. It has been commonplace for writers, including Sikhs, to describe the religion as a fusion or synthesis of Hindu and Muslim ideas. Such an interpretation neglects the inspirational contribution of the Sikh Gurus themselves and is seen by most Sikhs to deny the elements of revelation and grace which lie at the heart of the message of Guru Nanak and his successors. The view that Sikhism is a form of syncretism is almost universally rejected today.

Guru Nanak (1469–1539), the initiator of the Sikh movement, was born in Talwandi (now in Pakistan and called Nankana Sahib). He worked, probably as an accountant, in the service of Daulat Khan Lodi in the town of Sultanpur until his call to begin his preaching mission in 1499. This is not regarded by Sikhs as a conversion experience but a commissioning. The Guru, Sikhs believe, was born already in a state of perfection, as the result of God's will, not the consequence of his own *karma*. The purpose of his life was to bring the divine word to an age which had replaced direct knowledge and experience of God with **Hindu** ritualism and **Islamic** formalism.

Nanak travelled widely until about 1521 preaching the message of one God and one humanity in which differences of caste and class, gender, and colour as well as religion were irrelevant and contrary to the divine order. In these journeys he was often accompanied by a Muslim bard named Mardana. His message, and that of the other Gurus who continued his work, was given in devotional songs (*shabads*). These provide the content of the Sikh scriptures.

Guru Nanak taught that God is one. Though he was happy to use Hindu and Muslim names when referring to the deity he also used the term *Akal Purukh*, the Timeless One, and held the view that God was personal though neither male nor female. God as Creator, *Karta Purukh*, is an idea which features strongly in the Guru's teachings. God is ultimately ineffable but has become manifest as Word (*shabad*). God is often, therefore, described as the *Sat Guru*, the True Guru, who is the preceptor of all human kind.

The householder stage of life was the one which Guru Nanak commended and practised. In this way he not only included people of all castes but also outcastes or untouchables in his teaching. He also made work a virtue and laid the foundations for a movement based on the three principles of personal spirituality, honest work, and care for one's fellow human beings. Guru Nanak required his disciples to come together for congregational worship and mutual support. An institution known as *langar*, which he began and other Gurus developed, requires all Sikhs, and others who share in their worship, to eat together. Its negative purpose is to denounce the practices of some socio–religious groups whose members will only take food with and from members of their own fellowship; positively it affirms belief in one universal community. The food provided in *langar* is always vegetarian. A small handful of *karah parshad*, made of wholemeal flour, sugar, and ghee, prepared in an iron pan (*karaha*), hence the name, is also given to those who attend most Sikh functions. It serves the same purpose as *langar*.

It is unlikely that Guru Nanak's intention was to create another religion but by the time of his death the movement had assumed such a size and distinctiveness that he felt it necessary to appoint a successor. In all there were 10 Gurus, the line ending in 1708 when the last Guru, Gobind Singh, declared that in future Guruship would be invested in the scripture, now known as the *Guru Granth Sahib*, and the community, the Guru Panth, which adheres faithfully to the teachings contained in it. Anyone, man or woman, may read from the *Guru Granth Sahib* and conduct any Sikh ceremonies. The movement is totally lay, though a professional *granthi* (literally reader), may sometimes be appointed to conduct services and ceremonies and provide teaching.

The importance of the scripture has already been mentioned. It contains the compositions of six of the Gurus, Hindu and Muslim teachers such as Namdev, Kabir, Ravidas and Ramanand, and bards who played at the court of the fifth preceptor, Guru Arjan. Sikhs point to this as additional evidence of the inclusive nature of Sikhism. The text was compiled by Guru Arjan in 1604 and revised by the 10th Guru, Guru Gobind Singh, who also gave the Sikhs the physical form by which they are best known. In 1699 he introduced a new method of initiation. Members of this new family, the **Khalsa** (the Pure), were required to take certain moral vows and to wear the five Ks, five distinguishing features which in Punjabi all begin with the initial K. They are: (i) *kesh*, uncut hair, including body hair; (ii) *kirpan*, sword; (iii) *kaccha*, trousers, often worn in a short form as an undergarment; (iv) *kara*, steel wristlet worn on the right forearm; and (v) *kangha*, comb, used to keep the hair tidy and in order. Bodily hygiene is something which Sikhs emphasize strongly, whilst at the same time rejecting any belief in physical purity and pollution.

Sikhs are now to be found worldwide, especially in English-speaking countries. Most of them, some 13,000,000, still live in the Punjab area of India and have links with that part of the world. Punjabi is the spoken language of the community and is used in worship. The Sikh population worldwide is about 16,000,000. Britain's Sikhs number some 350–400,000, the largest group outside India.

In India itself many Sikhs, dissatisfied with promises of greater autonomy within the state, have called for the establishment of a completely independent Sikh state which they refer to as Khalistan (the land of the pure), in which the *khalsa* will rule supreme. The increasing militancy employed by some Sikh groups in attainment of these aims is a cause for concern for Hindus and moderate and non-*khalsa* Sikhs alike. Jarnail Singh Bhindranwale is perhaps the most prominent militant of recent years, closely associated with the All India Sikh Student Federation (AISSF) and the Damdani Taksal religious school, Bhindranwale, and many of his followers lost their lives when the Indian army stormed and descrated the Golden Temple, Amritsar in June 1984. Operation Blue Star, as it was named, and the massacre of over 2,700 Sikhs in Delhi in the wake of Indira Gandhi's assassination, have caused a deep sense of injury to almost all Sikhs. Sikh militancy therefore continues and many outrages have been committed. Such tragedy must, nevertheless, be placed against a background of rising Hindu fundamentalism.

Sino–American Buddhist Association (SABA). This eclectic yet very traditional **Buddhist** group was established by Tripitaka Master Hsuan Hua in 1968. The aim of the association is to provide Westerners with access to Chinese Buddhist teachings as transmitted within a valid ordination tradition. For this reason one of Hsuan Hua's first acts after founding the SABA was to send five of his American disciples to Taiwan in 1969 so they could receive the threefold ordination of Chinese tradition. The Association is now able to provide full ordination in America for those who aspire to the monastic life, and offers what is, perhaps, the most traditional and disciplined version of the Buddhist lifestyle in contemporary America. In the course of spreading its message it has taken on some substantial financial commitments (including $6,000,000 for the purchase of 237 acres plus buildings that form the basis for the City of Ten Thousand Buddhas near San Francisco), and it has plans for further expansion. Should all its projects come to fruition SABA could well become one of the most influential Buddhist groups in America today.

Siyam Nikaya. The oldest and most influential fraternity of **Theravada Buddhist** monks in Sri Lanka. It was founded in 1753 when monks from Siam (now Thailand) were invited to Sri Lanka to re-establish an authentic ordination lineage after an earlier form of monasticism had fallen into disrepute. Centred on the ancient capital of Kandy, the Siyam Nikaya once enjoyed the patronage of Sinhalese royalty and still retains considerable affluence. The Temple of the Tooth, containing an important relic of the Buddha, is administered by the fraternity. Traditionally ordination has only been possible for the landowning (*Goyigama*) caste and the Nikaya remains highly conservative. It has two principal sub-divisions based on the Malwatta and Asgiriya monasteries and a highly elaborate hierarchical structure. The current number of monks overall is about 12,000.

Slavonic Orthodox Church. See **Orthodox Church (Byzantine).**

Smartas. Smartas are a community of brahmins in South India who adhere to orthodox Hindu practice, maintaining caste distinctions and passing through, at least in theory, a series of four prescribed life-stages. The Smartas are so called because they follow the *smritis,* the "remembered", non-revelatory i.e. non-Vedic texts of **Hinduism.** Smartas are characterized by worship of five deities: Vishnu, Shiva, Durga, Surya, and Ganesha. The **Shakta** cult of the goddess Tripurasundari has been absorbed by some members of the group and worship of the Goddess's symbol, the *shri chakra,* is found in their temples. Although the Smartas are householders, they also practise renunciation into one of the **Dashanami** orders of Shankara.

Society for Companions of the Spirits. A Japanese new religious movement also known as **Reiyukai Kyodan.**

Society for the Establishment of Righteousness and Harmony. A Japanese new religious movement also known as **Rissho Koseikai.**

Society of Friends (Quakers). This movement began in England in the 1650s, when George Fox and the other early leaders of the group claimed an unmediated relationship with God which had no need of a "hireling ministry", or outward sacraments. The whole of life was deemed sacramental and no place was more sacred than any other. Friends decried the use of "steeplehouses" and preached that everyone, man or woman, had the opportunity to turn to the "inward light". There was "that of God" in everyone. Quaker "Meeting for Worship" was based in silence, allowing any to minister when led by the Holy Spirit. (The term "Quaker" was initially a nickname based on the way adherents trembled and shook during worship.) Business decisions were, and are, taken without votes as Friends seek to discern the will of God.

Friends refused to pay church tithes, to swear oaths (for they said they always told the truth and a passage in Matthew forbade swearing), and refused to acknowledge social rank. Friends only took their hats off to God and used "thee" and "thou" to everyone, infuriating those who would normally be addressed with the deferential "you".

Convinced that they had been called to restore "primitive **Christianity**" to a people in apostasy, Friends would disrupt church services or follow other "leadings" such as going naked for a sign. By 1660, it is estimated there were up to 80,000 Quakers in Britain and the restoration of the monarchy brought with it harsh persecution. The Quaker Act of 1661 and the Conventicle Act of 1664 put many Friends in prison. The adoption around this period of the Peace Testimony (the basis of Quaker pacifism) and the idea that the corporate approach to God had greater authority than the individual one (placing a sanction on individual ecstatic behaviour) reflected a more pragmatic approach.

By the beginning of the 18th century, Quakers in Britain had ceased to proselytize and were concerned with protecting the "gathered remnant" from the temptations of the world. Earlier customs now became rules and many were disowned for marrying a non-Friend or other offences, such as owning a piano. Barred from the Universities due to their non-conformity, Quakers turned to industry and are known today for their success in the chocolate industry, amongst others, and subsequent philanthropy. In the 19th century, British Friends underwent further periods of transition. Keen to mix as equals with their **Anglican** counterparts, wealthier Friends began to adopt a more Bible-based evangelism. The concept of the "inward light" was attacked as unscriptural. By 1860, with membership at an all-time low of some 13,000, the regulations about marrying out, and the wearing of "plain dress" and the use of "plain speech" had been abolished. Towards the end of the century, there was a theological shift away from Biblical authority to some of the early teachings of Friends. Quakerism in Britain today is characterized by a liberal attitude to belief (many British Quakers are not Christian), although a more sectarian attitude prevails in terms of behaviour.

Friends set up Pennsylvania in the 1680s as a "Holy Experiment" in divine government and religious toleration and were influential in the other American colonies. In the 19th century, American Quakerism underwent a series of schisms. Towards the end of the century, some Meetings began to see themselves as churches, adopted pastors and "programmed worship" (as opposed to the "unprogrammed" spontaneity of silence). However, Friends everywhere continue to believe in an unmediated relationship with God and the consequent abolition of the laity. Today, there are 280,000 Quakers worldwide, grouped within 66 autonomous "Yearly Meetings".

Society of Jesus. *See* **Jesuits**.

Society of Jewish Science (Society of Applied Judaism). Founded in New York in 1922 by Reform Rabbi, Morris Lichtenstein (1890–1938) as a Jewish version of **Christian Science,** and still currently active.

Society of Militant Clergy. The Society of Militant Clergy (Jam'iyat-i Ruhan-iyun-i Mobariz; also Jame'eh-ye Ruhaniyat-e Mobarez) is an Iranian organization whose roots go back before the revolution to 1976, when a nucleus formed around Ayatollah Beheshti. Since the 1979 revolution it has been pivotal in radicalizing the traditionally conservative **Shi'ite** clerical structure and organizing support for the ruling Islamic Republican Party. When the latter was dissolved in 1987, the Society's function as a political arm of the *ulama*, endorsing candidates for elections, increased. A channel of influence for many radicals, it opposed Iran's neutrality in the Gulf conflict of 1991, denouncing the United States. However, it failed to command popular support for its stance.

Soka Gakkai (Value Creating Society). Soka Gakkai was founded in its preliminary form on Nov. 18, 1930 by a Tokyo teacher, Makiguchi Tsunesaburo. Its religious foundations are in **Nichiren Buddhism.** Since 1952 it has been a juridically independent lay organization, related to **Nichirenshoshu.** Originally created as a forum for the educational theories of the founder, it has become a new religious movement based on Nichiren's belief that the benefits of spiritual practice can be reaped here and now.

In 1943 Makiguchi and his associates were imprisoned for violating the Peace Preservation Law (i.e. opposing State **Shinto**). After the war Soka Gakkai grew dynamically under the controversial leaders Toda Josei (1900–1958) and Ikeda Daisaku (b. 1928) and international membership is currently approaching 16,000,000.

In Japan, Soka Gakkai has a high public profile, with its impressive rallies and meetings, and extensive range of social reform programmes in keeping with Nichiren's utopian ideals for the country. It has launched a campaign for world peace, and in its international capacity endorses the ideals of the United Nations, in which it plays a consultative role. It has its own education system, including Soka University, and its emphasis on conversion accounts for its wide usage of the mass media, and the production of its own daily newspaper, *Seikyo Shimbun.* Until 1970 **Komeito** (the "Clean Government Party") was the political wing of Soka Gakkai.

Soka Gakkai, in accord with Nichirenshoshu, holds that positive social reform will take place when each individual realises the all-permeating Buddha-nature. This process has been defined as the "human revolution" and it is towards this end that all Nichiren Buddhism applies itself.

Soka Gakkai International (SGI). The international arm of **Soka Gakkai** with branches in about 115 countries. Nichirenshoshu of the UK is the British arm of the organization.

Son. Son is the Korean version of the ancient Chinese Buddhist *Ch'an* school and a close relative to **Rinzai Zen**. The Son tradition was taken to Korea during the unified Silla period (668–935 CE) by a monk called Pomnang who combined two Chinese traditions of Ch'an with the teachings of *The Awakening of Faith in the Mahayana*, a Chinese text.

During the 8th and 9th centuries CE nine schools of Son developed. Each had a headquarters on a mountain site and hence they came to be known as the Nine Mountains Schools. In the late 12th century the Son master Chinul (1158–1210) developed what is recognized as a distinctively Korean version of Son: the **Chogye Chong.** This was essentially a synthesis of Nine Mountains practices with Kongan (Japanese: *Koan*) techniques for cultivating sudden enlightenment, along with the teachings of various scholastic schools that had been introduced from China.

Under the Japanese, who annexed Korea in 1910, Buddhist monks were allowed to marry and by 1935 almost all of the senior incumbents in monasteries were married. This state of affairs was, however, anathema to traditionalists. After World War II a division emerged between the **T'aego Chong** (a faction representing married monks) and the Chogye Chong. In 1954 the South Korean government supported the Chogye Chong in its attempt to control the monasteries and now only celibate monks are allowed to become abbots. At the present time about half of the 45,000 or so Korean monks and nuns are married. They serve the needs of approximately 6,000,000 Korean Buddhists.

Today, the Son Buddhists of Korea are seeking to revitalize their distinctive synthesis of doctrines and practices whilst making their tradition relevant to the needs of people living in the modern world. They emphasize education and social involvement, run retreats for the laity, operate a number of newspapers and, at the Donnguk University, are sponsoring a systematic translation of Buddhist texts into Korean. **Buddhism** appears to be regenerating itself in modern Korea and at the heart of that regeneration lies the distinctive synthesis of thought and practice that is Son.

Son Chong. The unified **Son** school of Korean **Zen Buddhism**, renamed **Chogye Chong** in 1935.

Sotir. *See* **Zoe**.

Soto Zen. A Japanese form of **Buddhism** which places great stress on meditation.

Dogen (1200–1253) brought Soto to Japan from Sung China. He, like other Kamakura period innovators, spent some time at the **Tendai** centre on Mt Hiei. He travelled to China with Myozen, a disciple of the **Rinzai** founder, Eisai. Many sources suggest that he met with Eisai himself before his trip.

Soto puts near exclusive emphasis on the practice of *zazen*, sitting meditation. This is based on the principle that practice and attainment are essentially one and that enlightenment is not a goal which can be approached or grasped. In Dogen's words, "All existents are the Buddha nature". All sentient beings are potentially enlightened. So simply sitting in meditation, or going about one's daily tasks in accordance with the precepts and with awareness, is to live out the realization that *samsara* and *nirvana* are not separate but totally interrelated.

In his major work, the *Shobogenzo*, Dogen sought to express the nature of the intuitive transmission of Enlightenment outside words which tend to engage the intellectual mind only (hence his suspicion of the Rinzai practice of the *koan*). His concern was to precipitate the fundamental reorientation of perception towards Enlightenment, with as little distracting paraphernalia as possible.

Dogen, more than Eisai, wanted to purify **Zen** practice in Japan; to separate it from Tendai and the burgeoning Pure Land (**Jodoshu**) devotion of the time, and to remove Soto from Rinzai's shadow. Some time after his return from China, he left the capital for the remote Eiheiji in Echizen (now Fukui prefecture), which was to become Soto's centre for around 200 years.

Despite Dogen's puritanism, Soto embraced many aspects of folk religion throughout its history. This was partly because membership was drawn mostly from the agrarian classes, who were attracted by its simplicity.

Like all Buddhist schools in Japan, Soto has undergone periods of repression, particularly during the Tokugawa Shogunate (1603–1867), but has emerged to be one of the largest forms of Japanese Buddhism, with over 6,000,000 adherents, its own university, Komazawa, and ample training facilities for its monks. The restored Eiheiji and the Sojiji in Yokohama are joint head temples and the priesthood numbers around 15,000.

Both Rinzai and Soto Zen have achieved a solid footing in the West, initially through the efforts of such figures as Dr Daisetz Suzuki, Christmas Humphreys and Alan Watts during the 1950s and '60s, and more recently Dr Irmgard Schloegl (Ven. Myokyo-ni). Zen's minimalism appears to hold particular appeal for Westerners coping with the ever-expanding complexities of modern life, and the number of practice centres continues to grow both in Europe and in the United States. The Order of Buddhist Contemplatives is a Western, Soto-derived monastic order.

South American Traditional Religions. The total indigenous population of South America is well over 15,000,000. The majority are highland peoples such as the Quechua and Aymara of the Andes, whose total exceeds 11,000,000, while about 1,000,000 forest dwellers live in the Amazon region. All these peoples retain in varying degrees their pre-Christian religious views, many of which have been the subject of detailed studies by anthropologists and specialists in comparative religion and mythology. As in central America the contemporary situation of these peoples is bound up with their political survival, and religious and political issues are closely linked.

In Brazil the Amazonian tribes are some of the least assimilated indigenous peoples on the entire planet, continuing to hold to their way of life, including traditional religious outlook, free from European encroachment. With the development of the Amazon basin, however, this heritage is under intense threat and has led to a concerted politicization of the Amazon indians in which religious leaders have shown a strong commitment to protect and sustain their natural habitat and environment.

In 1989 an extraordinary convention took place under the auspices of Indian tribal leaders at Altamira, joined by many environmentalists and political leaders; the conference opened with a religious peace ceremony staged by the Xavante tribe from the South Amazon. The government of Brazil has since promised to review its ambitious "Plan 2010" which called for the development of virtually all the Amazon's water resources and the flooding of an area of rain forest the size of the UK.

The federation of the indigenous nationalities of Ecuador has declared itself willing to use armed struggled if the jungle regions of that country are not converted to an autonomous territory for their peoples, and Ecuador declared officially a multinational country.

Bolivia has the highest proportion of pre-Columbian religious traditions surviving, with 66 per cent of its population belonging to one of several indigenous cultures, such as the Aymara and the Quechua tribes descended from the Inca civilization. Traditions of magic, **witchcraft**, divination and therapeutic sorcery continue to play an important part in the lives of the impoverished descendants of Incan civilization. Among the agricultural peoples practising small-scale subsistence farming in Columbia, Bolivia and Chile, the modern-day descendants of the Incas remain closely bound up with the obligations imposed on men and women by the cycles of nature. In Peru the Sendero Luminoso (Shining Path) guerrilla movement is mostly made up of Indians from the highland regions, and the dispossession of Indian lands is one of the great motivating factors behind the unrest throughout the region. In Chile the Mapuche people of the highlands have fallen foul of both right- and left-wing attempts at assimilation, and continue to demand autonomy.

As in Central America, spirituality is closely linked to hallucinogenic and narcotic drugs, such as cocaine, the consumption of which remains an everyday reality to the native peoples. Such practices hark back to the Incan practices in which narcotics played an important part in divination through enabling the priesthood to contact the spiritual worlds.

One of the most intriguing survivals of South American **paganism** is that of the Tairona culture of northern Columbia's Atlantic coast along the Sierra Nevada. There the Kogi Indians have maintained, in almost complete isolation from contact with Western civilization, the spiritual and cultural traditions of their ancestors. The Kogi comprise a microcosm of pre-Columbian spirituality of great significance, in which the priests, the Mamas, devote themselves rigorously to the concentrated development of mental and spiritual energy (*aluna*), maintaining contact with the spiritual worlds on behalf of the community as a whole, performing the function of sacred guardianship.

Attitudes to sexuality among South American peoples generally were far more full-blooded and liberal than among their Spanish and Portuguese conquerors, as the large numbers of erotic objects, such as terracotta pots and figurines, testify.

In South America as in Central America it is to be hoped that recent changes towards democratization in the world at large will advance the cause of Indian emancipation, both spiritual and political, and there are signs that this is indeed the case. The large UN Conference on the Environment and Development in mid-1992 in Brazil marked a further watershed in the recognition of indigenous rights throughout the region. Native peoples have a vital role to play in the quest for patterns of sustainable development. The contemporary world has therefore, not surprisingly, seen a growing interest, reflected in publications and research, in the indigenous spirituality of South America.

Southern Baptists. The Southern Baptists are a denomination of the American branch of **Baptists.** The split between North and South in the USA came in 1845 when the board of the American Baptist Home Mission Society decreed that they could not appoint as a missionary anyone owning slaves. This led to a decision that it would be best if a separate and independent Southern Baptist Convention should be formed, consisting of 14 southern states who stated that slaveholders were no less eligible than others to serve as missionaries. During the American Civil War the Southern Baptist Convention publicly supported the Confederacy and afterwards voted to continue to function independently. Until World War II membership was confined to the southern states, but since then it has expanded across the USA.

Three factors distinguish the Southern Baptist Convention from other Baptist churches. Their theology is conservative and they speak out strongly on ethical issues. They have opposed gambling, pornography, homosexuality, violence on television, and abortion. They have also led campaigns against racial discrimination, anti-Semitism and religious persecution. The second feature is a deep concern for evangelism and missionary work: they have the largest number of missionaries of all the American denominations, and make full use of modern technology and communication techniques. Finally the stewardship of talents, and especially of money, is a central belief. This leads to high levels of giving by members of affiliated churches, ensuring the effectiveness of their work.

The evangelist Billy Graham comes from the Southern Baptist tradition and his methods and message reflect the above attitudes. Former president Jimmy Carter is also a Southern Baptist, and his election is a reminder of the fact that the Southern Baptists are now the largest American Protestant denomination.

Spiritual Baptists. This Afro–Protestant cult in Trinidad—also known as the Shouters—is similar to **Revival Zion** in Jamaica. Baptism by full immersion in a river or the sea occurs, but services do not feature the drumming which is prominent in Revival Zion and numerous other Afro–Caribbean religions (for instance **Kumina** and **Shango**). Moreover, the spirit possession that occurs involves, in most cases, the Holy Spirit only, and not the further range of spirits found in Revival Zion.

Spiritualists. Although spiritual mediums existed in Bible times (King Saul visited a medium at Endor to consult the dead prophet Samuel, I Sam. 28) modern Spiritualists go back to 1848, following the experiences of the family of John D. Fox in New York State, USA. After hearing mysterious tappings in their house his teenage daughter Kate set up a code of communication with the spirit believed to be causing the phenomenon—a man who had been murdered in the house. As an adult Kate became a medium in the Spiritualist Church.

Interest in the spirit world spread quickly. Spiritualism was brought to England in 1853 by David Richmond, starting in Yorkshire but soon spreading south. At one time the movement claimed 10,000,000 believers, including such notables as Sir Arthur Conan Doyle. A famous Victorian medium, D. D. Hume, demonstrated his powers in front of a gathering of eminent scientists and convinced many.

Spiritualists believe that God is Infinite Intelligence. They reject the deity of Christ but believe he was a medium. A medium is someone who is sensitive to vibrations from the "spirit world", where the disembodied spirits of the dead are believed to exist. He mediates with this spirit world at séances via a specific spirit called a "control". The means of communication vary, and may include a change of voice or automatic writing. Mediums can also specialize in clairvoyance (the knowledge of future or hidden events) or healing.

The largest group of adherents is in the USA, where the International General Association of Spiritualists has a membership of over 100,000. However there have been a number of splits in the movement. In the United Kingdom the Greater World Christian Spiritualist League has about 30,000 members, although the beliefs of Spiritualists have never been accepted by mainstream Christianity. The Spirtualists' National Union has a similar membership, but is open to non-Christians. Spiritualists were prominent in the Natural Law Party which put up candidates nationally (but unsuccessfully) in the 1992 UK

General Election. Their most well-known medium was Doris Stokes. Worldwide membership is about 500,000.

Spiritualists' National Union. *See* **Spiritualists.**

Sri Lankan Theravada. Buddhism was almost certainly brought to Sri Lanka by Mahinda, the missionary son of the converted Indian emperor Asoka Maurya, some time in the 3rd century BCE. Mahinda succeeded in converting the king of the time and ordained the first monks. His sister subsequently brought an ordination lineage for nuns. Sri Lanka has consequently been a Buddhist country for over 2,000 years, at least as far as the majority Sinhalese population is concerned. The Pali canon (*tripitaka*) was committed to writing on the island between 29–17 BCE. One of the most famous Buddhist writers, Buddhaghosa, moved to Sri Lanka from northern India in the 5th century to undertake the translation of Sinhala commentaries into Pali. While there he composed his classic treatise on the spiritual life, *The Path of Purification* (*Visuddhimagga*). From the 10th century we find evidence for the rise of an ascetic forest monk tradition which survives down to the present day. Divisions such as these can be traced back to about the beginnings of the Christian era and we know of royal attempts to reform the *sangha* in the 12th century. The three monastic fraternities (*nikayas*) today (i.e. **Siyam**, Amarapura and **Mahanikayas**), though only dating back to the 18th century, are heirs to some of these disputes. The influence of the *sangha* has ebbed and flowed across the centuries, though periods of stagnation have generally picked up from a fresh impetus supplied by fellow Theravadins in Thailand or Burma.

In the last hundred years or so, Sri Lankan Theravada has undergone many changes. Millennial movements have been relatively common, and **Theosophy** has played a significant role in a number of developments. Similarly, lay meditation and therapy of the type offered by the Siyane Vipassana Bhavana Samitiya has grown in prominence. The appearance of this-worldly movements such as the developmentally-oriented **Sarvodaya Sramadana** has been another feature of Buddhist modernism in the country, while sections of the Theravada *sangha* still regard themselves as the bulwark of national identity in a longstanding and bitter dispute with Tamil separatists in the north. Recently an ordination lineage for nuns has established itself again in the country after an absence of almost 1,000 years and, although not universally approved, the number of women coming forward for ordination is growing. About 12 million Sri Lankas are Buddhist, i.e. about 69 per cent of the population.

St Thomas Christians. *See* **Syro–Indian Churches.**

Subud. Subud—Susila Buddhi Dharma (or Susila Budi Darma) in full—is the only one of the numerous kebatinan movements that have proliferated in Indonesia this century to have become truly international. Founded in 1947, its origins lie in a revelation which is claimed to have occurred to Muhammad Subuh Sumohadiwidjojo—later known as Bapak ("Father") Subuh—in 1932, although a sense of spiritual awakening had begun already in 1925, and had been followed by extensive contacts with a teacher of the **Naqshabandiya Sufi** order.

The movement's emphasis is on *latihan*, practice, rather than theoretical teachings, although an authoritative summary of the latter is contained in the book which originated with Bapak Subuh in the 1940s and whose title is also that of the movement, *Susila Budi Darma* ("Susila"—right living according to God's will, "Budi"—an inner force inherent in human nature, and "Darma"—submission to God).

Subud advocates its form of spiritual practice as supportive of, and complementary to, the spirituality of other religions, rather than claiming to be a religion itself. For this reason it in 1979 withdrew from the umbrella *kebatinan* organization in Indonesia.

Since the mid-1950s, however, Subud has become well-known outside Indonesia, including in Europe and America. Bapak Subuh (1901–87) was invited to England from Indonesia in 1956 by Gurdjieff's chief English disciple John Bennett, and initially attracted many of Gurdjieff's and Ouspensky's students (*see* **Gurdjieffian Groups**). His system, consisting mainly of *latihan*, performed twice a week, involves letting the "divine power" take over the body and mind. Effects can include movement, dance, prayer and catharsis, often leading to increased well-being, and sometimes profound spiritual changes. Membership is open to anyone over 17, and is said to be about 10,000 worldwide (1,000 in Britain). There is no fee, but a voluntary donation of three per cent of one's income is suggested. Its enterprises include various social welfare projects and businesses worldwide.

Sufism. Sufis are traditionally described as the mystics of **Islam**, but this is in important respects misleading: Sufism covers quite a variety of beliefs and practices.

In early Islam, Sufis were pious Muslims who reacted to what they saw as the corruption bred by worldly success by practising austerities, and they marked their more ascetic lifestyle by wearing garments of wool—*suf*—hence Sufi.

Their spiritual concerns led them to focus on the inner life; and ever more elaborate theories of the possible states of the soul, and how to achieve them, were developed. Methods varied, but included singing and chanting as well as types of meditation. Interpretation of the goal varied too. The famous (or notorious) al-Hallaj apparently claimed identity with God, and was crucified in 922 CE for blasphemy. That kind of monistic mysticism was henceforth to be avoided, and Sufism had to keep within the bounds of Islamic law and traditional belief. Due to a considerable extent to the work of al-Ghazali (d. 1111), it secured an accepted place within Islam on those conditions (although they were not always adhered to: a notable exception was the monism of the Spaniard Ibn al-'Arabi, 1165–1240, with his theory of the "unity of all existence", *wahdat al-wujud*). It is in respect of this core development that Sufis are properly known as Muslim mystics. They also emphasized the love of God rather than his justice.

The methods of prayer and meditation were handed down from master to pupils. This was often facilitated by groups of Sufis living together in communities. In this way the Sufi orders emerged. Particular traditions, e.g. of *sama*—music performed for spiritual purposes—and forms of *dhikr* (or *zikr*)—rhythmic repetition, aloud or silently, of the names of God in order to attain ecstasy—were passed down from a given spiritual leader to succeeding generations of disciples who venerated his memory and gave him their personal allegiance. Such a chain of spiritual allegiance is known as a *silsila*. The founder is referred to as a *shaikh*—a term also used, along with others (*murshid, pir*), for subsequent spiritual guides within the orders at any particular time. Followers may be known as *murids*, and Sufis in general are sometimes called dervishes, as reflected in a label such as Whirling Dervishes which highlights a distinctive feature of the ritual of individual orders, in this case the **Mawlawiya**.

The number of orders has proliferated enormously. The vast majority are **Sunni**, but a few, like the **Ni'matullahiya**, are **Shi'ite**. Some, like the **Naqshabandiya** and the **Qadiriya**, are international in scope; others are regional, like the **Chishtiya,** Suhrawardiya and Shattariya, which have their focus in the Indian subcontinent, the Darqawiya and Tijaniya in Africa, or the Shadhiliya more particularly in North Africa and the Middle East; others are relatively local, like the Hamadsha in Morocco or the Kubrawiya in Turkmenistan, or else associated with certain countries in particular, like the **Muridiya** and Senegal, the Khatmiya and Sudan, or the **Sanusiya** and Libya.

The followers or disciples of a shaikh lived in, or visited and travelled between, Sufi centres which often received endowments from wealthy patrons and in some cases became elaborate complexes known as *zawiyas*. These might contain a mosque, college, library, refectory, and a lodging house for travellers, servants, and students. A more basic centre may be known as a *tekke, ribat* or *khanaqah*.

The tombs of the founders of orders in particular, but also of subsequent venerated *shaikhs*, were of major importance. They were likely to become the centre of a *zawiya* complex, and centres of pilgrimage. The anniversary of the death of the *shaikh*, the *'urs*, became the occasion of a great gathering of people, and a major festival. This is true still today, for example in the Mawlawiya, the **Bektashiya**, the Chishtiya, the **Badawiya**, and the Madariya. A host of other festivals and pilgrimages is associated with Sufism too: part of what some observers label "popular" or "folk" Islam as opposed to the "orthodox" Islam of Quran and *ulama*.

Here Sufism again became controversial. A very great number of tombs of holy men, usually referred to in English as saints, became the focus of shrine cults. Visitors implored the intercession of the saint on their behalf, or his miraculous intervention, whether for healing or some form of worldly success. Simply by touching his tomb the devotee would acquire some of his special sacred power, *baraka*. This is now a long way from mysticism. In North and West Africa the term **maraboutism** has been used in relation to this phenomenon, but it is an extremely widespread one, being common, say, in Pakistan and India, but also in the Muslim states of the former USSR. It incurred the intense hostility of the **Wahhabis**, and in Saudi Arabia the once common Sufi shrines have all been destroyed. In South Asia, attitudes to the saints remain a subject of often bitter controversy between the **Barelvis** and the **Deobandis**.

The vast majority of orders have remained "with the law" (*ba-shar'*), as stipulated centuries ago by al-Ghazali. A few, e.g. the **Malangs**, have developed "without the law" (*bi-shar'*), and their members may in truth be Muslim in name alone: one is here on the very fringe of Islam and Sufism alike.

The fortunes of the orders have fluctuated a good deal, but they (i.e. the *ba-shar'* ones) have been enormously influential in a variety of ways, sometimes through the education or social services they have provided, sometimes politically, and very often in the spreading of the faith—even if not always in a form approved of by the *ulama*, or modern reformers (e.g. the **Salafiya**), or today's Islamists (e.g. the **Muslim Brotherhood** and the **Jama'at-i Islami**).

Sukyo Mahikari. A sub-sect of the Japanese religious movement **Sekai Mahikari Bunmei Kyodan,** established in 1974 by an adopted daughter of the founder of the original group, Okada Sachiko.

Süleymancis. A Turkish Islamic renewal group founded by Süleyman Hilmi Tunahan (1888–1959), and similar in some ways to the **Nurcus**. A **Sufi** sheikh of the Nakşibendi order (**Naqshabandiya**), Süleyman opposed the Kemalist policy of establishing the Turkish state on a secular basis, and was arrested in 1933 for setting up Quranic schools as rivals to the state schools. Attempted state control of **Islam** in Turkey through a Directorate of Religious Affairs (*Diyanet Isleri Baskanligi*) was a particular target of criticism, and remains so amongst his followers today. Indeed Süleymancis, in expressing their disapproval of the secular state, refuse employment in government service. Nor will they become teachers in state schools, though they are active in running hostels for schoolchildren. In their quest for new members, their strategy resembles that of the Nurcus.

The Süleymancis, with a centre in Köln, are particularly influential among the Turkish community in Germany (being in this respect the envy of rival groups like the Nurcular and **Milli Görüs**), and this has led Diyanet to step up its opposition to the movement, which it currently denounces as heretical. The Süleymancis are also represented, in Islamic Cultural Centres, in most western European countries. In Turkey they have been the object of criticism, not only by Diyanet, but also by the **Alevis**.

Sunnism. Sunnis are variously described as mainstream or orthodox Muslims. They form the overwhelming majority of all Muslims. The designation Sunni is based on the word *sunna*, meaning the path set forth by Muhammad. This path is contained in the Quran, and in the authoritative collections of hadith—the reports of the sayings and actions of the Prophet. The shari'a, the religious law, is widely regarded as normative too. Sunnis recognize four schools of law, or four rites, as they are also known: the **Maliki, Hanafi, Shafi'i** and **Hanbali**.

Sunnis are defined negatively as not being **Shi'ites** (or **Ibadis**). However, they recognize Shi'ites as being Muslim, which they do not do with regard to members of the **Ahmadiya**.

Most of the numerous **sufi** orders that have developed within **Islam** are Sunni orders, but some Shi'ite ones also exist, so Sufism transcends the Sunni–Shi'ite distinction rather than forming a third category alongside the other two.

Within Sunnism a number of different movements and schools of thought are to be found. Of considerable significance are the **Wahhabis** of Saudi Arabia because of their trusteeship of the historic cities of Mecca and Medina. Among South Asian Muslims, two major groups are the **Barelvis** and the **Deobandis**, but there are also the **Ahl-i Hadith** and the **Ahl-i Quran**, while the **Tablighi Jama'at** is of wider appeal internationally.

The resurgence of Islam in recent years undoubtedly owes much to the revolution in Iran, a Shi'ite country, but it has certainly seen a proliferation of religio–political organizations in the Sunni world too—as well as vigorous activity by older-established ones such as the **Muslim Brotherhood** and the **Jama'at-i Islami**. The label "fundamentalist" is often used in this connection, but is not terribly satisfactory. The attitude to scripture that it characterizes is supposed to be held by all Muslims, not just the so-called fundamentalist ones; alternatively put, it is not their attitude to scripture that distinguishes the Muslim fundamentalists. In many cases it is their attitude to the *shari'a*, but this is not uniform either. Amongst Muslims themselves they are increasingly referred to as Islamists, a usage adopted here. The meaning remains vague—like many of their programmes—but it serves to pick out those religio–political organizations which aspire to establish an Islamic state as a means of transforming Muslim society. And outside Iran, most Islamists are Sunnis.

Svetambara Jainas (White-clad Jainas). One of the two major sects of Jainism so-called because their ascetics wear white robes. The practice of nudity has always been regarded as optional for Svetambara monks who, unlike the **Digambara Jainas**, consider that women are capable of the same spiritual and ascetic attainments as men. The fact that nuns are clothed presents no obstacle to liberation. Indeed, according to the Svetambara (but not the Digambara) account, the 19th *tirthankara*, Malli, was a woman. They have an extensive canonical literature, and a very large body of commentarial and philosophical texts in classical and vernacular languages.

The majority of Svetambaras have been, and remain, *murtipujakas* or "image worshippers". That is to say, lay religious practice is characterized by temple worship: the making of offerings and other devotional practices in the presence of images of the *tirthankaras* and their attendant deities.

Outside the rainy season, monks and nuns separately lead itinerant lives in small groups under the overall direction of an *acarya* or teacher. They beg food and water from householders two or three times daily, taking the alms away in small pots.

After the Muslim invasions, various "reforming" sects arose within the Svetambara community. One line of reform led, in the 17th century, to the formation of the Sthanakavasis ("dwellers in halls"), who came to assert that the canonical texts do not sanction image worship. Consequently, they took (and take) no part in temple ritual. A further division within this group led to the formation, in the 18th century, of the Terapanthis. In 1948, under the leadership of the monk Acarya Tulsi, Terapanthis began the Anuvrat Movement, with the purpose of spreading reformulated Jain values to all communities. Recently, an ex-Svetambara ascetic, Chitrabhanu, has acquired a following outside India, establishing a Jain meditation centre in the USA.

Today Svetambaras are especially influential in north-east India (Gujarat, Rajasthan and the Punjab). The ascetic community comprises approximately 4,400 nuns and 1,650 monks.

Swaminarayans. The **Hindu** followers of the ascetic Sahajanand (1781–1830) who came to be regarded as a manifestation of the Supreme God and thus given the name Swaminarayan. There are perhaps 5,000,000 members of this movement, mostly living in Gujarat, but there are members in other parts of India, especially in large urban centres, and in East Africa, the United Kingdom and the USA. The Swami Narayan Hindu Mission acts as an international umbrella organization.

Swami Narayan was born near Ayodhya in Uttar Pradesh, but spent most of his life in Gujarat. At the age of 20 he became the leader of an ascetic order which, in the next 30 years, he turned into a well-organized group made up of both ascetics and householder families. He was happy, in his lifetime, to be seen as an *avatara* of the Supreme God. In other ways he is one of the earliest Hindu reformers of the modern age: he opposed female infanticide and the practice of *sati* (the self-immolation of a widow upon her husband's funeral pyre) and was in favour of the remarriage of younger widows.

The chief Swaminarayan temples are in Gujarat, at Vadtal and Ahmedabad. The scriptures of the movement (along with some mainstream scriptures such as the *Vedas*), consist of Swami Narayan's writings and sermons. Spiritual guidance is undertaken by ascetics, but the overall leadership and control of practical affairs is in the hands of a householder, a descendant of one of the two nephews whom Swami Narayan chose as his successors.

The **Vaishnava** character of the movement manifests itself in three ways. One is that Swami Narayan is often identified with Krishna. Another is that the pattern of daily worship of the Swaminarayan temples is closely modelled upon that of the **Pushtimarga.** Thirdly, Swami Narayan saw himself as firmly within the philosophical tradition of Ramanuja's version of **Vedanta**, even though he was prepared to modify this in some ways.

The lifestyle of the Swaminarayan movement is puritanical. Men and women are rigidly separated in worship, and ascetics must be particularly careful to avoid any contact whatsoever with women. There is an insistence upon charitable works, social concern and high moral standards.

Since Swami Narayan's time there have been some schisms among his followers. The most important schismatic group is the Akshar Purushottam Sanstha, whose members revere one of Swami Narayan's first disciples, Gunatitanand, who is said to be the *akshar,* the abode in human form of the Supreme Person, and therefore an appropriate object of worship together with the Supreme Person.

Swedenborgianism. Emanuel Swedenborg (1688–1772), a Swedish scientist who developed a dominant interest in religion, became concerned to expound the hidden meaning of scripture and to communicate his own mystical/supernatural/ visionary experiences. According to his philosophy, the spirits of the dead, located in two groups with characteristics roughly corresponding to heaven and hell respectively, jointly constitute Maximus Homo, a huge human being. He judged Christ to be the highest form of humanity, but his views are not in general in line with Christian belief. He established the first New Church in London in 1787, which for a time became the basis for a flourishing worldwide movement. It still has a number of congregations in various parts of the world, and Swedenborgianism is seen as influencing the contemporary **New Age** movement.

Syrian Jacobite Church. Also known as the "Syrian Orthodox Church", the Syrian Jacobite Church is one of three main traditions among the **Oriental**

Orthodox Churches. It derives directly from the monophysite majority within the original Patriarchal Church of Antioch which in the 5th century rejected the authority of the Council of Chalcedon. The term "Jacobite" comes from the monk, Jacob Baradaeus, who in the 6th century renewed the monophysite tradition in Syria and rescued the Church from absorption into the **Orthodox Church (Byzantine)**. Its adherents once included almost all the Christians native to Syria and western Mesopotamia (Iraq), but a large proportion of this population later converted to **Islam**. Now living in predominantly Muslim countries, the Syrian Jacobite minority suffers from restrictions and insecurities unlikely to diminish in the face of nationalistic and fundamentalist Islam.

Heading the Church is a Patriarch of Antioch who now lives in Homs, in Syria. The liturgy follows the West Syrian (Antiochene) Liturgy of St James, which now combines Syriac with Arabic, and members number around 200,000. The Church also claims jurisdiction over Jacobite Christians living in North and South America (50,000) and in Southern India (*see* **Syro–Indian Churches**).

Syro–Indian Churches. Since at least the 5th century, and possibly much earlier, there has been a community of Christians on the Malabar coast of South West India (Kerala State). This community, probably established by Syrian missionaries, traditionally trace their origin to the missionary activity of St Thomas the Apostle. Also known as the Malabar Christians, or St Thomas Christians, they have had a complex history and now exist in at least five distinct groups.

Originally the community seems to have followed the beliefs of the **Nestorians** and maintained ecclesiastical contacts with the hierarchy in Iraq. Following the Portuguese colonization of South India in the 16th century, they joined themselves to the **Roman Catholic Church**, but in the following century undue pressure to adopt Western customs and usages alienated the community, which in 1653 broke with Rome. In 1662 the majority were persuaded to renew their union with Rome, while the remainder, prevented from rejoining the Nestorians, joined themselves to the **Syrian Jacobite Church**. In 1874, within the Roman Catholic group, a small minority split off from the Catholics to re-establish links with the Nestorians; these are the Mellusians, so named after Bishop Mello, their original leader.

In the 20th century, continuing disputes among the Syrian Jacobites produced new groupings. Around 1910 a split developed between those accepting the jurisdiction of the patriarch of Antioch and those placing themselves under their own locally elected catholicos. **Protestant** and in particular **Anglican** influence produced a small minority of Reformed Jacobites, who have appropriated the title Mar Thoma (St Thomas) Christians and who in recent years have been associated with the ecumenically inspired Church of South India. In 1930 a further group of Jacobites became reunited with Rome, this time retaining their Jacobite traditions and known as the Malankarese Uniate Church (Malankara being the old name for Malabar).

Thus there are now five distinct groups of Churches: (i) the original Malabar Catholics, numbering around 1,500,000, who use a Romanized version of the East Syrian Liturgy of Addai and Mari; (ii) a Jacobite (**Oriental Orthodox**) community, who use the West Syrian (or Antiochene) Liturgy, and who number around 500,000; (iii) the second Catholic group, the Malankarese Uniates, who also use the Antiochene liturgy, but translated into the vernacular Malayalam language. They number about 125,000; (iv) the nominally Nestorian Mellusians, now numbering only a few thousand; and (v) various Protestant Churches.

T

Tablighi Jama'at. Tablighi Jama'at, or "Missionary Society", which is also known as the Tahrik-i Iman (Faith Movement) and the Dini Dawat (Religious Mission), is probably the most popular reform movement in the Islamic world today. With the **Jama'at-i Islami** it is one of the two great **Islamic** movements to emerge from South Asia in the 20th century. The founder was Maulana Muhammad Ilyas (1885–1944), who came out of the **Deobandi** tradition. Dissatisfied by the Deobandi focus on those who were literate, he aimed to take the message of Islamic reform to the masses. His followers were required to adopt the following practices: (i) inculcating missionary spirit; (ii) acquiring and transmitting Islamic knowledge; (iii) enjoining what is right and forbidding what is wrong; and (iv) working together in mutual love.

In executing their mission members of the Tabligh go on tour in groups. They wear a specific uniform (a beard, Muslim cap, a long Indian shirt and trousers cut off above the ankles), and preach both door by door and in the local mosques. Their methods bear comparison to those of the **Salvation Army** of the Christian tradition. The movement is notable for its total focus on the renewal of faith, for its prohibition on the involvement of politics in their mission, for its avoidance of all religious controversy, and for its following of Islamic law as set out in the medieval law books. Since the death of Muhammad Ilyas, the Tabligh has spread throughout Asia, Africa and North America. In Europe it has had most success in France, Belgium and Britain, where its main centre is in Dewsbury, Yorkshire. It retains its links with Deobandi mosques in particular.

T'aego Chong. A Japanese-influenced school of Korean **Buddhism** which argues that monks should be allowed to marry. In 1954 the South Korean government decided against the T'aego Chong in their dispute with the traditionalist **Chogye Chong** and now only celibate monks are permitted to become abbots, though ordinary monks are still allowed to marry.

Tahrik-i Iman. Tahrik-i Iman, or Faith Movement, is an alternative name for the Indian—and now international—Muslim reform movement, the **Tablighi Jama'at.** It was the name preferred by the founder, Maulana Ilyas.

Tak Kaau. This is the Cantonese version of the Chinese new religious movement **De Jiao**.

al-Takfir wa'l-Hijra. Al-Takfir wa'l-Hijra emerged in the 1970s in Egypt as a radical offshoot from the **Muslim Brotherhood.** Shukri Mustafa (1942–78), a young agricultural student, was imprisoned in 1965 for distributing Brotherhood leaflets at Asyut University. It was the time of a wave of arrests following the discovery of a plot against Nasser centred on the leading ideologue of the Brothers, Sayyid Qutb. In prison Shukri Mustafa became disillusioned with the Brothers, and laid plans for a new movement before his release in 1971. He completed his studies and formed a group around him called the Society of Muslims. They believed, following Sayyid Qutb, that Egyptian society had strayed so far from Islam that it was no longer Muslim, but unbelieving. Therefore, they thought it necessary to practise *takfir*, the act of declaring someone an unbeliever, and *hijrah*, emigration away from an unbelieving community to live as an exclusive group of true believers. Hence their name: al-Takfir wa'l-Hijra.

The group's expenses were met largely by the remittances of members sent for short periods to work in Saudi Arabia and the Gulf. Members lived communally in furnished flats, married among themselves, and refused to send their children to state schools or to do military service. This was preparatory to the time when they would be strong enough to launch a *jihad* against corrupt un-Islamic society.

In January 1977 they began this phase, attacking nightclubs and bars in Cairo as their contribution to a more widespread pattern of rioting against the Sadat régime. In July they kidnapped and later murdered a former minister of religious endowments who had written against them. Security forces then hunted down and arrested hundreds of members of the group out of an estimated 3,000–5,000. Shukri Mustafa and four others were executed in March 1978.

Al-Takfir wa'l-Hijra appeared to have been crushed in 1978, but organizations of the same name were still active in 1991 among the Islamic opposition in Libya and Algeria, as well as among Palestinians under Israeli occupation. In Egypt, surviving members have apparently continued their activities in comparable groups such as al-Jihad (the **Jihad Organization**).

Tantrism. A tradition within **Hinduism** which looks to the scriptural authority of the *Tantras* (composed 400–800 CE) as opposed to the Vedas of orthodox Hinduism. Tantric ideas, images and practices pervade Hinduism, but one who accepts the authority of the Tantras seeks liberation and enjoyment through initiation by a Tantric *guru* into a school (*sampradaya*) and lineage. While many *Tantras* are **Shakta** in orientation there is not always a clear distinction between **Shaiva** and Shakta texts. There are also **Vaishnava** and **Jain** *Tantras* and a large body of **Buddhist** *Tantras*, translated into Tibetan and other Asian languages.

The most characteristic feature of tantric traditions is that a female force or power called Shakti is integral to their idea of deity. The absolute is often conceived and represented as Shiva in union with Shakti who, as it were, gives him life. Shakti is not subordinated to Shiva. She may take gentle or ferocious forms and these latter manifestations often demand blood sacrifice in contrast to the "pure" Hindu gods who accept only vegetarian offerings. Various centres of Goddess worship in India are places of pilgrimage for tantrics.

Three broad categories of tantrics might therefore be identified. Firstly at a village, low-caste level there is popular worship of tantric deities, usually female, ministered to by low-caste priests. Such cults will be concerned with possession and exorcism. Secondly there is private worship of Tantric deities by high caste, usually Brahmin, householder Hindus who have been initiated into a tantric tradition. Such a tantric might be quite orthodox but accept, on top of his Vedic obligations, the ritual obligations of his tantric lineage. A third group is that of the tantric ascetics such as the **Aghoris,** who live outside of the householder's world, perhaps in cremation grounds, practising tantric yoga and imitating their terrifying Lord.

The Tantric householder performs rituals and **yoga** designed to awaken the Shakti within the body called Kundalini. Such rituals might involve the purification of the body through its visualized destruction; the construction of a divine body by the use of magical formulae or *mantras,* the internal or mental worship of the deity; and finally external worship involving the offering of incense, flowers and food. This rite will be accompanied by the repetition of *mantras* and possibly by the use of five ritual ingredients (the five "m"s), namely wine (*madya*), meat (*mamsa*), fish (*matsya*), parched grain (*mudra*), perceived as an aphrodisiac, and caste-free sexual intercourse (*maithuna*). Alcohol, non-vegetarian food and sex outside of the constraints of marriage and caste, are taboos for orthodox brahmins. By a "right-hand" Tantric these ingredients are substituted by other acceptable ingredients, such as vegetables for meat, meditation for sex, while for a "left-hand" tantric they are taken literally. It is these ritual practices which have given tantrics a reputation of immorality among high-caste Hindus. The extent to which a Tantric householder will take part in sexual rites varies. Many Nepalese tantrics, for example, do not perform these rites but simply read the appropriate passage in the Sanskrit ritual manual.

Liberation is not barred to women nor to low-castes in Tantrism and there have been female tantric gurus. However at a practical level, the role of women is generally subordinated to men and images of the divine as female, so central to Tantra, are nevertheless male images.

Tantrism can be found mainly in Nepal, Bengal and Assam and there are respectable tantric traditions in south India.

Taoism. *See* **Chinese Folk Religion; Chinese Taoist Association.**

Taro cult. A spiritist movement in Papua New Guinea. It arose in 1914 when a prophetic figure, Buninia, following a visionary experience of his dead father's spirit, developed rites aimed at increasing the taro crops. Spirit possession, communal meals and ecstatic musical gatherings for singing and dancing are prominent features.

TBMSG. *See* **Trailokya Bauddha Mahasangha Sahagyaka Gana**.

Tendaishu. The Chinese *T'ien T'ai* tradition was introduced to Japan by Saicho (767–822 CE), laying the foundations for almost all future Buddhist developments. Highly prestigious, partly due to its proximity to the new capital (modern Kyoto), the Enryakuji complex on Mt Hiei became its centre, and at its height housed 30,000 monks in 3,000 temples.

Tendai embraced a wide range of rituals. Practices and scholarship in other schools, including **Zen** and Pure Land (*see* **Jodoshu**), were also undertaken on the mountain. Tendai's great influence in the Heian period (794–1160 CE) provided the foundation for the development of *Mahayana* **Buddhism** in

Japan. The Lotus Sutra is a central text for the school, although almost all the *Mahayana sutras* (brought from China by Saicho) are studied and venerated. Tendai is a monastic order, and practices are ascetic and meditative, directed towards the great pantheon of Buddhas and Bodhisattvas.

Tendai's support came from the aristocracy, so with their fall, the sect suffered greatly. Violence and schisms, in particular in the 9th century when Enchin founded the esoteric Tendai Jimonshu, have plagued Tendai's early history. Including all the splinter sects, there are now 5,000,000 Tendai believers, and ascetics still inhabit Mt Hiei.

Tenrikyo. A Japanese new religious movement, also known as the Religion of Heavenly Wisdom, Tenrikyo is one of the 13 sects of **Kyoha Shinto** and places great emphasis on healing through faith. Founded by Nakayama Miki (1798–1887), a farmer's wife and miracle worker, the movement today has about 3,000,000 followers, 17,000 churches and 20,000 mission stations worldwide. Nakayama taught a monotheistic and highly mythological version of **Shinto** which stressed that sickness (*mijo*) is the result of acts (*hokori*) which contradict the divine will of God the Parent, who is also known as Tenri O no Mikoto—the Lord of Heavenly Reason. From the age of 41 she regularly underwent possession by *kami* and in this condition she wrote the two principal scriptures of the sect. She is also said to have identified the site of the original birthplace of man. Iburi Izo (1833–1907) took over the leadership of Tenrikyo on the death of Nakayama and it is he who laid down the present structure of the church.

The twin aims of Tenrikyo are to deliver from suffering and to prepare the path for the establishment of a "perfect divine kingdom". The movement concerns itself with the observance of domestic rather than state values, perhaps as a result of its early history of persecution, and stresses the virtues of loyalty, charity, obligation and gratitude. Shrine building is regarded as an important duty and great emphasis is placed on sacred dance, most notably in the central rite known as the "salvation dance service".

Thai Theravada. Thailand's ability to avoid colonization during the last two centuries has been due primarily to two kings, Mongkut (1804–68) and Chulalongkorn (1868–1910). Both played a major part in reforming **Buddhism** to accommodate modernist influences to enable it to become a source of spiritual and ethical well-being.

Although Mongkut and Chulalongkorn inherited the respect and power ascribed by mainland South–East Asian Buddhist monarchs as successors of Asoka Maurya (the ideal Buddhist emperor of India), they rejected the accompanying cosmology according to which the king, as universal monarch, occupies the centremost position in a three-decker universe. Mongkut's detailed familiarity with Buddhism during his period as a monk enabled him to question many Thai Buddhist practices which were incompatible with the Pali canon. He re-ordained according to the strict and somewhat puritanical Mon tradition and effectively founded a new branch of the Sangha, known as the **Thammayutika Nikaya** ("the branch of those who adhere to the Dhamma"). The older group subsequently became known as **Mahanikaya** ("the great branch"). Though the absolute monarchy was abolished in 1932, monarchs continued to play a major role in providing stability in times of crisis.

The Thammayutika part of the Sangha gained influence among the educated élite and was paralleled in Cambodia, where a separate patriarch was eventually appointed for each branch. In Thailand both groups remained under a single Sangharaja and were governed by a council made up of senior representatives of each branch. Thammayut temples (or *wats*) exemplify some of Thai Buddhism's finest architecture, and include the Wat Bovorniwes in Bangkok, which houses Mahamakut Buddhist University and the Phra Dhammaduta missionary programme, which sends monks to other countries. Its nearby Mahanikaya equivalent, the Wat Mahathat, houses Mahachulalongkorn Buddhist University, which in recent years has pioneered development work among its up-country monks who ordain at an early age partly to secure a good education, ultimately migrating to Bangkok to obtain a degree.

During recent decades lay Buddhists have organized themselves into a variety of groups. The Buddhist Association of Thailand came into being in 1934 with the aims of encouraging the study and practice of Buddhism and the consequent promotion of social welfare work and public service. In 1950 the Young Buddhist Association of Thailand was founded with similar objectives among young people. By 1970 there were 73 provincial Buddhist associations affiliated to the Buddhist Association of Thailand, while their Young Buddhist counterparts numbered 44. By 1984 this had risen to 54.

The **World Fellowship of Buddhists** was set up in 1940 as an international organization to promote Buddhist causes and realise Buddhist goals. At its ninth general conference in 1969 it was decided that the permanent headquarters of the Federation should be located in Thailand.

The centralization of the Thai Sangha has not prevented it from encompassing a wide variety of viewpoints. Politically, Phra Kittiwudho's anti-communist stance represents one end of the spectrum, whereas leftist monks were obliged to take refuge during the repressive military *coups* of the mid-1970s. Sulak Sivaraksa, a leading lay intellectual and social critic, is representative of the latter.

From a much less political point of view Buddhadasa Bhikkhu (or Putatat, as he is known to most Thais) represents a progressive reformist approach which reinterprets traditional Buddhist doctrines in a practical and ethical manner which appeals especially to professional lay Buddhists and the younger scholar monks. Ironically, though, most Thais continue to believe in a variety of spirits ranging from the *winyan* (essentially "soul") to different sorts of *phii*, which inhabit the small spirit houses to be seen in most streets. 95 per cent of Thailand's population of c. 59 million are **Theravada** Buddhist.

Thammakaai Religious Foundation. A this-worldly Thai **Buddhist** movement founded in 1970 by Phra Thammachayo (1944–), an economics graduate and abbot of Wat Thammakai in the northern outskirts of Bangkok. His deputy, Phra Thattachiiwo, is well-known for driving his Mercedes on the traditional Buddhist morning alms round. The movement indulges in an open display of wealth and uses the media in a sophisticated manner to obtain funds. It invests heavily in property, land, tourism and oil and was responsible for one of Thailand's more recent financial scandals, the "Chamoi chit fund", which collapsed in 1986. It is said that Wat Thammakai itself needs about $600,000 per month in order to maintain its overheads. Thammachayo himself receives some support from senior monks of the conservative **Mahanikay.** He teaches a form of lay asceticism adapted from the Thai forest monk tradition and places great emphasis on a meditational method in which a crystal ball is visualized at the base of the stomach. This is said to represent the *dhamma*-body of the Buddha. Monks within the order are, distinctively, ordained for life and are in general very well educated. Gen. Aathik Kamlang-ek, the well-known ex-Commander-in-Chief of the Army, sacked for financial irregularities in 1986, is a prominent lay-follower.

Thammayutika Nikaya. Also known as the Thammayut or Dhammayut, this Theravada monastic fraternity controls 1,502 of the more than 28,000 monasteries in Thailand. Founded in the late 19th century as a reformed group within the *Sangha* by King Mongkut, a monk of 27 years standing, the Thammayut adheres to a strict interpretation of monastic discipline (*vinaya*). Despite its size, in comparison with its rival—the **Mahanikay**—the Thammayut exercises a disproportionate influence in **Buddhist** and national affairs. This is in part due to the way the order has been used by royal circles to increase the power of the monarchy. Senior members of the royal family still act as patrons and, despite the abolition of absolute monarchy in 1932, the order is still strongly establishment-oriented. With the rise in influence of the Mahanikay after 1932, the Thammayut has tended to align itself with the authoritarian side of the Thai political spectrum and has maintained close links with the military. The Thammayut and Mahanikay have few differences over matters of Buddhist doctrine, though the former supports the ancient and ascetic forest monk tradition more forcefully. Many monks of this tradition are popularly believed to possess supernatural powers of prophecy and healing. The Thammayut was found in Cambodia, where it was known as Thomayat, until its suppression by the Heng Samrin government in the 1970s.

Theosophical Society. The Theosophical Society was founded in America in 1875 by Helena Blavatsky (1831–91) and Henry S. Olcott (1832–1907), and later established its headquarters in Madras, India. Blavatsky claimed to have received the wisdom of the ages from Hidden Masters in Tibet, with whom she was in psychic communication. The teaching is a synthesis of **Hindu** and **Buddhist** mysticism with Western **occultism.** The society's motto is "There is no religion higher than truth", and it was the first movement to claim that all religions have the same goal. Although disparaged by some as a charlatan (for her claimed psychic powers), Blavatsky is generally acknowledged as the first Westerner to bring Indian religion and philosophy to the West in an accessible form, thus paving the way for later seekers. Theosophy also popularized the now widespread twin doctrines of *karma* and reincarnation.

Several schismatic offshoots occurred, including one in 1891 led by one of the original founders, William Q. Judge in Pasadena, California, and known today as the Theosophical Society International; and also the United Lodge of Theosophists, founded in the USA in 1909. Its best known offshoot, however, was **Anthroposophy;** and Blavatsky's successors, including Annie Besant, discovered and trained **Krishnamurti.**

The Theosophical Society is still going strong though with a predominantly elderly membership. Although it claims that esoteric wisdom is revealed only to the spiritual élite, many of its programmes are open to the public. Membership is open to anyone in sympathy with its objectives, although they need two members as sponsors.

Theravada Buddhism. The term Theravada is used for the distinct Buddhist movement which emerged from a less well-defined group known as the *Sthaviras* (i.e. elders) in India in the 3rd century BCE. The term means "way of the elders". Theravada Buddhism is based on the Pali canon, known as the *Tipitaka*, and stresses the central role of the *arhat* (the one who slays the warring passions), rather than the *bodhisattva*, which is taken up in Mahayana Buddhism.

Our knowledge of the history of **Buddhism** following the Buddha's death is mainly based on early scriptures and is incomplete.

The Indian emperor, Asoka Maurya, came to the throne probably in 268 BCE. He became a Buddhist, favouring the fledgling Theravada, following a bloody war in Kalinga; thereafter he set an example of virtuous kingship which became an important ideal for subsequent Hindu and Buddhist leaders (especially in mainland south-east Asia). Asoka's son, Mahinda, took Buddhism to Sri Lanka, where the Pali scriptures were written down and Theravada Buddhism began to take on a distinctive form.

As Buddhism declined in India, **Sri Lankan** (Sinhalese) **Theravada** Buddhists came to think of their island as especially blessed by the Buddha, and a legend grew up that he had actually visited there. They incorporated certain Hindu and Mahayana ideas into their tradition (e.g. the building of shrines to gods inside temples and the use of Buddha statues), but otherwise Theravada Buddhism remained largely unchanged for many centuries. Monarch and *sangha* co-operated together in a symbiotic relationship which was eventually imitated in Thailand, Cambodia, Burma and elsewhere.

Early Buddhism had emphasized meditation and careful adherence to the Pali scriptures. In time public festivals such as Vesak, the full moon in May, celebrating the Buddha's birth, enlightenment and decease, were incorporated into the tradition.

Monks and nuns made merit for the laity, and the Buddha statues became objects of personal piety. When Sinhalese Buddhism was transmitted to south-east Asia in the early centuries of the Christian era, these meritorious and pietistic elements were reinforced by existing animist and brahmanistic practices (e.g. the veneration of *nats* in Burma).

Theravada monasticism was regulated by the detailed Vinaya rules of the Pali canon. Since the *sangha* is based on a republican form of government established in the Buddha's time it is possible in theory, though difficult in practice, for the rules to be changed. In Thailand, where King Mongkut based his 19th-century Sangha reforms on strict adherence to the Vinaya, conservative influences have remained strong, though in recent years monks have managed to take on new and progressive development roles within the framework of their monastic tradition. Orders of nuns have lapsed in many places, though there are moves in some Theravada countries (e.g. Thailand) to restore them.

Theravada Buddhism is to be found in almost all parts of the world. Its adherents tend either to be nationals from Buddhist countries or European and north Americans who are attracted by meditation and the Theravada Buddhist way of life. (For contemporary information, *see* **Burmese Theravada;**

Cambodian Buddhism; Laotian Theravada; Sri Lankan Theravada; Thai Theravada; Vietnamese Buddhism.)

Thomayat. A Cambodian **Theravada** Buddhist monastic fraternity closely aligned to the Thai **Thammayutika Nikaya** and monarchical in outlook. It suffered accordingly under the Khmer Rouge- and Vietnamese-backed governments, but with the return of Prince Sihanouk to Cambodia its influence may recover to some extent.

Three HO. *See* **Sikh Dharma of the Western Hemisphere.**

Thuddama Nikaya. The largest monastic fraternity (*gaing*) within the **Burmese Theravada** Buddhist *Sangha* with approximately 250,000 ordained monks. Founded in the late 18th century by an ecclesiastical council called by King Bodawpaya, the order takes a fairly flexible view of monastic discipline in contrast to the more puritanical **Shwegyin Nikaya.**

Tibetan Buddhism. Buddhism initially arrived in Tibet, under royal patronage, in the 8th century. The first monastery, at Samye, was founded in 779. It seems that, at this early period, both Indian and Chinese forms of **Buddhism** were taught though, as the tradition developed, the former came to dominate. Tibetan Buddhism consequently shares many of the features of the Buddhism taught and practised in the great monastic universities of northern India at the end of the first millennium CE. In particular, **Tantrism** and scholastic versions of the *Mahayana* are widely found. Older, unreformed schools like the **Nyingmapas** have tended to stress the former while the **Gelugpas** place great emphasis on scholarly activity. Despite these differences, the Tantric element is integral to all schools of Tibetan Buddhism.

After China's 1950s' invasion of Tibet, about 100,000 Tibetans, including the Dalai Lama and many other leading lamas, escaped Tibet's sealed borders into India, Nepal and Bhutan. While attempting to re-establish the shattered remnants of their tradition in precarious South Asian refugee camps, they witnessed in horror the determined attempts of China's Red Guards to systematically eradicate every trace of Buddhist culture within Tibet.

In India their focal point is the 14th Dalai Lama, Tenzin Gyatso (b. 1935), who set up his headquarters in the Himalayan foothills north-west of Delhi in 1960. There are, however, other Tibetan Buddhist groups in India, concentrated mainly in the Himalayan and sub-Himalayan parts of the north-east, especially in the border areas of Arunachal Pradesh. At Tawang, for instance, there is a large Gelugpa monastery.

With Tibetan Buddhism on the verge of extinction, lamas in exile began teaching interested Westerners, first in India, then abroad. Often stateless persons, refugee lamas even now face serious travel restrictions, but by 1967 the first Western Tibetan Buddhist centre, Samye Ling, had opened in Scotland. Twenty-five years later, there are hundreds of Tibetan Buddhist centres and monasteries throughout Europe, North America, and Australasia, as well as some in East and South-East Asia. Smaller groups exist in Latin America and Southern Africa. Non-Tibetans are successfully becoming monks, nuns, and Buddhist scholars, as well as practising the strictly enclosed three- and twelve-year retreats demanded of serious meditators. The translation of Tibetan texts has become a flood, both within and outside the universities, while many Tibetan lamas, especially younger ones, now speak English.

The first Western incarnate lama, the **Karma Kagyudpa** school's Sangye Nyenpa, was recognized in the 1970s, son of an American poet and an English artist. Since then several others have been recognized, including a woman. Many of Tibetan Buddhism's leading lamas now regularly visit the West, some even living there permanently. This development is largely decentralized, each lama or tradition operating with total autonomy. Most of the Tibetan traditions have by now had some success in the West, but the Gelugpa and the Karma Kagyudpa schools have had the biggest initial impact.

Buddhism in present-day Tibet has, to a very limited extent, been revived since the early 1980s with the restoration of some important monasteries such as Drepung and Tashilhunpo under the auspices of the **Chinese Buddhist Association (CBA)**, though monastic numbers remain very low. The situation is unlikely to improve in the near future, particularly in the light of the Chinese government's continuing disapproval of "non-patriotic" religious activity.

Tiruvannamalai. *See* **Arunachala Ashram.**

Trailokya Bauddha Mahasangha Sahayaka Gana (TBMSG). Literally, the "Association of Friends of the Buddhist Order of the Three Realms". A modern Indian Buddhist liberation movement proclaiming a "Dhamma Revolution" amongst untouchables in Maharashtra and surrounding areas. Arising out of the background of Ambedkarite **Neo-Buddhism** (*see also* **Buddhist Society of India**), the Association was formally inaugurated in 1979. Founded by British followers of Mahasthavira Sangharakshita and financed by a branch of the **Friends of the Western Buddhist Order,** it consists of a monastic order of c. 150 members, the TBM, and a social-work branch, Bahujan Hitay. It seeks, primarily, to address the spiritual and practical needs of ex-Untouchables already converted to **Buddhism** after the mass conversions under Dr Ambedkar in 1956.

Transcendental Meditation (TM). Maharishi Mahesh Yogi (b. 1911) "the Giggling Guru", was the first of the post-war Indian *gurus* to capture the public imagination, when the Beatles and other showbusiness personalities learnt TM. He was also the first to offer young people an alternative to drugs for self-awareness. TM is a **Hindu** meditation technique, practised for 20 minutes twice a day, using a *mantra* to calm the mind. Mantras were originally believed to be individually allotted, though it is now known that there are only 16, allotted according to age. TM calls itself a science but not a religion (though critics see it as a Hindu revivalist movement). Empirical research has validated some of the claims for TM's physiological and psychological benefits, such as stress reduction, though not for the attainment of cosmic consciousness.

The Maharishi's Spiritual Regeneration Movement (later registered as a charity) originally had the aim of saving the world through meditation in three years. When this did not happen, the methods became more and more elaborate—and expensive—and the organization now comprises a worldwide, commercially successful chain of international centres and "universities" (300 in America, 60 in Britain). The movement claims that if one per cent of a city practises TM, the crime rate drops dramatically. This is called the Maharishi

Effect. Recent media attention has focused on its courses in *siddhis* (psychic powers), especially levitation.

It is claimed that millions of Westerners have learned TM, though many have subsequently stopped practising. Current practising meditators worldwide are estimated at 4,000,000 (100,000 in Britain, with about 100 full-time teachers). The technique is taking off in a big way, being taught in schools, prisons, and even business corporations.

Trappists. *See* **Cistercians.**

Tribal Religions of India. According to the 1981 census of India there are 414 different tribal groups in India (total population 51,628,638—about 7.8 per cent of the population of India). It is therefore manifestly impossible to describe in detail the characteristics of the religious beliefs and practices of all these tribes. But a study of these groups yields some general patterns, and it is with these common features that this article is concerned.

Theistic concepts: In common with most tribal people in other parts of the world, the tribes of India believe in, and worship, supernatural entities. Most of the Indian tribes are polytheistic, but have a conception of a supreme creator god, who is not much involved in the day to day affairs of the world—a kind of *Deus Otiosus*—who has created the world and then withdrawn from mundane concerns. The Alhou of the Sema Nagas, the Kittung of the Vanars, the Thakur Jiu of the Santhals are all examples of this remote high God. The tribal people however are more concerned with lesser deities, most of them associated with some element of their natural surroundings such as trees, rivers and hills. Some of them are malevolent spirits, causing diseases, natural calamities and misfortune. Worship is directed to these lesser spirits rather than to the supreme creator God, and the concern of tribal people is to appease and propitiate them with rituals of various kinds, including sacrifices. In addition most tribes worship departed members of their tribe, clan and family, some of the most famous and long-standing ancestors having reached almost divine status. There are no temples, but most tribes have shrines which are built either inside the household or in the open. According to most anthropologists the motivation for worship seems to be fear of the spirits, both divine and ancestral, to turn away their wrath, and to keep them at arm's length, so to speak. Most groups have priest-like functionaries, such as the Bhumka of the Gonds, and the Ato Naeke of the Santhals, who lead the rituals and whose duty is also to identify which of these spirits is responsible for illness or other misfortune.

Eschatology: Tribal people of India have quite complex conceptions regarding the human personality. Most believe in the existence of an extra-corporeal element, and as a matter of fact in more than one soul for each individual. The Konyak Nagas for example believe that one soul, the *mio,* remains attached to the body for some time after death, while another soul, the *yaha,* goes to the world of the ancestors, and yet another soul, the *biba,* appears to the living as a ghost. The *jiu* and *roa* of the Uraons is another example of multiple souls. Life after death is very similar to worldly existence, except that it is a dimmer and less happy world. Most tribal people are buried, not cremated, and they take care to bury some of the essential equipment with the dead for their eschatological life, such as their weapons. Almost invariably there is a second burial ceremony designed to properly rehabilitate the soul into the ancestral world. This may in some cases take place as late as six months after the first burial. Some tribes keep a part of the body, such as the skull, in the house, so that some element of the departed remains in the household, to be worshipped, and more commonly to be fed at the time of festivities. But generally the worship or feeding is designed to keep the ancestral spirit away from the family, and to ensure that it is not offended and bring sickness or some other calamity on its living members. Many tribes erect menhirs to the dead, and in exceptional cases to the living as well.

The soul's actions while living do not substantially affect its after life, in contrast to **Christianity** or **Islam**. However tribes do believe that the good and the sinful are distinguished in some way or other in the eschaton. The Sema Nagas, for instance, believe that good souls go east towards the rising sun, whereas the wicked go west to the setting sun. According to the Konyak, those who die abnormal deaths or have committed much wickedness in life follow a path to the ancestral world which is very difficult and troublesome, while the virtuous follow a less arduous path—the very opposite of Christian conceptions! But eventually both types land up in the same ancestral world. Life in the ancestral world is a shadowy version of the temporal world. The souls till, hunt and fight each other as they do here. The partners of the first marriage are man and wife in the hereafter also.

Morality and ethics: Tribal people in India are generally more honest, sincere and upright in their actions than their compatriots from more sophisticated societies, but often their norms of morality and ethics differ from the latter. The *gotuls* of the Nagas, for example, where adolescent boys and girls sleep together and gain some sexual experience before marriage, will be frowned upon by most non-tribal societies. Though many tribal groups have strict taboos regarding extra-marital sex and incest, sexual relations before marriage are not looked upon with severity, especially if the union does not result in children. Many tribes, the Mundas and the Sarna for example, believe that God led man and woman to the first marital act and blessed the union, and hence such union cannot be viewed as sinful action. Some anthropologists opine that among tribal people morality is dictated not so much by any intrinsic value that virtuous action might have but by the adverse consequences that immoral acts might bring, particularly from the gods and ancestral spirits. The Konyaks, for instance, believe that the supreme god Gawang has great concern for moral behaviour and acts as the guardian of the moral order.

Finally it should be mentioned that a process of Hinduization, or "Sanskritization" as Indian scholars term it, has affected the religious life of many Indian tribes. **Hindu** gods and goddesses and Hindu rituals are now being gradually incorporated into tribal religious praxis.

Tridharma. "Three teachings." A combination of the teachings of Buddha, Confucius and Lao Tzu which came into being in Jakarta in 1938. Its Chinese founder, Kwee Tekhoay, edited a magazine called *Moestika Dharma*, and initially called his new teaching Samkauw Hwee (three religions). Adherents of Tridharma maintain that their religion is not syncretistic but a combination of three distinct sets of teaching, and tend to be non-political. It is difficult to estimate their number, but it is probably in the region of a few thousand.

True Nichiren School. *See* **Nichirenshoshu.**

True Orthodox Church. (*See also* **Orthodox Church—Byzantine.**) The True Orthodox Church, also known as the Catacomb Church and the Tikhonite Church, claims to be the authentic successor of the **Russian Orthodox** Church as that existed prior to Communist rule, or more precisely up to 1927. At that time a declaration of loyalty to the Communist state by Metropolitan Sergi of Nizhni Novgorod marked the beginning of a new period of church-state relations, and the numerous priests and bishops who rejected this declaration were severely persecuted, generally being sent to the camps or shot. Survivors went underground, forming the True Orthodox Church, as it came to be known, separate from the Moscow Patriarchate.

Numbers of adherents were unknown due to the extreme secrecy maintained as a necessary condition of survival: even today members themselves lack an overall picture.

From time to time members were identified and brought to trial. In 1976, Metropolitan Gennadi was betrayed to the authorities: he had organized a network of underground monasteries in the Caucasus, and also a seminary. Members are reputed to revere Tsar Nicholas II and his family, murdered by the Bolsheviks. They are to be found in all parts of the former USSR.

Until 1976 the True Church was the only one recognized by the emigré Russian (Orthodox) Church Abroad, but relations subsequently cooled, and today many members of the True Orthodox Church are joining the **Free Russian Orthodox Church**, which is the branch of the emigré church now active within the former Soviet republics. Thus the future of the True Orthodox Church remains uncertain.

True Orthodox Church of Romania. This underground organization of the Communist period has, since the downfall of the Ceausescu régime, emerged into the open and begun an extensive programme of church-building. Metropolitan Silvestru, its leader, has appeared on Romanian television.

True Pure Land School. *See* **Jodoshinshu.**

Twelver Shi'ites. Following the death of Muhammad in 632, the **Islamic** community was at first ruled by a succession of three caliphs, ending with the assassination of 'Uthman in 656. During this period, however, a small group of Muslims remained loyal to the Prophet's cousin and son-in-law, 'Ali ibn Abi Talib, and insisted on his right to leadership of the community, which they claimed had been directly granted him by Muhammad. 'Ali himself was acknowledged Caliph on 'Uthman's death, holding the office until his own assassination in 661.

Leadership of the burgeoning Islamic empire now passed to the Umayyad dynasty, with its capital in Damascus, but a now much-expanded body of 'Alid loyalists (styling themselves Shi'a bayt 'Ali—the Party of the House of 'Ali) continued to promote the claims of the descendants of 'Ali (mainly his offspring from the Prophet's daughter Fatima), beginning with his sons Hasan and Husayn.

It is with the martyrdom of Husayn in the year 680 at Karbala that **Shi'ism** may be said to emerge as a distinct religious movement. His death still figures as the central event of religious history for Shi'ites, for whom his sufferings (and, more broadly, those of his family and descendants) have connotations similar to those of the passion of Christ in **Christianity**.

After Husayn's death, his successors (Imams) adopted a politically quietist stance. Various strands of Shi'ism developed under different leaders, some from other branches of the Prophet's family, but in time an identifiable mainstream emerged, generally designated Imami (i.e. Imam-centred) Shi'ism. The chief divisions in this early period were those of the **Zaydiya** after the fourth Imam, and the **Isma'iliya** after the sixth.

The death of the eleventh Imam, Hasan al-'Askari, in 874 led to controversy over the succession, since it was not clear that Hasan had left a son. One group maintained that the true Imam was a boy of four or five named Muhammad, who had been placed in hiding. For a period of some 70 years this hidden Imam could be communicated with only through a succession of four vice-regents or gates; but on the death of the last of these in 941 there began an indefinite era of "greater occultation", which still continues, in which the twelfth Imam remains alive in a supernatural realm, from which he exercises spiritual sovereignty.

The Imamis now maintained that there could never be more than twelve Imams (hence their designation as Ithna 'Asharis or Twelvers) and that the last of these would in due course emerge from hiding as the Mahdi to inaugurate an age of peace and the universal triumph of Shi'ite Islam.

Since then, authority within Twelver Shi'ism has lain with the clergy, who claim the right to act as representatives of the unrevealed Imam. Clerical authority developed considerably in the 18th and 19th centuries, with the triumph of the Usuli school, which emphasized the role of the clergy as sources of legal innovation. This laid the foundations for the establishment of a religious state in Iran following the revolution of 1979 led by Imam Khomeini.

In general, the Twelver Shi'a have been deprived of political power, with the notable exceptions of the Buyid rulers in Iran and Iraq, and the Safavis (from 1502), Qajars (1794–1925), and Pahlavi (1925–1979) dynasties in Iran. Nevertheless, Shi'ism has spread widely in the Islamic world, and it is estimated that there are today some 73,000,000 Twelvers, with substantial communities in Iran (34,000,000), Pakistan (12,000,000), India (10,000,000), Iraq (7,500,000), the former Soviet republics (4,000,000), and elsewhere. The large Shi'ite community in Lebanon has acquired considerable political significance in the past decade.

Mainstream Shi'ism has never diverged markedly from **Sunnism** in its basic religious beliefs or legal norms. God, the Prophet, the Quran, and the religious law are viewed almost identically in both groups. The chief differences lie in the fields of ritual, the role of the Imams, and the authority given to the clerical establishment. The Shi'a also have a wholly distinct canon of religious traditions (Hadith), derived from the Imams rather than the Prophet.

Distinctive Shi'ite practices include the performance of pilgrimages to the shrines of the Imams and their relatives (particularly the sacred sites in Iraq: Najaf, Karbala, and Kazimayn); the permissibility of temporary marriage (mut'a) and the concealment of religious belief; and the celebration of the events of Husayn's martyrdom during the month of Muharram in the form of passion plays, threnodies, and processions in which significant numbers of participants engage in ritual flagellation.

From purely political figures, the Imams developed the characteristics of direct intermediaries with the divinity or even, in more extreme contexts, earthly representations of the Godhead, having come to be regarded as pure and sinless. It is in and through the Imams (particularly Husayn) that the believer finds salvation, and it is through their activity that the universe is both created and sustained. Extreme views of this kind have generally been rejected by the more orthodox, and restricted to sectarian movements such as the **Nusayris**, but several have passed into the mainstream. During the Safavid period (1502–1722), such ideas were greatly matured in a sophisticated form of philosophical speculation (known as "divine wisdom") which was developed by Twelver thinkers in Iran. This theosophical tradition was developed in the 19th century by the Shaykhi school and laid the basis for the radical millenarianism of the **Babis** and the subsequent move away from Islam of the **Bahais.**

Among the Twelver clergy, certain individuals are singled out as exceptional authorities, known as "Centres of Imitation" (*maraji'-i taqlid*), to whom all other believers are expected to defer in matters of religious judgement. At times, this degree of authority has been centred in single individuals, and at others spread among several (as at present). There is, nevertheless, a general tendency to concentrate authority in one figure, as occurred in the case of Imam Khomeini after the Islamic Revolution. The future of mainstream Shi'ism depends in some measure on how it chooses to tackle the problem of where and how widely to locate religious authority and how far to identify it with political power.

Tz'u Hui T'ang. *See* **Compassion Society.**

U

Udasis. An order of ascetics which traces back its origins to Baba Siri Chand. (1494–1512), the elder son of Guru Nanak. It is now part of mainstream **Hinduism**, and has no links with **Sikhism.** In its centres (*akharas*) children learn Sanskrit and their temples have images of the principal Hindu deities. It is thought that the Udasis may have been influenced in their formative years by the teachings of the **Naths.** It is also said that members may have acted as Sikh *gurdwara* custodians through the 18th century.

UK Islamic Mission. A British organization arising out of the Pakistan-based **Jama'at-i Islami.** Founded in 1962, it has some 50 centres located in various parts of Britain. Islamic education for Muslim children is a major concern, and it provides speakers to schools and colleges. It co-operates with the **Islamic Foundation.**

Ukrainian Uniate Catholic Church. (*See also* **Orthodox Church—Byzantine.**) The "Uniate" Catholic Church of Ukraine was created by the Union of Brest-Litovsk in 1595–96. Whilst retaining allegiance to the **Roman Catholic Church,**

it was to conserve Orthodox liturgical and pastoral traditions, celebrate its rites in Old Church Slavonic, and permit its clergy, excepting Bishops, to marry. In modern times, it was termed, first, the Ukrainian Greek Catholic Church, and now the Eastern Rite Ukrainian Church. In order to neutralize it, Joseph Stalin compelled the Ukrainian Catholic Church to accept absorption into the Russian Orthodox Church. The Orthodox Patriarch of Moscow collaborated enthusiastically. At the Synod of Lvov, in 1946, the Ukrainian Church signed its own death warrant. During the 40 years of persecution which ensued, the 4,000,000–5,000,000 suppressed Ukrainian Catholic laity attended Orthodox services, if they participated at all. They retained a concealed loyalty to the Eastern Rite Church. In the mid-1980s, there were no active Eastern Rite clergy, all having been imprisoned or murdered. The tide may have been turned by the accession in the late 1970s of a Pope, the Polish John Paul II, who emphatically proclaimed the rights of religious believers under communism, and by the heroic example of men such as Iosp Terelya, who spent 20 years in Soviet labour camps and psychiatric hospitals. Christian resistance movements now became visible in the Ukraine. The most potent was the "Action Group for the Defence of the Rights of Believers and the Church", led by Terelya. The years 1988–1989 saw mass public demonstrations in support of the Ukrainian Catholic Church, with hundreds of thousands on the streets. There followed the registration of numerous formerly Orthodox parishes within Ukrainian Catholic jurisdiction. In 1989, because of *glasnost* in the Soviet Union, and just two days before President Gorbachev's historic meeting with John Paul II, the Ukrainian Catholic Church was legalized. A serious confrontation now looms between the remaining Orthodox hierarchy and the Ukrainian Catholics, who wish to reclaim their church buildings. A synod was held in 1990 to resolve the issue; it broke down amid recriminations about the "violent seizure" of churches. This resurgence of religion and nationalism has created fears of the revival of anti-Semitism.

Ultra-Orthodox Judaism. *See* **Haredi**.

Umbanda. This Brazilian religious movement, although often described as African (Afro-Brazilian), is in fact much less so than **Candomblé** both in terms of its content and membership. Found chiefly in the south of Brazil, Umbanda emerged in the 20th century as a syncretistic religion with little in the way of central unifying doctrine but incorporating Amerindian, **African traditional** and **Roman Catholic** beliefs and practices (including a priesthood), and also the spiritualism of Allan Kardec (well known in Brazil as **Kardecismo**). Salient elements include belief in reincarnation, with rebirth higher or lower in the socio-economic scale as appropriate punishment and reward for conduct in this life, and belief in harmful spirits who need to be placated.

Its membership is generally more affluent and more Euro-Brazilian than that of Candomblé, and unlike the latter it produces a range of publications which promote its cause. With over 20,000,000 adherents, it is a force to be reckoned with politically, being wooed at election time in particular, and has members up to government level. Again in contrast to Candomblé, some attempt has been made to establish a federation of congregational groups, so that it might become a truly national religion, although hitherto this is not a trend that has proved particularly successful.

At times Afro-Brazilian spiritist cults—which also include **Macumba**—have been persecuted, but today Umbanda enjoys legal recognition and is a still-growing force in Brazilian society.

Uniate (Uniat) Churches. (*See also* **Orthodox Church—Byzantine.**) In Eastern Europe and Asia there are a number of churches which are in communion with the **Roman Catholic Church** but which follow Orthodox rites, observe the Eastern calendar, and permit the marriage of clergy. They include the **Maronites, Syrians, Armenians, Chaldeans, Copts, Ethiopians,** and others. Some of these churches in the USSR (e.g. the **Ruthenian Church** and the **Ukrainian Uniate Church**) had been handed over by the Government to the Russian Orthodox Church, and since 1990 have been the subject of dispute between the two faith-communities. In Uzhgorodin, Western Ukraine, the local authorities intervened when the Orthodox were unwilling to return the cathedral to the Uniates. It arranged for a Roman Catholic Church to be refurbished in return for the handing back in 1991 of the cathedral to the Uniates. These are perhaps 13 million Uniate believers in the world today.

Unification Church. The Unification Church (UC) was founded by the Reverend Sun Myung Moon in 1954 in Korea as Tong Il movement. In the West it is popularly known as "the Moonies", while its official name is The Holy Spirit Association for the Unification of World Christianity (HSA UWC). There are many offshoots and branches, such as CARP, ICUS, CAUSA, etc.

In 1936 Moon received his mission in a vision, which is to establish God's Kingdom on earth. Over the following 20 years Moon is said to have communicated with God and other religious leaders, including Moses and Buddha, the result of which is *Divine Principle,* the movement's sacred text. The book offers a reinterpretation of the Bible, claiming that Jesus failed in his task of restoring the original state of man by establishing a "Perfect Family"; another messiah (believed to be Moon) must now accomplish this mission.

It was not before the early 1970s, when the founder himself arrived in the USA, that Unificationism began to take off. The movement pursued a strategy of active recruitment and high public profile: lecture tours, large rallies, mass weddings, international conferences, daily newspapers and businesses. Its strong anti-communist stance was represented in CAUSA, particularly active in Latin America. By the late 1970s the "Moonies" had become a household name, branded as a sinister "cult that breaks up families", coupled with allegations of brainwashing and "Heavenly Deception", that is street recruitment teams presenting themselves as conventional Christians. This image was exacerbated by the libel action which the Church brought unsuccessfully against the *Daily Mail* in the UK.

Despite active recruitment it is believed that the movement's full-time membership never exceeded 10–15,000 in the West. Estimates of actual membership in the UK today put it in the lower hundreds. With the "House Church" movement within the UC, members do not necessarily live communally or work full-time for the Church.

Since 1989 UC's activities have spread to Eastern Europe with conferences, youth services and English-teaching projects, the high point of which was a meeting of Moon with President Gorbachev in May 1990 during the UC-organized World Media Conference.

Unified Vietnamese Buddhist Church. Also known as the United Buddhist Association, this came into being as a result of the Vietnamese Buddhist Reunification Congress held in Saigon in December 1963. It united **Theravadins** and Mahayanists in a single organization presided over by a patriarch and governed by an assembly of elders consisting of 50 or so senior monks.

Although the majority of Vietnamese **Buddhists** are technically members of the Unified Vietnamese Buddhist Church, most speak of their religion in terms of *cung to tien ong ba* ("the cult of ancestors"). They follow the lunar calendar, and on the first and 15th of every month go to the temple and put incense sticks on altars in front of photographs of deceased relatives. They also eat vegetarian food on this occasion.

Unitarians. Unitarians reject the doctrine of the Trinity: that there is one God but three persons, Father, Son and Holy Spirit. By corollary they reject the divinity of Jesus Christ (the Son). The doctrine of the Trinity was first formalized at the Council of Nicea in AD 325, in response to the unitarian doctrines of Arius (Arianism). Since then unitarianism has been regarded as heresy.

Unitarianism was strong in Eastern Europe in the 16th and 17th centuries and was spread to England in 1652 by John Biddle of Gloucester, who was later banished to the Scilly Isles. The movement had a resurgence in the 18th-century Age of Reason; the scientist Joseph Priestley was a Unitarian leader. It spread to the United States which still has the largest number of Unitarians. In the 19th century, under the influence of James Martineau, the movement shifted its emphasis on the Bible to a basis of rationalism and scientific thought.

Unitarian churches today are independent and organized on a congregational basis. There is a tension between those who would regard themselves as Christians (although rejected by mainline **Christianity**) and those who reject most Christian dogma. Unitarians are often active in the community and have been prominent in civil rights movements. Worldwide membership is over 600,000.

United Church of Christ. This **Protestant** church came into existence in the USA in 1957 as a result of the union of the **Congregational** Christian Churches and the Evangelical Reformed Church, both of which, though products of various mergers, had colonial roots. It thus brought together th Puritan and Separatist tradition and the German pietist and evangelical traditions. This pluralist denomination has 1,700,000 members.

United Methodist Church. The dominant US form of **Methodism**.

United Reformed Church. The United Reformed Church represents a fusion of the **Presbyterians (Reformed)** and the **Congregationalists**.

United Synagogue. *See* **Orthodox Judaism.**

United Synagogue of America. *See* **Conservative Judaism.**

United Torah Judaism (UTJ) or **United Torah Party.** (*See also* **Orthodox Judaism; Shas; Zionism**.) The UTJ, a non-Zionist Israeli political party, a coalition of **Agudat Israel** and Degel Hatorah, was formed to contest the 1992 Israeli general election and secured four seats in the Knesset (Israeli parliament). The spiritual mentor of this Ultra-Orthodox **(Haredi)**, **Ashkenazi** party, Rabbi Eliezar Schach (1896–   ), is one of the leading figures in religious politics in Israel. The UTJ was an unsuccessful attempt to consolidate Ultra-Orthodox support, fragmented in the 1988 elections when Agudat Israel (largely Hasidic, gaining four seats in 1988) and the then newly formed Degel Hatorah (largely Lithuanian–Midnaggdic, gained two seats in 1988) split the Ultra-Orthodox vote. UTJ stood on a platform supportive of peace on the political level and the support of Haredi institutions on the communal front.

Unity Sect. Also known as I kuan-Tao, this Taiwanese ethical society incorporates **Buddhist**, **Confucian** and **Taoist** teachings. Its origins are obscure though it was probably founded as an independent entity in 1928 by Chang T'ien Jan in northern China. Sect members themselves claim an ancient ancestry for the movement and hold Confucius, Lao-Tzu and Bodhidharma to be early members of an unbroken apostolic line. The sect centres on the cult of the Venerable Mother from whose womb Buddhas of the past, present and future are said to emerge. Initiation within the sect causes a person's name to be erased from the rolls of purgatory and transferred to the records of the saved. Knowledge of the "three treasures" (*mantra*—the name of Amitabha Buddha, *mudra*—a bodily posture symbolically revealing the relation between humans and the Venerable Mother, and the Mysterious Gate—a point between the eyes) is also communicated during the initiation rite. The Unity sect encourages traditional religious exercises such as shadow boxing, meditation, chanting of scriptures and vegetarianism and places great emphasis on the education of its members. Texts held to be particularly worthy of study include the *Tao Te-Ching* and Sun Yat-Sen's *Three Principles of the People*. Because of allegations of Japanese collaboration during the war the Unity Sect only achieved legal status in 1983. Two main sub-sects exist. The first, the Lui-ist, was founded by Chang's second wife, Madame Lui. The other, the Sun-ist, looks to the authority of Sun Su-chen, Chang's mistress. There is considerable rivalry between the two groups.

V

Vaikhanasas. A Hindu **Vaishnava** community of South India. Although comprising only about 2,500 brahmin families in Tamil Nadu, Andhra Pradesh and Karnataka, the Vaikhanasas have an importance beyond their numbers because of their claim to an unbroken tradition of ritual performance which goes back to Vedic times. From references in ancient texts it seems likely that the community existed before the beginning of the Common Era, even though the oldest of their own texts date from no earlier than the fourth century CE.

Most of their literature deals with temple ritual and with the construction and dedication of temples and images.

Vaishnava Sahajiyas. An esoteric Bengali cult, formed by a blending of **Tantrism** and **Vaishnava** ideas and practices. The Sahajiyas regard their practices as the natural expression of human sexuality, which is a microcosm of the unity-in-duality which characterizes the universe as they see it. As such their ritual involves sexual intercourse between the practitioner and a married woman, in order to re-enact at a physical level the pure love between Krishna and Radha and to transform worldly desire (*kama*) into spiritual love (*prema*). Semen is not emitted but "redirected" through a channel thought to traverse the centre of the body, to the thousand petalled lotus at the crown of the head where the bliss of Krishna and Radha is enjoyed. The Sahajiyas adopt and interpret the theology of the Gaudiya Vaishnavas.

Most of our knowledge of the Vaishnava Sahajiyas is derived from the cult's texts. Since it has always been esoteric, and since Sahajiya practices are now illegal, it is difficult to know how many adherents, if any, it may still have today. There is some affinity between the Sahajiyas and the **Bauls**.

Vaishnavas. Worshippers of the **Hindu** god Vishnu, his various forms or *avatars*, of whom Krishna is highly prominent, and associated deities. An exceedingly complex and diverse phenomenon with no central organizing principle. A number of related movements fall under the heading of Vaishnava, e.g. **ISKCON, Ramanandis**, etc.

Valmikis. *See* **Balmikis**.

Value Creating Society. *See* **Soka Gakkai**.

Vedanta. This is the term used to describe one of the six classical schools of Indian philosophy, its name meaning literally "the end of the Vedas". The aphorisms which form the core of its teachings were first set down by the philosopher Badarayana early in the Common Era. Based on the *Upanishads*, and, ultimately, on the *Vedas*, Vedanta holds that the individual is one with Ultimate Reality, and the object of the religious quest is realization. Thus knowledge alone dispels the ignorance which obscures one's real nature and brings dissatisfaction with life. Vedanta concludes that human intellect is incapable of comprehending the Infinite by its very nature. This being the case, one may only rely on the direct intuitive experiences of the great sages as recorded in the *Upanishads* as the basis for realization of Reality.

What the *Upanishads* communicate is, however, open to diverse inter-pretation. As a result, Vedanta has sub-divided into three major schools. The oldest of these is *Advaita*, or non-dualism. This school found its greatest exponent in the 8th-century CE philosopher Shankara, who held that Ultimate Reality is integral and "unsplit." Consequently, all phenomena are illusory (*maya*). This illusion can be dispelled by means of meditative insight (*jñana*). So antithetical was this position to the religious sensibilities of the time that Shankara was branded by many as a crypto-Buddhist. Shankara was also said to have set up the major monastic institutions of India (*see* **Dashanamis**) and is held to be the spiritual progenitor of the still-influential Jagadgurus, or

Shankaracaryas, the titular heads of these institutions. In recent times, one of the most respected of these was Shri Candrasekharendra Sarasvati of the Kañci Kamakoti-pitha in South India. The position of Jagadguru is hereditary in certain families.

The second great school of Vedanta was founded by Ramanuja in approximately 1100 CE. In this school, the human soul is seen to be a fragment of all-pervasive Ultimate Reality and unconscious of it. Nevertheless, this soul possesses identity in its own right and will retain individuality and self-awareness on re-uniting with Ultimate Reality, but it is in all senses subordinate to that Reality which pre-existed all things and was their Creator. Religious dis-ease, for Ramanuja, is not only a function of ignorance, but more importantly of disbelief or lack of faith. Thus *bhakti*, or devotion, not *jñana*, is the essential factor in gaining liberation from suffering. Finally, there is the dualist school of Madhva founded in around 1250 CE. Madhva believed in a clear, substantial difference between Ultimate Reality and the individual soul. The soul, he held, was an active and responsible, if imperfect, agent in its own right. Only through the gracious intercession of Ultimate Reality, which Madhva identified with the god Vishnu, could the individual be saved from the endless rounds of rebirth.

The various schools of Vedanta are still active. Indeed, many of the ideas espoused by various reform movements in modern **Hinduism** draw heavily on their doctrines as the metaphysical foundations of their own programmes. Vedanta also forms the philosophical basis for many forms of **yoga** and it is central to the teachings of most contemporary Hindu gurus.

Vedanta Society. *See* **Ramakrishna Mission.**

Vietnamese Buddhism. Buddhism entered Vietnam towards the end of the second century AD when the country was under Chinese rule. Both **Theravada** and Mahayana Buddhism were taught and practised. **Confucianism** was the basis of the royal court, and **Taoism** probably formed the bridge between these elements and folk religion. This was achieved partly through **shamanistic** mediums (male and female) and partly via national and local deities.

Under French rule from the end of the 19th century, **Roman Catholicism** was no longer prohibited. Buddhist monks engaged periodically in acts of resistance to the French, and both monks and laymen were active in educational and reform programmes. There was renewed interest in Pure Land Buddhism (*see* **Jodoshu**). Associations for Buddhist studies were founded in Saigon (1931), Hué (1932) and Hanoi (1934).

Following French withdrawal from Vietnam and the partition of the country into north and south, Buddhist monks became increasingly involved in politics. In the south, on Visakha Puja Day (May 8), 1963, government troops of Saigon President Ngo Dinn Diem, a Catholic, tore down Buddhist flags; monks responded by leading political protests and hunger strikes. On June 11, 1963, Thich Quang Duc, a 73-year-old monk, performed self-immolation. He was followed by a number of monks, nuns and lay Buddhists. Among the demands of the Buddhists were the free practice and propagation of the Buddhist religion and equality under the law for Buddhists and Catholics. Madame Nhu, the President's sister-in-law, condemned the protesters as Communists. "If another monk barbecues himself, I will clap my hands" she said.

By the end of August 1963 the Buddhist headquarters had been overrun. But Buddhist opposition had paved the way for a successful coup against the Diem régime, which was overthrown on Nov. 1. By now the Buddhists were seen as a major political force in Vietnamese politics. The military therefore gave permission for them to hold the Vietnamese Buddhist Reunification Congress in 1963, which led to the establishment of the **Unified Vietnamese Buddhist Church.** This body united Theravadins and Mahayanists in a single ecclesiastical structure.

The Buddhist Chaplain Corps, responsible for the welfare of soldiers' families, came into being at about this time. In 1964, largely at the initiative of Thich Nhat Hanh, the new Church also set up the Institute of Higher Buddhist Studies within the Department of Education. This later became Van Hanh University in Saigon.

About 26 million persons were Buddhists, of which two million of South Vietnam's 12,000,000 Buddhists were distinctively Theravadin. The remainder practised a mixture of Mahayana Buddhism, Taoism and Confucianism. South Vietnamese Buddhist temples of all kinds then numbered 4,856.

Struggles continued between the Unified Buddhist Church and the Saigon government, though by 1968 the moderate faction, led by Thich Nhat Hanh, was on the ascendancy. Many Buddhists increasingly adopted a politically neutral stance, wanting neither Marxism nor Western materialism. There were also in the south some new religions, such as the Buddhist-inspired **Hoa Hao,** the synchretistic **Cao Dai,** and the highly politicised Binh Xuyen (now defunct) whose leaders were monks and laymen who had been educated in the local schools.

Vinaya Vardhana Society. Literally, "The Association for the Protection of Buddhist Discipline", a Sri Lankan **Theravada Buddhist** movement dedicated to the improvement of morals amongst the laity. Founded in 1932 by G. V. S. Jayasundera, the group is vehemently anti-clerical and excludes monks from membership. The society is hostile to all forms of superstition, including the veneration of Buddha images and encourages lay preaching of the *dharma.* Its heyday seems to have been in the 1950s. Violent opposition from the *Sangha* had an adverse effect on membership after this time though it still remains high in some, mainly urban, areas of the island. Members are expected to undergo quite severe temporary retreats and, unusually for Theravadins, there is considerable optimism about the possibility of the laity attaining *nirvana.*

Viniyoga. The modern tradition of Viniyoga, "the discipline of gradual progression", traces its origins back to the 9th-century **Vaishnava** saint, Nathamuni. The present leader of the movement is T.V.K. Desikachar, who promotes the tradition from his Yoga Mandiram in Madras. It was Desikachar's father, Prof. T. Krishnamacharya, who first made the teaching available to Western students.

A central teaching of Nathamuni's *Yoga Rahasya* is that **yoga** can be practised by all people, men and women, householders and renunciants. It also stresses that each person's practice of yoga should be tailored to their individual needs. For this reason much of the teaching is arranged on a one-to-one basis. Stress and pain are to be avoided. Ideally, each individual progresses physically, mentally and spiritually in small increments to produce a gradual and harmonious realization of their potential as a human being.

At the present time Viniyoga teachers can be found throughout Europe and the USA as well as in India. Each of these has received regular personal instruction from Desikachar himself and is involved in training others to teach within the tradition. Desikachar's British representative is Paul Harvey who runs the Centre for Yoga Studies in Bath and offers a four-year diploma course on Viniyoga for practising yoga teachers.

Vipassana Movements. *Vipassana*, or insight, was one of the two basic forms of meditation taught by the Buddha. Until recent times meditational training was almost exclusively restricted to the monastic *sangha*. Since World War II, insight training has become available for lay practice, especially in Burma. The initiators of this movement, each teaching their own variation on the traditional **Theravada Buddhist** method, such as Ledi Sayadaw, U Ba Kin, Mahasi Sayadaw and, more recently, U Goenka, justify lay involvement by pointing to the increasingly evil character of an age in which traditional categories have broken down. *Vipassana* practice has been promoted as a means to self-development, enhancing career prospects, good health and the like. U Goenka, in particular, has attracted significant numbers of western practitioners who are not required to renounce their previous faith. The movement has spread to other Theravada countries such as Sri Lanka. The Lanka Vipassana Bhavana Samitya, for example, promotes the teachings of Mahasi Sayadaw.

Virashaivas. *See* **Lingayats.**

Vishwa Hindu Parishad (VHP). Literally, the World Hindu Society. An organization of **Hindu** temples founded in the early part of the century. Religiously affiliated to the **Rashtriya Swayamsevak Sangh (RSS),** the VHP expanded massively in the 1980s on the back of a rising tide of Hindu militancy. Particularly active in the agitation against a Muslim mosque, believed to be built on the site of the birthplace of the god Rama in Ayodhya, the VHP takes some pride, along with the RSS and the **Bharatiya Janata Party (BJP),** in its eventual demolition by a Hindu mob in December 1992. The VHP is active in the UK.

Vizhitz Hasidism. (*See also* **Hasidism.**) Rabbi Menahem Mendel ben Hayyim Hager (1830–1884), who led the Jewish community of Vizhitz from 1854, founded this Hasidic movement. Famous as an amulet maker and miracle worker, he established Vizhitz as a centre of Hasidism. His grandson, Rabbi Israel (1860–1938) moved his Hasidism within the Austrian empire to Grosswardein (Hungary). A number of the Vizhitz dynasty moved to Israel (Bene Berak, Haifa, Jerusalem) where they have attempted to re-create pre-Holocaust Jewish Orthodox life in a new setting. The Vizhitz founded a number of *yeshivot* in Israel and there are communities centred around these.

Voodoo (Vodun). This is the name given to the syncretic mix of **African traditional** and **Roman Catholic** religion found in Haiti. In many respects it resembles **Candomblé, Santería, Shango** and those numerous expressions of African-Catholic systems of belief and practice found in the Caribbean and

Central and South (and to some extent North) America. Loa (lwa) is one of the principal terms used to refer to the numerous African gods and Catholic saints (the two groups having been conflated) on which this religion is based. (Vodun, or Vudu, is the name of a god in African religion in Togo and Benin.) Spirit possession rituals, involving trances in which a loa spirit possesses certain individuals, are of central significance.

Although it has retained fewer African myths than Candomblé, in Vodun too special songs are sung and dances performed in honour of each individual deity. Animal sacrifices are performed to elicit favours from them. Respect for the dead is extremely important in this as in all other new world varieties of African-Catholic religion. The dead are second in importance to the loa, and must not be angered. Sacrifices to the family dead co-exist with Roman Catholic funeral rites on the occasion of a bereavement.

The particular importance of Vodun in Haiti is partly the result of the successful slave rebellion of 1791, as a result of which it enjoyed considerable freedom to flourish. More recently it was sanctioned by President Duvalier (Papa Doc, 1957–1971) as a means of gaining black majority support over the Roman Catholic mulatto élite. Yet despite receiving official recognition as a religion in the constitution of 1987, there is currently evidence of some decline.

W

Wahhabism. Wahhabism is a strict, puritanical form of **Sunni Islam** associated in particular with Saudi Arabia, a state which it contributed to creating, and whose society it continues to help mould.

The fundamentalist reform movement of the Wahhabis first arose in the mid-18th century in the isolated region of Najd in central Arabia. Wahhabis are so-called after Muhammad b. 'Abd al-Wahhab (1703–92), the movement's founder. Ibn 'Abd al-Wahhab came from a family of religious scholars, and spent many years studying under teachers of different legal schools and Sufi orders in Medina and Basra before returning to preach in his native Najd. In 1744 he formed an alliance with a local prince, Muhammad b. Su'ud, and together they launched a *jihad* to extend their community, to enforce the Holy Law (Shari'a) and suppress what they held to be corrupt beliefs and practices, notably all aspects of **Sufism**, popular cults of saints and sorcery. **Shi'ism** was also attacked and in 1802 the Wahhabis were raiding deep into Iraq, sacking the Shi'ite holy city of Karbala. By 1805 they had seized control of the Hijaz, capturing the holy cities of Mecca and Medina.

On the orders of the Ottoman sultan, the viceroy of Egypt, Muhammad 'Ali, organized an expedition into Arabia, putting an end to the Wahhabi Su'udi state in 1818. The second such state re-emerged within central Arabia, only to be ended again in 1891, when its Su'udi rulers were sent into exile by a rival tribal leader. It was 1902 before 'Abd al-'Aziz b. Su'ud was able to win back Riyad, and with the enthusiastic support of the Wahhabi **Ikhwan** (Brethren) to expand the territory under his control until he succeeded in founding the present Kingdom of Saudi Arabia in 1932.

Wahhabis stress that their faith is the "religion of unity" and that other Muslims have gone astray from the strict assertion of the absolute unity of God. Shi'ites and Sufis are held to be especially guilty. Therefore, only Wahhabis can be considered by them as true Muslims. All others are unbelievers against whom it is legitimate to fight a *jihad*.

However, King 'Abd al-'Aziz effectively ended the practice of continuing *jihad* in the late 1920s, when he suppressed the Ikhwan in order to halt their attacks on non-Wahhabi pilgrims to Mecca, their raids against Shi'ites and British in Iraq, and their demands for the forcible conversion of the Shi'ite population of eastern Saudi Arabia. With the ending of *jihad* there has also been an end to the strict Wahhabi prohibition against all mixing with non-Wahhabis, thus enabling the introduction of a foreign work force in Saudi Arabia, and the free movement of Saudis abroad. Nevertheless, the Gulf War of 1991 strained the tolerance of strict Wahhabis to the limit, as it involved the stationing of large numbers of "unbelieving" forces on their land.

Wahhabis condemn everything that they regard as innovation, for example all doctrines and practices with no sanction in the Quran, the Tradition of the Prophet Muhammad, or the consensus of the earliest Muslim community. Thus they disapprove of Hellenistic-influenced Islamic philosophy, Sufi theosophy, Shi'ite concepts of the Imam, and speculative theology. Among prohibited acts are the celebration of the Prophet's birthday, seeking the intercession of saints and making offerings at their tombs, dancing and playing music, wearing gold and jewellery, and smoking tobacco. Although there has been relaxation in practice in contemporary Saudi Arabia, this has met with disapproval in some quarters. This was manifested in November 1979 in the seizure of the Holy Mosque at Mecca by dissident Wahhabi Ikhwan under the leadership of Juhaiman al-'Utaibi.

The **Hanbali** school of Holy Law is followed by the Wahhabis, but they are also ready to accept the views of other schools where they consider them to be more soundly based on the Quran and Tradition, or where the Hanbali school does not offer relevant guidance. They believe in the need for creative interpretation in matters of law not covered by the sacred texts or consensus of the early community, introducing scope for reform in a manner which has had a wide influence outside Wahhabi circles.

Warkaris or **Varkari Panth.** A **Hindu** devotional movement in Maharashtra, usually regarded as having been founded by Jnanesvar in the 13th century, but in fact so deeply rooted among the lower castes of Maharashtra that it is impossible to attribute its origin to any single source. The Supreme God of the Warkaris is Vitthal, also known as Vithoba, whom they worship in his chief shrine at Pandharpur in South Maharashtra. Indeed, the name of the *sampradaya* is derived from the word *vari* (pilgrimage), because this is such a central feature of their worship. The origins of Vitthal/Vithoba are uncertain, but the names used for him in Warkari hymns identify him with Krishna. The Warkari movement has produced several devotional poets, the best-known of whom are Namdev (1270–1350) and Tukaram (1608–1650). Although it has cultivated an oral style of expression rather than a written one, Jnanesvar's commentary in Marathi on the *Bhagavad-gita* has been handed down as an important text for the group. The Warkaris today are mostly householders. They avoid meat and alcohol, and belong mainly to low castes, as did many of their poet–saints and leaders. It is their pilgrimages, to Pandharpur and other shrines, which distinguish them most sharply from other groups. These are made on foot and in well-organized groups which carry representations of past saints and sing hymns as they go.

Watchtower Society. The movement once generally known as the Watchtower Society is today more generally known as the **Jehovah's Witnesses**.

Way International. Founded by Victor Paul Wierwille (1916–1986), formerly pastor of the "United Church of Christ". In 1942 he claimed to have received from God "the secret of a powerful and victorious life" and the "real" teaching of the "word" as given to Christ's apostles. This teaching, especially the fact that Christians should be financially prosperous and that the "right" believing will bring material rewards in abundance, is passed on by way of a study course, called the "Power for Abundant Living" (PFAL): 33 hours of recorded material which is studied in three weeks. The Bible is interpreted by the teachings of Wierwille, according to whom Jesus is the Son of God but not God the Son. Graduates of the PFAL course can move on to the intermediate and advanced courses. Then a member may become a "Word over the Word (WOW) Ambassador" so that he can recruit and set up groups. WOW ambassadors are expected to hold a part-time job and spend at least eight hours a week witnessing. A WOW ambassador may take a three-year course at the "Way Corps College" in Emporia, Kansas, which trains future leaders. The course is said to be austere and students are financially sponsored by other members, the annual fee in 1979 being over US$4,000.

The Way's international headquarters are in New Knoxville, Ohio. Since 1982, L. Craig Martindale has been its president. The organization claims to have trained 40,000 adepts in 40 countries. The structure of the movement is that of a tree. The headquarters in Ohio is the trunk, states and counties are limbs, cities are branches (British branch headquarters are in Manchester), house fellowships with about six members are known as twigs, and followers as leaves.

The financial assets are said to be considerable. A large proportion of the income is provided by course fees, college tuition and the sale of books, records, T-shirts, etc. Since 1976 it has published *The Way*. The Way's image of a "Biblical Research Centre" has helped it to escape being branded as a "cult".

Wee Frees. *See* **Free Presbyterian Church.**

Wesleyan Church. The theological teaching contained in the 44 published sermons of John Wesley, the founder of **Methodism,** have often been used as a title to indicate an emphasis on evangelism and holiness. In Britain the small Wesleyan Reform Union, centred on Sheffield, perpetuates one of the 19th century Methodist splits. The Wesleyan Holiness Church, based on Birmingham is one of the black churches. The Free Wesleyan Church of Tonga has the allegiance of 35 per cent of the island's population, including the King, and particularly promotes education and evangelism.

Wesleyan Methodism. *See* **Methodists.**

Whirling Dervishes. A popular name for a Turkish **Sufi** order, the **Mawlawiya**.

White Brotherhood. *See* **Great White Brotherhood.**

White Fathers. *See* **Cistercians.**

Wicca. This term is preferred by some to the alternative label, **Witchcraft.**

Winti. Winti—also known as Afkodré (Dutch *afgoderij*, "idolatry")—is the folk religion of the Creoles of Surinam, and continues to be important to many Surinamese currently resident in the Netherlands. Of African origin, it is a spirit-possession cult, dealing with everyday concerns such as illness or misfortune. A great variety of *wintis*, gods and spirits, and also the spirits of the dead, need to be placated and honoured, and their help sought. Their intervention in human lives is regular, and through their possession of mediums, both male and female, they can communicate with participants in the frequent rites that take place and which involve dancing, drumming and singing such as occurs too in Afro-Christian movements such as **Kumina** and **Shango.** For Surinamese Creoles, though, typically they juxtapose the practice of **Christianity** and Winti and have not effected a syncretic mixture of the two. A chief god, Anana, is frequently identified, however, with the Christian God. The *winti-pre*, or winti dance, is an important ritual for appeasing evil spirits: it lasts from the onset of darkness to dusk, and involves rituals honouring Mother Earth (*Marna Aisa*). The main religious mediator is the *bonoeman*, a medicine-man figure who supervises the winti dances and is skilled in traditional medicines and also magic.

A form of religion akin to Winti, but more systematically African in character, is practised by the Maroons—or Bush Negroes—of Surinam, descendants of escaped slaves who have lived in relative isolation in the interior.

Witchcraft. Witchcraft (the craft of the wise) or Wicca (wise—its Anglo-Saxon meaning is to bend or shape, i.e. those who can shape the unseen to their will), is regarded by many as the Old Religion. It has its origins in pre-Christian and pre-Celtic sources, and was traditionally worked in covens under one of the six ancient houses. Traditional craft was family-based and the lineage passed from mother to daughter. The teachings are traditionally passed on orally through its folklore and myth. A specific example of this occurs on All Hallows Eve when, as part of the celebration of Samhain (Oct. 31—adopted by the Christian faith as the Feast of All Souls), the lineage of an ancient house may be recounted.

Witches worship the Goddess under various names. She manifests as the Triple Goddess—maiden, mother and crone, and at other times as Goddess of earth, moon and sea. The Goddess represents the universal female. The Horned God, her counterpart, is also important—symbolizing creativity. In Christian times he was seen as the Devil because of his associations with fertility and nature worship.

Magic may be used for healing or for gaining some worldly success (e.g. a new job or a lover), but its use is governed by the Wiccan Rede: Except ye harm none, do what thou wilt.

Traditional craft is distinct from the approach of Gerald B. Gardner (1884–1960) and that developed subsequently by Maxine and Alex Sanders. Gardner, in the 1950s, began publishing rituals, or "Gardnerian" Rites, regarded by traditional witches as fragments of the whole craft and much more sexually explicit. Gardnerian craft has gained popularity rapidly since then in the United Kingdom, and even more so through the **Neo-Pagan** movement in America.

In the minds of the uninformed, Witchcraft may be wrongly construed as being equivalent to **Satanism.**

Won. A form of Korean **Buddhism** founded in 1916 by Pak Chung-bin (sometimes called Sao-Tae San) who, through the practice of rigorous asceticism, attained a Great Enlightenment in that year. Initially the movement consisted of just the founder and a few close disciples, but by 1924, when the group gave itself the title of the Society for the Study of the Buddha Law, its numbers had increased considerably. However, not until the end of Japanese occupation (1945) was it able to disseminate its teachings beyond its place of origin, the region of Iri in the south-western part of the country, and into Korea at large.

The term *won* means "round" and refers to the primary symbol of the movement: a black circle on a white background. This represents the Dharmabody (*Dharmakaya*) of the Buddha and hence the totality of existence. A primary concept of the Won tradition is adaptability. All its teachings are designed to make Buddhism accessible to ordinary people living in the modern world. Consequently, its centres are all located in the cities, its translations of Buddhist texts are in modern Korean, its rituals are simple and women play a prominent role in its activities.

Whilst essentially Buddhist, the Won tradition has drawn upon **Confucianism, Taoism, Chondo Gyo** and **Christianity** to achieve its aims. Unlike more traditional Buddhists, adherents of Won emphasize the importance of serving society, hence the movement has been active in the establishment of educational institutions from universities down to nursery schools. At the present time the Won movement can claim well over 500,000 members.

Word of Life (Livets Ord). An Evangelical Charismatic ministry, based in Uppsala, Sweden, and formed in 1983 by Ulf Ekman, previously a student priest in the Swedish **Lutheran** Church. The ministry includes a congregation and Bible school, an extensive media business (selling videos, tapes and books), a television studio, and a primary and secondary school. The congregation contains over 1,500 adult members, while the Bible school trains around 1,000 students a year. Probably the majority of adherents are under 40 years old.

Although it describes itself as a non-denominational church, the group is at the centre of a growing Faith Movement in Sweden. This involves perhaps 100 new congregations and 20,000 adherents.

Faith teaching in the United States and Sweden is frequently called the "Gospel of Prosperity". Financial prosperity and bodily health are held to be available to those who are "born-again", although it is stated that the "Last Days" may be approaching, and believers are encouraged to achieve material success in order to appropriate worldly resources for Christian ends.

The "Word of Life" is a significant expression of the contemporary growth and global spread of evangelical **Protestantism** and the Electronic Church.

The group has been accused by journalists, theologians and politicians of representing a politically right-wing ideology, opposed to the ideals of Social Democracy.

World Conference on Religion and Peace. This international network of people of different faiths united by a concern for peace and justice was initiated with a conference in Kyoto in 1970. The immediate practical concern was to promote peace initiatives in the Vietnam war. Subsequent conferences were held in Leuven (1974), Princeton (1979), Nairobi (1984) and Melbourne (1989). The international headquarters of the organization, formerly in Geneva, is now in New York in order to facilitate its contributions to the UN (it is a Category II United Nations Non-Governmental Organization associated with the Economic and Social Council). It has established an international network of local groups, and is seeking to establish an interreligious aid programme for refugees. It supports programmes of peace education, and links its concern with promoting positive disarmament measures with analyses of the international economic and political structures which perpetuate injustice and poverty. Conflicts which are rooted in religious allegiances, or which take on that guise, are its particular concern.

World Congress of Christian Fundamentalists. The keynote address of the 1990 World Congress of Christian Fundamentalists, held in London, was delivered by the veteran American Evangelical, Dr Bob Jones, chancellor of Bob Jones University. The definition of Fundamentalism put forward by a committee which included the Rev. Ian Paisley of Northern Ireland and printed in the Congress programme stated that "A fundamentalist is a born-again believer in the Lord Jesus Christ who maintains an unmovable allegiance to the inerrant, infallible, and verbally inspired Bible". Previous World Congresses resolved to reaffirm the unique and special place of the Authorized (King James) Version of 1611 and condemn all modern versions such as the New English Bible, Revised Standard Version, Good News Bible and the New International Version. Apostasy and compromise which were to be found in dialogue with Roman Catholics, Jews and other religions, have also been rejected. The **Roman Catholic Church** is claimed to be revealed in Scripture as "the mother of harlots and abominations" (Revelation 17:5).

World Congress of Faiths. This organization exists to promote inter-faith activity and understanding of the kind that began in 1893 with the World Parliament of Religions held in Chicago. The moving spirit behind its establishment was Sir Francis Younghusband, leader of a British military expedition to Tibet in the early years of the century, who was influenced in part by the 1933 gathering of a World Fellowship of Faiths in Chicago held in conscious imitation of the earlier World Parliament gathering.

Although no follow-up occurred in the United States, Younghusband was encouraged to organize a World Congress of Faiths in London in 1936, and this then inaugurated a permanent organization under the same name. Younghusband had developed a personal philosophy of his own, and this perspective, according to which there was an underlying unity of experience beneath the surface differences between religions, has been one major strand in the work of the Congress throughout its life. It has sought to promote a shared recognition of spiritual reality through shared understanding by members of different faiths, without, however, seeking to generate a new synthetic faith.

A more recent focus of interest has been the search for a global ethic, in which the relationship between human rights and religious traditions is explored. An interest in seeking common moral values contained in the different world religions became prominent from the 1960s onwards, inspired in the first instance by the then chairman, Baron Reginald Sorensen.

Inter-faith dialogue is today far more common than when the Congress began its work, but remains a central concern of Congress members. For others, the aim of inter-faith dialogue may be primarily, or indeed exclusively one of removing misunderstandings and promoting tolerance, but within the Congress there is the added dimension of the search for a shared truth.

With the development of multi-religious societies in Europe in particular, the Congress has taken an interest in the inclusion of a world religions perspective in religious education.

An annual conference is held, the journal *World Faiths* is published, and a substantial number of inter-faith services have been organized. The headquarters are in London.

World Council of Churches. Formally inaugurated at Amsterdam in 1948, the World Council of Churches began as an international fellowship of autonomous **Protestant** and **Oriental Orthodox** churches which "accept our Lord Jesus Christ as God and Saviour". It marked the fusion of two strands: Faith and Order, concerned with the common expression of the Christian faith, without compromising the doctrinal integrity of any particular denomination, and Life and Work which attempted a Christian response to social, political, and economic problems. The discussions at Amsterdam were inevitably coloured by the experience of World War II, the threat of Communism, and the neo-orthodox Theology of Karl Barth. Its headquarters was set up in Geneva and its first General Secretary was the Dutchman W. A. Visser 't Hooft.

The reality of world political and economic power was recognized in the decision to hold the second congress at Evanston, USA in 1954, but it was the third congress in New Delhi in 1961 which marked a watershed through the vastly increased representation from the Third World which included 11 African churches, many of which owed little to Western missions. Criticism of the doctrinal basis of the WCC that it was not sufficiently Trinitarian, was addressed at this congress by the addition of a reference to the scriptures and to "their common calling to the glory of the one God, Father, Son and Holy Spirit".

At New Delhi reconsideration was also given to the use of the word "churches" in the WCC's title and stress was increasingly placed on the notion that "churches" applies only to diverse manifestations of the one Holy, Catholic Church. It was the 1975 Congress at Nairobi which called for "visible unity in one faith and in one eucharistic fellowship". The acceptance of this goal was eased by creative thinking about "reconciled diversity" and "conciliar fellowship" which led up to the Lima text on Baptism, Eucharist, and Ministry.

In 1968 the Uppsala assembly accepted a trusteeship over creation, "guarding, developing and sharing its resources", and coming to the conclusion that "Christ takes the side of the poor and oppressed". A few weeks later, the **Roman Catholic** Episcopal Conference of Latin America, meeting at Medellín in

Colombia, declared that the Church should take an option for the poor. This parallel thinking had been institutionalized in the creation of a joint Roman Catholic and WCC secretariat and committee on the issues of society, development and peace (SODEPAX).

The 1975 Assembly in Nairobi agreed to what in Britain became a highly controversial *Programme to Combat Racism*, and in the wake of the oil crisis, to a "just, participatory and sustainable society". This was carried further at Vancouver in 1983 when the fellowship was extended in response to pressure from women, youth, the physically disabled, and children for their voices to be heard. The 1991 Assembly in Australia seemed to some critics to move too far in accepting the religious experiences of social and cultural minorities like Australian Aboriginals and American Indians.

In 1993 a new General Secretary, Dr Konrad Raiser, took office at a time of restructuring, partly in response to diminishing financial resources. He brings to the post a strong awareness of the disquiet expressed by the Orthodox at recent developments.

World Fellowship of Buddhists (WFB). First established in 1950 by G. P. Malalasekere and sponsored by the All Ceylon Buddhist Congress, this is predominantly a non-denominational lay organization. Its aim is to carry on the spirit of the historical **Buddhist** councils as an expression of true religious ecumenism. At its first World Buddhist conference in Colombo, Sri Lanka (1951), lay and monastic representatives from 27 countries, covering nearly all Buddhist schools, were in attendance. Its headquarters has been in Bangkok since 1969 and there are 82 active regional centres throughout the world. The WFB is involved in social and humanitarian programmes, supports the establishment of Buddhist education and has been instrumental in developing Lumbini in southern Nepal, the birthplace of the Buddha, as a major pilgrimage site. It maintains a large number of missionary centres around the globe. About 50 monks per year are supported in this work. The organization publishes a journal, the *WFB Review,* and a book series in Thai and English. The WFB flag, comprising the five colours of the Buddha's halo, is much used by Buddhists today. It was designed by Col. Olcott, a leading **Theosophist,** in the 1880s.

World Hindu Society. *See* **Vishwa Hindu Parishad.**

World Islamic Call Society. This Libyan-based would-be rival to the Saudi-based **Muslim World League** is still more commonly known by its original and simpler title, the **Islamic Call Society.** It promotes Qaddafi's atypical interpretation of **Islam**, and his view of modern Western societies as centres of Christian hostility to Islam in the manner of the medieval Crusaders.

World Jewish Congress. International association of Jewish representative bodies founded in 1936 in Geneva "to assure the survival and foster the unity of the Jewish people". Presently there are representatives from more than 60 countries. The Congress has addressed issues of concern to Jews worldwide, such as War Crimes after the Holocaust; compensation from Germany after 1945; anti-semitism. Its research branch, the Institute of Jewish Affairs, is in London.

World Messianity. The English rendering of **Sekai Kyuseikyo,** a Japanese new religious movement.

World Muslim Congress. The World Muslim Congress (Mu'tamar al-'Alam al-Islami) is one of the main international Islamic organizations, along with the **Muslim World League** and the **Organization of the Islamic Conference.** Founded in 1926 during an international Muslim conference in Mecca, subsequent conferences were held in Jerusalem in 1931 and Karachi in 1949 and 1951. Its present structure was established at the last of these, and Karachi remains its main base.

Primarily a cultural organization to promote unity and co-operation among Muslims, it is seen by some observers as one of the ways in which Pakistan seeks to establish important Islamic credentials rivalling those of Saudi Arabia. Most of its activities have now been assumed, however, by the Saudi-based Muslim World League.

There are five regional offices internationally, in Senegal, Somalia, Lebanon, Malaysia and the Philippines.

World True Light Civilization. The English form of **Sekai Mahikari Bunmei Kyodan,** a Japanese new religious movement.

World Union for Progressive Judaism. Founded in London in 1926 in order to foster the cause of Progressive Judaism (**Reform Judaism** and Liberal Judaism), the World Union moved its headquarters to Jerusalem in 1973 and includes the recognition of Jewish religious pluralism in Israel among its aims. It represents communities in more than 20 countries worldwide.

Worldwide Church of God. Also known as **Armstrongism**, after the founder Herbert W. Armstrong, who founded the Church in Oregon in 1933 as the Radio Church of God. He had left his ministry at a Seventh Day **Adventist** Church in Missouri. Since 1947, the international headquarters have been in Pasadena, California. With the acquisition of a property near St Albans in 1959 the WCG started its activities in Britain. As in America, the media (pirate radio stations, magazines and newspapers) were used to make the Church known. Today, it boasts 800 congregations in 120 countries. In Britain 22 full-time ministers look after 3,000 baptized members. The UK headquarters are in Borehamwood, Hertfordshire.

However, with the death of Armstrong's wife Lorna (1967), schisms and power struggles occurred, exacerbated by allegations of moral and financial misconduct in the leadership. Armstrong himself was accused of dictatorial and totalitarian style of leadership. Several splinter groups broke away, among them one led by Armstrong's son, Garner Ted Armstrong, who set up his Church of God International in 1978, with its UK headquarters in Lincoln.

The organizational structure of the WCG is hierarchical, with offices only open to men. Armstrong was the head bearing the title "Apostle"; after his death in 1986, he was succeeded by Joseph W. Tkach, called "Pastor-General". Total membership of baptized members is claimed to be 94,000 worldwide. The WCG gives a literal interpretation of the Bible, lays great store by prophecy, teaches the Second Advent of Christ, celebrates Saturday as the day of rest, observes Jewish Holy Days (Passover, Atonement, Tabernacles, etc.), claiming that Easter and Christmas are unbiblical. In its teachings of ethics and morality the Church appears conservative, emphasizing marriage and family life. Adherents eat kosher food. There is a stress on spiritual healing, with some members discouraging the use of modern medicine, although others see no contradiction between the two. Funds are raised through tithing and appeals for "offerings". The movement's main publication is *Plain Truth,* a monthly magazine with a purported circulation of 2,000,000 copies in six languages. The Ambassador College (founded in 1947) in Texas offers four-year undergraduate courses in humanities, training ministers and personnel for the Church.

Y

'Yan Tatsine ('Yan Isala). The 'Yan Tatsine is a Nigerian **Islamic** sect which shot to prominence in December 1980 when large-scale rioting broke out in Kano. Followers of Alhaji Muhammadu Marwa, known as Maitatsine—Hausa for "he with powers of cursing"—fought pitched battles with police and army, resulting in several thousand dead, including Marwa himself (who had gradually built up a large following over the previous 20 years). The sect, which preaches a radical denunciation of materialism and privilege—and curses or damns (hence the name it acquired) all who are attached to modern materialist objects from bicycles and watches to economic wealth—recruits among refugees from Chad and Niger as well as among poor rural migrants to the cities and alienated wandering Quranic students (*gardawa*) and teachers (*mallams*). It has continued in existence despite the disaster of 1980, which was precipitated by the sect's attempt to take over the Friday mosque in Kano as a prelude to an insurrectionary attempt to establish control of Kano itself, and further outbreaks of violence occurred in 1982 (in Maiduguri and Kaduna), 1984 (in Yola), and 1985 (in Gombe).

There are certain similarities between the 'Yan Tatsine (meaning followers of Maitatsine, but sometimes also known simply as Maitatsine, or as 'Yan Izala) and the **Ikhwan** who occupied the mosque in Mecca in 1979.

Yazidis. A small but widely-dispersed religious and tribal community mainly found in western Iran, Iraq, and Syria; Kurdish-speaking but distinct from the main body of Kurds. The origins of the cult are obscure, but it seems to involve a syncretistic mixture of early Iranian beliefs, **Christian**, Muslim (including **Sufi**), and related doctrines and practices. The Yazidis are often mistakenly referred to as "Devil-Worshippers" through a misunderstanding of their dualistic belief system in which the creation and continuation of the world are shared by God and Malik Taus, the peacock angel. Although some Muslim writers have regarded them as an Islamic sect, this does not appear to be historically or doctrinally accurate. The cult possesses a large priestly class and has distinct prayers, pilgrimages, festivals, and other rituals. There is a small body of sacred literature in Arabic, accessible only to the senior priesthood.

Current conditions in Iraq and Iran make it difficult to say with any precision what the fate of the Yazidis has been in recent years.

Yoga. Yoga is perhaps the best known of the six orthodox Hundu philosophical systems. Supposedly founded by the ancient sage Yajñavalka, the system was first codified in the *Yogasutra*, traditionally ascribed to Patanjali who redacted the work in approximately 200 CE. Yoga is often seen as the practical embodiment of the Samkhya school of philosophy, but it forms a part of most forms of Hindu meditative practice. Early Yoga downplays the importance of God, and references to God in Patanjali may well be later interpolations. This is not to say that later schools of thought which appropriated yoga's "technology" for their own purposes did not introduce theological elements, but rather the primary aim of yoga has always been to teach the means by which the individual human soul may gain release from the phenomenal world regardless of the existence or non-existence of a personal deity. This is accomplished through the "eight limbs of yoga". Those who practice these techniques believe that these "limbs" result in the individual's liberation from rebirth in the world. The first of these techniques is *yama*, external control and restraint of the senses. Next is *niyama*, internal control of the mind through meditation. This is followed by *asana*, the well-known bodily postures of yoga, and *pranayama*, control of the breath. These lead to *pratyahara*, control of the senses and *dharana*, meditation. As these deepen, the practitioner enters the states of *dhyana*, contemplation, and finally *samadhi*, super-consciousness.

There are a number of different schools of yoga which have different emphases. *Karma-yoga* is primarily concerned with salvation through works or action in the world. *Bhakti-yoga* places its emphasis on devotion to the gods and salvation through faith. *Jñana-yoga* focuses on the pursuit of wisdom. These three forms of yoga are mentioned, and their practice sanctified, in the *Bhagavad Gita*. The esoteric *laya-yoga* deals with the acquisition of magical powers through the activation of the subtle centres of the body. *Hatha-yoga* is concerned with physical culture, while *raja-yoga* emphasizes spiritual aspects of the system. *Hatha-yoga* is perhaps the system most recognizable to the Westerner. Raja, or "royal" yoga lays far more stress on the psychological and spiritual elements of yoga than does *hatha-yoga*. Here one might also note the various "yogic" practices, such as *kundalini yoga*, practised by the non-traditional schools of **Hinduism**, such as **Tantrism**. Yoga is one of the most prevalent forms of Hindu religious practice and forms a significant part of the teachings of most contemporary Hindu gurus. In the West, many organizations such as the **Self-Realization Fellowship, Siddha Yoga, Viniyoga** and Iyengar Yoga have promoted one or more aspect of these ancient teachings.

Z

Zar Cult. The zar cult is to be found in the Nile area in Egypt and the Sudan, in Somalia (where the zar is known as the sar), and in Ethiopia (where it appears to have originated). It is a spiritist cult, or spirit possession cult, similar to others found across Sudanic Africa from Ethiopia to Senegal. The *zar* is a spirit believed to possess women, causing depression or frustration. The afflicted woman engages a *shaykha*, or female religious specialist (although on occasion it may be a male), before whom she dances, speaking in the voice of the *zar*, and acting out its character. There may also be blood sacrifice. The *shaykha* then diagnoses the root of the problem, and relieves the woman of her affliction by suggesting a way of appeasing the spirit.

Confined almost exclusively to women, the *zar* cult tends to be despised by the men (themselves often members of **Sufi** orders).

Zaydis. The smallest of the main branches of **Shi'ite** Islam. The sect originated in allegiance to Zayd ibn 'Ali (d. 740), a brother of the fifth mainstream *Imam*. Unlike the **Imami** leaders, Zayd advocated armed rebellion to establish Shi'ite rule, and was himself killed in an abortive uprising. Zaydi states were established in Tabaristan (864–928) and Yemen (from 893 to the present, with interruptions). In doctrinal and legal matters, the Zaydis come closest of all the Shi'a to **Sunni** orthodoxy. During this century, attempts to intensify a traditionalist religious rule in Yemen have been modified by wider political conditions in the country and its division in 1970. Zaydis form about 40 per cent of the population of the former Yemen Arab Republic, with their traditional centres in the northern and central highlands and the eastern desert.

Zen. An important form of Japanese Mahayana Buddhism. The word *zen* means meditation and is a translation of the Chinese term *ch'an*. The Ch'an tradition arrived rather late in Japan, though earlier forms of **Buddhism**, particularly **Tendaishu, Hossoshu** and **Kegonshu,** eased the way by making rigorous meditation practice more familiar to the Japanese people. Myoan Eisai (1141–1215) is generally regarded as the founder of Zen. Travelling to China in 1168 and studying under masters of the Lin-chi (Jap. **Rinzai**) tradition, Eisai gained enlightenment and established the first Zen temple at Hakada, on the southern island of Kyushu, in 1194. He later directed the influential Kenninji temple in Kyoto at which Zen practices were taught alongside those of the Tendai and **Shingon** schools. His disciples successfully purged Zen of doctrines associated with the older schools of Japanese Buddhism and a variety of Chinese Lin-chi (Rinzai) masters were encouraged to visit Japan to complete this work in the late Kamakura period.

Soto Zen was brought from China, during the Sung period, by Dogen Kigen (1200–1253). Since that time the Koshoji near Kyoto has been its major temple. Soto is characterized by the centrality of *zazen* (sitting meditation) in its practice, while Rinzai gives great prominence to meditation on the *koan* (public utterance). Both schools have continued to flourish down to modern times, though the former was riven by schism throughout the 13th century. After a period of stagnation, Soto began a renaissance in the 17th century. Its spread throughout Japan has led to it becoming the second biggest Buddhist school, the largest being **Nichirenshoshu.** Another Zen school, the **Obaku,** owes its existence to the missionary activities of Chinese monks during the Tokugawa Shogunate (1603–1867). Established first in Kyushu and soon after (1661) in Kyoto, the Rinzai-based Obaku has remained reasonably small.

In the Middle Ages literature, calligraphy, painting and garden creation flourished, particularly in connection with the Rinzai Five Mountain (*gozan*) movement centred on Kyoto and Kamakura. Similarly, the way of tea (*sado*) owes its existence to a variety of Rinzai masters based at the Daitokuji temple, Kyoto during the 16th century. Finally two Zen practitioners of the Edo period deserve mention. Takuan Soho (1573–1645) was Japan's greatest teacher of swordsmanship and is regarded as an important influence on the later chivalric tradition. Basho (1644–1694) is the most prominent exponent of the *haiku* poetic form. His naturalism is a recurring theme in later Zen-inspired culture. In the Meiji period (1868–1912) non-Shinto religion was briefly suppressed, though Rinzai, Soto and Obaku have continued to receive support since that time. In recent years a good deal of interest in Zen has developed in the West in response to the opening of Japan to the outside world. The writings of D. T. Suzuki and the beat poets of 1950s America have been influential in this regard. Similarly, the Order of Buddhist Contemplatives is one of the many quasi-independent Western-Buddhist-based Zen movements to emerge in the last few decades.

Zionism. Zionism is the modern political movement which supports the Jews' re-establishing a national centre in their ancestral homeland. Contemporary Zionists disagree about the necessity of every Jew living in the State of Israel but all support its existence. Since the Romans' destruction of the Temple (70 CE) and subsequent exiling of the Jews, traditional **Judaism** hoped for a return to the Land of Israel. Zionism as a political movement, however, began at the end of the 19th century under the leadership of Theodor Herzl (1860–1904). Although a group of Russian Jews created the *Hibbat Zion* ("love of Zion") movement to create agricultural villages in the Land of Israel following the 1881 Russian pogroms, it was Herzl who created a Jewish nationalist movement which united Jews from many lands and put their quest for a secure home on the international agenda.

Zionism was a response to both internal and external events in the lives of modern Jews. It began as a response to the failure of emancipation to provide full equality for all citizens, it becoming clear that Jews were expected to give up much of their identity in order to "fit in" but, as the pogroms, Dreyfus Affair, and later Holocaust showed, even this was not enough. Internally, many Jews began to question both the passivity of many Orthodox Jewish leaders as well as others' assimilationist tendencies.

Against this backdrop, Herzl began his activities, organizing the first Zionist conference in Basle, Switzerland (1897). Herzl worked tirelessly on the project, seeking international support for a state for the Jews. Herzl held the movement together despite internal divisions over the place of traditional Judaism in Zionism and a British proposal to give the Jews Uganda—a plan which Herzl backed only as a temporary measure but which was rejected by the movement. Herzl's early death stunned the organization.

Nonetheless, Zionists kept immigrating. The 1904–1906 Second Aliyah ("ascendants", i.e. immigrants to the Land of Israel) from Russia included an influential group of secular socialists who sought to re-shape the Jews by making them into communal farmers. This structure eventually became the **Kibbutz** ("collective farm") movement which became the symbol of Zionism pioneerism. *Kibbutzim* were established by the prominent *ha-Shorner ha-Tza'ir*

("The Young Guard") movement as well as *ha-Kibbutz ha-Me'uhed* ("the united *kibbutz*") and *Kibbutz ha-Dati* ("the religious *kibbutz*"). The secular lifestyle of most *kibbutzim* outraged the majority of traditional Jews who insisted that only God could save the Jews. One of the few early religious Zionists, Rabbi Abraham Isaac Kook (1865–1935), embraced the pioneers, arguing that their "insolence" was actually a harbinger of the Messianic era.

World War I radically affected the Middle East with the defeat of the Ottoman Empire. During the war, in 1917, the British issued the *Balfour Declaration* which expressed support for "a national home in Palestine for the Jewish people". Although later British governments would attempt to limit Jewish rights, their support at this point was important for Zionism.

Four main trends developed among Jews in the *Yishuv* ("the dwelling," the Jews living in the Land of Israel). Of the Zionist "new" *Yishuv*, the largest were the Socialists, which dominated *Yishuv* and Israeli politics until 1977. Led by men such as Berl Katznelson (1887–1944) and David Ben-Gurion (1886–1973), much of the infrastructure of present-day Israel was created, such as the federation of labor unions, the Histadrut. In 1930, the various unions formed Mapai, which after merging with smaller parties became Ma'arach (Alignment, or Labour).

Opposed to them were the Revisionists, led by Ze'ev (Vladimir) Jabotinsky (1880–1940), who rejected socialism and a 1937 plan partitioning Mandatory Palestine into a Jewish and an Arab state. The movement evolved into the Herut party led by Menahem Begin, which, except for the years 1967–1970 (from the 1967 Middle-East crisis to a dispute over the question of withdrawal from the territories), was in opposition to Labour-led coalitions until 1977 when Herut, at the centre of the larger Likud party defeated the Left. Since 1977, the Likud has either led or shared power in ruling coalitions.

The third trend, Religious Zionism, was represented by Mizrahi (an acronym for *Merkaz Ruhani*, "spiritual centre"), the forerunner to the National Religious Party (*see* **Mafdal**). Founded in 1902, Mizrahi was the only traditionalist group to join the World Zionist Organization. While most religious Zionists did not consider Zionism to be concerned with the Jews' redemption, the influential Rabbi A. I. Kook, noted above, did. His son, Rabbi Tzvi Yehudah Kook (1891–1982), continued this line of thought, seeing the Six-Day War as confirmation that the redemptive process was unfolding. He and his students affected Israeli society by creating **Gush Emunim** ("bloc of the faithful"), which led the broader-based settlement movement in the occupied territories. Although the National Religious Party currently strongly supports the settlement movement, a minority of religious Israelis, clustered around the *Oz ve-Shalom* (strength and peace) and *Netivot Shalom* (paths of peace) movements, supports a more conciliatory approach.

The fourth group is comprised of non- or anti-Zionists. In 1919 they attached themselves to **Agudat Israel** (bloc of Israel), whose overall policy did not oppose Jewish nationalism but disagreed with Zionism's disregard for diaspora Judaism and its general secularity. The Jerusalemite chapter, however, was much more opposed to Zionism than overall movement. Yet as the Yishuv developed, Agudat Israel began having more contacts and interactions with Zionism, prompting an isolationist faction, the Edah Haredit ("haredit community"), to bolt the party (*see* **Orthodox Judaism**). Today, Agudat Yisrael, despite philosophically opposing Zionism, takes part in the Israeli political system, and in recent years, participating in governmental coalitions in return for religious concessions. Recently, the party has splintered. In 1984, Sephardi members formed a new party, in response to perceived discrimination by Agudat Israel's **Ashkenazi** leadership. In 1988, Agudat Yisrael became further divided when Rabbi Eliezer Schach supported the formation of the Degel Hatorah (Torah Flag) party to combat what he saw as the undue influence of **Lubavich Hasidism** in the party.

Zionist Churches. This is the label used primarily in a South African context to refer to African independent churches of the prophet-healing type. Whereas the so-called **Ethiopian Churches** largely reproduced the dominant Western forms of **Christianity**, and were often based on group secessions from the European-run churches, the Zionist churches, which began to appear from the 1920s onwards, were typically founded by a charismatic leader, developed distinctive patterns of worship (e.g. with drumming and dancing) and emphasized gifts of prophecy and healing in the manner of the **Pentecostals.** In Nigeria the same kinds of churches are referred to as **Aladura** churches. They exercise a powerful appeal, and there are thought to be several hundreds of them. (*See also* **African Religious Movements.**)

Zoe. Zoe ("Life") is the oldest and most influential of the several evangelical and reform movements that have been a notable feature of Orthodox Christianity in Greece since the beginning of the 20th century. Founded in 1907 by the archimandrite (monastic priest) and preacher Eusebius Matthopoulos (1849–1929), together with four other theologians, it entered the public arena in 1911 with the first publication of the periodical *Zoe,* from which the movement takes its name. Against a background of nominal **Christianity** and lax religious observance among a population served by a largely uneducated clergy, Zoe aimed to renew Orthodox Christian values among all sections of Greek society, particularly through preaching and Bible study; to encourage closer participation in the Church's sacramental life (especially through more frequent confession and communion); and to reform certain elements of Church worship and custom. Extremely well organized, the movement has pursued its aims in all sectors and age groups of the Greek population, through preaching, teaching, publishing, and social work.

Based in Athens, Zoe is registered as a private and voluntary corporation; it has no official Church ties or State support. At its centre is the Zoe Brotherhood, a body of theologically trained individuals organized along monastic lines and consisting mainly of unmarried laymen who undertake a life of poverty, obedience and chastity (though no strictly binding vows). Its members refuse all ecclesiastical preferments. They pursue their activities throughout Greece, initiating Bible study groups, organizing catechism classes, and working through various affiliated organizations. There is also a Women's Association, Eusebia.

Relations between Zoe and the Greek Church have been mixed. As an independent religious organization Zoe is easily perceived as a rival, or as a Church within the Church (rather as **Opus Dei** has been regarded in **Roman Catholicism**). At the same time the more secular Greeks find it easy to despise Zoe for its moralistic and pietistic attitudes. On the other hand many among the clergy have welcomed and encouraged the work of Zoe, regarding its aims and achievements as one with their own. In 1930 the success of Zoe and other movements encouraged the official hierarchy to set up its own "home missionary" movement, the Apostoliki Diakonia ("Apostolic Service"), though this now co-operates with Zoe in the organization of catechism classes.

Despite its inherently conservative character, Zoe has undergone significant development. In 1960 changes within the movement led a conservative faction to defect and set up a rival organization, Sotir ("Salvation"), whose activities parallel those of Zoe though in a more puritanical and in some respects fanatical mode. In recent years Zoe theologians have become more aware of western theology, and to some extent influenced by it, and an interest in ecumenical issues is slowly developing. The main impact of Zoe has been in urban Greece, among the middle classes from whom the members of the Brotherhood themselves are drawn.

Zoroastrians. Followers of the ancient religion established by the Iranian "prophet" Zarathustra (known in the West as Zoroaster) who lived in Iran, c. 1000 BCE. They sometimes refer to themselves as Mazdayasnians, "worshippers of Ahura Mazda", the "wise lord" and entirely good God (and so Mazdaism). Their early history is obscure, but from the 6th century BCE until the coming of **Islam** in the 7th century CE theirs was the most important, perhaps the official state religion in three successive Iranian empires.

After the Arab invasions, Zoroastrians suffered persistent persecution and were marginalized numerically, economically and geographically. The faithful remnants of **Irani Zoroastrians** were forced to retreat to remote Iranian villages where they subsisted in poverty. As a result of these conditions, some Zoroastrians left Iran in the 10th century CE, eventually establishing a community in north-west India where they became known as **Parsis** ("Persians"). For those left in Iran, there was a brief improvement under the Pahlavi dynasty (1925–1979). Parsis now constitute the largest group of Zoroastrians (approximately 100,000 compared to: Iran, 30,000; Pakistan 4,000; Britain and North America 6,000).

The traditional teachings of Zoroastrianism are contained in its holy text, the *Avesta*, associated with Zarathustra himself. Of equal importance is the Pahlavi literature (about the 9th century CE). The central insight of the religion is that the world and human beings are the field in which the cosmic struggle between good and evil takes place. On the one side of this radical ethical dualism is the good God, Ahura Mazda, on the other the evil Angra Mainyu. Both at the cosmic and at the individual levels, the good or evil nature of things is the result of free moral choice. Human beings are at the centre of this struggle, and it is their duty to care for the creation of God (that is the spiritual and the material world) and to fight evil in all its forms. In the long term, the favourable outcome of this struggle is not in doubt. Zoroastrians also believe in heaven, hell, resurrection of the dead, and a final judgement, ideas that may have had a substantial influence on the Semitic religions.

Fire, representing God, plays the central role in Zoroastrian worship or sacrifice (*yasna*). It is tended by hereditary priests; physical and moral purity is essential to the ritual. Originally focused on the ever-burning hearth fire, such worship has constituted a temple cult since the 4th century BCE. Boys and girls are initiated into the Zoroastrian community before puberty, when they are invested with a sacred shirt (*sudre*) and cord (*kusti*). Since it is considered to be the work of evil, death also involves substantial purificatory rituals.

Traditionally, Zoroastrians do not accept converts and favour marriage between blood relations (usually cousins). Similarly, they do not proselytize. Today a steady decline in their numerical strength has made them increasingly self-conscious about the essential nature of their community and religion and their need to preserve it.